# BEHOLD

My Story

Marco Martin

BEHOLD
My Story
All Rights Reserved.
Copyright © 2023 Marco Martin
v2.0

The opinions expressed in this manuscript are solely the opinions of the author and do not represent the opinions or thoughts of the publisher. The author has represented and warranted full ownership and/or legal right to publish all the materials in this book.

This book may not be reproduced, transmitted, or stored in whole or in part by any means, including graphic, electronic, or mechanical without the express written consent of the publisher except in the case of brief quotations embodied in critical articles and reviews.

Creative Writing 101 Publishing

ISBN: 979-8-218-95969-2

Cover Photo © 2023 www.gettyimages.com. All rights reserved - used with permission.

PRINTED IN THE UNITED STATES OF AMERICA

"Kunta Kinte, behold the only thing greater than yourself."
ROOTS by Alex Haley

*Dedicated to Mama, who suggested I write my autobiography.*

# Table of Contents

Prologue ................................................................................. i

Act 1, Scene 2: Monologue ................................................... 1
Act 2, Scene 3: Dialogue ...................................................... 16
Act 3, Scene 4: Teenage Love ............................................... 31
Act 4, Scene 5: March 5, 1986 .............................................. 37
Act 5, Scene 6: Teeny-Boppers .............................................. 41
Act 6, Scene 7: October 13, 1987 .......................................... 53

Season 7, Episode 8: College Hill .......................................... 65
Season 8, Episode 9: Malcolm X ........................................... 87
Season 9, Episode 10: Islam ................................................. 111
Season 10, Episode 11: Criminal Justice ............................... 127
Season 11, Episode 12: Girl Scout Cookies ........................... 147
Season 12, Episode 13: Correctional Officer ......................... 163
Season 13, Episode 14: Misunderstood ................................. 192

Chapter 14, Part 15: Jailbird ................................................. 204
Chapter 15, Part 16: Capital Murder ..................................... 222
Chapter 16, Part 17: The Trial .............................................. 248
Chapter 17, Part 18: Inmate Number 298601 ........................ 275
Chapter 18, Part 19: Residue ................................................ 292
Chapter 19, Part 20: Redeemed ............................................ 305
Chapter 20, Part 21: Epilogue .............................................. 318

# Prologue

My father, Shawn, left my mother. He abandoned, all of us. I had, no idea, he was leaving, that fateful day. Without warning, I was "Whammed!" When I came home, from school that day, there wasn't any sign, he had ever lived there.

There wasn't an inconsolable, candid conversation, or explainable excuse. There wasn't a goodbye, note, or sit-down talk. All of his belongings were gone. An empty man's cave, or den room, where he used to sit or stand. An empty space, where he used to be. Nowhere to be found. No father.

Suddenly, I was catapulted, into confusion. I was thrusted, into the throes of being, "the man of the house."

She always said, "He changed, the moment they crossed the border," for their new home, in the commonwealth state of Virginia. The man in love, sweetly, holding "I love you" notes to the camera was becoming indifferent. The Marine soldier, who survived the jungle overseas, was vanishing before her.

"How come, we don't go to church?" I'd ask my parents.

"That's because, the biggest devils are in the church," they taught me.

My parents didn't believe in dragging me to church, or forcing me to go. So, we didn't attend. I didn't come from a religious group, sect, or spiritual background. I learned early on, about (some) religious people's two-face hypocrisy.

I always assumed, my dad wanted a woman, much like his own mother. She was old-fashioned, humble, church-going, God-fearing, sweet, gentle, homebody, who tirelessly cared for her family. My mother had those same qualities.

Mama played the piano, for her church choir, growing up. Sometimes, she'd play the piano, in our house, for our listening pleasure. She could, amazingly, read the musical piano notes. Sometimes, she'd listen to church service on Sunday, on tv or radio.

She cooked us, three square-meals a day, during those days. Before I headed for school, and after she came home from work, she'd cooked. Steak, fried chicken, homemade hamburgers, pancakes, waffles, grilled balcony, bacon, grilled cheese sandwiches, pork chops, beef liver, you name it.

She, relentlessly, cleaned clothes and washed dishes. She, restlessly, sewed on the sewing machine, and made her own clothes, respectively.

Believe it or not, we had canine pets.

There were earlier times, my dad, did so much as, playfully, hug mama from behind, or surprise mama with a kiss. It forced me to giggle with glee, at the sight of my happy parents, when I was toddler. Dad would, affectionately, call her Von.

"It wasn't all bad," an abused victim, may say. There were backyard cookouts on the grill. Occasional friends would stop by. Funny-looking, funny-smelling cigarettes were, sometimes, left in the den's ashtrays. Dad would play Teddy Pendergrass or Marvin Gaye, R&B music from the patio speaker. He'd change his own engine oil. The garage had its own private telephone line from the house.

Plenty of Christmas cheer. Window lights aglow. Many delightful decorations. We had a tremendous amount of Christmas toys and presents, under the live tree. Dad made homemade vanilla ice cream. "We rich," I'd say as a kid.

My parents would, quickly, discourage me from saying that. My mother would often tell me, she grew up poor. "Money doesn't grow on trees," she would say.

"Do you want to be a policeman like your daddy?" family, friends and neighbors would say.

"Yeah," I'd say, of course, as a small boy.

"My daddy's a policeman," I'd proudly say, to anyone who cared.

People, in those days, had the utmost respect for his professional career. I blamed his chosen, one-sided, stressful, line of work, the way the family was.

One time, he wasn't speaking to Mama. Let alone, sharing the master bedroom with her. He'd move to the guest bedroom. For the first time, in 1984, Dad, decidedly, moved out of our home with, mysteriously, another woman, in their shared apartment. After pleading for forgiveness, he moved back in with us, a year later.

Needless to say, my mother, Etta, was baked in humility, and humiliation. (Giving you something to chew on.) She was quiet, but quick-witted. Humble, but hardworking. Nervous, but neat. Faithful, but fearful. Short, but stood tall. Lonesome, but loving.

Absorbed in his thoughts. My father, when he was there, would walk around the house, with a mean look. Apparently, he wasn't happy. My parents had plenty, so I thought, in their shared bank account. Yet, more often than not, he had a chiseled, mad face. Life of the party, funny, socialite, and a ladies' man, "out there," but a tyrannical giant "in here."

Dad brought women over to the house, during our school, and work hours. It was in broad daylight.

Mama would get tips, from an anonymous caller, at work.

"Do you know, your husband is bringing women to the house?" the caller would say.

The neighbors, reportedly, saw what was going on. My father would deny it.

He was sweet and charming with the ladies. "He could charm the cherries, off a cherry tree," as the saying goes. Rumor had it, my father had an abortion or miscarriage with "someone."

Slowly, but surely, my parent's marriage was drifting apart. It was like a ship going out to sea, or all to see. In his civilian clothes, my dad was bold enough to afford, my younger siblings and I, in his excursions with his women. His "friend" Cassie once bought, my brother and I, matching red and green winter hats and gloves for Christmas. She was younger than him, street-wise, and outspoken like him.

We, practically, begged for his attention, to no avail. He was stoic, distant and aloof. With us here, at the house, anyway. Not to mention, I had an older (half) brother, Antonio. Same father, different mothers. My dad had him, before my parents were married. He too, was growing up in the Carolinas, without his biological father around. Dad, seemingly, was bored with the family, he made.

He would, usually, sleep most of the day away, or left home, to be with our nearby neighbor, fellow motorcyclist, and his best friend, Mr. Hall.

On the few occasions, when my dad did go, anywhere with us, he would, grumpily, rush us along. He'd take us home, only to dump us. Then he'd go out himself. It was as though, saved by the bell. He'd throw on nice clothes, and heavy cologne. He'd explain it as going "under cover" due to his police assignment. He'd stay gone, for hours. All night, sometimes.

My father, went as far as getting the same Christmas gifts for my mother and sister, as he did for his "mystery woman" and her daughter. (How do I know)? When I was a kid, I would sneak through my father's things, in his dresser drawer.

If I may be so bold, I needed to know, why he acted the way he acted. I read through his red hardback memo book, with two separate Christmas lists. This family and his mysterious "other family."

Being honest, my father, acted like, he didn't have time for his children. For a spell, I couldn't bring myself to call him "Daddy" when I was kid. I'd speak to him, when he was in earshot, but I wouldn't give him that title. I, simply, didn't feel comfortable with the man. From where I was standing, he, hardly, wanted to spend time with me. He, certainly, didn't seem to want a relationship with me. When he was, actually, there, in the home, it was horrible.

He would intimidate the "fear of God" in us. Particularly, towards my bunk bed-sharing, younger brother, Mel and I. We would, nervously, scurry to clean our room, or there would be hell to pay. We would be frantic, or shiver like cocoa leaves, at the very sight of him, pulling up in the driveway. I developed a nervous twitch. I didn't want him to take that thick, black leather belt and whip my backside. Even to this day, I have a hard time, trusting people, especially, with stoic demeanor men.

Being right up his alley, a little bird told me, that my father had a vasectomy. Yet, he knew Etta wanted another daughter, after my sister, Dreeka. My parents, both came from a family of four, three other siblings each. Finally, my mother, courageously, filed for divorce in 1987. It was, finally, regardless of what others may think of her, in their hometown. My parents' divorce was finalized in 1988. Before the insurance company knew the wiser, my father used my mother's insurance to get his vasectomy reversed.

Apparently, so he could have children with his new wife.

Years prior, my mother tried to talk to him. She'd confront him, on why he was never home.

"If I had something worth coming home to, maybe I'd come home," my father said to her, keeping his promiscuity up.

It was a hidden combination of pain on her, that I scarcely knew. When it was time for his weekly socials, my dad told my mama that there was going to be "late night activities," so he was able to spend the weekend at a hotel. A blind man could see, what was going on.

My mother was recommended, by her divorce lawyer, to hire a private detective. To prove infidelity in court, he, discreetly, took pictures. He snapped camera shots of my dad's "other woman" in a see-through negligee, with the two of them together, in a hotel, somewhere, in the west end of town.

Controlling her anger, my mother used the risqué pictures, for the divorce as planned. She wanted to tell the truth of their marriage, not to gloat.

As a star witness, my father once beat my mother up, right in front of me. She decided to visit their small, southern hometown, in South Carolina without his permission. (I remember, to this day). I witnessed the whole thing. It was in the den room, after my maternal aunt, North, left. I was five-years-old. I stood in the doorway. She looked scared. She looked, directly, into my eyes, helpless. There were other occasional glitches, I'm sure. Usually, their arguments were behind the closed bedroom door. So I knew little, next to nothing. Yet, there were times, I did see them in action.

"Say it again! Say it again!" dared my father, to my mother, I'd hear.

I was there, when there was a call to the police. Two uniformed police officers standing, in our house, at our front door. Being fellow counterparts of his, they left our home, without incident. It was in the realm of, "Ma'am, do you want to press charges?" She, reluctantly, said no. That was that.

My mother worked in bookkeeping. She was an accountant, for a well-known telephone company, C&P Telephone. When she was pregnant, with the three of us, my dad hardly showed any interest. I can't imagine why. My father had plenty of friends and friendly acquaintances. I could only wonder. Did they knew of the times, he hit my mother, whenever he felt she wasn't in compliance?

He was always, anxiously, upset whenever my baby brother and I stay home from school, if we were sick. (I wonder why). He'd looked after us by ordering us to bed for hours, without any television on. It was a deterrent, to say the least.

"If you're sick, you're sick, right?" he'd say.

Then there was the time, when I walked in and saw my father feeding "another woman" a banquet of chicken. He, literally, was putting food in her mouth, no less.

It could have been an actual blizzard going on. The weather folks would be on television, advising people to stay home. My father was conceptional, and went out anyway. Apparently, "someone else" was important to him. Night after night, he was breaching his marriage contract.

My mama went to church, one Sunday. Suddenly, a woman sat beside her. It was on the condition of telling her, about my father seeing another woman. Mama approached him about it. He denied it.

Someone called my mother on the phone, one day. No caller I.D.

"Do you know your husband have women at the house, when you're not at home?" she said grimly.

One of my friends confirmed to me, that he saw a woman, at the area of the house. With room to spare, a neighbor told my mother, if only she would "coming home, on her lunch break," she would've seen a lot.

In a ray of sunshine, in broad daylight, my dad was messing around, with a neighbor's cousin. Too busy to save the marriage, it would have been more considerate, for Dad to just leave. It was if he wanted to provoke my mother, into telling him to leave. (He, obviously, wanted to get caught). It was if though, so my dad could tell his folks that he had no choice, but to leave. My mother, apparently, wouldn't give him the satisfaction. Etta knew. (She had to, I thought).

Or, how about the time, when my father wrote that letter to my uncle, Joe? He told him that he got a another woman pregnant. My mama saw the letter. She confronted my dad. Calmly, he explained that if Uncle Joe knew of his "experiences," maybe we wouldn't be gay any longer. He consoled her, with something as silly as that.

On another occasion, my father warned me to stop, or "Can it!" I was a kid. I was seeing things. I was hearing things. He threatened me. Should I tell my mother, he had another woman in the house. I warned my mother, anyhow. She deserved better.

Needless to say, he treated my mama "like dirt." It was all a con job. Whenever my paternal grandparents would visit, he treated her lovely. As soon as my relatives left, Dad went back to his "old hat" ways.

One time, my paternal folks from South Carolina called, unexpectedly. They liked to surprise us. They said, they were coming up here, the following day. It was like, keeping my father captured. He was furious! He told my mother, he was going on a "fishing trip." When his folks arrived, Dad stayed outside, sulking and working in the yard.

My paternal grandmama had to ask my mama, "Is he upset?" that they drove up.

"No," said my mother. "He just wanted to get the yard work done," excusing his bad behavior.

That's not the half of it. Dad took his frustrations out on me. Oftentimes, he'd tell me to clean my room. I was doing so. I made the mistake to talk to Mel, for a minute. Dad attacked me. He struck me In the back of my head, with his fist. On my case, he knocked me to the floor. He started choking me.

"Mama!" I cried, knowing she wasn't there, thinking I was going to die.

Correct to assume, I never quite got over my father's rejection of me. Argumentatively, from the womb, I felt rejected. Seeds of hatred and mistrust. Is it any wonder, why I acted so negative at times? The countless bullying, towards my younger siblings. The bad, dysfunctional relationships. The impulsive decisions . The poor self-esteem and the juggernaut self-doubts. The juggling with suicidal thoughts, as big as the autumn sky. I was, thoroughly, and emotionally scarred.

From a chamber of secrets, my father threw a baby bottle at my mother. It was during a card game. She made a bad play, which cramped his style. Right in front of another couple. If you can believe that.

Once, my mama, ideally, was talking about, going to her hometown in the south. It was on front of friend of my father's. The friend, jokingly, asked could his wife go too.

"Sure, she can go," said my mother.

"Listen to her. She's saying 'Yes,' but as soon as you leave, she'll be saying, 'Why she want to go?" said my father, humiliating her in front of company.

My mother made more money than my father. It wasn't any banter, boast, or bragging. A threat to his charter manhood, perhaps? My mother, his matrimonial wife, never once, made an issue out of it.

He wanted to get caught, it seemed. People who cheat, usually, keep their private affairs, private. They don't dominate their secret affairs, around the children. Not for the world to see, with no respect to the "marriage."

From the moment my parents arrived to the commonwealth, my father became a changed man. With a promising job of carrying a gun, billy club stick, and telling people what to do, it seemed a good place to be.

It wasn't before, two months later, when my mother dreaded her stay with him. She called her hometown, because she wanted to go home. My father's usual bitter flavor of treating her so, badly, was becoming unpalatable. It was the accumulating of holidays of leaving her, alone. The flourishing foul moods. The cursed days, when my mother, Etta, was pregnant with me.

There was the incident, when she wanted to go the store, with my father. They only had one, shared car at the time. She was cooped in their, then apartment, all day. She, merely, wanted to get out for awhile. My father became furious, throwing the keys at her.

"I'm tired of being married! I want my freedom," he easily said to her, too many times.

Or, was it the time, when the county sheriff showed up? He was at the house with paperwork from my father's lawyer. It stated that, if my mother didn't come up with a "reasonable offer," for buying him out, the house would be sold. The two of them could split the profits. Both of them were on the deed to the house. Another dagger to the heart. Was my father willing, to put his three children, out into the street?

The divorce became, affectively, hard for everyone involved. Through negotiations, and foretelling, with the lawyers, my parents reached an agreement about the house. My mother could keep our two-story, five-bedroom house, if my father wouldn't have to pay, absolutely, "no child support." Nor, medical coverage for the children. He elected, not to have any financial responsibility for us, once the divorce was made.

Somehow, on a foundation of love, and a lot of pain, we survived. We were on a very lean budget. Mama had to use her gas station credit card, to get us something to eat, or groceries, sometimes. Suddenly, all the bills, the house, the car, she alone had to handle, on her own. The food, she had to handle, on her own. The other unforeseen, miscellaneous expenses became my mother's problems, alone. My mother became eligible, for a life of struggle.

Meanwhile, my father was enjoying his new-found freedom. Our Christmas-time in December, suddenly, looked like it was in recession. My father seemed, to forget about Mel and I. We weren't, exactly, on speaking terms, with him. Nor did Dad, reach out to us. Dreeka, alone, was invited, involved or enjoyed icebreaker moments, or quality-time, with Dad, his new wife, Cassie, their daughter, and our now, new (half) sister, Chrissie.

I felt alone, with, definitely, no one to talk to. It, definitely, took courage to live, and not harm myself, with the hurtful things, painful comments, and relentless teasing, about my overweight. My well-being was held in the balance. I needed to be brave, but instead, I became a bully, towards my younger siblings. Feelings of facing a cold, cruel, judgmental world, on my young shoulders. No father.

Our neighbor, Mr. Pig was progressive, but a sloppy-second. However, he's the one, who taught me, how to change the tire on a car. He taught me, how to tie a necktie. He taught me, never, (ever) give up.

"Don't take no, for an answer," was his approach.

Mr. Pig drilled that in me, when it came to looking for a job. He was more than an old, nosey neighborhood, drinking his can of beer, on his front porch steps. He taught me valuable lessons. I didn't have a father "around," or took the time. So I appreciated it. His son, Paul, was my hero, because of all the white women he was dating.

Mr. Pig would say,"Marco, come here," inviting me near.

There were other detectable "red flags" or signs of a grossing, failing marriage with my parents.

"You look like a raccoon," said my father, which caused my mother to fall on the floor, crying.

"You talk like you have mouth full of spit," he also said, in a demeaning way.

The entire marriage was abusive like that.

"You smell like Noxema. That stuff don't smell good," my father said to hurt her.

"What's that smell?" he'd say, as though my mother's perfume smelled, like garbage or something.

There was no denying it. Especially, when it came to one restaurant experience. My father took us to this steakhouse place. Erasing my mother's heart, he ordered nothing for himself. He sat and watched us eat. Being the "X-generation," I didn't get it. He rushed us, only to deposit us back home, and then went out himself.

Other strange things like that happened. The family sat in the car, at the fairgrounds, to watch the fireworks, being that it was a national holiday. He brought us home, dumped us, and went out. His usual pattern.

There were numerous occasions, when my mother would be trying to share something, about what happened at home, work, or on the news. My father would show "no interest" in what she had to say.

"You finish?" he would say in jest, then walk away.

"Don't touch me," in would say in their bedroom, claiming a headache.

It wasn't by design, when one day, my mother was in my room, and somehow the word "girlfriend" was mentioned. My father, in his usual way, stormed in. He said, he would hit her, if she said, something else to me, "…In front of this child." Right in front of me, my father threatened my mother. I told my mama, I would have "done something to him." I promised her that. As I grew older, I wouldn't have let, anything, happen to her. I was ready to protect her, from him. She was glad, it didn't come to that point.

Our lives were destroyed. It was a floodgate of emotions. Hence, the chip on my shoulder. There were times, when there was no communication with him. He would, actually, walk out of a room, whenever my mother would walk in.

My parent's marriage became unglued. It was devoid of respect, as other women called the house. My mother handed him the phone, thinking it was job related, or asking for legal advice. From the expansion of his voice, she could tell. It was something he wanted to say, without letting her know, what was going on.

Dad played my mama, " like a game of golf." He would get a "discreet" phone call, and suddenly leave. With a diamond in the back, my mama decided to do a little detective work, on their distorted marriage. Once,

Dad got one of "those" phone calls. She drove to this particular house. Sure enough, my dad's car was parked out front. Mama walked up to the door, and knocked.

"Is he here?" she asked the elder woman behind the door.

She didn't invite my mother in. My dad came to the door, digging himself deeper. Staring at each other, my mother turned around and left. The house belonged to my now half-sister, Chrissy's grandmother.

My sister, Dreeka, and Cassie's older daughter, Tammy, went to the same daycare. Now, dig this. The house was only a street over, from the daycare facility.

Not that mama was looking, but she happen to stumble across a letter, which directed her attention. One line, fairly, stated, "The reason I was able to get away, with so much, is because she stupid enough to believe everything I say."

Giving my mother, one to grow on, a neighbor disclosed something to her. After my father abandoned us, he admitted it. He knew my dad was living with his girlfriend, in a neighborhood, practically, across the street from ours. In a house with his "other family."

Speaking of phones. The man who carried a gun for a living, put a house phone in the garage, independently, for privacy. So at my discretion, by accident, I picked up the phone to use it. My father became fast and furious with me.

He later came up with, the shallow idea, of getting call-waiting. So, if my mother should happen to call, he wouldn't miss his other call, from his other woman.

Make no illusion an about it. The female, my father was seeing, had an apartment, within walking distance. Occasionally, my younger siblings and I, went over there. (The first time he moved out. Not the final time.) I warned my mother, that the lady over there was his "girlfriend." My mother asked him about this. He came up with a handy lie. He said the woman, over there, was his "roommate's girlfriend." He gave mama his best regards.

It seven or eight months later, Dad called, saying he wanted to get back together. My mother wanted to believe there was a fiber of decency left in him. She took him back in. It was later, when she found out, apparently, the "roommate's girlfriend" and him got into an argument. It forced him, to need a place to stay.

When my father left for good, the last time, my mother, harmoniously, went over to "the house" nearby, once more.

"What is it?" the "other woman" said, as though she was being distracted.

The two of them never, actually, met. It was, finally, face to face. Obviously, she knew, who my mama was. It, certainly, was not the "stranger" way, to greet someone. It was though, she knew all about her.

During my parent's marriage, early on, my father stopped wearing his wedding band. So many lies were told to his folks down south.

"Nobody around here cares anything about you! You might as well leave," my mother, allegedly, said, which was, totally, not true.

Lies were told. Heavy duty lies, such as my father, the disciplinarian, wasn't allowed to discipline us, the children. Lies that belonged in a dog kennel. Such as, my mother haven't been a wife to him in months.

Don't get me wrong. My mother was no angel. With me, anyway, she would be snappy, sarcastic and stoic, sometimes. She could have a pessimist personality, or taking everything, personally. She would be anal, without apology. She could speak, sharply, or impulsively. She was, usually, obsessing, or overly sensitive, at times. Mama could be unnerving, with nervousness. She was overwhelming, with worrying.. Yet, no one, deserves to be smacked around by her husband, used, abused, lied to, and cheated on like that.

After a few months, when my father was court ordered, to pay child support, before the divorce was finalized, other things were said.

"Here's yours! Do what you want," my mother was, supposedly, to have said to us.

It was misconduct. Hence the phrase, "Those children run that house," we heard, about us, through the grapevine.

Was it the morning, when my father was on the war path with me, as usual? Accidentally, I left some shoes or something, on the steps. I was just a kid. My father went after me. I was distressed. My mother was leaving for work. I was, literally, terrified. I was begging my mama, not to leave me. I just knew, it was not a natural situation. I shouldn't be scared to death of my dad. Perhaps, it may explain why I ran away from home, several times.

Was it when we became a dysfunctional family, when my parents arrived here? Just starting out, they moved into an apartment, near a garage landfill. Rats were everywhere. My parents saw one or two a day, over a three week period. My mother was terrified, needless to say. Found one rat in the clothes hamper.

"I hope you wake up, with a dead rat, laying on your stomach," said my father.

Hideous thing to say. She didn't know what molded such behavior.

There was the time, when my mother was in the hospital. She was about to give birth to Dreeka, the baby of the family, with induce labor. My mother was crying and crying , because of her hallow marriage. My maternal grandma asked, what was wrong. Mama couldn't, hardly, bring herself to tell her, that my father showed no interest, in her pregnancy. No interest in their, supposedly, monogamous relationship.

The horizon of a divorce was near. In the courtroom, my father's lawyer said, my parents needed to work things out, for the sake of the children.

"She's too sick!" my father labeled her, to him.

When my mother was pregnant with me, her first born, my father showed, hardly, any interest as well. When it was time, for her to get "me" to the hospital, he told a, friendly, couple they knew, to do it, because he was at work. A hue of humanity would've been nice. There wasn't the typical enthusiasm as with new fathers. Such as,"My son is going to be a lawyer !" No, nothing.

There were other defining moments. There's not enough hydrogen to explain it all.

Or did things fall apart, when I was recommended therapy? I was acting "legendary" in school. The therapist wanted to get some background information. Particularly, genuine, good family experiences with my dad. As strange as it may sound, my mother could not think of any. Only idle thoughts of him being cruel, with evil intentions.

Maybe it was the fact, that my mama had to teach herself, how to drive a black, 1971 Ford Mustang. She, alone, worked the levers, on their only stick-shift car, with black leather interior.

"You drive the car, when I tell you, you can drive it!" my father once said, to his amusement.

My mother wasn't going for that.

"No, hell I won't!" my mama said, about the mean, American-made machine. "Ain't no damn car, going to sit out there, in front of my damn door, and I can't drive it, and I got to help pay for it! I'm going to get in it, and drive it, or I'm going to tear, the damn thing up! It doesn't make me one bit, of damn difference!"

My mother got into that car, that day. She self-taught herself, how to brake, on a busy traffic, or a steep, hilled street. She drove the life of that car, everyday, for the next four years, until it was traded in. Mystified, my mother didn't even know, he was buying the car at all. Dad bought a straight-shift car, without her consent, knowing my mother "couldn't drive it." My mother learned anyway, by herself.

*8 years old*

*ACT 1, SCENE 2*

# Monologue

"HOWDY," AS MY mother would say. I'm Marco. I was born, on a Monday, at 7:20 pm, on February 8, 1971. The same day as my father's birthday. When life gives you lemons, make limousines, I say. I was born at Richmond Memorial hospital. It's now defunct.

My parents are from the same hometown. They were high school sweethearts. My maternal grandmother's maiden name, is the same last name, of my father's.

My maternal grandfather, David, died from a gunshot wound, when I was six-months old. I never got the chance, to know him. I'd hear stories. He had a drinking problem, and a gambling problem. Of course, there was the famous story, my grandmother, Maggie, threw a pot of boiling, hot water on him, during a heated argument. Another violent household.

Once, my mother needed moral support to visit him, where he was staying. My grandparents were separated. I was a newborn baby, and my mother wanted to introduce, him to me. My father refused to go in. My mother decided not to go in as well. Six months later, my grandfather was killed.

My mother was the valedictorian, in her senior class, at Westside High School. She majored, in mathematics, at South Carolina State University.

My father served his country, and was stationed in 'Nam. He didn't share much of his war experience, to his children.

My parents got married June 24, 1969. It was during my mother's Junior year, in college. 1970, my father moved here, to the commonwealth state, after he got out of military service. He was promised a job. Specifically, they were recruiting Black police officers, in the city. My father moved here, with only $27 in his pocket. Meanwhile, he lived in a YMCA shelter, awaiting my mother.

As a baby, my mother assured me, with all the loss, love and nectar she could muster. Nightly, my mother kept me in her arms, and in her heart. With my "vacationing" father, it was like being lodged between a rock and a hard place.

My parents moved to a house, in a predominantly Black, middle class neighborhood, two years later. I was two-years-old. Mr. Pig, our nosey, but friendly neighbor, would tell me old stories. He said that all the White people moved out, when Black people moved in the neighborhood.

It was a nice, quiet neighborhood. In a new, fence-less, two-story house. Beige, with brown shudders. In a lullaby, I was lonely, being the only child. My non-combatant mother spoiled me. She took tons of pictures.

When I was three-years-old, I would, actually, go into the utility room. It was where the washer and dryer was kept. With the lights off, the door closed behind me, sitting on the steps it provided, I'd pray for a younger brother. Soon after, Mel was born. Eventually, he moved into the bunk bed, directly, above me.

As small children, Mel and I became a force to be reckoned with. We were like a machete in a rainforest, knocking down everything in our path.

"You two, are the most disrespectful children, I have ever seen, in my life!" cried my mother, in her usual Zayre's department store.

Without paying for it, of course, we would eat candy, right on the spot. My brother and I would take superhero action-figure dolls, right out the package, and play with it. As children, we would curse and swear. We'd rip and run, throughout the stores. We'd, totally, embarrass our mother. We stole toys. We tried on clothes. We knocked things over. Our father wasn't around. Mel and I was so disruptive. A plain-dress security guard notified my mother, if we don't stop, we would no longer be allowed, in their store. It brought my mother to tears.

My mother would, sometimes, leave us in the car. She'd promise to be back soon. We would curse out obscenities at unassuming pedestrians going by.

"White people! Black people! Unite!" I would yell, my personal favorite, a majority of the time, at a local store near you.

Ordinarily, my father would give us butt-whippings, if he was informed. With those thick, black leather belts. I nearly went into shock, from the pain. Like a maniac, I would get whippings, constantly. Because of that, I vowed, that I would never hit my children, with no physical pain to punish them.

I was so disruptive, in my first ever, nursery school. I was asked to leave, by the school administrators. Eventually, my parents put me, in yet, another nursery school, Bethlehem. It was in the basement, of a nearby church. Mrs. Stevens would hit my hand, with a measuring ruler, or paintbrush handle, when I would get out of line. Of course, the school taught me, my A's, B's and C's and numbers. They held Christmas pageants. The children would race up, to the pastor of the church, whom we all, lovingly, call "Daddy." Mrs. Stevens would grab my cute cheeks, which made all the children giggle.

My parents' southern hometown was no exception. I would get major butt-whippings down there too. Every year, we'd go. Sometimes, all hot summer. A week, sometimes. My parents, and us children, would spend time there.

My maternal aunt, North, would join us in the fun. She lived in Jersey. I wasn't sure, she knew of my parent's marital problems.

"Hey, Pee Wee," my father, affectionately nicknamed her.

"Von" was my mother, on occasion.

"Boy, you look, just like your daddy!" my paternal grandparents would say, as I walked through their door.

I looked forward, to being with my family in the south. The summer heat was, unbearably, hot. Nearly, everyone was wearing tank tops, cut-off shorts and flip flop shoes.

I was, completely, comfortable with its Anderson, small-town hospitality, southern accent and southern charm. I felt at home in South Carolina. People were friendly, laidback and easygoing there. I was in awe, when people would, politely, wave, to us, but they didn't know us.

I often wished, I would've grew up there, with all my fun-loving cousins. Unlike here, which I felt, perhaps, people were, unnecessarily, uptight and had a bad attitude. I would smile. I was proud. Happy to be there. It was a humbling experience.

"You gonna be a policeman, when you grow up?" they would say.

I'd nod my head, "Yes," as I was, practically, expected to do. I was massaging my father's ego.

My paternal grandmother, Mattie Ruth, was sweet as can be. She'd fix me something to eat, at a moment's notice. She introduced me to coffee, as a kid. She made the best sweet tea, and red Kool-Aid. She let me put ketchup, on the great spaghetti she made. The sweetest person, I have ever met.

We had loads of fun. We drank beers. We'd get drunk. I'd ride around or go out, with my paternal cousins. My father's sister, Mae, children. As kids, we'd walk to a small store across the street and purchase "penny candy."

On Independence Day, we'd throw lit firecrackers, at each other. My cousin Baby would play loud music and drive, terrifyingly, fast. There was Shee, Baby's older sister. It was good times. He was a few years older than me. Fist and Jonathan, my cousins, were party-goers too. Jonathan suffered from Sickle Cell.

I was, eternally, grateful to my paternal uncle, Kenn. He always took off from his job, to show us kids, a great time, whenever we were in town. He would take us to the movies, swimming, roller skating, you name it.

I admired Kenn's willingness to be friendly. He was funny and talked to everyone he met. I was very impressed with that. I was amazed. That struck a resounding cord in me. He didn't care, if they were Black or White. He was very fun to be around. He was considerate and playful. My mother and aunt, North, simply adored him.

People, who have a lot of money, don't impress me, unless they're giving me some. I'm not, nearly, impressed with how smart someone is. Especially, if they're arrogant with it. However, I am impressed with, how kind someone is, to all others. So, there he was, in the flesh, being kind to everyone. I promised myself, if I ever had a son, I'd name him, Kenn.

That may explain, why I get misty-eyed, over civil rights leader,

Martin Luther King Jr. every year on his national holiday. Goodwill to all, impresses me.

Uncle Joe, on the other hand, was more quiet and reserved.

Everyone in my father's family would, playfully, pick on my "grouchy" granddaddy, John. He loved his old cowboy movies, and didn't want to be disturbed. He worked land maintenance, for a electric power plant company, Duke Power, for many years. He liked to "read" my superhero comic books. He'd make homemade ice cream, in a churner, by turning its handle, a hundred times. He grew up on a cow farm, and rode horses when he was younger.

Occasionally, as kids, my grandmother and him would whip us, with a long, orange, race track strip, made for toy cars.

Mel and I would, clarify, which grandma we were referring to, by using their last name.

My maternal grandmother, Maggie, was a bit stern. (She didn't play that). Living alone, she would walk miles, to go to the neighborhood store, or even further, to pay bills, downtown.

My two maternal uncles, Reggie and (David) Sanford, lived with their wives and children, on the west coast.

On a fixed income, Grandma didn't have much, but she kept her house, nice and neat.

"You can do a lot with a broom," she once said. In which, her own mother, my great-grandmother, Viola, taught her, "Where there's a will, there's a way."

She didn't like her young grandchildren, jumping on her bed mattress. She didn't like her young grandchildren, going in and out the house. She kept law and order, by invading our legs, with a "switch." That was a skinny branch or twig from the hedges. We had to, personally, pick one out for ourselves, for punishment. If it was deemed too small by her, we would have to, reasonably, pick out another, for own whipping. She also had a skinny, leather strap, hung on the wall.

"...And it better not be too small either!" my mother's mother would say.

She had a green thumb, for plants. She grew a small garden, tomatoes and squash, in her backyard. She had a peach tree, and often prepared peach dishes, on our plates. She made grits croquettes, salmon croquettes, for breakfast. She enjoyed watching sports on television. She smoked her cigarettes, but later quit, only because the price went up. She was full of tenacity and demanded respect.

If it wasn't for my maternal grandmother, the mosquitoes, also, tore our legs up. We had to play outside, on grandmama's swing set. To pass the time, we'd walk to the store. Sometimes, we'd walk on a nearby train track. The train crossed once or twice a day. Couldn't help but hear it, as loud as it was. We'd play with my next door cousins. My grandfather and his brother, which was my mother's uncle, had houses beside each other.

My maternal grandma was, generally, strict. So, Mel and I would try our best, to get back to our father's side of the family, as, quickly, as possible.

Our older brother, Antonio, was always in my heart.

"Where's Tee?" I'd ask, first thing, at my paternal grandparents.

My grandma had his phone number. I'd make it a point to see him. Grandma would "spoil us rotten." She sliced us delicious cakes, she baked herself. She'd reach in her pocketbook, to give us coins, to buy candy. Sleeping on the couch, directly, under the soothing window fan, was the most coziest feeling in the world.

Though Mel and I were far from home, we were still young and rebellious.

"We rich! We rich!" I'd say to my other young cousins.

"Don't be telling them that!" my father would admonish.

"In Virginia, we got this...In Virginia, we got that," I would brag, proud of my home state.

Getting on their nerves, I'm sure.

"Alright now, Marco. You want to go back, to your other grandma's house?" warned the elders.

My father's family would threaten us with that. It was "boring" at my mother's mother house. We felt there was nothing to do there.

My grandmama, Maggie, had a gold tooth. She gossiped, with other women, while smoking her cigarette. She listened to her church service, the Reverend Ike, every Sunday.

I could, finally, hear my own mama say, "Mmm-hmm," or "Yeah, child," when she was around the ladies in her family. It was nice seeing my mother, comfortable, in her hometown element.

My uncle, Reggie, was quiet, with long, Jheri curl hair. He delivered the U.S. Mail. He coached his sons' football team. He visited South Carolina, yearly, too.

Naturally, we would have to visit my mother's cousin, Louise, since we were in town. As usual, on our last night in Anderson, we'd see my mother's uncle. They, simply, called him "Unck." Short for uncle. He had the same name as my father.

"Boy, you look, just like your daddy," I would hear from him. "Boy, you getting big!" he would say.

Whenever we got outside anywhere, I would beg, and beg, my mother for candy or a toy.

"You the most begging child, I have ever seen, in my life!" my maternal grandmother said.

Sometimes, my mother would buy me something, in a jiffy. Other times, my grandmother would intervene, in the middle of our conversation.

"…You're spoiling that child!" she said, out of her mouth.

My mother's mother, Maggie, was the type of person, who said whatever was on her mind. She didn't bite her tongue, or held back. It didn't matter, how joyless, it may have sound. It could be at my mother's expense as well.

My father could be seen drinking a beer, with Mae or her husband, Clarence. They worked at the factory mills.

Also, before we left, for home, mama and my aunt, North, would haul their clothes at the laundry mat, down the street. A man, who was, respectfully, known as Pee Wee, worked on, or fixed, the laundry room machines. He wore a coin pouch around his waste, for change. He had a crippled hand and had a limp walk. He attended school with them, and knew them when.

My aunt, wouldn't wear any junk or cheap-looking stuff. She would wear stylish, name brand clothes. She'd wear Jordache or Calvin Klein's jeans. She wouldn't shop at certain stores. The minute she had my cousin, Nikki, all that changed. Eventually, she went for the more affordable, clearance items she could find. My aunt wouldn't allow stores to cheat her, monetarily, too. She'd demand every dime, she was owed, from the cash register. She worked as a social worker.

Quick to paddle my behind, anytime, or anywhere, I wouldn't have traded, my life with my maternal grandmother, any different. On the eight-hour drive, going back home, I would, somehow, feel sorry for her. She lived alone, and faced everything, by herself. One daughter in Virginia. The other daughter in New Jersey. Her two sons, in California. My mother assured me, she had plenty to do. She had her plants, small garden, peach trees, puzzle books.

My palms would become sweaty, at the thought of my father's violence and intimidation. In spite of our safe return, my mother would have her worries. It was a loosely based marriage. Things went back into their private affairs. Now away from all the family. Things were, right under her nose. My parents would go back into their regularly, separate, scheduled program. Mel and I would reacquaint ourselves, with our light blue room, with our Star Wars bedcover.. My aunt, who in earlier times, would ride down south, with us, would catch the Greyhound bus, or fly from here, at Byrd Airport.

"What's up, Walt?" I would say, to my next-door neighbor.

I told him about the small, golden trophy I won. It was for remembering the names, of every chapter title, in the Bible, at my paternal grandma's church. The summer cookouts, we had. The firecrackers we popped. That was illegal in Virginia, at the time. He proposed we go outside and play. I'd rip and run, up and down the street, in my cut-off shorts and tank tops. Once, my siblings and I caught a plane, to spend the summer at South Carolina. Another time, we caught the Greyhound bus to go south.

Walter would laugh, and get me to laugh along with him. For the smallest things, or for no apparent reason at all. We would, passionately, ride our bikes, here and there. As kids, we'd would do nutty things, like climb to the roof of my house, by way of the backyard patio cover. We'd climb to the top of the gym's roof, at the nearby middle school, by way of its slanted columns.

When my father wasn't home, of course, we'd get on my father's motorcycle, pretending we were going somewhere, fast. Between the fence of my house, and our back neighbor's fence, we would, literally, suck the sweet nectar from honeysuckle flowers. Not too far from us, we'd walk there, and eat blackberries. We'd capture fireflies in Mason jars.

Occasionally, after school, Mrs, Smith, an elderly Black woman, would keep us, until our parents came home. She was the neighbor, who lived, directly, behind us.

Walter was an only child. His father was a truck driver. Whenever he would see a tractor trailer truck, Walter would raise his clinching fist, up and down, signaling the driver to blow his horn. Remarkably, they obliged to our delight. His mother was a nurse.

There were a gang of other kids in the neighborhood. The prospect of the woods, close by, was ours for the taking. A sage, or pathologist, wouldn't be able to tell you, why we did it. We rode our bikes on dangerous, dirt trail of rocks, ramps and hills. There were fallen trees, and wild animals. "The Woods" as we called it, had a creek. It offered crayfish, which looked, exactly, like miniature lobsters.

Also, there were fishermen and a small pond, centered in our neighborhood. Sometimes, we'd go there and hang out. Other times, Walter and I would help ourselves to some cheese puffs, or a sandwich of peanut butter and jelly.

Being the environmental, animal lover that I am, I'd collect bugs in one of my mother's Mason jars. I'd have to punch holes in the lid, so the bug can survive. Usually, mama kept her jars with fruits and veggies, preserved, air-tight. That was something my grandmother did too. I suppose, for a "rainy day."

Eventually, my father got me a German Shepherd puppy. I named him, "Chico," I loved that dog. He was kept outside, in a doghouse. I'd spend hours with him. Feeding him, giving him treats, and running around the yard with him. It broke my heart, when we went the following summer to South Carolina. We gave him to Mrs. Smith, to keep him. I was told, my dog got tangled in his rope, and died, when we got back from our trip.

BEHOLD

When I was a kid, I was always snooping around. I was too scared, to mess with my dad's stereo, eight-track cassette tapes. However, I did, in my free time, sneaked my father's record collection. I'd, sneakily, listen to his Richard Pryor, concert records, and laugh. I'd listen to his James Brown '.45's records. My parents saved their 1960's record albums. Both of their names were written on the album cover. I guess, if anyone borrowed them, there wouldn't be any confusion.

I would peep into my dad's Playboy, and Penthouse magazines. He kept them in the cricket-infested garage. Sometimes, I would show them to Walter. With the women, having a peculiar thing, between their legs, I kept coming back for more. Getting an adrenaline rush, I moved up the ladder, to dad's VHS cassette tapes. I was scared to death, thinking, at any moment, Dad would pull up in the driveway.

Miraculously, I never did find his police-issued gun, to play with. (Thank God).

As long as my father was, supposedly, working long hours, for a pension, one day, I was okay. Whenever he was home, there were unpredictability, bouts of violence. It could be him, punching a hole in the wall with the back of the tv, or staring at me, eating. I'd quiver like a scorpion's tail.

My mother would relate to me stories, how she grew up poor. Sometimes, the only thing, merely, to eat was a loaf of bread. The lights would be turned off, and no money, for the electricity bill.

"You don't know, what's it like to be poor," she would say it me, should I complain about food or something.

As I watched The Muppet Show, my mother would sew her own clothes. She'd, proudly, show me the thick, colorful, hand-made, woven quilt, her mother made.

Sometimes, on a Saturday, we would go downtown, on the corner of Seventeen and Main Street. We'd stroll to the Farmer's Market, for fresh fruits and vegetables. It was one of the perks, of her being raised in the south. Mama would pick through or squeeze fruits.

Her eyes would radiate, when she would talk about the Jim Crow laws. She lived in a racially, segregated, separated south.

"Y'all don't know what's it like, to go a "Colored" water fountain, or a "Colored" back entrance, to a movie," she would tell Mel and I.

At the Farmer's Market, we might see our neighbors, Mrs. Green, or Mrs. Miller. In the hot seat, of my mother's beige '76 Ford Elite, we went.

I might hear, how my father was the only person, in high school, with a brand new '65 car, in 1965. He earned it, by working full time at a Kentucky Fried Chicken restaurant. (My uncle Joe raised chickens, by the way, to earn money, by selling chicken eggs.) Dad also, then, worked at a car wash too.

The summers seemed to go, so quickly.

"Marco Polo," kids teased.

"Boy…Hey, boy! You're going to school?" pestered Mr. Pig, in his raspy voice.

I'd nod my head, "Yes," in a sensible way.

"…Good!" he would say, as I noticed him, holding a can of beer.

Mr. Pig was a train conductor. He'd always give me, friendly, advice. Whether I, exactly, wanted it or not. "Never give up. Try, try again." (How can I forget)?

"…I pick on you, because I like you. You know that, don't you?"

His son and daughter, several years older, would look on.

I'd carry my, Hot Wheels cars, lunch box to my elementary school, during my kindergarten and first grade. My mother would fix us cereal, pieces of bacon and toast. We'd gulp it down, with either apple or orange juice.

I'll never forget, my second grade teacher, Mrs. Horton made me pee on myself. See, you couldn't just, get up and go to the bathroom. You'll get in trouble. So, I kept pitching my hand up, for permission to leave the classroom. Oddly, she would never call on me. (I know, she saw my hand.) I was so embarrassed. She recommended, I see a doctor. My father took me, and I got some pills, for my "little problem."

"Your daddy a policeman?" the kids at school would recite.

They didn't know, how shallow our relationship was.

"You scared for him?" they would say, which made his job description plausible.

They had no idea, for months, I wouldn't call my father, "Daddy." I was tired of him whipping me, all the time. The looking mean, or intimidating us, was too much. I was scared of him, and what he might do.

Mrs. Jackson, from the Third Grade, rings a bell. It was Halloween. She wore her, actual, karate clothes to school. She, really, did know martial arts. I won the Bookworm contest in her class. It was for reading the most books, which included, having to do a book report, on the book too.

For Halloween night, my father would do it up big. He'd carve out a face, in a fat pumpkin. He'd place a candle in it. We'd hang a life-size, paper skeleton on the door. (Creepy, huh)? We'd turn on the porch light, a must. We'd wait for the kids to come, for their candy. Mel dressed up like Batman. I was Superman. I'd shepherd Mel around with our pumpkin-shape, Trick-or-Treat plastic containers.

My father was, extremely, popular. Everywhere we went, someone knew him. The point I'm trying to make, he coached us along, distant and aloof.

The most profound thing, I have ever witnessed, was from the movie, Roots.

"Kunta Kente, behold the only thing greater than yourself."

That was " lightning in a bottle." I caught it. "Only God is greater!" His father said this, as he lifted his infant son, to the heavens above. Little did he know, that his son, Kunta, would someday be stolen. He was sent, politically, to an incorrect land for generations.

Without the head shrinks, and occasional pops on the head, I've always wanted to relax, with my own family, I created. I wanted to make up for what I never had, with my father.

Anyway, it was, nearly, Christmas, when my father picked up a certain woman in the car, who gave Mel and I, signature red and green, brimmed, stocking caps. We always had a huge Christmas, when my father remained with us. Things haven't been the same since, with little potluck. It was a very special, magical time. Lots of presents, under a heavily, decorated evergreen tree. Many toys. Candy was everywhere. Lights in the windows. I rented my time. I could, hardly, wait for Santa Clause to come. So many sizable gifts. Kids from the neighborhood, like David and Willie, would visit us, to see what we got.

# MONOLOGUE

On my 8th birthday, taking precautionary measures, the county schools were closed, because of the heavy snow. My father gave me a birthday present. It was Michael Jackson's then Greatest Hits album. He seemed as young as me, on the album cover. I slapped it on my record player, with glee. It was magic. With predictability, I couldn't contain myself. I danced and singed, in my bedroom slippers. I've been a Michael Jackson fan, ever since. I would play that one, single album, for hours. I loved music. I'd always play it. I had plenty of mixtapes, I'd record off the radio. I thought I was going to be a disc jockey someday.

Older people said, I was smart. I loved to read books. No longer tame, I'd make myself useful by reading. As a kid, I would smuggle, "borrow," or steal, tastefully written, Judy Blume books. They were considered "girl books" from the school's library. I'd, discreetly, return them back. I guess, I was too embarrassed to, regularly, check them out, at the library counter, but I liked them.

Unquestionably, It was the author, Judy Blume, that sparked my interest, in creative writing. I thought her books were, wonderfully, vulnerable, and personal. It was delightful and insightful. I loved the narrator's point of view stuff. After that, with valor, I dabbled with poetry, myself. I'd do a little writing on my own, here and there. There was something very satisfying, powerful, and permanent, about putting my thoughts, on paper. I wrote short stories. It gave me joy, to play with words, or fool with word play.

It was the summer of 1979. I couldn't believe what I was hearing, coming from David's mouth. He was another neighborhood kid. Despite his vast knowledge about football, he knew the whole, entire, Sugar Hill's "Rapper's Delight" song. It was amazing.

New kids were on the block. I got in solid, with his next-door neighbors or "cousins," Vin and Gerry. They were brothers. We got along great. Meanwhile, Walter, my neighbor, gravitated towards Greg. He lived down the street, in the other direction .

I introduced my new friends to my brother, and baby sis, Dree. Like The Temptations, we were inseparable. Vin and Gerry were good-natured, easygoing, laidback, and "country."

Greg, however, was a "city slicker," previously, from another neighborhood. He invited mischief, but polite and well-mannered with parents. Sometimes, he'd hang with his other neighborhood friend, Bernie. Both of their families worked a well-known tobacco company, Phillip Morris. Bernie had a birthmark, black ear. We wouldn't dare, talk about it.

I did a short stint, with a (predominantly White) Cub Scouts of America troop. It was a source of fun. I learned the hierarchy of God, Country and Honor. The Den Mother baked us cookies and poured us lemonade. We dressed in our Blues. The Scout Master, who supplied us with the Cub Scout Manual taught us survival skills. We learned skills about the forest, first aide remedies, and the importance of helping others. We made wooden, hand-made, go-cars. We raced them in a competition, with other troops. My car was black, No. 8. Vin and Gerry, and I tried to be in the Cub Scouts, with their cousins in Petersburg, but it never panned out. I think our parents, wasn't willing to drive that far.

My father's best friend was in the same neighborhood too. They did everything together. "Where you saw one, you saw the other." On the spare of the moment, they would go on motorcycle trips. There was bowling, fishing expeditions. They'd borrow each other's tools. Our family and Mr. Hall's family went together, to Washington DC's National Zoo and Baltimore's Aquarium. Theirs was a testimony of true friendship.

Naturally, I hung around Mr. Hall's son, Chucka. He was a habitual "fibber." However, I was speechless, at all the great toys he had. He was an only child, with a vivid imagination. He was very theatrical. Chucka had all the Star Wars action-figures, so we got along beautiful.

However, when I was saw Superman: The Movie, I became a die-hard Superman, superhero fan too.

My mother is deaf, in her left ear. She would seldom drive us, to visit my aunt, in New Jersey. North had a Doberman pincher, in her apartment. My mother, certainly, wasn't wild about that. From North's, eight-story, apartment building, you could see the Manhattan skyline.

My aunt would take us sightseeing. New York City was exciting. We were, finally, in The Big Apple. Huge buildings kissed or licked the sky. It was splashed with tall skyscrapers, flashing lights, loud car horns, huge signs, bold people, and thick fog. I loved it! Spunky as she wants to be, my maternal grandmother tagged along too. We, thoughtfully, visited grandma's (half) sister, Aunt Elizabeth in Harlem. We saw The Apollo theater. Once, she prepared us some "nasty" tasting sandwiches. We, discreetly, spat what remained, in our napkins.

Also, we rode the artistic, or graffitied, crowded subway. With our ears popping, the elevator, quickly, flew us, to the top of one the world-famous, World Trade Center towers. The ferryboat swam, to the Statue of Liberty. We staged ourselves, in the middle of Times Square. We drove the Brooklyn Bridge.

Being steadfast, we visited grandma's sister, Aunt Cleo, in North Carolina. With her living in the mountains, our ears would tingle, from the anticipation of going up and down.

*ACT 2, SCENE 3*

# Dialogue

IT'S NOT AN old wives' tale, or being stingy with the facts. My father took the family to the lake.

There was a sliding board, which led into the water. Mel and I, being children, got on the it. Mel flew into the murky water. He took a long time, to resurface. I felt toil and troubled. I knew something was wrong. I whisked in the water, after Mel. I believed, I saved his life. True story.

It's also true, I was very protective of Mel. Especially, when I was in the 4$^{th}$ Grade and 5$^{th}$ Grade. I got into, so many fights over my little brother. If any kid, from the neighborhood, and I mean any, talked Mel, I would strike. Without thinking twice. It wasn't my brother's fault. They'd say something, perhaps, about his big forehead, buck teeth, or round stomach.

Love transcends all things. Hard times make a person wise.

On the big, yellow school bus, in the 4$^{th}$ Grade, nobody wanted to sit beside Rita. Not to mention, if she strutted over, to their seat. The guys would laugh at her, making her cry. The kids thought, she was a bit "off" or slow. It was beyond reason. I didn't knock her, or make fun of her. I was nice to her. We were from the same neighborhood. Rita felt comfortable with me. Of course, naturally, the kids said, I must like her.

No, I had my eyes, on that pretty young thing called, Mia. She had a troop of admirers. I kept glancing at her in class. It wrecked my school work. I had it bad. Eventually, the teacher called my parents, to say I wasn't "succeeding in my studies." She was my little crush. Mama, with her woman's intuition, knew. So, eating my candied yams, at the dinner table, I tried to put Mia's long, sultry hair out of my mind.

5$^{th}$ Grade was no exception. Mia was still cute. She had a best friend,

Monique. They stuck together, like twins. In 5th Grade, students exchanged classes, for each class period.

Each 5th Grade teacher had a reoccurring theme, plastered, on their classroom walls. Mrs. Thomas taught English. She provided her room, with pictures of dogs. Mr. Reynolds, History. He supplemented his walls with Charlie Brown and the Peanut Gallery. Mrs. Cook, Math and Science. She showed us the meaning of panda bears.

Mel began doing things "unbecoming" of a boy. He was playing with Dreeka's dolls. He was making a mess, with mama's makeup. He'd suck lollipops, peculiarly. My dad wasn't having it.

I spent so much time with Walter, Vin, and Gerry. We'd play Atari video games for hours. We'd walk to Eastgate Mall, Sears department store, to play its arcade's video games. I felt a little, lonely at school. They were a year, or two older than me. They were, already, at middle school. It was depressing.

I'll never forget. All the students had to go into the Multipurpose Room, under advisement, to sit still or remain quiet. The school was showcasing student talent. We were in for a treat. Every year, the PTA sponsored plays. I was one myself, but somehow, this was different. Rose, her sister, and Ron, came unto the stage, like suspects.

Suddenly, Earth, Wind, and Fire's "Let's Groove" song was on the airwaves. It electrified us. The dance trio took each other's hand, popped and locked. It was the first time, I seen "breakdancing." They slid across the floor, doing Michael Jackson's Moonwalk.

Then, there was the Spring of '81. It was the morning, I became a loyal Prince fan. Getting ready for school, I put the tv on MTV. Music videos, as usual. It catered, to my Rock and Roll needs. Sue me.

Prince's "Controversy" video was on. He was "different." He was "odd," but cool. That lead guitar player, with the black trench coat, heeled boots, meant business. I became an instant fan. He dressed "weird," but the confidence, he displayed was unfounded. I was sympathetic to his cause. I was learning to love, all genres of music, through Prince.

He was R&B, Rock, Jazz and of course, Pop. He was Little Richard, James Brown, Jimmy Hendrix, all rolled up into one. He could dance, sing, and scream. White people, Black people in his band. Yes! I loved that. He put everything on the table. It was unspeakable, "before his time" talent. Girls liked him.

I began wearing a gold necklace, imitating my dad. I wanted to be cool. I started to pimp walk, like Prince. I started to wear my shirt collar, flipped up, like Prince. Rick James was funky, but Prince became my idol, my "main man." Like clockwork, everyday after school, I would call local, radio host, Kirby Carmichael, on his popular, AM radio show. I'd request that mesmerizing "Controversy" song. I'd get Walter to request the song too.

Whenever we were away in South Carolina, I'd visit my cousin, Tina as well. Amateur hour. Next door, to maternal grandmother.

"Open your mouth, when you talk!" my aunt, North, would say, if I mumbled my words.

(Where was the nearest balcony)?

"You're going to eat, all of that?" she would say, if I reached, for an extra piece of chicken.

( I wanted to be absent).

At the time, I had an infinity for buttons. They were, usually, celebrity pictures, celebratory pinned to one's shirt, hat, coat, whatever. I was wearing one, with the lead singer of the rock group, Joan Jett and The Blackhearts. "I Love Rock and Roll," was my song.

She happens to be White.

"Who's that?" North said, eyeing my button, with a raised eyebrow.

However, North said, I was "great with children." She told me, I'd make a "good father, someday." My personality, perhaps. I was always "young at heart" with an "old soul."

I had another dog, named "King." He was white and black fur. He was German shepherd, mixed with something else. I hated to leave him behind, in a barricaded fence, whenever I went to school. Somehow, he "mysteriously" decided, to up, and run away from home, never to be seen again. I couldn't prove it, but I always believed, a certain someone, got tired of buying dog food, or spending money for shots, and let him go, far from the house.

"I laugh, to keep from crying," was my motto.

When I was in the 6th Grade, I'd do anything for a chuckle. I wasn't getting any attention from my father. I'd act a fool, or silly, in school. Mr. Robinson, the 6th Grade, assistant principal, administered in- school detention to me, plenty of times. I rather "be laughed with, than laughed at."

Occasionally, Dad would throw me, Conan the Barbarian, and The Incredible Hulk, comic books. However, the hurt, of a stoic father, was becoming unbearable. Sometimes, I'd claim myself, "running away." I'd pack a suitcase, and leave. Without any money, or place to stay, afraid, I didn't get far, and turn back.

I spent a lot of time with Vin. We did everything together. The morning would begin, by me going to his house. Sometimes, he'd make us late, getting ready for school. Their house was eclectic, with clumsy household appliances. Apparently, their father, who worked for G&E was going to fix them. Vin and Gerry couldn't stand their stepmom. Soon, they had a baby brother.

Girls, girls, girls. It was all we talked about. It was agony, watching Vin get all the girls. I'd be the shy "wallpaper" or warming the bench. Females, seemingly, didn't give me, the time of day. I assumed, it was because of my weight.

I didn't fit in. I was a Black kid, who often watched American Bandstand, and MTV. I loved pop music videos. Of course, I'd, usually, watch BET and Soul Train too.

I wasn't apart of the "cool kids." I wasn't a "bad boy." I wasn't talking "slang." I certainly, wasn't "hip." I didn't have the "nice" clothes. I felt, I was "too White" for Black kids, but I was "too Black" for White kids.

"Marco likes that White boy music," the guys would tease.

I'd cry, in my pillow, every night. I wanted a girlfriend too. The only girl, who seemed to like me, or pay me any mind, was Rita. She was the girl, nobody wanted, unless, she was willing to give them a little "nookie." I wanted more, than easy "hanky-panky."

It didn't stop me, from being the classroom clown. I was the practical joker. I wanted applauds or my classmates approval. I must've been a headache to my teachers.

It seemed, the only luck I had, was when the guys and I went to the annual rap music "shows," festivals. Some shows were held at the Richmond Coliseum. Sometimes, at the Arthur Ashe Center. With various, New York hip-hop artists on stage, loud bass speakers, the place was packed, with teenagers. Plenty of fights, and lots of weed. In the dark, girls would grind dance with me.

I'd gain confidence, from smoking a stick of marijuana. It was, casually, passed around on the dance floor. It was the size of a miniature cigar, or caterpillar's cocoon. Getting high, was peer pressure..

Vin, of course, would get plenty of girl's phone numbers. I was, extremely, shy, quiet, and self-conscious. I hated my fat body. So, I wouldn't get any numbers. Nor did I try.

"I wish my mama, never gave birth to me!" I would cry, crying myself to sleep.

In further collateral damage, I was recommended family counseling, if I wanted to remain at the school. Embarrassed, I kept, seeing a" shrink" or therapist, a family secret. The neighborhood guys would have, certainly, labeled me "inky dink" or mental, for doing so. I couldn't take the chance. That would've been social suicide.

I was encouraged, to write my feelings, in a daily journal. I'd frequent the Barnes and Noble bookstore, at Eastgate mall.

With no money, I'd steal the small diaries, or journal books, the store afforded. I also dreamed of having my own published book, in there someday. I was amazed, all the books and authors.

I'd go to Fairfield public library. I'd dream something I wrote, would be in there someday. I'd check out books. As a kid, I loved to read MAD magazine. I loved the comical satire.

I was 12-years-old, getting high. There was smoking "reefer" before school. There was smoking "grass" after school. Strictly, for kicks and giggles.

We'd "blow guns" to each other. That's, directly, inhaling, from the actual marijuana smoke itself. The other guy, would forcefully, blow, the marijuana stick, turned inwardly, from inside his mouth, while pushing the weed smoke, directly, to our nose.

Sometimes we'd, simply, "puff, puff, pass" the marijuana, to the next guy. We'd all chip in, for a $10 "dime bag" or $5 "nickel bag." Occasionally, someone would sneak out, their parents beer, or cigarettes. We'd walk to middle school, high, "buzzing" or feeling good. Amazingly, no one failed school, or got "bad grades."

I wasn't the only one, causing havoc, in the classroom. Other juvenile delinquents, once made Mrs. Griffin, the 6$^{th}$ Grade math teacher, burst into tears. She ran out the door, in the middle of class. The students laughed, hysterically.

"You should be ashamed of yourselves!" Mr. Knox said to us.

He was a real nutcracker. He was another school assistant principal.

With no comment about my therapy sessions, the guys and I played games of pool, and video games at the nearby arcade, Wizard's.

Sometimes, we'd go to the nearby, Total Plus store. We'd buy chewing gum, Bubble Yum.

I'd steal candy, especially, chocolate, candy bars. I got caught once, stuffing chocolate, in my umbrella. The store manager told me, "don't come back," or he'll call the police.

Guys like, Cent or Willie would brag about a certain girl, they talked into, unbuttoning their blouse. They would credit their communication skills. I'd listen, in anguish, because it wasn't, successfully, happening for me. We'd all gawk and stare at girls' booty and bodies, as they walked by. It was compensation for them "looking so good."

With a bone to pick, there were, occasionally, skirmishes, arguments, fights and "knuckle sandwiches" exchanged with neighboring guys, I grew up with. "He pushed your mama, off a cliff!" moments. Someone would instigate it, and you certainly, could never, (ever) back down, or be scared to fight back.

Sometimes, we'd, playfully, "slap box" or assimilate our boxing skills. Sometimes we'd wrestle, for fun.

Greg was always antagonistic, or picking at me. I couldn't understand why. I was always on the borderline of smashing his face, into compost. Being a boxing fan, I "studied techniques" by watching Muhammad Ali.

"I wish Greg, would touch me! I'll mess him up!" I'd tell my mama, out of frustration.

"Greg's not crazy. He's not going to touch you. He'll try to beat you down, with words," she'll console me.

My mama would also tell me, "Anybody, who spends all of their time, putting down people, aren't happy with themselves."

After we rolled ourselves, out of money, at the Wizard's arcade, the neighborhood guys and I would concern ourselves with Album Den. It was a music, record store, at the same shopping center. We'd spend, or waste time, looking at the latest vinyl album covers, cassette tapes, or posters. I even thought, maybe someday, I'd work at a record store.

Sometimes, we'd walk to the nearby Taco Bell. I loved their Mexican Pizza. McDonald's too, sometimes. We'd play at the outside basketball court, at the middle school. I'd play "defense" with hands up, in the way, distracting opponent. Vin would tell us "locker room" stories of a girl, that showed herself to him. We'd all condone his actions, with the inappropriate grins, laughs and questions.

Willie and I must've massacred, or broke, 20 to 25, large, classroom windows, at our deserted, middle school, over the weekend. We threw rocks, through the windows, smashing glass everywhere, thinking it was funny. Willie graffitied, or tagged, one brick wall, with white spray paint.

Greg "ratted" me out, saying he saw me, climb the school's highly wired, fence. That forced the police to confront me, alone. It was school property. The police called my father, the policeman. I agreed, I walked through the school, to the rear of the school, to play basketball, but that was it. "It wasn't me." I had a bruised ego with "Greg trying to tell on me." Without a connection, cameras, or evidence to say otherwise, the police ended their questioning, and let me go. I just knew, I'd be arrested and butchered my life away. Thrown in a juvenile detention center somewhere, but it didn't happened.

I was, constantly, going to see my therapist, on a regular basis. She was a, lovely, (White) woman. I was attracted to her. (For goodness sake). Then she transferred, to another office, out of town. That turned my trust, into counseling, to ashes. I went, a couple of times afterwards, but it was like, dragging a camel from its water. I consulted my mother. I stopped going. I, simply, couldn't pour my heart out, like I did, with the lady therapist.

Vin and I would walk to Eastgate, to check out the girls' "assets." We'd first, truck through Thalhimer's. It was an expensive clothing, anchor store, but they also sold donuts. (Who doesn't like donuts)? We'd canonize the ice cream parlor, the mall had. We'd check out, the name brand shoes, at the A&N store. Of course, the arcade, in Sears.

In 1982, was when Prince came out with his 1999 album. Baby! I was hooked. I was, definitely, then his biggest fan then, for life. His music was so cool! I wanted concert tickets, when Prince was, finally, coming to Richmond Coliseum. My father wouldn't let me go. He said I was "too young."

I also was a big fan of the popular "Minneapolis Sound." They were the musical protégés of Prince. Shelia E. and others. I had plenty of wall posters. It was, practically, a music shrine in my room. I had The Time, looking cool. I had Vanity 6, looking sexy. Of course, a Prince poster too.

Greg concocted a story, of how he'll trade me a mixtape, that he made. It was to have, all the latest rap songs. He wanted my, The Time poster. I said, "Okay," like a complete moron. So stupid! I've always regretted that decision. I could've kept the poster, and tape music off the radio, myself.

One Christmas, my aunt, North, bought me an aquarium. It was full of exotic fish. Goldfish, black goldfish, and kissing fish. They swam like beautiful, hypnotic, celestial bodies. The fish tank kept leaking. Eventually, my father gave the fish away, my pets, to a fisherman, at our neighborhood pond.

My uncle, Joe, lived with us, for a spell. He stayed in the guest room. He worked as a bank teller. He wore a pink, champagne colored suit to work.

Soon, Joe got his apartment, and lived with a friend. I heard babbling about them being gay. Dad wouldn't allow Joe's "friend" in the house. He'd have to wait outside, in the car. Then Joe moved from Richmond and lived his life in Denver, Colorado. I didn't see Joe, for many moons. The word "faggot" was never, ever, allowed in my parent's house, respectfully.

The 7$^{th}$ Grade was doomed from the start. With my dad running the house, with a clinched fist, I was going "cuckoo." Walter and Greg would dress in different, colored Izod shirts, with matching socks. My mama thought, paying for "that small alligator" was, ridiculously, high. I felt like, I may as well get my clothes, from a flee market. (I couldn't win.)

We'd all wear penny loafers. I would, literally, put a penny inside of mine. I'd place the coin, in the front of the shoe, above the tassel. We'd all would put some sort of coin, in our shoes. I made sure, I'd polish my shoes, with shoe polish. Nice and shiny.

From time to time, my parents would drop Mel and I off, The Boys Club of Richmond. It was in the west end area of town. We didn't mind going, sometime, but not all day long. We endured, before most people have, their morning cup of Joe. Mel and I would play board games, air hockey, card games. The place had an inside, and outside swimming pool. There was a basketball court.

Every year, The Boys Club would sponsor, a two-week getaway, Camp Little Hawk. Reluctantly, we had to go. My father thought it was good, for Mel and I to be away from home, camping with other kids.

We'd go on nature, hiking trails. We'd go swimming, in a pool, canoeing, in a lake. We'd make hand crafts, and socialize, with other boys, we didn't know. At night, there would be a camp fire. We'd roast marshmallows, while the camp coordinator, told us scary stories.

Mel at the time, had a few neighborhood friends, but their friendship soon ended.

So, in the 7th Grade, there was a White, Italian girl, who I thought was, absolutely, "dynamite." I'd watch her flow on the court. She was a Lady Falcon. She was on the girl's basketball team. I had this, huge crush on her. I thought, she had all the curvatures. It didn't matter to me, if Tiff was "ivory," and I happened to be "ebony." I'd, foolishly, in love, walk her home, daily. She lived on the "other side of the lake," which is still, the same neighborhood. I cherished the school picture she gave me. My egotistical friends couldn't, possibly, see what I would want, with a White girl.

"Tiff, can I have your phone number?" I begged.

"I'm not allowed to give it out, Marco," she would say.

I got my piece of pie. Rita and I exchanged phone digits. Eventually, she moved to another house, in another neighborhood. It wasn't too far. I'd walk over there, a lot. I met her whole family. I met her older brother, Afro. Soon after, he killed himself, with a gunshot to the head. Her mama worked at AT&T telephone company.

Passing the time in school, I got hyped up by other students, to put a tack in the teacher's chair. Let's say, I desperately, wanted to fit in.

During my second semester, in the 7th Grade, I think it was the last straw. Someone, I don't know who, wrote a "love letter" to my teacher, Mrs. Arnold. It, honestly, wasn't me. Yet, it was "wrote" by me, which it was not.

With that being said, I was sent to the Special Education classroom, for the "Emotionally Disturbed." It was for, all day, of my entire classes. It was social suicide. I was hurt and humiliated. I was, highly, embarrassed. It was "deception." I was "rejected."

"Inky dink!" the kids would bark, outside the Special Education window. "Retard!" I'd hear from inside.

Needless to say, I was frightened to be seen, anywhere, near, that classroom. We'd go to lunch, beforehand, separately, from the "regular" students. I didn't want to be synonymous with being "crazy." Apparently, Chucka didn't have a problem with it. He was in the same, exact, classroom I was in. There was only about seven of "us" in there.

Meanwhile, Rita was in Special Education, for the "Learning Disturbed." The other classroom. Other students, humorously, or maliciously, referred to it as "L.D." Kids were ruthless. There was no "cut" card

I knew, in my heart, I "didn't belong" in Special Ed class. They had the wrong guy, sort of speak. Mrs. Mason and her teacher assistant, taught us, individually, at our assigned, seated cubicles. (Great, I can hide.) Rumor had it, Mrs. Mason was married to a White man.

I mostly, hung out with Jewels. He had a temper. He was a ticking, time bomb. He was ready to "fight like a fugitive." Lamanda, a fellow classmate, knew the definition of sassy.

I spent a lot of time, visiting Ms. Johnson. She was my school counselor. It was incumbent, that I see her, in her office, everyday. She was a pretty woman, who reminded me, of the distressed lady, in Michael Jackson's Thriller video. I was depressed. I blamed myself, for trying too hard, to be funny. I shouldn't have, deliberately, went out my way, to make friends.

Ms. Johnson always gave me, friendly, advice. She said, I should think about writing, in a journal. So, I did. She also gave me talks, on low-self esteem. Mine was on the floor, at that point. We talked about personal matters as well. I had so many questions and concerns.

She painted a "beautiful art gallery" for me. It was one of promise and hope. I thought, in a more perfect, democratic society, "It would be nice, if people didn't act so mean." Ms. Johnson was great at enunciating her words. She taught me, "It's okay, to be different."

With what, little confidence, I did have, was gone, from being in "that class." As a result, I became, extremely, shy and quiet. I started to eat, more and more. Food was comfortable and comforting. I'd get lost in movies, particularly , science fiction movies. I was no longer, the little engine that could. Tiff and I drifted apart. Again, I was embarrassed, I was in Special Ed. I felt isolated, from the rest of the world. My social life plummeted. My friendships, with the guys, was superficial, generic at best.

Once, Walter and I tried out a paper route, with the local, evening paper. It was The Richmond News Leader. We delivered the newspapers, as promised, to Jarrett's apartments, after school. When it came time, to collect the money for the paper, a lot of tenants, didn't trust, giving their hard-earned cash, to two twelve-year-olds. Our manager, didn't want to pay us either. So, we quit. With the money, we did get from the tenants, we bought ourselves candy.

Making good, out of a bad thing. I continued to write in my diary, I stole from, the nearby Barnes and Noble bookstore.

Once, Mel and I would "borrow" cash from mama's pocketbook. We would steal, a little at a time, without it being noticed. Then we got greedy. My mother, finally, found us out. It was shameful.

"Get out of my sight!" said my father.

He said, he was "too mad" to whip us. Rarely, did my mother whip us, but she did that time. What makes it so bad, my parents gave us, weekly, allowances. (Wow).

In those days, I'd be wearing suede, Puma sneakers, with the fat shoestrings. I'd wear the clear, square-shaped "Gazelles," nonprescription glasses. Of course, long sleeve Puma shirts. I'd wear 9.25 silver necklaces. (I loved that Italian horn charm). I bought my silver, from a Broad Street, downtown vender. We'd catch the GRTC bus. Naturally, I'd wear my gray Kangol cap, or white Kangol bucket hat. Maybe a white, furry, rabbit's foot keychain, for luck.

I felt worthy, whenever I was with the neighborhood fellas. In fact, we'd be over Walter's house, experimenting, with Kool cigarettes. It made me choke. We'd play Run DMC, loudly, while getting high, smoking marijuana. Our horns were showing. We'd try to out drink each other. We'd see, who could hold their liquor, without being drunk. The guys and I would go to teenager house parties.

Greg and Willie, both had custom-made, brass, belt buckles, with their name on them. Hip-hop culture. A thing of envy. Also, they gave us the weed, we needed. Once, some guys gave us some cocaine to try. We all snorted, the white, powdery substance. (Peer pressure). The cocaine gave me a gruesome, feeling in my nose. (It hurt.) It was a very discombobulated, discomforting feeling. I never tried that again.

The guys would, openly, share their latest, sensual encounters or stories. Bragging rights.

Once, in front of Walter, Rita talked against my mother, which made him laugh. Instantly, I smacked Rita, causing her to fall on the ground. (No, I'm not proud of that).

"Okay, Marco! Okay, Marco!" she panicked, from the ground.

"Don't you ever, talk about my mama like that!" I roared at her.

I got into another fight, while I was at school. I hung back, after the bell rang. I waited on the basketball court. This kid, had some sort of dissent about me. He "dissed" me. I got in his face. I knocked the chip off his shoulder. I danced around, punching him, while not letting him get too near. With harmony, style and grace. I won.

"Muhammad Ali!" a guy, strictly, called me for the next several of days.

I mostly, hung around Vin, when I got home from school. On account of him, being a couple of grades higher than me. Sometimes, I would find myself with Walter. He, usually, acted one way with me, and another with other people.

"Marco, if I didn't know you, I'd be scared of you," Bernie once said.

That was weird, considering he was the guy, nobody in the neighborhood wanted to cross. He was the one, everybody respected. He had the connections or many rough-looking cousins. I wasn't sure, in my head, if he was being serious. The guys at school would rap, freestyle, and someone, or me, would "beatbox." That was the art of making drum percussion sounds, with your mouth. I once saw Bernie, breakdancing a "windmill" on the floor, using flat cardboard.

It was summer '84, and school was out. Prince's Purple Rain album and movie was, finally, released. Everyone said, Morris Day "stole" the movie. He was great, but I begged to differ. My father took us to see the movie, along with another woman, by the way. I sat, close to the screen. My dad and her, sat in the back, somewhere.

When it was time to go, I was, usually, the main one, who wanted to go. I couldn't wait, to go to South Carolina. It was my family's annual tradition. At my maternal grandmother's house, I must've ate everything on the hog.

"Grandma, can you make some pig's feet?" I'd beg, for my personal favorite.

My uncle, Kenn, put the key in the ignition, of his brown, new '84 Ford Taurus. The music volume would go, all the way up.

"Hot damn!" Kenn would say, especially when his favorite song, "Sussidio" by Phil Collins was on.

He cherished his nieces and nephews. He didn't have children of his own. Kenn would drive the car, incredibly, fast. He worked at a mill. He shared a trailer, with my cousin, Baby. My cousin was a produce manager, at the Bi-Lo grocery store. As kids, we'd all be over there, at the trailer park. I was having the time of my life, kissing every moment. I'd look through Kenn's collection of movies, VHS video tapes. I'd negotiate with my other cousins, Jonathan and Fist, what movies we should watch. Kenn had a high regard, for scary movies. Kenn would let us drink beer. I was thirteen. We'd drink Budweiser beer or Miller.

If my paternal grandparents' porch light was out, we'd consider it too late, to disturb them. We'd turn around, to go back to Kenn's trailer. We'd get drunk again.

Baby cared for his girlfriend, Brina, but they would argue. He was making good money. He had a certain, goodness or morality about him. He was, respectfully, humane like Kenn, when it came to dealing with people.

My cousin, Shee, was living with her boyfriend, Brad. He was a cook, at Brady's restaurant. They had a daughter, my cousin, Tamika.

My dad always had good hygiene. On the last leg of summer, he took us kids, to Water Country USA in Williamsburg. It was a water park, with water rides, slides, a giant pool that made waves. He brought a woman with him, who had multiple children of her own. I was young, not stupid. I didn't make a fuss, about the women, as long as I was involved, with my Dad.

8th Grade, I spent the whole day, and the whole year, in Special Education for the "Emotionally Disturbed." As if, things couldn't get any worse. I'd wear my Levi's blue jeans, hoping a nice girl would notice, the small tag, on my butt. (I was wearing name brand.) Everybody, who was anyone, was talking about the must-see, movies, Beat Street and Breakin'. My personal favorite was Breakin' which was starring Kelly, Ozone and Turbo.

I was in, immeasurable, pain at school. It was hard, to lift my head. It broke my spirit, that I was still, in Special Ed. I "wasn't supposed to be in there." Yes, I made a mistake. (Who hasn't?) Noticeably, the students at school, were more arrogant and self-centered, the older we got. I was an "outcast." The remarks, I'd hear about my weight was, really, bothering me. I didn't want to live, in a cold, cruel nation of young people, any longer. I thought I wanted to kill myself, as selfish as it may sound. I felt so lonely. All the neighborhood guys I knew, went on to high school. I'd even take a sarcastic remark from Greg, at that point.

    Which brings me to the time, he didn't want to pay me, when I let him borrow our lawnmower. He wanted to cut a neighbor's grass, to earn money. He promised, he'd pay me, some of the money, because I'm supplying the lawnmower. He refused to pay me, anything afterwards. So, I fought him, in front of his house. (I was standing up for myself).

*ACT 3, SCENE 4*

# Teenage Love

RITA WAS, PRACTICALLY, giving her stuff away. It seemed like every Tom, Dick and Harry was getting with her. You'd think it was her livelihood. That was a turn-off, and it made me lose respect for her.

Her big booty cousin, Margi, would be at the house, often. The house would smell like marijuana, as soon as her mother would put the needle on a jazz record, especially Sade. Rita and I shared a few laughs. Sometimes, I'd lie to her, to escape. She didn't, ever, want me to go. She'd call me, a lot, all the time. I thought, it was getting on my nerves.

"My mama, wants me to go to the store with her," I'd lie.

Thinking that Rita would call, I'd be missing over at Vin's house. We'd play Combat, Asteroids, Pac-Man, Donkey Kong on his Atari, for hours. I'd try to come home at a decent time.

If my father was home, I'd have a lump in my throat. It was an indescribable fear, my father put in me. At his discretion, without a real explanation to my mother, to where he was going, he'd leave. He was notorious for putting me on punishment. I'd lose tv or phone privileges. Or worst, I wasn't able to go outside, for a week.

I always vowed to myself, if I had babies of my own, I'd be the best Dad, ever. I'd make time for them. I wouldn't shift away from their lives, making them feel like oatmeal.

If was, actually, in a grocery store, I'd get my mother to buy me Right On! and Black Beat magazines. They featured, or were flooded with '80s music, innovative hip-hop artists, actors, actresses, original interviews, and R&B entertainers. Marketable teen sensations.

Frustrated and friendless about school, I would say, off the wall, insults to my siblings. I was a masterpiece for disaster, I felt. So, I opted to take it out on them. I was so hurt, internally. My mama was the only family I thought I could turn to.

I was a living, breathing organism. I wanted to prove that to the world. I was considered fat, and hate myself for it.

However, I was still seeing Ms. Johnson, at least once a day. I could not invented a better friend. Though I was supposed to be seeing Ms. Hill, the 8th Grade counselor, they amended the rules, it being okay. I begged Ms. Hill, who was the lead counselor, not to put me in Special Ed, in high school. Ms. Hill said, there was "nothing she could do."

For Christmas that year, my mother gave me a gold, jagged-edge cross, with Jesus depicted on it. I loved it! It became my good luck charm. That cross meant more to me, than my beloved, square, multicolored, interchangeable, Rubik's Cube. It meant more to me, than the first cassette tape, I ever purchased, Whodini's Escape album. You couldn't pay me, to take that gold necklace, cross charm, off. I wore it, outwardly, on all of my shirts.

Ms. Johnson did a great job, keeping me grounded.

"The only reason, I come in here, everyday, is so I can get out of class," I once said to her.

Obviously , I didn't mean it, and was having a bad day. (What was I thinking?) I needed her! I liked her! Ms. Johnson looked so hurt. I can't believe, I said something, so stupid. This is the same lady, who practically, gave me a standing ovation, when I walked in her office. She always treated me, as though I was a joy to be around. She had a "million dollar smile."

When everything was said and done, it was nothing personal, but I wanted to get away from Mrs. Mason, and her teacher's aide, Mrs. Stevens. Not to mention, the class I was, absolutely, miserable in. There was "nothing wrong with me."

Burying the hatchet, I begged, pleaded, and cried, to my father. I needed his help. He just "had to" stop them, from putting me in Special Ed, the upcoming school year. I was horrified, of being "in that" during high school. My father made a few phone calls. In an unprecedented, small miracle, I only had to be in "one" class period of it, in 9th Grade. I promised to act right. However, I thought, I'd have to time it just right, so no one will see me, go in there. Anything else, would be "preposterous."

My parents wanted to paint my room. They gave me the bigger room. It was the guest room, Joe stayed in. They sent us to South Carolina, for the entire summer. Mel, Dree and I got on a plane, on our own. I was "scared to death" to look out the passenger window.

I strained to have a good time, with the family in South Carolina. I had so much on my mind. I wanted things to go perfect. I wanted to "look good" for high school. Not to mention, my mama would only get affordable, clearance, "on sale" clothes.

When it was the "alternate week" when we stayed with my maternal grandmother, Mel would walk with me downtown, to window shop. I needed to be textured. I needed name brand clothes, so I thought. I'd beg my mother for the money. Eventually, the funds revealed itself in the mail.

My grandma, Maggie, didn't believe in sitting us at the table, before it was time. On any given summer night, she would be rooting for Reggie Jackson, the baseball player. Watching sports, was one of the few times, she would "let her hair down."

As the days progressed, we trotted over to my dad's side of the family. Without missing a beat, Baby would tell me, about all the different girls he had. As far as I was concerned, he was a pro with the ladies. Unlike me, who was "sabotaged" with only one girl, Rita, who I didn't, necessarily, want to be with. She was too "promiscuous" for me.

Kenn was still passionate about life as ever.

It just so happened, the family wanted to go to Charleston, South Carolina. It was beautiful. Palm trees, beach resorts. We all stayed in a hotel, eating salami sandwiches, and other stuff. My cousins and I were impatient. We wanted to get into the pool. Unfortunately, my granddaddy didn't go. He, usually, complained about his "bad leg." (Wild horses couldn't pull him away from that tv, I thought.) The room was furnished with a, fully, equipped oven and stove. My grandma, Mattie Ruth, would sometimes cook or warm things up.

Prince's new video, Raspberry Beret, was on tv. My first time ever seeing it, was there, in the hotel.

"Look at him. He looks like a faggot," I said.

(What was that about?) Why was I covering up the fact, I was Prince's biggest fan, is beyond me. Everyone, sort of looked, at my grandmother, for her reaction. She was "sweet as tree sap." Bear in mind, my grandmother was a deeply, religious woman. My family was, practically, Puritans, respectfully, when she was around.

Later on, at Kenn's place, we were drinking beer, like a couple of goodfellas. He had something to tell me, when he thought, I was drunk enough. It was just him and I.

"Marco, you know, I'm gay, right?" Kenn admitted.

Of course, that didn't change my feelings, or respect for my uncle, not one iota.

"Naw. Uh, uh," I denied.

In less than a pin stripe, Kenn showed me, pictures. They were scenes of gay men, in adult magazines, adult films, to prove his point. I didn't care, if he was a drag queen. He was still my uncle. Now it was all coming together to me, like pieces of a puzzle. The GQ fashion magazines, the White guys, his friends, that came over. Not that it mattered.

Before I knew it, mama and North was in Anderson too. My uncle Reggie and his wife, Cedell also. My cousin, Sissy was a "wild child." Fun and unpredictable. My other cousin, Carl and I went to see the movie, Weird Science. I was a movie buff, so it was great.

My favorite movie that year, was The Last Dragon. It was starring Prince's ex-girlfriend and protégé, Vanity. I saw it with Walter, on Grace Street.

I couldn't believe my ears, when I heard, my paternal aunt, Mae Francis, shot her husband, in the stomach with a .12 gage shotgun. She had an abusive husband. He survived. Everybody, usually, bad-mouthed him.

When I finally, did get back home in Virginia, at the end of summer. All the guys in my neighborhood, had mopeds. (Wow.) Naturally, I wanted one too. Vin and Gerry shared a dirt bike.

"You're not old enough," my father said.

Perfect. I was only 14-years-old, not 16, as required. Of course, that didn't stop the guys from riding, simply, because I couldn't. They left me, as they went on their youthful excursions.

I was too heavy, to ride from behind. Like a culprit, high school was right around the corner. I was so nervous. I shouldn't have been. Especially, with everyone I grew up with and know, would be there too.

I'd see Paul, Mr. Pig's son, with girls coming over to visit him. He was so cool to me, with his long, gray trench coat on. I wanted to be like that.

It was, finally, 9th Grade. I was going to The Springs. First day of high school. I was just glad, I had on my white striped, blue suede, Adidas shoes on, at least. It was radical, catching a school bus, for the first time, in years. I'd walk to my old middle school.

The guys and I secluded ourselves, against a wall, as we would watch, the ladies walk by. I was shy. I was intimidated at so much beauty. I was, really, a Freshman. Before the tardy bell rang, I rammed myself inside the classroom. I seized a seat. It felt great, being in "general population" again. Though I was considered, "D-level" classes. I'll take it.

There were so many pretty girls, Mia too. At any rate, I was sentenced, to one period class, of Special Ed, so I had to go. By that time, Chucka moved out of of the neighborhood, with his mother. Mr. Hall remained behind. My father and Mr. Hall, stopped hanging around each other, for some unknown reason.

Mr. Branch was the teacher of "that class." He wasn't in the best shape, himself. He'd give me a sermon, for always being late for his class. I wasn't about, to let anyone see me go in there. It was a big deal.

All the fellas, ever talked about, was the different girls they were having. I'd put up a brave face, around the guys, but when I was in my, newly painted, red room, it was another story.

I made up my mind, I didn't need a lot of girls. I just wanted that one, special girl, in my life. I'd dreamily, listen to R&B, slow jams, wishing I had someone, to offer romantic moments with. I'd look at pop videos, wishing I was having a fun time.

I'd cry and cry, because my special lady seemed to be, nowhere to be found. I'd drown myself, in Funyuns, watching Star Trek: The Next Generation episodes, alone, on a Saturday night. I just wanted to be accepted, "me for me."

"What's wrong with me?" I would say between tears. "I want a girl-friend! Why can't I get girls?"

I learned my lesson. I was no longer pulling pranks, practical jokes, and disruptive in class. I became, really, reserved and quiet.

Vin recognized my problem. He suggested, I should lose weight.

"Big people run in the family," I'd excused myself.

He used to tease me, that I sounded like Michael Jackson, because of my soft-spoken voice. Yet, on the phone, girls seemed to like it. Especially, when I was going through puberty. I could express myself, better over the phone. Vin would try to recruit some of his girl-friends, to go on a double date with me. I was, painfully, unsure of myself.

Rita continued to call. I'd lie. I would tell I'm coming over, when I wouldn't. I'd just hang up the phone, sometimes. Mostly, I wouldn't pick up the phone. I didn't want to be with a girl, who was like a doorknob. "Everyone gets a turn." What choice did I have? I had no other alternative. Certainly, no one was bursting the door down, to see me. If I did go to Rita's house, it was just to keep her in my pocket. Back burner, sort of speak.

The school pep rally at Springs were great. The cheerleaders, the Springer football team players was pumped up, by the school band on Fridays. Gerry was in the band, by the way. Guys would be yelling. The girls would be screaming. People would be dancing in the bleachers. That night, the guys and I would walk around, at the home games. Of course, we'd try to talk to girls on the visiting team. We wouldn't have a clue, or care about the score.

*ACT 4, SCENE 5*

# March 5, 1986

MY MOTHER GOT a phone call. It was early morning, from my family down south. My uncle Kenn died. I was devastated. It was as if, someone stabbed my back with a knife.

My father came home, in his police uniform. My mother told him the bad news, about his brother.

"Oh, no!" he said, wailing in her arms.

It was the first time, I ever seen my father cry.

My parents encouraged me to go to school. My first period was 9th Grade English. The teacher made her roll call, as all teachers do.

"Here," I said, registering present, after hearing my name.

After that, I started crying in class. The teacher excused me, to go see the school psychologist, that deals with "death in the family." I had permission to go home.

Like pollen, Kenn was gone in the wind. It was the first time, someone I knew, a family member, I was close to, died. I was traumatized. I struggled with Kenn's death. I reflected on his shorten life, at 26. My mother took me to JC Penny's, for some a suit, dress clothes. I didn't, ordinarily, go to church.

It was a long, quiet drive, down Interstate 85. I didn't understand, how this could happen, to such a good man.

"If Kenn won't with that White boy, this wouldn't have happened!" I angrily said once, along the way.

That wasn't like me, to play the race card. Nor was I prejudice, in any way. I celebrated diversity and different cultures.

I was desperate. I wanted answers. Remarkably, we were again reminded, in North Carolina, when we heard the news of Kenn's fatal accident, on the radio. More sniffs and cries.

The guy, who drove Kenn's car, wasn't hurt at all. He lived, without a scratch. That was unshakable. My uncle wasn't wearing, the shoulder harness part, of the seatbelt. That broke his neck, on impact, as the driver hit the column, of a train track's bridge, over the street.

"I know, there were things, you could talk to Kenn about, that you couldn't talk to me about," my father said to me.

When we got to grandma's house, there was, unusually, a yellow ribbon, hanging from the porch light. When it was time to visit the body, at the funeral home, I could, hardly, go in. A mortuary assistant, quietly, snickered at me, because I was so reluctant, to walk in. My mother had to hold my hand. My uncle, dead. At Kenn's casket, I stood there in silence. I wanted to stamp my feet, in anguish.

On the way to the funeral, I cried so hard, I didn't remember getting inside the limousine. My aunt was in despair.

"I'm here, Mae," my father said.

It was the first funeral, I ever been to. The man, who made the best pies, was gone. No one, could repeat, or take his place. Like me, Kenn struggled with his weight.

Family and friends preceded, in a long caravan of cars. Traffickers pulled over, out of respect. Produced in me, was a feeling of hopelessness. My uncle was "slaughtered" and there was nothing, I could do about it.

Immediate-family dominated the first rows of the church. Family also resided by the coffin, in a slow, slothful way. The smell of many flowers, filled the air. It was a day, that tanned out hearts forever. After the repass, grandma showed us around Kenn's trailer. She wanted to have, some of his belongings, his clothes.

"I feel like I'm stealing from him," I said as grandma, snatched up some of his shirts, she wished me to have.

"Kenn would have wanted you to have them," my mama, quickly, assured me.

I valued Kenn. He was a very social being. I wanted to be like that.

I became upset at Dreeka and Tamika. We just buried Kenn, but I "couldn't tell" they knew, with them. They were, busily, playing and jumping around, as young children do. It was was though, "They didn't have to eat their vegetables." In solitude, mama told me, "they're young" and don't know any better. Dreeka was only 6-years-old at the time.

We said our goodbyes. Baby was the only one in Kenn's trailer now. We ventured back north, to Virginia, in great sorrow.

Undoubtedly, Kenn's death sparked the beginning, of my spiritual journey. The concept of death, filled me with terror. I invested my time and energy in watching The 700 Club, Pat Robertson, and other television evangelicals. The crying spams of Tammy Faye Baker, the tenacity of Jimmy Swaggart, the audacity of Dr. Frederick Price, you name it. Suddenly, I was watching it all. I spent countless hours, reading the Bible.

*16 years old*

*ACT 5, SCENE 6*

# Teeny-Boppers

VIGOROUSLY, WITHOUT A spell check, I wrote my first, full story, Groovin. It was a "Romeo and Juliet" story of a black guy, dating a white girl. Love conquers all. I paid a fee, to have this company type it. I was dreaming of being a writer someday.

Jesus became my religion. In spite of my damn vocabulary, I bought a big picture frame, from Jody's Music, a really, religious music store, that sold musical instruments. It was a picture of Jesus, kneeling on the ground, with his hands clamped together, over a huge rock, as though he was praying. It was, prominently, hung on my wall. I must have stared at that picture, for hours. It gave me peace and purpose.

1986 was full of surprises. Often, Greg and I would, splendidly, skip school. He assured me, he'd forge a signature on a note, on behalf of my parents. It would say, I was "sick" the previous day. Greg wanted to get with Kat. I'd tag along. I was invited, because she thought, I was a "barrel of laughs." I kept her laughing. Kat knew Rita too.

At 5 o'clock sharp, every weekday, I would watch Dance Party USA. I loved that show. It was on the USA cable network. It was, considerably, a knockoff, of Dick Clark's American Bandstand. Like a Russian spy, I wouldn't miss it, for the world. Quiet as kept, I would watch Casey Casem's Top 40 show. I listen to him on the radio too.

Trashing the idea of school, Walter and I would often stagger in, tardy. Sometimes, we'd throw our book bags over our backs, and waste time, purposely, missing the school bus. We'd walk to McDonald's or a local "Mom and Pop" store, on our slow route, to school.

I started hanging around, Carl. He was Paul's cousin. He was bowlegged. He had a tide of girls, after him. They thought, he was cute. Guys thought, he was cool.

"I need me a Cheddar Melt!" he'd always say, flashing his gold tooth smile. We'd walk to McDonald's and get ourselves a Cheddar Melt sandwich, a McBLT or a Barbecue Rib.

"Monkey see, monkey do" I suppose. Greg got one. Willie got a gold tooth. I wanted a gold tooth too.

"Ain't no son of mine, gonna be walking around, looking like a hoodlum!" said my father.

That was a "no."

Vin would tiptoe us around, in his dad's Chevrolet Camero. That car, badly, needed help. It had no air conditioning. The door, barely, wanted to close shut. Yet, it got us from point A to point B.

I was, usually, in a all-black baseball hat, or navy blue Yankees hat. I would "go off" or liked it, when I spotted a girl, in fishnet stockings or pantyhose. I wanted someone classy, not, necessarily, sassy. I definitely, didn't want a girl, with a bad attitude. That was the worst.

Kenn's tomb was always on my mind. Though I was having fun, with the guys, I wouldn't allow myself, to forget about him.

We'd whistle at girls, with a straight face. Vin would drive us, to our hangouts, like Byrd Park, in the west end. It was a hot spot. Especially, on Sunday evenings. It would be a long procession of cars, going in the park. People would, slowly, drive their, newly, waxed or washed cars. Some had chrome rimmed tires. Other cars would drive through, with loud, booming hip-hop music, through their windows. Of course, plenty of great girls, walking around.

Friday and Saturday nights, we'd ride up to the McDonald's, on Broad Street. People would get food and mingle. Onlookers, looking cool, standing by the car. We may have decided to go to Hardee's on the Boulevard. Another hangout spot. It was great, but it was torture, at the same time.

"Get the girl, get the number." It was all, anyone cared about. I didn't want to be judge, about my weight. It was a game, and I was in "the floor is lava" game troubles.

Our nearby roller skating rink, "Skate Land," wasn't our thing any longer. That was, usually, for middle schoolers. Radio DJ, Kirby Carmichael would host, sometimes, there too, then.

I kept a strong will, trying to be, cool as a cucumber, relaxed. Carl, who went to another high school, would talk to girls, right beside me.

Also, we went to "The Strip." It was on Leigh Street, behind DMV. People raced their, loudly, revved up cars.

Trans Ams would zoom pass us.

Paying our dues, for no particular reason at all, Carl and I would catch the bus for 6th Street Market Place. It was a midtown "tourist" attraction, small shops, food court, live jazz music. He lived with, his younger sister and grandmother, in a townhouse, beside MLK Bridge.

I was in my own world.. I continued to write, in my diary.

I got into one fight, during high school. Vin instigated it. During lunch, Kevin butted in front of me, in the lunchroom line. Perhaps, he thought it was okay, since we were from, the same neighborhood. Vin and I quickly, cut school, in his dad's good, old, burgundy Camero.

"The whole school saw, Kevin cut in front of you! I know, you're not, going out like that! You have to do something, or you'll look like a punk!" said Vin.

Taking me for a loop, I felt, I had a wretched decision to make. So, it was either fight Kevin, or people would be, taking me for a joke. Kevin was, considerably, tall, a basketball player, and in the 11th Grade. I was, merely, a Freshman. When he, finally, came home, I picked a fight with him. Like a WWE pro wrestler, I body slammed him, to the ground. We rumbled, exchanged blows. Out of nowhere, Kevin yanked me, in the back of the head, with a brick. In summary, without a twinkle of stars, it didn't hurt. Adrenaline rush, I guess.

"You won!" Vin said to me, proudly.

"He's retarded!" Kevin hurled at me, after the fight.

"I ain't like Kevin anyway," some people at school, would say to me.

"You beat a Junior!" I'd hear.

I felt like I was born again, the next day. Everyone at school, praised me, for beating Kevin. I was standing up for myself. I earned their respect. I was a Freshman, who claimed victory, over a Junior. (In hindsight, it's not something, I'm proud of.)

However, what I am, very proud of, is when the fellas and I went to see the movie, Krush Groove. It was playing at Henrico Movie Theater. I was with Willie, Bernie, Greg, and a guy, Charlie, from another neighborhood.

"What did you say to me?" suddenly, one of us, said to another moviegoer, dragging us in.

It was directed, to a White classmate of mine, after the movie was over. Obviously, they were picking on him, simply, because he was White. I knew him, from school. Nice guy. He was, completely, innocent. They surrounded him, like hell hounds. The kid tried to zigzag or run for his safety. In an element of surprise, someone "stole him" or sucker punched him, when he wasn't looking. Like vicious, wild dogs, the group, repeatedly, punched him, stomped, or kicked him, outside, near the box office, ticket stand. I REFUSED. I wasn't apart of that! He didn't stand a chance. Before we were in a police line-up, we ran off. As though, I was apart of their ruthless, and relentless assault, they all got mad at me.

"Marco, why you didn't do anything?"

"He didn't do anything to me!" I said.

The kid, they beat up, looked so unhappy at school. I felt sorry, for him. It, virtually, was turning into a Black versus White thing, at school. I wasn't about that. Race, or color, didn't matter to me. If I liked a certain girl at school, they guys would have to ask me, whether the girl was White or Black. If the girl was White, they didn't want to hear about it. If she was Black, they'd be all ears, because that was considered okay. They would get with a White girl, but they wouldn't "go with her" or date her. They, certainly, wouldn't marry one.

"What color she is?" they'd ask me.

Most of the guys, around my way, was prejudiced, against White guys, or White people, in general. That wasn't me.

Unfortunately, I seen more fights at school. Primarily, at the hands of Black people. Without a snag, many guys would unload, their fistfight, or feet, on one, individual. They were getting their butt kicked.

In school hallways, things got ugly. The "double banking" fights, two versus one. Getting "jumped" or ambushed, by more than one, was appalling. It, certainly, wasn't a fair fight.

Incidentally, the management at the Henrico theater, apparently, decided not to premiere "Black movies" there again. Especially, after the "double banking" I was, nearly, apart of, but wasn't.

That summer, I met a girl named, Ree. She abducted me, with her eyes. She thought, I was cute. She was a year, younger than me. We exchanged, phone numbers. Eventually, she invited me, to her house. Same neighborhood, but further down, on the "other side," of the pond. It was sweet. It was great, being with another girl, other than Rita. Her younger sister, Leigh, did not like me, at all. I don't know why. Chiefly, because of my weight, I suppose. (Who knows)? Ree and I was together, talking all summer. I'd visit often, phone calls.

However, when school started, she was to be a Freshman. I was a Sophomore. She acted like, she didn't know me, around other people, at school. Ree stopped talking to me. Suddenly, she wanted nothing, to do with me. She was afraid of what others may think, I think. Heartstrings..

Also, that summer, my father drove us to Walt Disney World, in Florida. It took us two days, to get there. We stopped at a hotel, on the eastern side, of South Carolina. I was baffled with joy, inside the magician kingdom. We'd conform, into long lines, to wait, for those wonderful rides. Somehow, my dad was throwing acid on the situation. Again, he seemed unhappy. He'd rush us along.

"Look at her. She's acting like a little girl," my father said to me, about my mother.

Once at the hotel, my dad was on Mel's case, about the way he was churning a lollipop, inside his mouth. Mel, quickly, adopted and stopped, from something my father said, outside the hotel room.

Walt Disney World was huge. It took us three days, to see it all. I owed myself to go back, and enjoy.

On the way back, from our vacation, my father picked up a hitchhiker, walking along the highway. The total, complete stranger was dressed as a fellow Marine. (Talk about, Semper Fi).

Also, that same, clammy afternoon, we visited South Carolina State University. That was mama's and North's college. Naturally, we stayed in

Anderson, the following week.

Dad took us, to my parents' 20th anniversary high school reunion. It was nice, seeing the people, my parents grew up with. Kids were everywhere, running around, the barbecue. The food was agreeable. My parents alone, went to a dance benefit. We stayed with relatives.

Baby and his new wife, Brina, moved into a house. I drank a six-pack of beer, by myself. I got so drunk, I couldn't walk straight. I, barely, knew my own name. I passed out. Alarmingly, my father came over to the house, the next morning. I, immediately, acted sober. No signs of a hangover. Baby gave me some coffee, to sober me, before we went over to our grandma's house.

Before I started the 10th Grade, I had another favor, to ask my father to make. I no longer, had to attend, the Special Education. However, I told him, the "D-Level" classes weren't, exactly, challenging enough either. A lot of the students in "D-Level" were unfocused, lazy, and only cared about, the latest hip-hop music. I knew, I could work, harder and smarter. Before I knew it, I wasn't colliding at a lower level any longer. I was placed in "C-Level" classes.

Walter and I decided, to join the Springer Football team then. In the blazing, hot sun, we went to all the football practices. Our neighbor, David was on the team too. During school hours, David always carried a briefcase. I thought it was great. Assuming, it made him "look serious" about his academics.

Walter and I was on "third-string" on the team. We didn't get any playing time, on the field. My only game I was in, was a scrimmage game, which "doesn't really count." I tackled, the opposing team's quarterback, before he got a chance, to throw the ball. Walter quit the team. Soon, after a couple of weeks, I quit too.

"Beating a blank," or better than nothing, Vin and I both got jobs, Shoney's restaurant, Eastgate mall. I lied about my age. I said, I was 16, whereas I was, merely, 15. I forged my birth certificate, with white out. Typed in another birth year, ending in "0." Copied that, and "wallah."

I was making, little over $3 an hour, minimum wage. I was a busboy, cleaning off tables.

# TEENY-BOPPERS

I would steal the tips, which was meant for the waitresses. I'd, merely, just swipe the money, discreetly, in my busboy bucket, when I cleaned the tables. All the other busboys did it too. Like a comedian, I thought it was funny. When things got hectic, I'd help wash dishes too. Vin didn't last long. Shoney's was my first, real job, not including the paper route. I hung in there, for a couple of weeks later. Without Vin there, it wasn't the same. Soon, I quit too. I managed to save up, for this electric blue, with white stripes, Adidas jacket. I bought a watch too.

With little money in our pockets, Vin and I went to the annual Virginia State Fair. (Weirdly, whenever the fair, came to town, it would always rain.) So, I must've had a blister on my foot, because my leg was hurting, killing me. Our parents, showed us no mercy. We didn't have a ride home, afterwards. Vin said he "knew someone" in the area, that could offer us a ride home. Thinking it was cool, I was limping, the whole way. Suddenly, it was about 20 guys, quickly, heading our way.

"Run!" he said. "Come on, run!"

Vin ran off, leaving me behind. I could, barely, move, because of my sore leg. I was surrounded.

"My grandma lives here! My grandma…" I lied, because, I was, apparently, in the wrong neighborhood.

I was hit, with a single, body blow to the stomach. Kneeling, to the ground, in agony, they stole, my new watch. They stole, my new Adidas jacket. It was my first time, wearing them both. I was boiling mad, that happened to me.

My mother, initially, thought I made the whole thing up. As though, I just wanted a ride, in the middle of the night. She apologized.

Guys from the neighborhood said, I should have fought Vin, for leaving me. Not falling into that trip again, I didn't.

Actually, years before, that wasn't the first time, being "jumped" happened to me. A few of the guys and I went to see Rita. Our neighborhood, Heckler, and the Bridge was "beefing" or didn't like each other, somewhat. Out of nowhere, some Bridge guys charged after us. Something didn't feel right. Somehow, I was alone, left behind. I was surrounded. Bird "stole me," which caused me to drop, to the ground.

I was 15-years-old. I felt, discouraged, from the book publisher. They wanted me, to send them money. (What?) In order to publish, my book Groovin'. Of course, I didn't have the funds. My dream of being a writer, came to screeching halt. It was deferred, a hill to climb. I felt like an unsung hero. So, I thought, I better pick something else too, besides being a writer. Just in case, it didn't work out.

"I'm going to be somebody!" I would tell Kat.

"Boy, you crazy!" she would confess.

No longer in Special Ed. Class, in the 10th Grade. I made up my mind, I wanted a job, whereas I need to wear, a shirt and tie. I wanted to be, independently, important. I wanted to use my brain. I developed a high regard, for intellectual types. I started to respect, smart people, and eloquent speakers. So, I decided, I wanted to be a reporter, someday. It seemed more practical. Only if, being a writer, wasn't realistic, or became, a far fetched idea. The idea of Journalism was "something to fall back on" or pay bills.

I got my class ring, during my Sophomore year. It was a gold, class ring of 1989, with amethyst stone, diamond-cut, zodiac sign, "Aquarius," on one side, and had "Journalism," on the other.

Breathless. A classmate, named Becky (White girl) and her (White) friends, invited me to this, laidback, teenager nightclub called, The Cellar Door. It was on Broad Street.

I had to, practically, beg Vin, Walter and Carl to go with me, to a racially "mixed club." I had to reassure them, plenty of girls would be there, White and Black. They, finally, approved. I was a happy camper.

The club had a huge, video screen, hovering above the dance floor. I thought, it was the coolest thing. It was my kind of club. It was my kind of atmosphere.

It was, distinctly, showing, Janet Jackson's "Control" song. They played, Human League's "Human" video. Also, Doug E. Fresh's "All the Way to Heaven" was a showstopper, among others.

The Cellar Door was beautiful. As promised, it orchestrated pop music, with different races of people. We went several times. I wanted to dance, have fun, be myself. I didn't want to be upset, or uptight, like I was in the other clubs. Unlike the Ebony Island, where arguments, shootouts, and bruised egos occurred.

Apparently, the club wasn't doing as well, as I thought. Soon, Race Track, an automotive store, took its place. The club was shut down. That was a "pain in the butt." The Cellar Door was the first club, I ever been to. Going there, on Friday or Saturday nights, was now a memory. My neighbor, Paul, went there too.

All jokes aside, Mel was, constantly, being harassed in school. His teachers would call, or write, my parents a note. They said my brother was having an "identity crisis " with other students. Mel told me, the kids were leading a campaign, to fight him. He feared for his life. He was scared, that fighting him, would become contagious, or inspire other students, to fight him too.

I would meet Mel, at his school, after school ended, and "double dog dare" ANYONE to lay a finger, on my brother. I didn't care, how many people it was, to fight us. I would have fought them all. I was ready. I can tell you that.

Meanwhile, Dreeka would have her friends, Dannie, Apple, Issa, and Shay would come over to the house, occasionally, after school.

My second period, was Spanish class. Not to "toot my own horn" but I always had, an appreciation, for different cultures. In front of me, sat a pretty (White) girl. Her name was Tina. Like the song, "Tina" by Georgio that came out, that same year. We would chitchat, throughout class. I liked her. Somehow, Greg got ahold of her. He bragged to me about it. It, nearly, gave me a heart attack. I was thinking, "You don't even like White girls!" I knew, Greg was only using her. So, I told Tina about it. She, apparently, liked Greg. Eventually, she listened, to what I had to say. She cried. I felt bad for her.

I also, felt sorry, for the worms and frogs, we had to dissect, in Biology class. No animal, deserves that type of treatment. (Smile.)

With the aurora, freshness of Spring, I put in for a summer job, at Kings Dominion. An amusement park seemed like a great, fun place to work. I wanted to meet people. It was a welcomed "Broadway show." Problem was, I was 16, without a car.

I wasn't gathering, shopping carts, or bagging groceries, at Winn Dixie, any longer. I wasn't allowed to accept tips, for doing my job, such as loading groceries, in people's cars. Of course, I did, accept tips. Since I was terminated, for working or moving "too slow," it seemed like, the ideal thing to do. My father knew the manager, so I was, quickly, hired. 6 months later, quickly fired.

I was 16-years-old. Thanks to Coach Parker, from Fairfield Middle school. He took me on my first driver's test, in Driver's Ed class. Finally, I had my driver's license. (That was a big deal.) I had nothing, to show for it. If it wasn't for Vin, driving us in that raggedy car, we, hardly, would have got around.

The word was out! There was a new, racially "mixed club" called, TJ Finnigan's, on Staples Mill Road.

We partied there, with vengeance. Without a mirrored disco ball, or chandelier, we did the latest dance craze. Having my crew with me, everything was cool. Everyone "went off" or stormed the dance floor, when Eric B. and Rakim's "I know You Got Soul" played.

DJ Stormin' Norman was, constantly, chatting hype, on the mike. He was also the host of a local video show.

Once a guy, named Ant, in school, asked me a rather silly question, became my name, and my brother name, start with an, "M."

"Marco, are you a Muslim?" he said.

"You see this?" I said, holding my gold cross, necklace, for all to see. "I ain't no damn Muslim!"

"Sorry, I didn't mean to offend you," he said.

Well, I got the job at Kings Dominion. Charter bus included. As usual, my employment there, soon fizzled out. They assigned me, to The Barbecue Pit. I was serving pork. A lot of cute girls dropped in.

Eager to please, or make a friend, I sat with this (White) girl on the bus. She was fluent in gothic clothes, and punk rock music.

Like I said, my cushion job, came to an end. I'd always tell people, I got into a fight, over the rapper, LL Cool J. At the restaurant, we could bring our personal cassette tapes from home. We'd play them on the cassette player, held in the back of the store.

Someone stole a coworker's tape. He was playing his music that day. We all enjoyed it. It happened to be LL Cool J. I had the same cassette at home, myself. I felt bad for the guy. So, I thought I'd be a "Good Samaritan" and bring my own music, the next day. Especially, since I had the same album, he was playing, and now missing. I was thinking, "We can play mine, then."

"Marco, stole my tape!...I'm going to mess you up!" I'd hear, he was saying all day.

The girls I worked with, kept telling me, to ignore it. I got along great, with them. Finally, I couldn't bear it any longer.

"You ain't going to do nothing to me!" I said.

I couldn't take it anymore. In front of all the customers, and everyone, we got into a fight. We wrestled to the ground. He got in, a sucker punch. Before I got a chance, to anything to him, the park's security guards broke us.

"I'm Marco Martin!...I'm Marco Martin" I kept saying, over and over.

I was being escorted, to the front gate. A kind lady offered me, some water. She thought, I was hyperventilating. With all the commotion going on, security called my father, to pick me up. Needless to say, I was fired. Fighting was the "kiss of death" at the job. I was let go, despite my elocution, or being innocent. I was involved.

It was that same year, when I caught my father, "red handed," at the other woman's house. With nothing to do, and a driver's license, my mother let me go for a joyride, in her car. Dree and her friend jumped in the car too. Turning up the bass, on the radio, I drove my mother's 1984, blue, Buick Century to the Meadows, a neighboring neighborhood. I was just, riding around, arbitrarily, passing the time.

Dad left for work, in his police uniform, hours earlier. Evidently, he didn't, actually, go to work , but he was working in her yard, in jeans and a white T-shirt on. My dad froze when he saw me. I flew home, to tell my mama. I had, a story, to tell her. By definition, I was putting myself in danger, but I didn't care.

Vin enlisted into the Army. He was two years older than me.

I had to repeat, 10$^{th}$ Grade English, in summer school. I thought, maybe, I could enlist in the Army too. I wanted to travel, see the world. The military could pay for college. It was a win-win situation.

"They won't take you," Vin said. "You have to lose weight first," he said.

I let that, discourage me. I didn't go into the military, without talking to an actual recruiter myself.

That's not the half of it.

"If you don't lose weight, I'm not sure, we can hang out anymore," Vin once said, to me, awhile before.

I was crushed. I was flabbergasted. We were supposed to be "boys" or best friends. We were "road dogs" I thought. We always hung out together, despite what anyone thought, I thought. I was his sidekick, while he competed, and got all the girls. He was Batman, but I was Robin.

*ACT 6, SCENE 7*

# October 13, 1987

WORDS CANNOT COPY, the way I was feeling. So, it's scrupulous, to even try. Without a goodbye, or a trace of his belongings, (if you don't count the records, he decided to leave behind) my father was gone. The man, who punched me, in the face, because I messed with his adult movies, in the VCR player, left us. The man, who punched me in the face, because I popped popcorn, in the microwave, after school, wasn't there anymore. The man, who said, "Don't do it for me," when I joined the football team, the year before, disappeared.

My mama, became one, with pain. Mel and I were of the opinion, maybe, we were better off, without our father in our lives. Officially, we were abandoned by him anyway.

Technically, I was still a pedestrian. I was determined, more than ever, to get myself a car. Money was scarce. We suffered a food shortage. My mother, who had no help, in our well-being, surrendered to credit cards. Once, mama charged, two grocery bags worth of food, to her Amoco gas station, credit card.

Somehow, my father wrote, and called Dreeka, but not his two sons, living in the same home.

Greg would say, "Talk to your father. He's still, your father."

"I don't see him, trying to talk to me!" I'd say.

I'd try to describe, what a person, I thought my dad was, at the time, but it was no use to him. Tenaciously, I'd listen to my old-school music, or "old soul" sounding, Terrence Trent Darby. I'd be in a Virginia (Cavalier) sweatshirt. I'd eat, voraciously, trying to drown, my loneliness away. As the new, man of the house, I had to do something. I wanted to help carry my family along.

I got employed at Bonanza, family steakhouse restaurant. It was across the street, from my former job, Shoney's. Mr. Wood, the manager, drove a small, orange BMW. Neighbors, from down the street, worked there too. It was a family affair. Barry and his two sisters were there. Barry cooked the grill. His sister took orders. His older sister, was assistant manager. I washed dishes, as usual. I figured, if I work there, it'll enhance my chance, to get a car.

Eventually, I became lighthearted. I was happy, that I was no longer being, sucker punched, in the face by Dad.

"I'm tired of you hitting me!" I once said to him, after I was punched, for not cleaning my room, fast enough.

It was the very, first time, I have (ever) spoke up to him. Remarkably, my dad didn't retaliate. Shortly, thereafter, was when he left our family. It was, quickly, becoming a hostile, "him or me" environment. Some kids blame themselves, when their parents separated or divorced. Not me. I was, actually, glad, he decided to leave.

My mother had to scramble, for gas money, when her "plastic" was, completely, maxed out. To make matters worse, her department at her then, AT&T accounting job, was moving into an office space downtown. Now, she has to pay, for parking space too.

I was in the 11$^{th}$ Grade. I had thoughts, of killing myself. (What else?) I was depressed, because of the way things were going, with the young ladies. I was so hurt by that. Painfully, obvious, they didn't seem to be interested in me, so I thought. I became sullen and withdrawn. I felt, I wanted to die.I wanted the pain to stop. However, I didn't want to hurt my mother, I told myself. Blaming it on my "fat" genetics, didn't help either.

I was trying to think, which euphemism, would be less painful. It seemed like Kenn's spirit was trying to tell me something. Every night, I would wake up from sleep. I'd look at my desk, and it would read, 3:30 in the morning. That was the exact time, I was told, Kenn died, exactly.

I was made out of glass. I was fragile, vulnerable, and easily, breakable. I was supersensitive, about the least, little thing. I'd cry in the pillow,

OCTOBER 13, 1987

because of girls, and my father. I felt like, I lost my soul. I didn't know, who I was.

Why, am I here? Why, me? Why, am I going through this? I would apologize to God, between sobs. I felt, evidently, He was mad at me. At school, I felt like I didn't belong, with the other kids. I felt, I couldn't relate. I detected laughs, and jokes, about me, during school.

Again, I would turn to the Gospel. I would watch, Pastor Steve Parson, on tv. He was, head executive of the Richmond Christian Center. He seemed like a nice guy. He'd pray or "speak in tongues." He'd lay his "healing hands on the sick." The tv show, Amen, made me, actually, want to go to his church, in person.

It seemed Mel's goal to embarrass us, wherever we went. He would wear mix-match socks, gloves. He would do anything, out of the ordinary, for attention. He'd overdress. He'd underdress.

I had a few, favorite classes in 11th Grade. Marketing, was a hands-on business model class. Drama, we did a remake, play production, "She's So Hot" which, originally, starred Marilyn Monroe and Jack Lemmon. I loved acting.

Undoubtedly, the highlight of 1988 was when, I saw Prince, in concert. He came to the Richmond Coliseum, on his Lovesexy tour. Thank goodness, Mel and I got tickets. You'd think, I'd be going off, or losing my mind, when I saw Prince, live. I was playing it cool, taking it all in stride.

At first glance, he appeared, to be driving, an old, white 1966 Ford Thunderbird, as he entered on stage. It was the one in his "Alphabet Street" music video. He played his guitar, he danced, he sang. The stage was centered, directly, in the middle of the Coliseum floor.

Overwhelmingly, it was a nice show. It was everything that I could hope for. It was everything that I expected. Everyone dressed, extremely, well. The music was fun, funky, sassy, sexy. Races of every color, enjoying the Black "Rock and Roll" legend on stage. I was proud. It was just like I imagined it to be. We all, warmly, shouted, screamed, clapped and embraced Prince. Life was purple and grand again.

Shelia E. was the drummer. Plus, she's a singer, in her own rite. Cat, the dancer, had on sexy, white, knee-high boots, a short, digressing mini-skirt, and large, hoop earrings.

The next day, I greeted school, with a "too small" Prince T-shirt. They didn't have a larger size.

I had to beg Mel, for us to go church. I didn't want, to go alone. I wanted to be, among the aithful at the Richmond Cristian Center. He grumbled, but, finally, we went.

I instantly, made a connection there. The words, "Jesus Is Lord" was, prominently, fanned over the pulpit. I had a gut feeling, I was home. All those hours, listening to sermons on tv wasn't in vain, I thought. It didn't matter, if I was fat, for the first time in my life. The first hour was the choir, peacefully, singing praises. The second half, was the pastor preaching. When the church congregation dismantled, after service, a lot of fine, feminine, well-to-do women, happen to walk by. I wanted to go, again and again.

It was the rap group, Public Enemy that took my political consciousness, to new heights. I got a kick out of Flava Flav, whenever he would say, "Yeaaaah, boyeee!" He was the hype man, the entertainment. Chuck D. would, seriously, inform us about the social conditions of out miserable, little planet.

Mel didn't want to go to church with me anymore. Especially, after he wrote the pastor a letter. The pastor answered, "It's not okay to be gay." I didn't want to go, by myself. So, eventually, I stopped going to church. I put thoughts, about going to church, on hold.

Wanting some, much needed, female friends in my life, I submitted my name, in the February 1988 edition, of Black Beat magazine, pen pals section.

I entered my name, age 17, favorite artists, Prince, Luther Vandross, and Run DMC, hobbies, writing poems and short stories.

It was a dream come true. I got so many pen pal letters, from girls, all over the world! Plenty of pictures. Lots of mail! It was great. It made me feel happy, to get so much attention, from girls. I made a few phone calls, to Dayton, Ohio. I was, really, liking a girl from Boonesville, Mississippi. One pen pal person, sent me a bootleg, cassette tape, copy of Prince's unreleased "Black Album." (Wow.)

## OCTOBER 13, 1987

I was still working long hours at Bonanza, after school. I, finally, got a car! It was an affordable, beige, four-door, 1982 Ford Grenada. I picked it up from the local Heckler Chevrolet dealer. It was my first car, but a hinderance, is what it was. It was a "lemon." The seat wasn't comfortable either. It hurt my back. I was, constantly, out of an abundance of caution, taking it to Pep Boys, for them to mess over the parts.

At home, I'd take my frustrations out on family. Like my father, I would punch a hole in the wall, because the students at school, treated me so lame. I would call Mel, "faggot" whenever I was upset. I would call Madrika, "ugly" whenever I was hurt. I wanted the Grim Reaper, the dark horseman, to visit me. (Clearing my larynx.) I made my family, scared of me. Even to the point, my mother thought I might, eventually, hit her.

I wanted to be treated, like a human being, from the other kids. I was "fat." That was the proverbial tip of the iceberg.

Rumors leaked at school, that I had a bad hygiene problem. If someone farted, or smell musty, people's eyes would go, in my direction. Simply, because, I was the biggest one in class. Multiple times, I'd get embarrassed. It wasn't me, "cutting the mustard."

If that wasn't bad enough, my mother couldn't afford to buy us expensive fashion, name brand clothes, like Air Jordan's. So, I'd try, to turn it around, by wearing my "church shoes." I'd wear dress slacks, and a dress shirt, all the time. One girl, called me "Luther Vandross," commenting on my "conservative look." I took it as a compliment.

"Thank you, sir. May I have another?" I should've said, mockingly, from all the insults.

Though, my Junior year was, immensely, painful at school, I still had my pen pals. After awhile, the novelty of it, wore off. They wrote less. I wrote less.

My "best friend," Vin was in the Army, seeing the world. Obviously, he was moving on.

When the pen pals was falling apart, I began turning to African American pride, and Black history.

It was political conscious rappers, such as Chuck D. (Public Enemy) that opened my eyes, to the myth of White Supremacy. I was learning from them. I wanted to know more about, the fearless leader, The Honorable Minister Louis Farrakhan.

Once, I was in a car, riding with Walter, Bernie and another guy. The fella said something very derogatory, about Muslims.

"Don't be talking about Muslims like that!" I said, ready to fight, which was, completely, unlike me.

I don't know what came over me. I wasn't even Muslim! I didn't know a thing, about the religion, Islam, or whatever they believed in. (Imagine that.)

"Farrakhan, is a prophet, I think you ought to listen to," a lyric from Public Enemy's "It takes a Nation of Millions to Hold Us Back" album.

Naturally, when I, finally, did get a chance, to watch Louis Farrakhan on tv, I was very impressed. The minister was very interesting, needless to say. He had an inbred logic about him. The way he talked about God was new and approved, as I have never seen before. Not to mention, the beautiful, black women in long, white gowns, sitting in the auditorium.

Martin Luther King Jr. was my hero. I always refer to him as "Dr. King" out of respect.

"If I was born back then, I'd do what I wanted to do!" I would say as a kid.

"Oh, no you wouldn't!" condemn my parents, who knew first hand, it was about survival.

Meanwhile, I was still messing with Rita. I was sad inside. I wanted a real, romantic relationship, with someone. I wanted an actual girlfriend.

It was Mel's friend, Clarence, who introduced me to the all-Black rock group, Living Colour. I became a big fan. I thought, MTV, and Rolling Stone painted them, as a novelty act, but I knew better. Corey Glover had great vocals, the heavy, guitar riffs were great. With that, Living Colour, made me appreciate, and go deeper into the past, with Jimmy Hendrix. His guitar playing was phenomenal.

At that point, I wasn't wearing braces, or a retainer, any longer. Mrs. Knox, who was married to Mr. Knox, from Fairfield, was a bit weird, or eccentric. Yet, she was, annoyingly, sweet to me, during her Chemistry class.

OCTOBER 13, 1987

"Psst, Marco. See if you can get the answers, from Mrs. Knox," my classmates would say, during class.

The other students would try to look at my test answers. Mrs. Knox would, actually, give me the answers. Happily, she'd help me with quiz questions, if I "got stuck." Without any manipulation on my part, she would, blatantly, do it. My other classmates, obviously, would get offended.

My school year, semester, was coming to a close. Marketing class held a banquet, along with other county schools, at the Richmond Marriot hotel, downtown. We all had to dress, in business attire. As employees, we all entered a contest, writing an essay, about our managers. My manager won an award plaque, because of the essay I wrote. He hung it in his office.

That summer, my mother was going through, a bitter divorce. Finally, she filed paperwork, from my dad, who treated her, like a doormat, all those years. She was doing the right thing. However, I couldn't help, but feel rejection, from my father. With him only contacting Dree, I felt, he didn't care. It tore me apart.

In the 12th Grade, during my Senior year, it became, fashionably, acceptable to wear African heritage medallions, around our necks. Mere plastic, but it meant something. It was the continent of Africa, colored red, black, and green. I wore mine, proudly, like a cherished organ. It felt invigorating! Mentally, it was the first time, I showed, outwardly, racial pride. I took it one step further. I'd wear my African medallion, or my African beads. Black people, who acted ignorant, or arrogant, were not "enlightened," as far as I was concerned then.

It was time, I started planning, for my future. I didn't want to be a janitor. (That much, was certain). Not that there's anything wrong, with being a janitor. The tv show, A Different World, and Spike Lee's movie, School Daze, had me thinking about attending an, historically, Black college. Namely, Virginia Union University, or Virginia State University. I asked the schools for brochures. I even wore a VUU sweatshirt.

In a metamorphosis, I began, really, appreciating the beauty of Black girls at school. Black girls, in their fashion statement, wore burgundy, knee-high Agnes boots. They wore Agnes earrings. They wore, Gucci, or Louis Vuitton too.

I was allowed to leave school, earlier. It became part time, everyday. I joined the work force, sooner. Thanks to the Marketing class, and with enough class credits.

In the midst of all those people, I still felt lonely. Everyone, I grew up with, graduated. Except, for Greg. He had to repeat 12th Grade. Surprisingly, he was nicer to me that year.

Gerry enlisted into the Army too.

When Vin was in town, it was, actually, no better. When he visited me, I could tell, he changed. I, hardly, recognize him anymore. The Army made him different, I thought. My childhood friend, seemed to be just that. They guy, I grew up with, grew apart.

I didn't have a real, religious background. I had "no place to go." I developed a soft spot, for Jews and Judaism. I heard horrible stories, about Adolf Hitler, and Nazi Germany. I too, felt like an outcast. I too, was different, a stranger.

Occasionally, I'd get a haircut, at Essence. Usually, I'd go to the barber, Malik. He was a tall, bearded guy. Curiously, he'd wear a certain, thin, white, skull cap. He did my mother's hair as well.

I'd hide behind my nonprescription, reading glasses. I minced few words. Suffering from a broken heart, I was scared of rejection. Diets didn't work. Sometimes, I'd hear comments that I was, possibly, gay. Justifiably, I wanted my Senior year, to hurry up and end. I wanted to be of age, out of the house, and on my own.

Once or twice, I'd take my old, pale-looking car to the Richmond Christian Center. I longed to hear Scripture. Pastor Steve Parson was great. He was friends with Pastor Fred Price, from tv. He didn't believe, pampering the congregation. He told it like it was. Ushers were pretzeled everywhere, passing out the collection plates, once or twice, during service.

I didn't know anyone there. The church was huge. Nice people, fancy place. Everyone was sitting pretty. I didn't have the money, great career, own nice home, luxury car, or an expensive 3-piece suit, to show off. I didn't have the superficial, sense of importance, or air of fortitude. So, without any "church hurt," or something anyone said, or did, I stopped going, all together, again.

OCTOBER 13, 1987

So, without a parachute, I jumped. Out there, proceeding to take matters, in my own hand. I caused a riot, between my sister and I, when it came to boys. I became overprotective. I threatened one boy, Reginald, with a baseball bat. I was going bananas. I didn't have a close friend, or a girl, loving me. I felt responsible, for my sister, of her self esteem, or any prospects she had. I tried to sabotage, as dubious as it may seem. I didn't like Madrika having a key to the house. It wasn't because, I didn't trust her. I didn't trust boys, males, men, for that matter.

Christmas that year was interesting. I got an African pendant. I also got a red, black, and green flag. North, knowing I had a fondness for ancient Egyptian, gave me a bag, with Egyptian images on it. Mel bought me a gold, Nefertiti charm. I almost cried, on the spot. It was so beautiful. Eventually, it turned up missing. I believed, one of my sister's friends stole it. Being a special time, with North and Nikki, we'd ride around, looking at different Christmas lights. A must-see was the decorations was at the Omni hotel, downtown.

In 1989, Bonanza, my job, went into bankruptcy. I never did receive, my last, two weeks worth salary.

Like a Patriot missile, I quickly, needed a job.

I no longer wanted to beat Greg to a pulp, with his little, smart remarks. He was, happily, earning money as a Barber in Essence, along with my barber, Malik.

The Senior prom was coming up. Like any other red-blooded American, I wanted to go. I, purely, didn't know what to say, to get a date. I was in denial, of self-worth. I was too scared, to ask a girl out. I didn't feel, I was qualified. I had, no scheme. I had, no people. So, I stayed home. The only thing to quench my memory, of classmates, was my, yearly, yearbook.

I blamed myself, for being so quiet. It was my fault, I didn't have any dates. So, I stuck delicious food, in front of me. Food became my lucky, raffle ticket. It made me, feel good. Food didn't judge me.

At that point, the only time, I drank alcohol, or got high, was when I was visiting relatives, in South Carolina. The more I ate, the sadder I got. The sadder I got, the more I ate.

After the secretary, sent my mama, the final, divorce decree in March, she tried her best to move on. Mama became our personal angel. She tried to fix things, on her own. She'd mowed the grass.

My dad, became a phantom, of our irrational past. Naturally, Mel and I weren't sentimental, when dad got remarried that year, May 27, 1989. Unexpectedly, my cousins showed up here, for the wedding nuptials.

"You're not going?" they said to me, already in their tuxedos, after the fact.

He didn't invited me! I had no idea, my father got married. Probably, wouldn't have went, if I did. I don't know, but I wasn't asked. The wedding reception was being held in the Confederate Hills country club.

"No," I told them, pigeon-toed.

The only record, I had of my father, was when I looked in the mirror. Considering, how hurtful it could have been, I didn't turn out too shabby. Eventually, I got tired of feeling, pity for myself.

Going through her collection of Black Beat magazines, (a year later) I got a letter from Leigh. She wanted to be pen pals. Like a shark's fin, on the surface, of a deep blue sea, her letter came out of nowhere. I was okay with that. At any rate, we called each other, long-distance (collect calls.) We talked for hours. All day. All night. It felt great.

She was from Brooklyn, New York. My heart would shimmer, at the thought of her. The poetry in the R&B songs, had special meaning to me now. Leigh was like a reflection of myself.

Shortly, we developed feelings, for each other. Without playing games, we registered, what we had as the real thing. Leah and I had so much in common. We shuddered at the same things. We both ate pork. What affected one, was relevant, to both of us. I longed, to see her. She sent me post cards.

I loved her, and anything, to do with her. I loved New York City. I loved her northern accent. She loved my "country accent" as well. She was a big fan of model, Cindy Crawford, actress, Marilyn Monroe, and country singer, Reba McEntire. Leigh was sweet, somewhere naïve. She never smoked pot. I was sort of a rebel, a skeptic.

The only thing, I wouldn't accept, was her pushing or "preaching" her Jehovah Witness beliefs, at me. It made us argue. If I talked about

OCTOBER 13, 1987

slavery, and the effects, it had on our people, Leigh wasn't interested. She preferred, I talk about something else.

In due time, I got a job at Hardee's. I was flipping burgers. Working there was slow. Hardly, any customers.

I turned my essay in, to my 12th Grade English teacher, with a smile. I assumed, because of my permanent tan, she uttered something about me "cheating." I guess she thought, I couldn't have, possibly, wrote it myself. Without so much as a sneeze, or taunt, I took it as a compliment.

I'd vanish in the sofa, wishing Leigh was there with me. The most I could do, was look through my telescope, hoping she was looking at the same stars.

Like a vegetable, in the hospital, I did bad, on my pre-Scholastic Altitude Test. I figured, maybe, I could go to community college, J Sargeant Reynolds. They didn't require an SAT, and I could transfer, to a 4-year University, somewhere later. I wanted to go into Mass Communications, despite people thinking, I "didn't speak, clearly, enough." I looked at journalists, Bryant Gumble, Frederick Douglass, and Ida B. Wells, for inspiration.

My uncle Joe suffered from a kidney failure.

My maternal grandmother suffered from Glaucoma. She went, to my high school graduation. I never seen my grandma cry before, considering, how stern she used to be.

"All the stuff, that boy went through," she cried.

I stood, directly, behind Greg, in the graduation, ceremony line. He got on me, for not inviting my father, to the ceremony. I was thinking, "My father doesn't invite me anywhere."

I had on my green camouflage, Swatch watch. Not to mention, I tied my own tie, thanks to neighbor Mr. Pig. I felt vindicated, walking across that graduation stage. I was so ready for, "spice and everything nice." Theoretically, I made it my chance, for a new life. Mel and I went to see, the new Star Trek V : The Final Frontier movie, that evening.

Two week later, Greg killed himself. I could not believe it! His nephew, Tim, found the body, hanged in the garage. I didn't go to the actual funeral. However, I made sure, I went to the funeral home, sign the book, and saw

BEHOLD

the body. Greg's death was, simply, too hard to deal with. Also, I made sure, I visited his gravesite, when I was ready, in my own time.

Summer of 1989, I looked for higher wages, in retail sales. I'd ask for job applications, in a shirt and tie. I was a hawk, looking for any small thing I could find. I also sought a job at, Peaches Records store, because I love, all types of music. (Who better, right?) I stayed, job hunting, in the west end, part of town, since it was my favorite area.

I'd rent action movies, from the movie rental store, Block Busters, or Movie Time. Eventually, old, Kung Fu genres. "Shaolin versus Lama," or "The Five Deadly Venoms." Kung Fu fighting monks, or drunk Kung Fu masters. Of course, Bruce Lee's "Enter the Dragon." I fell in love, with Chinese food, Chinese dragons, and Asian culture. I thought Asian women were, totally, beautiful.

*SEASON 7, EPISODE 8*

# College Hill

WHEN I WASN'T at war, I'd visit Rita. Food stains and roaches were everywhere, in her Jarret apartment. She inherited $10,000, from her father's life insurance policy. She also, had a baby boy.

Not too long after Greg's suicide, our neighbor Mrs. Miller lost her life, to a heart attack.

I was thunderstruck. I watched the EMS people, try to resuscitate, work on her, outside. They brought her out topless, but I didn't notice. I just wanted her saved. At her funeral, I made sure, I wore the, red necktie, she bought me, as a graduation present.

Also, it was the same red necktie, I wore across the graduation stage.

I, nearly, starved that summer, preparing for school. I just wanted everything, to go right, that first day of college, on a Wednesday. To my surprise, Chucka, who I grew up with, and attended Special Ed with, was there at "Reynolds" too. (It was the Parham Road campus.) I haven't seen him, in four years. He wore sterling silver rings, while I titillated the fashion world, with my gold rings, necklaces, and watch. We both were taking the Liberal Arts program. We were like brothers. We hung out together, immediately, like old times.

I reinvented myself. I no longer cared, what anyone had to say, or felt. I was starting over! I thought, I was cool, wearing, my black shirt, black shorts, black leather boots. For the first time, in my life, I wore that outfit, because, "I wanted to!" I was doing my own thing, and I, certainly, didn't want, to be "quiet" any longer. I was going to college, with a more "mature" crowd. I wasn't going to let people's thoughts, or opinions, about me, run or ruin me. No, I was done with that.

Chucka was shy himself, when it came to talking to the ladies. He had a thing for (White) women, from afar. He had crushes, but the girl didn't know it. (Sounds familiar?)

We'd watch women, but no interaction. (I'm not doing this anymore, I'd tell myself.) We agreed, Black women had "attitude."

It felt nice, having a close friend again. Like me, Chucka went to the video arcade, to win. We hung out. We were going to the movies. We'd walk around South Park mall. We'd eat in Pizza Hut.

I drove, to his trailer park in Chester. It was a 30-minute drive. He lived with his mother, and her boyfriend. I'd spend the night.

Chucka had so many great hip-hop albums. He had two turntables, and a microphone. He had aspirations to be a DJ someday. His DJ name was "Dev-01." He also had, an impressive adult magazine collection.

Whether she noticed me or not, I didn't know. In my math subject class, was the prettiest young lady, in the whole school. Her name, Tiffany. Just the sight of her, I would breathe hard. I would tremble.

Worse than that, I knew, I insisted, I was going to try, to talk to her. (What's the worst that can happen?) I was done, with that "shy stuff." I wasn't in high school anymore! I wanted to put the "fat stigma" behind me. "If she say no, she say no." became my motto. "It's not the end of the world," became my mantra. "Life goes on," became my slogan. "Just ask the next girl,." became my mission statement.

I stopped wearing my 1989 class ring, by the way. (Why?) Not in high school!

Leigh was still writing me. She wanted to do this, and that, when we, finally, meet. That was fine and dandy, but she was so far away. I was succumbing to the females, closest to me.

I couldn't take it anymore. I didn't want the sun, to set another day, without me asking Tiffany, out on a date. Dammit, I had to try! I may not see her again, after this semester, I told myself. 1989 was going to be my year. The first time I (ever) ask a woman out. Practically, following her, into the college bookstore, I made up my mind. It took, every fiber of courage, I had. I was so nervous. This is it!

"Tiffany, you want to go to a movie, or something?" I said, assuming she might be free Saturday night.

It was the bravest thing, I have ever done, but she didn't know that. It was so untypical of me.

"I'm seeing somebody, right now," Tiffany said.

I should have known. She was young, beautiful, and could, possibly, supply all of my needs. Tiffany was nice. Though she said, "no," I was very happy with myself, for at least trying. (I would never have done that in high school.)

After that, the unthinkable happened. I sat behind her in class. So, before class started, she would, actually, turn around in her seat, every time, to say hello.

"Hi, Marco," she would say, forcing our eyes to meet.

It was no hard feelings. I wish I could take her out, for eggs and waffles. Our 8:00am class was a real bummer.

Leigh was in the back of mind, and I accepted that. "Just don't lie to her," and I didn't. It was fun going to Reynolds. It was great, meeting new people. My school work was suffering. I wasn't taking homework assignments, seriously. I, hardly, studied. I was making, poor grades, which, nearly, suspended me. Under advisement, I took more notes, during class.

I was still sweltering, in my Hardee's uniform, after school.

I did my best, to synchronize or do my homework. It was no use. Unmercifully, I bombed my tests.

With my tail, between my legs, I felt like giving up. Besides, the bad grades would average in, or go into my overall, grade point average. There was no "replacement" or redo class. One can take a class over, but the "bad grade class" was still, averaged in, anyway. That was Reynolds, for you.

I was getting a taste, of manhood, and independence. However, the nightmares of the past was bidding at me. Painful memories still affected me. It influenced me. They controlled me.

It was absurd, the way we grew up. Same as me, Mel would roam, in dad's dresser drawer, to get better acquainted.

"Thank God! It's about time," Mel and I felt, when my father left us.

At the same time, I was bent out of shape, that I didn't have a father to confide in. I found comfort, in nothing.

"I'm going for a 'fault divorce,' even if it is more expensive," my mother said to her lawyer, the year before.

My mother realized, that if she has to go through life's adventures alone, so be it.

"No woman would give a man, pictures like that, somebody else had taken," the lawyer said.

Her name, Ms. Scarborough.

"Yes," my mother said.

If it came to it, that neighbor would have to be subpoenaed.

Dreeka was the only one, enjoying commercial success, or relationship with "her daddy." It wasn't her fault. It didn't take the CIA, to see, I was bitter about that.

My mother heard so many, blasted stories. She didn't know, what to believe. I had so many complaints and cries myself, but I knew, I didn't want to get my answers, in a liquor bottle, and become an alcoholic. Or worse, a drug dependent. Not, simply, recreational marijuana. Of course, I didn't need, to overindulge on food.

In all honesty, I was, definitely, depressed my father, in his white, 1982 Ford LTD, wasn't there to pick me up as well. I allowed myself, to be blue over that, for years.

No, my mother didn't know, for a fact, he was messing around. She had suspicions, which he always denied. I felt, completely, helpless without my father around. My mother, refused to feel like that.

"I don't have time, for people walking around here, talking about, 'They don't know how to do it, or 'don't know what to do' without trying," she said to me.

My mother wanted, to change the lock, on the front door. I said, "I didn't know how."

"If I have to change this lock all by myself, then so be it! But I'm changing this lock! Today!"

We had work to do, especially, after my father left us, out to dry. We had to fend for ourselves.

"Where are the instructions, mama?" I said.

"Here they are. Now help me, figure this stuff out," she boldly said.

We took about 45 minutes, or so, to put the new doorknob on, but we, actually, did it.

"See what we can do. You can do anything, if you put your mind to it. All you have to do is try.

My father attempted, to get in the house, after he moved out.

"I'm over to the house. I want you to know, you can't keep me out of this house. You've changed the lock on the door? Until we get a decree, I have every right, to come into this house. If I want to move my shit back in here today, I can do it. You can't keep me out of this house," my father said, later.

"Why are you over there?" said my mother, after they both knew, the marriage was over.

"I have some things, I need to get," he said.

"What things? I'll get them for you."

Finally, my dad said, he needed the stepladder. He asked my mother where it was. My mother said it was upstairs, in the attic. He'll have to wait, that evening or tomorrow.

"I'll talk to you, later. Bye," my mother said, considering, her time bracket, for personal calls at work.

I was furious, when my mama told that story. I was, especially, conscious of how cruel, he could be.

"He hasn't changed, one bit! After those times, he called acting so nice. I thought he, maybe wanted to come back in here, or at least, keep in pleasant contact with us. All that was nothing, but a front. He's still the same person! He's never coming back in here, no matter what any court, judge, or lawyer says! He's never coming back in here! He's still trying to be boss. Listen to how he talked to you! He still has no consideration for others," I said.

When my parents talked again, my mother told him about his left-over furniture. My father said, he wasn't taking it "no damn place." He told my mother, she could get rid of it herself.

It was like hitting a brick wall. It was important, that my dad get served, with divorce papers, first. My mother was going bonkers, waiting around for the private investigator, to report something.

"He may move," Mel said, dropping that on her.

My mother was going through so much, emotional pain, and physical pain. She tried to explain, to my paternal grandmother what happened.

"This is what he wants. He made his choice. He's going to blame it on me, but he made his choice, and we lost," my mother attempted to her.

12:15 am. Sunday. The phone rang.

"You'll never get him back," said a female voice, unapologetically.

As soon as my mother heard that, she hung up. Even after my mother confronted her, face to face, and she said, "What is it?" years prior, my mother did not know her voice.

"I hope you can see now, it was him, and not the other person," my maternal grandmother said, to my mother.

Being, brutally, honest, my grandmother said, other hurtful things as well.

"There's only one reason, a man goes out yonder, and you know what I'm talk about. Your mama works everyday, and she be tired. And if he had to have it everyday, and she's too tired, he just goes out yonder and get it," she once told me.

My mother endured everything grandma "didn't exactly say." Also, the "strange" remarks she did say, with a grain of salt.

My parents split, totally, stressed my mother out. It raised her blood pressure. She explained it to her doctor.

"I've been, like a walking time bomb, for three months now, because my husband and I separated, about three months ago," she told her daughter. "A more truthful way of stating it, is that he walked out on me and my three children, three months ago."

Applauding the doctor, he wrote exactly that, for my mother's records. "Husband walked out on her and three children, three months ago."

"No wonder, you're under so much stress," said her doctor. "I didn't realize this. I knew it had to be something. You got your hands full. I'm glad you told me."

I would do things, like rip my sister's pictures up of my father. Especially, the hand-drawn one, of him in his police uniform. It "was" hung up, in the den. A "one of a kind," gone forever.

My mama said, I can leave the house, if I don't stop. She reminded me, after all, that my father is not dead, no matter how many memories I try to rip up.

"Sometimes, I wish he was," I said.

I was a real Cabbage Head, when it came to my father. I hated him, for treating us like that. I resented him, for leaving. Being a photocopy of my father's looks, I gave everybody a harder time still.

"We've got to start acting like a family. We're all we got. We got to stick together." I said, once I got myself together.

"Did he really said that?" Dreeka said.

I opted for change. I was tired of feeling like a Canadian quarter, in an American town.

"Okay, maybe I am hurt," I said, coming out of costume. "Hurt is not the right word. I'm mad! I'm just mad, about all the things, he did to us. I guess, I just took things out on y'all. I promise, I'm going to be a better son, and a better brother."

"I wonder, how long this is going to last," said Mel, as though I was pulling his leg. "Probably, until tomorrow, until he starts ripping up pictures again."

I was driving my sister batty, by painting my canvass of ill feelings, about our father. I would call her a "traitor" or "Benedict Arnold" for seeing him, whenever, she alone, was invited to be with him.

"I'm afraid, I might start, hating Daddy," Dreeka cried.

She was hearing so much negative stuff, particularly, from me. With no money in sight, we were flat broke. Mama was struggling, to pay everything, by herself.

"It's not fair! He walked out on us, but we're the ones, who have to suffer," I said, about my father.

No "hello" or effort from my dad. No nothing. I was hurt. Mel and I referred to him as " Dreeka daddy," simply, by his first name.

My faith in God, and mankind, went down the drain. My days of worshipping Jesus, a man, were, officially, over.

One birthday, my cousin Baby called, to wish me,Happy Birthday. He was our grandparents house. I talked to them as well. Mel heard that Dad went to South Carolina, recently. Mel called him, by his first name.

Apparently, they said, "Who?"

"Dreeka's father," Mel said.

Occasionally, Dreeka and I would have candid talks, on why she thought our dad left. Without any argument.

"Not that I think he was right, but probably, because mama wouldn't give him any s-e-x," she said, spelling it out, for us.

"What?" my mama said, overhearing our conversation. "I'm not going to go into any details, but nothing, absolutely, nothing, could be further from the truth. That's probably, what he tells everybody, and probably, everybody thinks that, but that's not true. He's the one, who had all the headaches, and was always tired. Sometimes, I wonder if he was a real man. That's all I'm going to say about it. But that's not the reason."

My mama going on, about her s-e-x life made me embarrassed.

"Can't you talk about something else? I don't want to hear about my mama doing things like that," I said.

(I know what you're thinking. "How do you think, you got here)?

"I have nothing else to say, except that NOTHING could be further from the truth." Mama said.

"I talked to Dree, calmly, and she answered everything I asked her," I said, later on.

"That's what I've been trying to tell you," my mother said. "You don't have to go crazy. As long as you're screaming, and yelling at her, and calling her everything low, under the sun, calling her names, she's not going to cooperate with you. She's not going to talk to you. All you're doing is pushing her closer to her daddy. Give her a chance. She'll, eventually, realize all these things on her own. See how much more you got out of her, by acting calmly?"

I would ask Dree, does she realizes, our father doesn't call her?

"Well, I call him all the time. I don't give him a chance to call me," she, casually, said.

Sure, we had our crying spells, but we shared a few laughs. Once when we were in the store, Dree handed my mama a card. On the front of it, was the face of a woman, with in tears. It read:

"You're hurt right now. He's gone, but try to be an adult, and hope he finds what he deserves."

My mother figured, the inside would read, something philosophical like, keep the faith, or be strong, or things will get better. Instead it read:

"Herpes, head lice and leprosy."

It was great, seeing my mother laugh again. After all, my father was in my mother's life for over 20 years.

"You have something, that he doesn't have," one of us said. "Us."

Again, it was great, going to college. It was fun, being young, and going for it. I had my whole life, ahead of me. Hopefully, college was going to be my "silver bullet" to a good job someday. I had hopes and dreams. Desperately, I wanted to make something out of myself. I didn't mind working, a dead-end, minimum wage job, as long as I was going to school.

Who knows? Maybe, I'd meet a open-minded woman, (who loves me, for me) and have a couple of kids someday, I thought.

However, my past, became my constant companion. It was like, my feet were stuck in cement. I couldn't go forward. I didn't want to look back. The world was a cruel place, and I wanted to rise above it.

For example, when my father was about to kill me one day, my maternal grandmother chooses sides, without discussing, with anyone, what happened.

"You just don't want, anybody saying anything, about your children," grandma scowled at my mother. You did not ask (my father) what happened."

She was referring to the incident, when my mama heard, all this commotion from upstairs. She ran to see what was the matter. She had to pull my father, from off of me. I was through with it. It didn't matter anymore.

"We need to talk about this," Mama later said to him.

"There's nothing to talk about. You had no business interring." Dad said.

I'm throwing a curveball here, but I lived in fear of my father. I was, authentically, nervous around him. I was a child, afraid. It felt like, I was in police custody, and I was becoming an introvert.

BEHOLD

My mother wanted it hers what happened from both sides. She asked my father, did I do something, first.

"What kind of question is that?" he said, as though he was offended by word "first."

Getting back to the conversation earlier, my mother and grandmother had. My grandmother said, I provoked my father, into hitting me like that. That was, absolutely, not true. No kid deserves to be "man handled." (Even boxers wear gloves).

"Yes, he may provoked him, by going into Miguel's room, and talking, but not with any body gesture," said my mama, referring to the time, my father told me to clean up my room. "He never told that Marco did."

"And you didn't ask," said my grandma, missing the point.

Like my mama would always say, "If it ain't one thing, it's something else."

Our cars were acting terrible, always breaking down. Mr. Pig would give, friendly, advice.

Dreeka was wishing, I would get off her case. Her and (stepsister) Tammy bought our father a "soon to be a father" card. Evidently, he was expecting another baby. My (half) sister Chrissie grew up, without me, not knowing me.

My mother wanted to get some major house improvement done. The insurance man, said my father would also have to be present' for the estimate. Simply, because his name was on the house deed, at the time.

"No," my mother said, flatly, without her usual sweet cinnamon flavor. "No, I rather not do that."

"We're learning, I told my mother.

Every week, we'd cope with something new, without help.

At the moment, I was still, not going on dates. Rita didn't count. Leigh was hundreds of miles away. However, I did look forward to the Halloween Ball, sponsored by Reynolds. I was prepared, to meet or ask someone out. With, hardly, anyone in there, I soon left. (I tried.) Holidays were the "kiss of death." I felt, loneliness. I'd be at home, watching a movie favorite like, Conan the Barbarian, wishing I had that special lady, especially.

My mother wrote Cassie, Dad's new wife a note, when she found out, she did Dree's hair.

"Don't ever touch my daughter's hair again!" it said, declining to go any further.

"If you would take time, to comb her hair, then no one else would have to do your job! Since you are her mother!" my father replied back.

I could hear the bass in his voice, from the note. Back and forth, nasty notes would be passed, between my mother and Cassie.

"Don't write me no more stupid letters," she wrote to mama.

Repeating what my father's wife wrote, my mama said back to her, "This is grammatically incorrect! Perhaps, an English class is in order. Don't write me! Don't call me!"

Food for thought, my mother wrote a note, to my father, giving him plenty to gobble down.

"If you aren't afraid to do so, you'll read this BEFORE you rip it up! I've been both mother and father to theses children ALL their lives, so don't even try to undermine what I do as THEIR MOTHER. Get your daughter to open up to you and let tell you how much you've hurt her. As far as your sons are concerned, THEY SAID you DIED two years ago! Good luck in the future DEAD MAN! Don't ever again send me a note or letter of any kind. I DON'T want any communication with you at all. I've made my point! I want this exchange of notes to stop! Get the child support payments here on time in the future or we're going to court. If either of you start to take things out on Dree, then your true colors will definitely come through and she'll see you both for what you are. You only have one more person to lose in your life! Keep up the good work! You're almost there!"

Alienating their relationship even further, my father wrote back anyhow.

I didn't read and don't want to, so don't write me a letter again. Please contact your lawyer for any future contacts."

Taking action, my mother wrote back.

"This belongs to you! After all, you started this! I had NOT SAID ONE WORD TO YOU! YOU'RE THE ONE WHO CHOSE TO WRITE ME. Don't send this back, particular not through your daughter."

Using Dreeka for gossip, she became the common denominator in their lives. Short, to the point phone calls were made on her behalf. My father would ask if my sister was home.

"No," my mother would tell him.

He'd ask, if she would tell her, he called.

"Yes."

Without desperation, Mel would answer the phone.

"Is Dree there?" Dad would, simply, say.

"No," Mel replied.

"Thank you," Dad returned.

During that time, Mel was in high school. The students was going ape, thinking my brother was "fruity." He was being harassed and bullied. Mel was feeling alone. So, he would call me, everyday, at his lunchtime, so he wouldn't have to sit by himself. My brother depended on me, to help him get through it. I happily accepted it.

Learning to love me for me, I gave up on exercise. Caring about what others thought, gave me nothing but grief.

Other things, other experiences, derived from my parent's phone calls.

"First, let me ask you, have you paid that $325 owed on that insurance?" said my mama.

"I've paid, some of it." said my dad.

" How much have you paid?" Mama said.

(No answer).

"Are you ever going to tell me, why you used my insurance? What did you use my insurance for?"

"I have every right to use that insurance, just like you're using MY house," Dad guaranteed.

"You really got some nerve! Call back, in a little while to talk to Dree. I'm on the phone right now."

My father didn't have inquiries, pleasantries, or so much a better idea "Hi," for Mel and I.

My parent's divorce became effective, March 14, 1989. However, it was through them, I learned the value of voting. It was because of them, I became interested in politics. I found it very interesting. Being a "bleeding-heart liberal" and 18-years-old, I voting for the first time. I voted for the first, Black-elected Virginia Governor, L. Douglass Wilder. It felt beautiful. It was incredible, really being an adult, and voting Democrat.

Coming from a gutter of emotions, Mama, Dree, Mel, and I were determined, to have some fun. Mel was a diehard Janet Jackson fan. We went to, TWO of her concerts in Washington DC, (really, Landover, Maryland.) It was the Rhythm Nation tour. It was great show.

It was a 1990, a new decade. No more, letting people dictate, who we are. It was a great concert. Janet had a whole factory of dancers behind her.

MC Hammer was taking the world by storm. He was doing the same thing, with an onslaught of dancers. Chucka and I went to his show in the Richmond Coliseum.

Somehow, Chucka, or should I say, Dev-01, got in good with the school's DJ, in the student lounge area. The one they had, would play cassette tapes, withspeakers, during "peak hours."

We volunteered, to play our own personal (Black) music, for the school. I was happy "representing our people."

I went to a predominately White school. There were times, I'd be the only Black Person in class. It made me cling, to my Black heritage, even more.

I was still wearing, my blue jean book bag, with the African continent, colored red, black, and green, sewed in it.

I stuck out like a sore thumb, but I was proud, none the less. I felt, my diction was good enough, but I didn't use big, fancy words to impress anyone, nor did I read announcements, on the microphone, like my White counterparts.

I just, simply, wanted to play good music. So I hardly, said anything, behind the booth. I'd run my show, as long as two hours sometimes. Chucka, pretty much, left me, by myself. (Why, I don't know.) It was his idea, his thing.

My father wasn't in my life, but I still had my health.

Keep in mind, I was into, politically, conscious rap music. I'd play Public Enemy, X-Clan, Ice Cube, or Sister Souljah. So, every now, and then, I'd sneak in my midday program, a "message song."

"Can you play something else?" a White guy asked me, walking to the booth where I was.

As disagreeable, as that may have been, it stopped me in my tracks. Was the lyrics "too Black, too strong?" I was, slightly, embarrassed. Did I come across as a racist, or a bigot? I didn't want to be fenced in. I wasn't a prejudice person. I didn't want to be seen as anti-White, when I, certainly, wasn't.

The world was filled with heinous crimes against humanity. I didn't understand. I didn't know why people could be so heartless. From where I was standing, people didn't seem to care, unless it was about materialistic things.

Where was God in all of this? Did He exist?

If I may continue, sure, it great hanging out with Chucka. Once, we went to Virginia Beach. We eyed the women, while drinking wine coolers. Yet, something was missing.

Sure, Vin would take us to clubs like, Armani's (formerly known as DJ Lounge). We went to The Slip, downtown. We visited Fevers. We stopped at 24/7 club in Petersburg. Also, a club near his military base, in Newport News. However, something was missing. Carl was cool, but something was missing. Walter, or Gerry, was okay, but I knew, something was missing.

Men were dogs, I thought. I did not trust men. Maybe, because of my experience, growing up. I was dissatisfied. I wanted more out of life than getting women's phone numbers, having fun, getting high, or drunk. I wanted more out of life. What? I didn't, exactly, know. I didn't have, a peace of mind.

Don't get me wrong. Women, absolutely, enchanted me. They're so beautiful! I love women. The more feminine, the better. I was, completely, in awe, infatuated and comfortable, with females. I just, simply, wanted to be with, the right lady. I didn't want to be anyone's secret, or necessarily, private affair. I wanted a girl, to believe in me, love me. I didn't want to be, an afterthought, a choice, or treated, like a piece of meat.

I helped my brother, to forge his ID. I taught Mel, how to white out, type in, and copy his birth certificate. He was only 15, but he needed to be 16. We both got jobs at the Hardee's, not too far from my college. Two things, Mel wanted. A state- of- the- art CD stereo, from Circuit City store, and a car.

I bought me 1986, golden brown, Buick Skylark. It had an all digital dashboard! I loved that. I drove it fast, like a homicidal maniac. I was a speed demon. The police gave me, speeding ticket after speeding ticket.

I needed more flexibility, in my working hours. My grades were suffering, like a hole in the roof.

So, I dived in at the job across the street, from Hardee's, which was Wendy's. They put me, on the salad bar. I had to mop up, any fluid, I may have seen on the floor, in the bathroom. The manager kept me, cleaning the bathroom. It was a humbling experience, to say the least. Customers would, actually, look down, shaking their heads, at my miserable job position. I was forced to clean, disgusting urinals and toilets. I considered it "paying my dues." It was "only temporary." ( I'm going to school). I was getting an education, so it really didn't matter, I'd tell myself. It seemed dubious at times, but I find education, is very important.

It wasn't before long, when Leigh and I became, attached to each other. We ignored the fact, we were so far from each other. She was a fragile, virgin woman, who was willing to move to Virginia. I could be my total self, around her. She didn't care about my weight, more importantly. It was impetuous that we be together. I wasn't taking "no" for an answer. She gave me the impression, she'd do anything for me. It was so innocent. So elementary, the love we had.

As usual, I was running late to my Journalism class. To me, we were a special breed of students, enveloped in political thought. They had great communication skills. Everybody in there, wanted to, somehow, embellish as a reporter one day. Perfectly, honest, I was intimidated. I was in a galore of thoughts. I doubted, if I could be as good, or enunciate, like the rest of the people. I wanted employment at the Richmond Times-Dispatch, like everyone else. Yet, I needed to gather confidence, which I didn't have. I felt as an individual, that I could write, but speaking, in front of other people, was a different ballgame. It was fear, my dear.

Rita's middle name being "Infidelity," I'd go over there, to liven things up. I'd visit her then townhouse in Hilltop. Projects on south side. Drug dealers on every corner. I'd, quickly, go in her house. I would play with her son and daughter. Though she was, carelessly, rough, whenever she would discipline her kids, I envied her. Here I was, working some minimum wage, dead-end job, busting my butt to school. Meanwhile, she sat around, collecting WIC and welfare, getting high and drunk, and being with different dudes all the time. I'd soon leave. (Leigh, way up in Brooklyn).

It was no joke or metaphor, the bank from the car dealership, would call me, all the time, without interruption. I needed my car, but I wasn't able to make my payments, on time.

Not to be sneezed at, I wanted a wife, someday, I thought. However, Leigh's voice began to irritate me on the phone. She began Brooklyn College. Yet, as much as I wanted her to stop, she continued to, relentlessly, give me Jehovah Witness teachings, Such as, God the Father, God the Son, God the Holy Ghost. I wanted to hear about her other adventures, like her school. The more she pulled, the more I pushed. I didn't want to hear about her religion, all the time. I was tired, of hearing about heaven. It got to the point, where I was sick of hearing about God. At least, coming from her. It was insufferable. She would not let up! If I did decide, to talk about God, I would argue, that there's only, One God. I'd argue against, the Trinity concept she was talking about.

My mother would often buy, The Final Call newspapers, from the Nation of Islam. The men would be on a busy, street intersection, selling the paper, for only $1. So, I began, curiously, reading them. Of course, I wanted to see, what Louis Farrakhan had to say.

My mother didn't believe in judging other races. She didn't make mockery, out of other religions. For that, I am, particularly, grateful. It would have been justified, but she didn't curse either (unless she was upset).

It seemed, the moments I spent with Chucka, our friendship, was going more and more downhill. I felt, I was being taken for granted. I didn't mind taking him home, but I didn't like, being used for a ride either. I would leave campus, on purpose, deserting him. Things weren't always bad. Once, we went to a comic bookstore at Willow Lawn. We were like two kids again, admiring our favorite superheroes. He bought a huge collection of comic drawn, topless women cards. I did the same. They were, tastefully, drawn.

Sometimes, I'd glance at police cars, to see if it was, actually, my dad. Yet, I thought, I hated my father. I felt, "I'll see him, whenever I see him." Be it the morgue, or otherwise.

I was no longer the type of guy, to get on my knees to pray. I wasn't the type to feel, I have to belong to an organization. I didn't need someone telling me, how to be. I most, certainly, didn't have time, for some superficial, sanctimonious "holier than thou" person, thinking they're better than me, or other people, because they're "knowledgeable," or "saved," and therefore, sanctified. I wanted to do, what I wanted to do, when I wanted to do it.

My siblings and I had our issues. I would eat, my problems away. (Little Debbie's Pecan Pies). Dree refused to do any labor around the house. Mel was wishing, he was never born. He didn't have any friends then. I sort of knew why, or what was happening with him.

In 1991, I did something nice for myself. I got my left ear pierced. It stung, incidentally, but it felt great doing something, I've always wanted to do.

In Mel's painted, purple and green, room, I caught him watching, a taped episode of Geraldo's talk show. It was a topic about gay teenagers. They were discussing their personal hardships.

"He got a necklace like you, Mel," I said.

I was oblivious to what it, actually, meant. Mel, who had the same, rainbow-colored accessory, then put his television on mute. Clearly, there was something he wanted to say.

"I'm gay, Marco," he cried. "I was afraid, if I told you, you wouldn't be my brother anymore."

I reflected on the awful times, I called him a "faggot," if I became mad at him. My heart leaped. My brain nagged at me. I was perplexed. I had so many questions.

"You'll always be my brother!" I cried. " I don't care what nobody say."

We hugged. We cried.

"I always knew," I said.

"How?" Mel said, naturally.

"You got that nice car, and never talk about girls."

We both laughed.

He just bought a new, red 1991 Geo Tracker. It was a stick-shift, he didn't know how to drive, at first. Mr. Hall (Dad's former friend), taught him how to drive it.

Mel felt liberated, that he finally told me the truth. Especially, with no negativity, from me. I didn't, exactly, like the idea, of my brother, being in a particular lifestyle, but he was still, my brother, none the less. That's all that mattered. One thing for certain, two things for sure, Mel played the coolest techno, club music, I have ever heard.

With Mel, working at Kings Dominion, I got a newfangled dishwasher job, at Red Lobster. The waitresses and waiters were, absolutely, stuck up. The restaurant was, predominantly, White. Sometimes, I'd overhear racist remarks. They didn't give us, dishwashers, any breaks.

So, I'd go into their walk-in refrigerator, to steal food. I ate plenty of their Lobster Tails, and custard pies. Eventually, I was fired for working, too slow. Before I was let go, I managed to save up enough, for a Greyhound Bus ticket. I wanted to visit Leigh.

We wanted to see each other. The plan was, I'd catch the bus to New Jersey. My aunt (North) would drive me to Brooklyn, to see my "pen pal." I wanted it to be a great summer. I wanted things to go, smoothly.

"It's like you're going on a blind date," my mother said, at the bus station.

I didn't care. I was like a pilgrim, that needed to go. I was a lizard coming out of its hole. I needed to do this, on my mind own, for the first time. Trying to talk me out of going, was nonsense. My mind was made up.

I got on the bus, proud of myself. I was living my life. I had my Walkman. I had some of my favorite cassette tapes. Also, I had chicken, wrapped in aluminum foil. My eyes enjoyed the scenery, Washington DC, Baltimore. The world wasn't, necessarily, loveless. I had an obligation to fulfill, and that was to be myself. I was providing a point, as the bus lunged forward. I had to do something on my own. It was like I was, more or less, an aspiring writer, taking his ideas to Hollywood. I had the magnificent feeling, that I was doing the right thing.

The bus got us, passengers, to the port in New Jersey, safe and sound. Of course, I loved to see, from North's apartment, Manhattan skyline. From the window, I loved to see, the beloved Twin Towers, holding their post. I tried, not to show it. I was, completely, nervous. While I was trying to organize my luggage, I knew, I was about to, finally, meet Leigh the next day.

Of course, Saturday morning, insecurity poured over me, like a used tissue. I wasn't sure, if Leigh saw me, would she still want to marry me. North was trying to give me tips, on what I ought to be like. Namely, just be myself.

Once we crossed the Brooklyn bridge, we went to Crown Heights. There was no turning back. Not surprisingly, Leigh was shy. I introduced myself to Leigh's, elderly, mother. We, quickly, went to her room, while North and her Leigh's mother chatted. It was weird, I didn't get a chance to her younger brother and father, who was in their Brooklyn brownstone as well.

Leigh showed me her scrapbook, of her favorite celebrities. It was nice, getting preferential treatment. She wasn't overbearing. It felt wonderful. It was the best present, I could have hoped for. When it time to leave, I could have cried. It wasn't about looks, but the beauty, we had inside. I felt like praying.

Sunday, the next day, I went back to Leigh's house, to reclaim what was, rightfully, mine. Somebody suggested, we go out, to get something to eat. It was making my mouth saliva. We went to a quaint, little restaurant, in a prominent area of Brooklyn, just the four of us. Afterwards, Leigh and I pardoned ourselves, up her staircase, to her room. She promised me, she would come down to Virginia, the next year. There was no scuffle of words. No statements of rudeness. Well, she did, playfully, call me "Nestle Crunch bar," because of the razor bumps, I had on the back of my hairline, on my neck. Saying goodbye, was like being a battle-scarred battleship. I went out, into the unknown sea.

North drove us around New York's skyscrapers and high rises. I saw all the famous stories. We pushed our way towards Harlem. Even at night, there was a sea of people. After years of watching the Apollo Theatre on tv, on Saturday nights, I was, directly, in front of it.

"You want to get out, and walk?" said North.

I was like, yeah, why not? So, there I was, walking around, among strangers. Some merchants was selling merchandise, quality items, on a section of 125th Street.

It was a struggle to leave. Before I caught the bus for home, North and I went on a quest, to find me a flat-top, African-style hat. I wanted something to remember, my Black heritage. Countless hours, I stared at my New York City poster, in my room.

After wasting, so much time in school, I decided, to get my priorities straight. I applied myself. I started to get good grades. However, I had a hard time, because of my previous grades, actually, pulling my grade point average up.

Mel made a new friend, named Mike, from Kings Dominion. He happened to be White, which didn't bother me. Then it seemed, suddenly, Mel had all these White people, like Amanda, and Wally, coming over to the house. Naturally, I quivered inside, at the sight of complete, total strangers, in our humble home. It felt like an "intrusion," for lack of a better word.

Once, I asked Mel, to hang out.

"Mel, do you want to go to a movie or something?"

"I have to see what my friends are going to do, first," he said.

It's not like, he already made plans. I was crushed! Of all the things, I did for him. All the fights, I got into over him. Those times, I protected him, when they protested him. I was there for him, when he didn't have any friends, to speak of. So, I began to resent his new friends. Not because, they were White either. Separating truth, from fiction. It was because Mel, subsequently, put his friends, before me, his own brother. I felt betrayed. Suddenly, I'm being treated, like a dirty rag, or a forgotten, loyal servant, who sufficed, while he ran the streets, rampant, with his friends.

Meanwhile, I was shackled at home, with lack of friends. Seemingly, the guys I grew up with, outgrew each other, moved, or moved on. Sometimes, I'd ride to the park, but it was no fun, by myself. I was a baby, without a rattle. I was a guy, who shaved for nothing. Sometimes, I'd accompany my mother to the store, K-Mart, Williamsburg Pottery, etc.

Seeing Kunta Kinte on a slave ship, it meant I was watching Roots movie again. Not surprisingly, I cried again. I became short winded, as I watched Kinta, being suspended on a a rope, whipped into slavery. My soul recommended, I be all I can be. I needed to study, learn, and do what I could, to help people. African people were shut out from their ancestral home, their culture, their language, their God. They were swindled into slavery, by adversarial African tribes, Arabs, and Whites. That brings me to the point, when I was the only Black person in my Western Civilization history class. The teacher herself, had racial overtones.

"They enslaved each other, and don't let nobody tell you differently!" said the instructor.

Was she redeeming herself, at my expense? Smooth as silk, she would say derogatory statements, synonymous with Native Americans. I just sat there, quietly, like a reformed Black man, listening to that crap. My instructor would sing that tainted mess, while I sat there, peacefully. The only thing I regret, I didn't walk out. Maybe, tell the school, in protest, or curse her out, regardless, if other students were taping it or not. Her job was to teach, not spread her bias views, about the past. I decided, the sleazy woman, who proudly, drank her tea, wasn't worth it.

Admittedly, I hung around Horse, who sold drugs. He knew, I didn't want to get involved, in any way, with that. He respected that. He would tell me war stories, of what it was like being shot at, and him shooting back. He respected me, for going to school, and not turning out, like he did. Horse wanted to repent. I would smirk, knowing his tendency to sell pharmaceuticals, wasn't going to stop, no time soon. Horse was the kind of guy, who cared about his reputation.

Horse had it bad, when it came to the ladies. If he saw a cute girl, he couldn't be silent. He had to talk to her. With him being Vin's "cousin," we hung out more and more. I grew up sheltered. Some would say, spoiled.

BEHOLD

Horse would tell me, I should be thankful, I didn't have to rob retail stores, like him.

Somehow, as opposite as we both were, we became great friends. He explained to me, the drug business. He'd "flip" or double, what he paid for the drugs, and then sell them, at a marketable price, for profit. The downfall, being robbed, going to jail, or being killed.

Vin, I found out, also sold drugs, in the Army. Apparently, military pay, wasn't as souped up, as it was supposed to be. I know, because of the conversations Vin and Horse would have, in Vin's car. The hairs on my neck would rise. Specially, hearing what they would do, if someone threatened them.

*SEASON 8, EPISODE 9*

# Malcolm X

IT WAS SPRING of 1992. Leigh paid for an all-expenses paid, round trip bus ticket, to see me, in my neck of the woods. Like a spider, awaiting its food, I welcomed her, into my web. It was a Thursday, I'll never forget. I took her sack, threw it in the trunk of my car, and drove, quickly, to a romantic spot, anywhere, where we could be alone.

We were at my old high school. Suddenly, a police car pulled up beside us. I thought we were toast, with those bright lights, shining in on us.

"This private property," he said, giving us a break.

Finally, I drove Leigh to my home, feeling like a fool. So embarrassing. It felt like a captain going down, with the ship.

"I trust you," Leigh said.

I was in another zone. There was little turbulence, along the way. We reached an understanding. We did the right thing. We were two consenting adults, as we retired to our separate rooms.

The next morning, my mother was due at work. My brother and sister went to school. My vehicle was parked, right outside. Whenever the urge, we could go wherever she wanted. Ordinarily, I wouldn't be with a woman, but there she was. It felt great. I wanted to capture the moment. My eyes noticed every violet flower. I was a volcano, ready to explode. I had so much love to give. I was making minimum wage, but Leigh didn't care. I didn't have the "flyest" or nicest wardrobe, but it didn't matter. For the first time, I felt alive. I felt like a human being, dancing under a waterfall. On top of it all, my weight didn't seem to bother me.

I took Leigh to the movies. We saw, "Wayne's World." It was an afternoon matinee, so the movie tickets were, considerably, cheaper. Since I didn't have much money, I also took Leigh to Byrd Park. I wanted to let go, be free. We had fun. I, playfully, chased her through the park. In public, we became one. We coincided. We held hands. We were two human beings, truly, experiencing the opposite sex, for the first time. Colors of black, brown, pink, and occasionally, milky white went into action. Yet, this was red. It was love.

On a budget, the next day, I took Leigh to the sexiest movie, I could find. We saw, "Basic Instinct," starring Sharon Stone and Michael Douglas. I didn't want to see another comedy. I was in the mood for a suspense thriller. I was a gentleman. I let her bite off, my candy bar. For the first time in my life, I was in a committed relationship. It was wonderful! Leigh was my companion. Cupid took an aim at my heart, and I was going for it. In the back of my mind, I knew it was a blaze, that would soon have to be put out.

Sooner or later, she'd headed back home, to Brooklyn. I didn't care, if Leigh didn't have the greatest skin dexterity or complexion. It didn't matter, if her face was blotchy. As white as Dove soap, I loved her.

A few days later, I wanted to get off the old block. I took Leigh to Washington DC. She never been there. It was, only, an hour and a half drive from the house. Mel tagged along too.

"Nice legs!" he shouted from the car, to a man in shorts, in DC.

I alluded to Leigh in conversation. I pretended, I didn't hear, what I just heard. We went to a record store, that Mel, somehow knew about. On our way back, we stopped by Potomac Mills, which is a huge mall, outside of DC.

It was the day, of the Rodney King, police brutality verdict. The four White policemen, who, severely, beat him, with blunt force trauma were acquitted. They were, completely, exonerated. It was all over the news, when we got home. "No justice, no peace," was the slogan. Black people were rioting in the Los Angeles area. Amateur videos captured Blacks and Latinos having a bonanza, looting stores. Black leaders, confessed their frustrations.

I felt, if I was among the looters, I would have done, the same thing. I too, would have threw glass bottles. Church congregations held prayer.

People held candles. I was furious! Suddenly, the riots of the 1960s didn't seem so much, like ancient history. There's civil unrest in our times too. However, Leigh didn't share the same sentiments. I put the brakes on my feelings about her. I made the conscious decision, she was a "sell-out." I was already upset, she ran back and told Dree everything, like our private conversations.

It was like the Civil Rights Movement, all over again. Bridging the age gap, young people everywhere wore, Malcolm X T-shirts, Malcolm X baseball caps. Everywhere I went, Malcolm X was a constant reminder.

Reluctantly, I let Leigh go back home. After a couple of months went by, she anticipated, she maybe pregnant. I was upset. I was scared. We toiled over, and over, on what to do. I wanted children, someday, but I felt it wasn't the right time. I didn't have any money. She didn't have any money. Leigh and I were so far from each other. Especially, because of my father, I wanted to be there for my child. We cried. We argued. I, finally, talked her into getting an abortion. We felt, it was the right thing to do, at the time. I sent her $250, in the mail, to get it done, without her parents knowing about it. Leigh got it done, before she went into her second trimester. The most I could do was apologize, for not, actually, being there, beside her.

Afterwards, the abortion traumatized Leigh. She felt guilty. I felt guilty. We cried buckets. Regrettably, Leigh broke up with me. She said, she was going to be join a convent.

I was, completely, devastated on the mistake we made. I was hurt. I was so hurt, Leigh and I were over. I felt like, I was nothing more than a kitchen appliance, that wasn't plugged up, without Leigh. I was something, long forgotten, in a bathroom cabinet, without Leigh. The lady, I invited into my heart, was no more.

Hanging around Horse, he helped me develop an attitude about women. He'd call women, "bitches," "ho's" or "sluts." He always had a macho man bravado. Unfortunately, I'd refer to women, the same way he did.

I drove him, everywhere. We could, easily, be found on Canal Street. He'd, usually, wear his cotton shirts. As long as I wasn't mixed up, with his drug dealer stuff, I was fine. We drank plenty of Old English malt liquor. That was my personal favorite. Of course, we drank it, directly, from the glass bottle.

Putting a cap on things, I felt, fat as a cow. I was straight as an arrow, with carnal desires. I didn't iron creases in my pants anymore. (Why)? Because, who cares? I admired Horse, with the amount of women he was catching. He took his .25 mm pistol, everywhere. He wouldn't leave home without it. I would cringe, whenever he brought it out. Sometimes, he'd play with it. He was always, avoiding the police. He was always, talking about fighting, or chocking someone. Occasionally, he'd do jail time. He had an assortment of friends. I felt lucky, to be centered in there, somewhere. He swore, he was going to hook me up, with a woman, one day.

With all the fanfare, and hoopla, about Malcolm X that year, I decided to get my hands on, The Autobiography of Malcolm X as told to Alex Haley. I began, tirelessly, reading about his life, from cover to cover. Suddenly, to me, Malcolm X became more than a fashion choice, or passing fad, on a cheap T-shirt. I appreciated his uncompromising conviction, for the truth.

I became interested, in this thing, called "Islam." Malcolm X was convinced, it was the cure, for ending racism. It brought me chills, to read about his pilgrimage, to the holy city of Makkah. I too, wanted true brotherhood, regardless of color.

Eventually, I'd circle back to Rita's place. She lived in Mosby Court, which had a notorious reputation. Since the two of us, were just friends, I asked her to hook me up with someone. Rita introduced me to her friend, Pam. She had a baby daughter. I had a ball. I'd buy Pam and her brother, beer. I'd be over their house, in the projects, for hours, getting drunk. I was smoking marijuana. I felt comfortable. I felt good. I drove Pam to see the movie, "The Bodyguard," starring Whitney Houston and Kevin Costner. As though clarinets, were blowing in the air, I really started to like Pam. She said, she was into White men, but I acted "different." When it came to me, she said, she wasn't ready for a relationship. I grinned and bared it. (I did try).

"All these White people in here!" slipped Pam' brother.

We were at the movie lobby, awaiting to see "Single White Female," starring Bridget Fonda.

"Excuse me!" said a single White female, who overheard him, and was offended.

I was so embarrassed. I wanted to bury my head, in the nearest waste paper basket. We were at the Byrd Theater. It's one of the oldest running, but prestigious, movie theaters in Richmond. It on Cary Street. It's, absolutely, beautiful inside.

By the way, when the coast was clear, I got another earring piercing. This time, in my right ear. I thought it was hip, cool. I wanted to be different.

Also, when I was working Western Sizzling, I got the nerve, to ask Jennifer out on a date. She was a waitress. She was pretty, White, quiet, with gorgeous eyes.

Prince and the New Power Generation gave a concert, at the Richmond Mosque. Tickets were sold out, immediately. That meant his biggest fan, couldn't get in. So, Mel and I went downtown, to check out the people. However, I did go in the concert hall, to buy a souvenir. I ended up with a Prince T-shirt. That wasn't good enough. I had to see Prince himself. We, actually, went to the back of the theater. I saw a long, black limousine parked, and wouldn't move. Soon, Prince's dancers and his band came out. Prince was nowhere to be found.

"Where's Mayte?" I asked one of Prince's dancers.

I was addressing Tony M. That was Prince's occasional hip-hop artist, and dancer. Of course, I recognized him, from the music videos. He indicated she's coming.

"Can I have your autograph?" I said.

"You got a pen?" he said.

I didn't have one on me. Mayte soon came out to the limousine. She was, absolutely, breathtaking. She also, was his dancer. She was an absolute angel. She was so beautiful!

It wasn't the first time, I was star struck-struck. The year before, Dreeka and I went to Churchhill Music, to get an autograph from Ice Cube. Mind you, we just saw the movie, "Boyz in the Hood." I was nervous, meeting Ice Cube. I got him to sign, one of my cassette tapes, of his, "AmeriKKKa's Most Wanted." It was his first, solo studio album, after breaking up with NWA.

"Can you sign, my other tape?" I asked, because I also, brought an EP of his.

He said, he couldn't. There was a long line of other fans, awaiting an appearance, or autograph too.

Speaking of rap stars, Gerry and I saw Tupac, in concert. He did a show, at a club, named Ivory's. Tupac was an up-and-coming rapper, in 1992. His songs "Keep Your Head Up" and "Brenda's Got a Baby" was getting plenty of radio airplay. On stage, he had on, a beige Karl Kani designer shirt. The club was jammed packed. Not surprisingly, there was a fight, in the middle of the crowd, while Tupac was doing his thing.

Pam introduced me to her friend, Snow. She was fresh out of jail. Snow's drug of choice was heroin. She was a complete addict. She had to have it.

I must've been desperate for love and romance. I would do degenerate things, like drive Snow to the corner, to get her drugs. I would escort her to the grocery store. So, she could steal meats and diapers, to sell. I would be her lookout, while she stole clothes, from the mall.

"You're my lucky charm," she once told me.

I must've been delirious. Evaporating my credit card, I charged her clothes to wear. She continued her heroin habit. I'd watch her grapple items from the store. Then later, return the stolen items for money. She'd pretend she lost her receipt. She made hundreds of dollars that way.

Snow shot up her drugs, with a buddy of hers, in the next room. She didn't want me to watch her, get high. I would, quietly, drink beer, while she exhaled in the other room. She was 8 or 9 years older than me. Her mother was in her kid's legal guardian. We were just friends. We both knew, sooner or later, she was going back to jail. Stealing was a dirty disease.

I harassed my family for weeks, for us to see the movie, "Malcolm X," starring Denzel Washington. I knew in my heart, it was one of the most important films ever made. I devoured every scene. I took in every word.

When the ending credits, at the movie, started to roll, we stood up. My tears began to fall. I cried and cried. My family hasten to hug me, patting me on the back.

I knew, exactly, in my heart, on that very spot, where I stood. I WANT TO BE A MUSLIM. Under no compulsion, coercion, and with free will. I was clueless. All I felt, Islam seems "clean" and "pure." I didn't understand it. I didn't know why. I didn't know how, or which way, to turn. What do you do? Where do you go? Who do you talk to? I was lost in the sauce. I was anything, but diligent about it. I didn't search or research. I didn't look any further. However, I tucked the idea of Islam, in the back of my mind. It was like a family heirloom. Out of sight, out of mind.

Though I was disappointed in my father, and how my part-time, schedule at school, was going, I proudly, voted for Bill Clinton. He was so down-to-earth, he was considered our "first Black president." I wore my black leather, baseball cap, with the gold "X." Afterwards, I wore the "I voted" sticker. I got ferocious looks at school, which seemed to say, "Well, you know, who he voted for."

One of my coworkers, at Western Sizzling, couldn't believe what he heard.

"Marco, I liked you! I really liked you!" he said in discord, when he found out, who I voted for.

He was a White guy, who wasn't looking for a fight, or a hit.

In 1993, I disengaged myself, from my community college, Reynolds, all together. I believed, I was doing the right thing, by quitting school. Sure, I was going to miss the women, but I was disoriented. I tried to pull my grade point average, but it was no use. I was tired of wasting time.

Mel was flamboyant or proud, of his lifestyle. He was still my brother, regardless. My brother moved in with his boyfriend, Fawn. He left mother's house, to be with him. My mother said, "Violence didn't solve anything." He was, hardly, 18 and just graduated high school. Our relationship as brothers was already flimsy, as it was. I felt helpless, and humiliated. I felt, I lost him, not because he was gay, but to his gayness. (If that makes any sense). Virtually, he was cutting us all off, I thought. I was dizzy, with emotions. I was flustered, with sadness. I thought, I hated "that White boy," or should I say, older man. I felt his guy, manipulated my brother, to be with him. However, there was nothing, I could do. Mel made his choice.

When it came to Dreeka, I would do formidable things, like cut the tv off, when her, and her boyfriend, Curt, would be watching it. I'd immobilized their phone conversation, wanting to instill his fear of me. With boys sniffing around my sister, I acted overprotective and impetuous. I was pushing her over the edge, of her hating me, I guess. What's more frightening, I purchased a .25 handgun. (You never know).

That year, the family went to the Gay Pride Parade, in Washington DC, to support Mel. There were bus loads of people. We caught the metro train, at one point. Suddenly, Dree started singing out loud.

"If you're happy and you know it, clap your hands!" she sang, inclining the people on the train, to do the same.

Being in the nation's capital, I couldn't resist the urge to see a museum. I wanted to see the stuffed elephant in The Museum of Natural History. So, Dree and I went sightseeing .

The streets were full of protesters. Men in drag, men in pink. Rainbow colored signs tickled the sky. Lesbians wore purple. Some women, consequently, took their shirts off. Some of them, walked around the park topless. There were many celebrity endorsements. Lots of politicians for Equal Rights, talking from furry microphones.

We pointed our index finger, in recognition of Jesse Jackson. Seeing him, embodied the whole experience. With the reverend there, I knew it wasn't a game. Mel seized the opportunity, and ran over to him. Determined not to leave empty-handed, Mel got his picture taken, with Jesse Jackson. Proud of that moment, Mel hung his enlarged photo, on the wall, for all to gaze at.

Other heterosexual people, infiltrated throughout the day, supporting their love ones. We, certainly, weren't alone.

"We're here! We're queer! Get over it!" people shouted, to no end.

Many cried. Many danced their troubles away. It was a day, I will always remember. I had the enormous feeling, I did something great for humanity. I respected those gay people, for being themselves. Also, for having the "kahunas" of being proud, of who they were. Who in their right mind, would chose to be ridiculed, taunted, teased, shunned, offended, embarrassed, upset or hurt, if they didn't have to?

Actually, in 1993, I didn't know what, I was going to do, with the rest of my life. I had a job, with Old Country Buffet. I washed dishes. I was too young, for a midlife crises, but it was, painstakingly, unclear on what I should do next.

"Why don't you just, start all over?" my aunt North suggested.

The idea of school again, was irresistible. It started as a miniature thing, to think about. Then the idea of a "redo" grew, into a cute, cuddly panda bear. The kind of creature, you can't take your eyes off of. Rolling the dice, I tried my hand at Virginia Commonwealth University. I liked their diversity. Not too White. Not too Black. (Just right). I was, slightly, older, but I took the SAT exam at Tucker High School. Like a miscarriage, it didn't go too well. A pretty counselor at VCU said, I would have to be on "probation" or part-time, my first, two semesters, that year. So, I got in! I almost went into paralysis, when I accepted. I was so happy, I could have smoked a joint. I felt so fortunate, to have a second chance. I knew, I would have to study, "for real" this time. The great thing about VCU was, they would "erase" the earlier grade, if I had to take the class over.

Mel, cordially, invited me, to go with him to a gay club. I made the decision to go. Simply, to spend quality time with him.

"What if a guy, tries to talk to me?" I said, nervously.

It seemed juvenile, but I had concerns.

"Just tell them, you're not like that, or you're with me," he said.

So, after a few drinks, we went to Club Pyramid. It was on the Boulevard. It was predominantly White. I liked the techno, pop music. I was a little moody, not knowing what to expect. Would someone be pecking my nerves? Looking at the other club patrons, it wasn't so bad. Mel sensing my tension, suggested we go dancing. Eventually, I became at ease. Ironically, I had the feeling, I could relate. I too, knew what it was like, to be rejected. I too was judged, by the way I looked.

Occasionally, I thought about Leigh. (Putting the tv on mute), Vin and I, actually, snuck up to Brooklyn, New York to see her. We met a couple of girls, at a party, in Newport News. They wore nice perfume. They were from Atlantic City. We promised them, we would drive up there, someday. Vin knew which one he liked. Liking older women, I took the other one. She felt, she was too old for me. We were desperate to meet them again in New Jersey. Vin talked me into, driving my car. I met Leigh, to see how she was doing.

In Atlantic City, we lost a few casino games. The sea salt in the air, was enough, to make me nauseous.

With little persuasion, from Vin's girl, I smoked weed with her.

"You're cool, Marco," she said, feeling liberated.

Walter was fresh out of prison, for a (ransom note) robbery, at a Wendy's restaurant. Amazingly, his family got him a new, black 1993 Nissan Pathfinder. After two years in prison, I thought, that was phenomenal.

There was plenty of drinking, while driving. Noticeably, Walter was bitter and self-centered. He wasn't the same guy, I grew up with. Next, Carl and him wanted to meet some girls. So, I took them over to the Afton projects, where Rita lived. Dubious drug dealers. Police raids were the norm.

"Marco, are you gay?" Walter, suddenly, asked me, after a few sessions, of us going over to Rita's.

(Huh)? "What a pickle," I thought. I was appalled. I couldn't believe what I was hearing. That was a hard pill to swallow, coming from a guy, I knew all my life. I explained, just because my brother is like that, it doesn't, necessarily, make me like that.

There were times, I felt like a loaf, because I was still, living with my mother. So, I went on a crash diet, to look good for school. I felt obligated, to feel good about myself.

That summer, Walter and I got jobs at Steve's and Sons. It was a wooden, door-making place. Dust was flying everywhere. "Dusty and musty," at the end of each working day. It was a magnet, for guys, recently, released from prison, or on probation. We often had to work overtime, sometimes Saturday. I had the pleasure of being a "door flipper." I had to count 20-20-18, the number of door "skins" to flip on the conveyor belt.

There was the time, whereas I, accidentally, stepped on a long, rusty nail. It was sticking out, a piece of wood pallet, on the floor. I was in so much pain. I had to get a tetanus shot.

The postmark of it was when a fellow coworker, White guy, Rob, invited me to go to a club with him. The club was in Washington DC. His White girlfriend and another Black guy, I didn't know, tagged along. We had fun. We drank so much beer, I wondered how, would we get home. It was, powerfully, attractive, being around so many races of people, in a club again. The club was huge. There were three different dance floors.

I was eager to go to my new school. As, quickly, as my summer job at Steve's and Sons came, it was over. I doubted, if I'd return the following year. We preserved our sanity, by making corner store merchants rich, from our binge drinking. The power of the warehouse foreman was gone. The priceless, frustrated looks, the assistant foreman, Jamerson, would give, when he realized, we were behind, in our door production, was now a memory. The colorful profanity and metaphors was now, in the past. Breathing in dust, or the lack of oxygen was over. The intense heat, which could cure a disease, came to an end. Walter and I went our separate ways, with me, going to school, and him, working warehouse jobs. I was able to match him up with Angie, through Rita.

So, in the Fall Semester of 1993, I had the satisfaction of, actually, going to VCU. I was proud of myself, for not giving up. It wasn't Yale, but it was a great school. It wasn't located, in an upscale neighborhood area, but "it'll do." I'd go to Station Break, a video arcade, near campus, between classes. I wasn't sure, if I'd be around a bunch of snobby people again or not, but I chose Social Work, as my class major. My minor was Afro-American Studies, (Black history). I wanted to "make a difference," as cliché as that sounds. I wanted to help people. The idea of working with children, or at-risk youth, brewed in my mind, for years. I thought it would be fun. Scrawny ones, fat ones, I wanted to see children brainstorm over pictures, school work, while I out my two-cents in.

Seemingly, losing a lot of weight, I felt more confident. Especially, with the large quantity of woman at VCU. I felt secure, to ask the prettiest student in Dr. Drake's, Introduction to African-American Studies, out on a date. She sat, directly, behind me, in class. Without a quibble or hesitation, Shida said, "yes." Somehow, I wasn't intimidated.

"I love Black men," Shida would admit. "I love Black music."

She had an exotic look to her. She was an Arab woman, with long, dark hair. She was exquisite, with an excellent taste in clothes. She was very interesting, and very nice to look at. Also, she was from France, so she had an accent. She was so sweet, so nice. No bad attitude. I gave subtle hints, that I liked her. Yet, I was crazy about her! On our first date, I took her to a show, at the Richmond Marriott. She wanted to see the singer, Joe, in concert, so off we went.

I was happy to be her shadow, on a sunny day. I would have done ANYTHING for Shida. I thought I was falling in love. I considered her my "first real love." I was, completely, infatuated with her. I let her ravish through the little money I had. I bought her, whatever she wanted. Like a gardener, with cutting shears, I became what she wanted. I leaped for her, knowing no bounds. I didn't give a hoot about nothing, except Shida's happiness. Her perfume, her long, silky, jet black hair, drove me wild. Yet, she would tell me, "she's not ready," for a relationship.

I trusted Shida, without any suspicion. We, occasionally, kissed. Her words licked my ears. Her voice and every syllable, was delightful to hear. I couldn't get her out of my system, nor did I want to.

Shida confided in me, her family in France, were Muslim. However, she didn't practice. She was single, and taking classes in America. She was in Richmond, of all places. She was living her life. As far as I was concerned, the world regurgitated on me, up until that point, or until I met her. I had no skill set or much to offer. It was great, being with a gorgeous woman. An Arab, on top of that.

Religiously, there wasn't much, I could say. I didn't know much, about Islam myself. I didn't lose sleep over it, but Shida teased me with the little she did know. I wanted to know more.

I let Shida dump her problems on me. I wanted her to know, she could tell me anything. I wanted her to know, her place is with me. She didn't smoke. She was perfect! She was my tender, yellow flower. At Shida's request, I would be at her dorm, on campus, quick, fast, and a hurry. Whatever concerned her, was my terror too. Whatever needed to be resolved, I was a good soldier. I didn't ask questions. I did what I was asked. I was just thankful, someone that fine, so pretty, was giving me attention.

Yet, without retaliation, or without so much, as an argument, I sometimes felt, Shida was holding something back. Something wasn't there, or quite right. Deep down in my spirit, I felt, I wasn't in on it, whatever it was.

Love is blind. So, love revoked my other senses as well, when it came to Shida. I gave her sovereignty control of my thinking. It was like chewing on gristle. Tough, but tasty. Like in any other ritual, of getting my heart broken, I ignored the signs. I treated it as a speck in my eye, and kept it moving.

Shida was a good-looking girl. I felt threatened by other guys. She'd reassure me, she wasn't interested in other men, which made my spine tingle. Like the pope in a tiara, I wasn't making sense. I sacrificed my time for her. I spreaded my self thin, trying to please her. I took Shida, wherever she wanted to go. It could have been Timbuktu, for all I cared. I salvaged nothing.

I gave her my all. I asked Shida to marry me. She said, "yes." I was happy as French toast.

I saw plenty of step shows, on campus, between classes. Suddenly, a fraternity, or a sorority, would be "stepping" or doing their choreographed dancing. So, I decided to pledge the "purple and gold," Omega Psi Fi fraternity. I wanted to be a "Q-Dog." They seemed to be the boldest and the raunchiest. The pledges had to memorize, who the three, founding fathers, of Omega Psi Fi, were. We had to remember, the Greek alphabet. We had to help, organize a party. We once played basketball, in a juvenile detention center. I refused, to throw in the towel. I had to endure, their pathetic name-calling. I didn't take it, personally. I thought it was amusing, because it was to be expected. Due to the hazardous hazing, the following semester, the Omega Psi Fi chapter was shut down, until further notice. It was pending, under investigation.

Eventually, I didn't pay for parking any longer. I was done, with the VCU Student Parking, or its campus deck parking. I discovered, I could park for free, in the Oregon Hill neighborhood. It was a few blocks away, from the school, but I didn't have to pay anything.

White women, in particular, would, actually, cross the street, whenever they saw me walking near, or from, where I parked my car. (Why)? Because I'm a Black man? That, really, bothered me. It was as though, they thought, I might rape them, or rob them. I couldn't understand it. I was, simply, going to VCU, getting an education, like anyone else. I wasn't bothering anyone. With my backpack on, filled with school books, I wasn't hurting a fly. I most, certainly, wasn't going to hurt anyone. It was sickening to watch. It hurt my feelings. I was put under the same umbrella of someone, they would suspect. I was being viewed as a possible criminal.

I talked to my mother about it. She would tell me, the women, who crossed the street, didn't know me, and don't take it, personally.

I needed answers. I needed understanding. I needed to be involved. The Nation of Islam was selling The Final Call newspapers, near the VCU campus. As usual, they'd be at the busy, intersection on Broad Street, weaving through stopped traffic. Mama, occasionally, used to buy their newspapers. So, they were a familiar, or welcoming thing to see, for sore eyes. I did an unprecedented thing. I started buying The Final Calls myself. I felt, I was keeping up, with the times. I wanted to read more about racism, racial discrimination, racial bias, racial profiling, and all the prejudices that go with it. Apparently, I was buying enough, that one of the Nation of Islam guys, invited me, personally, to their meetings.

"Brother, why don't you, come on down, to the temple?" he encouraged me.

He was referring to Mosque No. 24. It was on Brooklyn Park Boulevard. It was all, I needed to hear. I was desperate for the truth. I got directions from the man, in the suit and bow tie. Eventually, I went there. I was patted down, upon entering the building. I was searched around my waist, for possible weapons. Nobody warned me, how great I would feel. I was waved, to the front row. Everyone went through the same security. It was good, all the way.

"All praise is due to Allah!" the minister said, from behind the podium, along with, what appeared to be, his two body guards, on either side of him.

Yes! I couldn't agree more! I was on the verge of exploding, with agreement. The truth was vibrant. It was crystal clear. The men were sharp, militant, and disciplined. The women were in violation, for being so darn beautiful. After the service, I felt so welcomed. I have never in my life, felt so respected!

"I want to be a Muslim. I've always wanted to be a Muslim," I said.

"Yes, sir!" they would address me.

Not since Leigh, has anyone called me, "Sir." She gave me the nickname, Sir, because I long for respect. I wanted to be taken, seriously. I felt whole, as I stood by the closed window-binders. The guys reached into their pockets, and bought me a bean pie. Especially, when I said, I didn't have any money. That meant a lot to me. They didn't know me! Also, they gave me a cassette tape with The Minister Louis Farrakhan on it. Being that it was December, it was their annual Nation of Islam's Ramadan. I fasted, the entire, next day, without eating, a single thing.

As it turns out, I went more, and more, to the Nation of Islam mosque. I was trying to "get it." They made it seem, absolutely, imperative I give up beer. I wanted to collapse, when they said, I should give up pork. However, I accomplished, a few things. I was being nicer, to my family. I wanted to believe in Islam. Yet, there were some things, I needed to comb through, first. Sure, racism exists, but I didn't want to hate anyone. That wasn't me. Like adhesive, I tried to cling on. I wanted to belong to something, bigger than me. The Nation of Islam, and what little, I knew about Islam, was my last hope.

"That devil! That blue-eyed devil!" the speaker would bestow on the audience.

That's how they referred to the White man. Also, they would direct our attention to American slavery, its oppression, and the country's embedded White Supremacy. Sometimes, a chalkboard was used, as a visual aid, to make a point. Members of the audience would stand, or clap. Some shouted back.

"Teach hard! Make it plain! Allahu Akbar!"

We had to write a letter, explaining why, if we wanted to, officially, join the Nation of Islam. It was to be mailed, to the national headquarters, in Chicago. It was a way, of loosening the shackles of slavery. It was dropping, the "slave master's name." We would receive, a registered "X" as our last name, if we made that commitment, (hence Malcolm X).

"That bagel-eating, hook-nose Jew!" the minister would say, in agitation.

I have never heard such, racial rhetoric. Beside the minister, would be his two, trusted body guards. It made the air, itself, still. With sustain, or without blemish, the men in bow ties, would be in perfect unison or compliance, like toy soldiers. I was nervous, to make any sudden moves, as the Fruit of Islam, (men) would eye the crowd.

I was proud to be Black. I wasn't anti-White. I wrestled, with what, they were teaching. I would often, voice my concerns, after the service.

"All of them?" I would question, about our White counterparts.

I couldn't conceive, or believe, all White people were, inherently, bad. No more than I would accept, all Black people were, innately, good. I didn't want to spend the rest of my life, angry, at White human beings.

"They're all devils, even their babies!" a well-spoken guy, who also condemned.

The teachings of The Honorable Elijah Muhammad were not to be amended. It was like, being in a bonfire. I felt confused.

"You just need to study more, Brother Marco," another one amplified.

I read books, such as "Message to the Blackman." I read, "Our Savior Has Arrived." I still wasn't, in complete agreement.

Meanwhile, I was enjoying my new school. I wanted nothing more, than a shot of brandy. VCU was anything, but conservative, when it came to fashion statements. I loved the anonymous faces, of all the different races.

"We're not Arabs, bumping our heads, five times a day!" an invited speaker would say, burning bridges.

I didn't know what they were getting at, or talking about. The ministers wore, neatly, pressed suits. They would often tear down, The US Constitution, skeptical of politicians, or "Reverend Chicken-wing," (clergyman or pastors). It became a broken record, being drilled in us, about the thick layer of racism, in this country. Undoubtedly, the followers felt, they were a living example, of what it was, to be a Muslim. They felt that people, who "bucked" or disagreed, on the teachings, were "lost" or sell-outs. They were considered traitors, to the Black race. In the back of my mind, I would think, "These were the very people, who had Malcolm X killed."

Still no word, from Dad. My father could've be dead somewhere, for all I knew.

Sometimes, I'd converse with Brother Anthony. He appreciated me, for at least, supporting the leader, Minister Louis Farrakhan. Like a baby calf, I milked Farrakhan's speeches, for all it was worth. Louis Farrakhan was the reason, I wanted to be a Muslim, in the first place. Like a sugarcane, he could "do no wrong." He was no counterfeit bill, sort of speak.

It was 1994. Mosque No. 24, as it was called, arranged for its followers, and supporters, to catch a charter bus, to Washington DC. It was for, an all-men speech, to see Louis Farrakhan, on stage.

Shida was still, in the limelight, but I was learning, to do things for myself. She wasn't a "cracker" (not my words) or White, so it was deemed "okay." When she found out, I was going, to The Nation of Islam, she became, visibly, upset. She said it wasn't "true Islam." She said, Islam was for everyone, regardless of color.

"I wish, I could start my own mosque, where color doesn't matter!" I said, as naïve as that sounds.

Every article, I read, or video, I ever seen, or tape, I ever listened to, was in no comparison to, actually, being there. News reporters, news cameras, of every kind, was there. Besides going to a music concert, it was the largest assembly, I have ever been to. Taking every precaution, the Fruit of Islam men, were spread everywhere, like melted cheese. The crowd, the militant stepping drills on stage, assured me, I was at the right place. Some people were awarded certificates, for their outstanding work and devotion.

When Louis Farrakhan was on stage, it was obvious, he was to be guarded, at all cost. The guys and I felt privileged, to be in the same room, with him. We were willing, to give all our charity to him. Farrakhan gave a shout out, to former Washington DC mayor, Marion Barry, who was, currently, facing drug charges. He also spoke, highly, of prophets, the men of God.

An autograph, would have been, out of the question, but I sat there mesmerized. I was dazzled, by Farrakhan's speech, and control of the crowd. He had a chip on his shoulder, because of America's domestic policy on Black people. He spoke of an upcoming, "Million Man March," for the following year.

There were awkward moments. I would explain to my mother, "Muslims believe in Jesus." I would mention Islam, whenever I could.

I was baffled, at the parking citations, I would get. I would try, to park closer to VCU. I'd go to "study jams" with other fellow classmates. As time went on, I was still getting, deadly, looks, walking to, and from school. As though, I was a bandit or something. I clawed my way, through some of those classes. Classes were demanding. Teachers were challenging. Students had to be outstanding. I refused, to let my life, decay and not have, some fun. I wish, I would've went to sporting events, or Ram basketball games. However, I wasn't into team sports then.

My favorite instructor became Dr. Drake. He was upfront. He spoke his mind. He didn't sugarcoat it. That's what I liked about him. He continued to bark politics, Black history, and of a closefisted Civil Rights Movement.

"All those people, like Farrakhan, who talk about, going back to Africa, ain't going nowhere!" he'd say. "They're going to live, right here, in America! You can go to Africa, if you want to! But they don't see us, as their brothers and sisters, over there."

(He really said that). Dr. Drake was like a "bat out of hell," sometimes. He was a radical, college student himself in the 1960's, who became "conservative" in his old age. He reminded me of "peach cobbler, with a cherry on top." He was a little defiant.

I was going for my Social Work degree. To me, it was essential. I was going for the "gold," which wasn't going to be "just delivered to me." I had to earn it. Victory was my only option. I had to graduate. I, simply, had to.

I gravitated around Shida, as much as possible. Deportation was the last thing, on our mind. With her perfect body, she required little exercise. I, practically, worshipped the ground, she walked on. That describes the extension of our disguised relationship. Her and I were destined for failure. Her face was my moon. Was I, her sun? She told half-truths. I was Shida's remote control device, that was expected, not to fail. Unbeknownst to me, I was behind her handiwork. She'd dial other phone numbers. She gave me false information. I worked hard to please her. Yet, I was digging myself in, deeper and deeper. Some of those far fetched stories, she told me, were ridiculous. I should've stopped, and ask myself, "Why?"

Without any diplomacy, or fear, Shida's White boyfriend, called me, on the phone. He said, they were sleeping together. He said, he had proof, on video tape. I didn't know, what to think.

"If I'm lying, come see, if I'm lying," he said.

I knew the address, because I would, often, drop her off there. She told me, she was "friends with the guy's ex-girlfriend," who happened to stay there as well. That's what I was, originally, told. I didn't know, if the guy was jealous, with had a plan, to kill me, or what. I didn't know, what the deal was. Somehow, I had to know. I had to, find out the truth. I knew, I had to go over there.

Of course, I was hurt.

"I can't believe, you're hurting, Marco! You're hurting him!" Shida cried, as though, she didn't want me to find out, like this.

A part of me, was interested in seeing their "roll in the hay." At least, the man was honest. I was crushed. I was devastated. I hoisted myself, out of the chair, not knowing what to do next. Thinking of the position I was in, I went outside. My knees buckled, from under me. I fell to the ground. Sure, I wanted to give the guy, a left hook. Yet, my sadness, wouldn't let my temper, get the best of me. My mind was racing. The florist? The house, I wanted us to move in? I wanted to be her husband. It was all, for nothing. It was all, lies. I needed a doctor, because I had a broken heart.

I was still, oddly enough, fond of Shida. Like a fool, I took her to a friend's house in Virginia Beach. It was a drastic move. Apparently, her boyfriend had trust issues. They got into a heated argument, and kicked her out of the house. She had no other place to go. She needed my help. My heart was on my forearm. I took her, to the only ideal, doable place, for her.

Going forward, on the highway with her, I was wondering, if we could have a conversation, about the video. I couldn't believe, I was so "green" or stupid. I didn't have a bad attitude. I thought about her. She was saying, she was wrong. She cried, and I didn't know what to do, with that. It felt like, the worst pain, imaginable.

"I'm sorry, Marco. I never meant to hurt you," Shida cried.

I put her at ease. I let her know, I was okay. However, I was "fraternizing with the enemy." I couldn't trust her. I was impatient, to put this thing behind me. I wanted to get on, with my life. I had an education, to think about. I didn't want to do anything rash. It fried my brain, why, she would do that to me. It wasn't implied by me, but for all I knew, the guy, in Virginia Beach, could have been, banging her too.

After all was said, and done, I had to elbow my way, through my emotions. Somehow, I didn't want anyone, to get a chance, to take me for a fool, ever again. The world became a frozen wasteland. It was punishment, without Shida. Like an elevator, my days were up and down. They became fundamental, as basic as that may sound.

At any rate, that balmy summer, my uncle Joe, put a relaxer, in his hair. It was a "wave hair" kit, which contained hair lye, for men.

I just got my heart broken. I wanted to treat myself. I needed something different. I needed a new look. I wanted something cool, just for me. I was tired of feeling disenfranchised.

So, I got Joe, to do the same, to my hair, when I visited South Carolina. I loved it! Somehow, I thought having "good hair" would increase my chances, with the ladies. Like a person, in the emergency room, my mother, absolutely, hated it. Being that my hair, appeared straight, and since, I wasn't gay, there was only one, other explanation.

"You're not White!" she would say.

My hair was only an extension, of how I felt inside. I wanted to do something, to help me from feeling like, an empty, used bottle of gin. Or worse, a germ, nobody wanted to be around.

My hair influenced me to disentangle myself, finally, from the Nation of Islam. The rhetoric, and the racism was hard to glaze over. I no longer wanted, to cause injury to my soul. My equipment, the very Holy Quran itself, which I brought at Mosque No. 24, contradicted the concepts, the ministers spat out. I didn't see the glory of hating White people. My instincts told me, something wasn't right. So, eventually, I stopped going. I was tired of their bitterness, and grim faces. I became sick of the paranoia. I was tired of the cynical approach to authority figures, above the Mexican border. Life is a precious package. I didn't want, to spend the rest of it, distrustful of White folks. "All White folks," for that matter.

Yet, before I went to the point of no-return, I took "pale-face" (not my sentiments), Shida and my mother, to see Minister Louis Farrakhan, at the Richmond Coliseum, when we were still "an item." Again, Farrakhan was drumming up support, for the Million Man March, which he wanted, to be held in Washington DC, sometime in 1995. Shida, mama and I, stood and clapped, incidentally, at one point, with something Farrakhan said. We were, actually, caught on camera doing so. In doing so, we were, immortalized on a Farrakhan speech. I bought the tape, from the Nation of Islam, and was surprised to see us.

Also, I'll never forget, when the Nation of Islam escorted me to see Sister Souljah. She gave a lecture at VCU. Sister Souljah kept looking at me out of curiosity like, "Who are you?" The Fruit of Islam sat either side of me. I was, directly, in the middle of them.

Though Shida was gone, she wasn't forgotten. I thought of the time, I suddenly, introduced her to my dad. He was sitting in his police vehicle, at (Eastgate Mall), Fairfield Commons Mall parking lot. He looked startled, not knowing, what to expect from me. It was like, cutting the boiling water pot, down. I wanted him to see I was doing okay, WITHOUT him.

Though Shida led me on, I still cared about her. To me, she was my first love. We continued, to hang out together. She was adamant, remaining friends. She insisted, our friendship, meant a lot to her. Not to mention, her jealous boyfriend, monitored her every move. It drove him nuts! He was getting a taste, of his own medicine. Obviously, he didn't trust her.

I mopped up my tears, as best as I could. I wanted inner peace. If Islam meant, I would have to hate people, judge people, or knit and attitude for non-Muslims, I wanted no part of it. I peeked inside, the Nation of Islam, and didn't like what I saw. For lack of a better word, it was hate. The "love teachings," or self-love of the Black man rhetoric, I found to be reckless. I wallowed in the murky waters, whenever they wished to take me there. But no longer! They often doomed, the destruction of America, due to its sins. Pennywise, if I had a dime, for the abusive language of other religions, cultural differences, I'd be a rich man.

Maybe, Islam wasn't for me, I thought. I began eating pork, which is, expressively, forbidden in Islam. I was in protest of it. I didn't know what to do. My perception of the religion of Islam was tainted. It was like, dirty laundry. I wanted it, off of me. The lessons taught, by the Nation of Islam drove me crazy. They wanted to be separated, from the White man. They would say, they don't believe in some, "mystery God" or "spook God, in the sky." It was as though, "the unseen" was superstitious nonsense. I didn't know where to turn.

However, the Nation of Islam was all I knew. It was all, what, anyone that I knew, was familiar with. I believed in the Quran, as the word of God. I thought, it was "neat." I knew little, if anything, about the Prophet, (peace be upon him), who the Holy Quran was, actually, revealed to, in the first place. I wanted to know more, but nobody could give me a concise answer. Prayers were, clearly, "good to do," but not, necessarily, mandatory. It was obscured, or to be taught later.

Putting a lid on things, I nestled harder, to what I knew. Nobody was going to tell me what to do, what to read, what to think, where to go, and how to get there. I was fed up with superficial people, interpretations, religion, and the blurry photograph it gave me.

*Muslim*

*SEASON 9, EPISODE 10*

# Islam

VIRTUALLY, IN LIMBO, I was like a "fiend on nicotine." I tried, to piece myself together. I was, perfectly, content, not being associated, with anything, in particular, at all. I was a nomad, happily, roaming the desert. I was picking and choosing, "where I be."

Continuing my minor, in African-American Studies, I took a class on "History of Africa." Its platform was instructed by Mr. Jones.

Making the students loony, Mr. Jones asked us, to write a topic paper. Then for us, to make an appointment, to meet him, at his office. Essentially, he wanted us to pitch our ideas, into an approved, essay. I felt lucky, because I had a personal experience with NOI. So, I decided, to write about Malcolm X, particularly, of his post-Nation of Islam era. I wanted to explain Malcolm X, and Pan-Africanist views. Also, he wanted to bring attention to America's police-state, to the United Nations.

"Spike Lee's movie, Malcolm X, made me want to be a Muslim," I said, to Mr. Jones, in his office.

It was September 1994. The paper was due in October, which wasn't too far off.

"Oh, yeah? How so?" he said, to make small-talk.

My teacher then wanted to know, about the prohibition on pork.

"It's unclean," I said, which was no more than that.

From the look on his face, he wasn't impressed.

"I was going to the Nation of Islam, but I didn't believe, in a lot of the teachings," I confessed, as someone, who was writing a post-NOI essay on Malcolm X, especially, with his trip overseas.

Mr. Jones didn't know it. Neither did I. The next statement he said, changed my life, forever.

"Why don't you look, in the Yellow Pages? I'm sure, there's a Muslim organization, who doesn't teach that sort of thing," he encouraged.

I didn't think of that. Like a couch potato, I sat on the idea, for a few days. I was okay, in my own world. I was in my own Mardi Gras. I was wearing gold earrings, gold jewelry, purple jeans, purple dress shirts. Not to mention, lye-relaxed hair. I thought, I was being sexy, cool.

It was a Wednesday afternoon. Like an orthopedic shoe, I took those first steps. I looked in the phone book, under churches. I looked under the headline of "ISLAM." I couldn't believe, I haven't done anything, as simple as that, before.

MASJIDULLAH. (Huh)? What is that? I thought, it was a most unusual, funny-looking name. I thought, it was weird, but I had to find out. I was skeptical. What did it, actually, mean? Out of curiosity, I mashed the digits on my phone. Nervously, I didn't know what to expect. I was ready to hang it up. I didn't know, what sort of person, was on the other end, of the phone conversation. Militant? Racial? Radical? Whoever it was, if they said ANYTHING, I didn't like, it was over. If they said ANYTHING, remotely, racist, I was done with Islam.

"How do y'all feel about White people?" I said.

It the first thing I said, when the person answered the phone.

"They are a creation of Allah's. Just as we are, a creation of Allah's," said the man, with the thick, African accent.

(Okay). Good answer. Clearly, skin color didn't matter. Nor did money, clothes, appearances, or educational background, or lack thereof. I wasn't going to tolerate ANY crap. I didn't want to hear ANY muck, thrown at America. I asked other questions as well. Brother Saadiq, finally, invited me to the "masjid" (mosque) or place of prayer.

On the way there, I was nervous, like a groom, heading for matrimony. I parked my car, at the corner, convenience store, across the street. The masjid looked, ordinarily, like any other house. It could've used a premium touch. It was sort of shabby-looking, in a drug-infested neighborhood, if you ask me. The only difference, was a small wooden memoir, which read MASJIDULLAH. Suddenly, I was overwhelmed. I was hoping

# ISLAM

for the best, but I thought of the worst. Like a mermaid, who didn't want to get caught, I drove away.

Fear of the unknown, overtook me. I was in the prime of my young life, at 23-years-old. Hesitantly, I didn't want to be burden down. Especially, with another man's ideology, of what I should be like. Saadiq called me, the minute I got home.

"What happened?" he said. 'We're all here, waiting on you.'

I could hear the sincerity, in his voice. He wasn't about making a profit.

"I got nervous," I said.

"That was Shaytan! (The Devil). Don't let Shaytan, do that to you. Please, come back, so we can talk.'

Hesitating, I finally, made it there, that night. When I walked inside the masjid, no one was there, to pat me down. No security checkpoint. Apparently, the people were praying. I stood in the entrance, all alone. I reached for door handle, ready to walk away, again.

Suddenly, the Muslims ran downstairs to meet me. Brother Saadiq was in a white turban. He had a full beard. He looked as though, he trotted through, the sands of the Saharan Desert. He invited me to their dinner. He was, merely, four years older. Malik, who used to cut my hair, was there. He had to leave. Al-Amin, who was the same age as me, stayed.

They placed a mat, on the floor. Next, they sat the chipped cups, worn plates, and old bowls, on top of the tattered floor mat. That was my first sign, it wasn't about appearances. It didn't bother me, in the slightest bit. At least, they weren't superficial, putting on airs, or holding up appearances. Curiously, there wasn't any forks or spoons. They said it was "sunnah."

I was a guest, who they treated well. I felt quite welcomed. I was, completely, comfortable. We sat on the floor. I thought, it was wonderful and natural. It felt right, peaceful, and supposedly so.It wasn't weird or "foreign." Saadiq managed to stabilized the rice, with his fingers. He began to eat, after he uttered "Bismillah." (In the Name of God). Everyone did the same, including me. It felt great. It was, totally, agreeable, eating with our fingers. (Index finger, middle finger, and thumb). I was a pit bull, with a thousand and one questions. I wanted to know about Prophet Muhammad (peace be upon him). I had no idea, about the "sunnah" or way of doing things.

Saadiq, happily, answered every one of my questions. Of course, skin color didn't matter. He was from Sudan. Arabic was his native language. He was my first, ever impression, of "true," (orthodox), "Sunni" Muslim or (original) Islam. He was, absolutely, the most humble, God-fearing person, I have ever met. He wasn't anything like a terrorist. He wasn't an extremist. He didn't blame the media. He didn't hammer threats like, "Death to America." He was thin, meek, and proud. He didn't scapegoat, or blame his problems, on White people. He didn't try to dazzle me, with statistical data. He didn't use psychic, head games about slavery. He didn't stifle me, with long explanations.

When I, finally, left, I promised them I'd return, the next day. MASJIDULLAH felt good. It was, predominantly, African-American. They were all heart. It was like "punishment," when I had to go.

The next day, that Thursday, I raced to the masjid, as if my life depended on it. It was all a blur. It was a scrimmage game, that meant nothing, until I got myself, back at the masjid. That peaceful place! It was "the quiet," before the storm. I wanted to rid myself, of every hurt, and disappointment, I ever had. However, I had a little "seasickness." I wondered, if I was going in right direction. I'm not perfect, and had so much to work on. I lived a quarter of a century. I felt, I had nothing to show for it. All I had was tears and fears.

It was again, time for prayer. Everyone was lined up, straight, in a row, facing Makkah. They were shoulder to shoulder, heel to heel. Someone invited me, to join the rank with them. I had no idea, what to say or do.

"Just think about Allah," another said to me.

I followed their lead. In sequence, we all stood, bowed, kneeled, and prostrated, with our heads to the floor. At the same time, I had the subtle feeling, what I wanted to do with the rest of my life. Without being forced into anything, or without compulsion. I wanted to be a Muslim. The believers and I gathered together, after prayer.

"Repeat after me," said Saadiq. "Ash-hadu in laa illaha ill Allah. Ash-hadu anna Muhammad ur-Rasul Allah."

That is to say, translated to mean, "I testify, there is no other deity worthy of worship, except God. I testify, Muhammad is the Messenger of God."

It was wonderful. I gained, more than enough, real friends. I had true brothers. They rained hugs, and a sessions of introductions, on me. Random thoughts, of feeling like a nobody, were flung to the shadows. It was a natural feeling. Dark clouds and ravens, no longer circled me. I kept an open mind, to everything I heard. I readily accepted it all.

"We need to give him a name," said Al-Amin.

"What does 'Muhammad Ali' mean?" I said, being that I was a boxing fan.

"Muhammad means, one worthy of praise. Ali means, one of high rank," Saadiq said, assuring me, about the Arabic. "You like that name?"

"We'll call you, Muhammad Ali then!" Al-Amin said.

"Yeah, but change it around," I said.

So, from that day forward, throughout the Muslim world, I became known as "Ali Muhammad," or simply, "Ali." To fellow Muslims, I'd introduce myself as such. My "new name" meant a lot, because it meant, I was someone of importance. "High ranking" and "praise worthy." I wanted to leap and shoot for the stars. I had a Muslim name, of my very own! I was proud. I was happy. I was at peace.

It was great being around guys, who didn't do surveys, on what girls, looked the best. They weren't as superficial as that. Remarkably, they didn't care about my car, clothes, or my weight. The reception, the brothers welcomed me into, was beyond words. They were careful, not to shove, too much information, at me, too soon. There was so much to learn, and unlearn. Undoubtedly, nothing was more important, than being submissive to God.

Mustapha helped me recite, over and over, the opening chapter of the Quran. We went over it, until I got it right. He also helped me, with other short chapters, to recite as well. It was redundant, but it was a matter of praying, totally, in Arabic. He was happy to help me, as though Allah was putting it on his tab, or blessing him, for helping me, a new Brother.

"You know, Brother. Muslim men don't wear earrings," he said, suddenly.

# BEHOLD

I was so impressed, I thought maybe, I should move to a Muslim country. However, Brothers told me there's corruption everywhere. Even in Muslim countries.

Without hesitation, immediately, I took my gold earrings out of both ears, on the spot. Also, I was informed, Muslim men don't wear gold. I stopped wearing gold jewelry. In fact, I sold my gold necklace, gold watch, and gold rings, at a pawn shop, for a miserable price. It was explained to me, a story, about the nonbelievers of Makkah. They tried to bribe Prophet Muhammad (peace be upon him) with gold treasures, marriage to their women, and making him a king, to be talked about for generations. He rejected it all, for the mission, and the duty that God placed on him.

There was so much niceness! Some of the Brothers invited me to spend the night, in the masjid. It didn't take an art dealer to see, some of them were homeless, and stayed at the mosque, for whatever reason. I relinquished my "slice of heaven." I said, maybe, I'd spend the night, some other time. Brothers like Abdur-Rahman, and Shaheed, made me feel comfortable. We talked over tea. From the looks of things, I could tell, how poor they were. Yet, they were rich in spirit. They were full of love, peace, and compassion. That's what mattered.

It was like a smack in the face, when I walked out the masjid's front door. Seeing a drug dealer, on the corner pay phone, reminded me, I was in a rough, part of town.

It was also upsetting, no one told me about Islam! This beautiful way of life. I had no idea about Islam. Little did I know, when my mother was, arbitrarily, purchasing Final Calls, I'd someday be Muslim.

"As-Salaamu alaykum," was said, as I departed from the mosque.

That ancient, Arabic saying, sounded so smooth and tender. Especially, because it was for all the right reasons. I felt rescued. Somehow, I was snubbing out the terror, which goes on throughout the world. My family in Virginia, was respectful, when I told them the good news. They seemed glad of what I did, and what I became.

The next day, was my first "Jummuah" or Friday congregational prayer. I was astonished at the different colors, nationalities, and accents. People from all over the world, different cultures, foreign countries. There were so many men, women, and children, that weren't there, my first two nights.

It was, absolutely, beautiful. Everyone had on beautiful clothes, African, Middle Eastern, or an everyday shirt and jeans. There was no judgement. The place smelled of wonderful incense, and oils. Naturally, we sat on the carpet floor, awaiting the "imam." He's the spiritual guide, or prayer leader of the masjid. It felt so "suppose-to-be." It felt right.

The imam, Shaykh Muhammad, was from Ghana. He too had an accent. He was the only one, standing and talking. He gave thanks, and warned us, for the retribution of our sins. It was great. I didn't want to be anywhere, but there. I was taking it all in, and enjoying the ride.

After service, the believers would greet each other, with "salaams," and smiles. They'd shake hands, and chitchat. Brothers would sell bean pies (my favorite), incenses, oils, kufis, or prayer rugs. Sisiters would sell home-cook veggie, chicken or fish dinners, to raise funds for the masjid.

The more I went to the masjid, the less I resented my father. I wanted to bury the hatchet, and rightfully, honor him. Though we weren't speaking.

I couldn't ask, for better people, to be around. They had, seemingly, pure intentions. They were honest to goodness. The men were adamant of their "kufi" or Islamic skull cap. They'd wear long, white robes, or various colors. The Muslims wore beautiful clothes. They wore long tops, or lose clothing. They didn't care, their attire was "different," and not necessarily, mainstream or "the norm." I was astonished, by their faithfulness. I was in a threshold of love and acceptance.

Brotherhood was the rule. Good deeds were envied. Arabic was valued. The women were humble. Undoubtedly, I was in another world. The Muslim world. Backbiting or gossip wasn't tolerated. No drinking alcohol, or getting high with drugs. A lot of them dressed bland, if not boring. Several of them, made a point of not watching tv. (Maybe the news). Some didn't listen to music. Many didn't want pictures, or images, of anything around. They didn't want to be distracted. They, merely, wanted prayer and studying. Of course, I wasn't anything near, on that level, yet.

The time, or the tick-tocks on a clock didn't matter, as long as I was in the masjid. It gave me peace and solitude. I felt, completely, safe there.

BEHOLD

I felt guarded, by angels. More importantly, I was free to be me, without, worldly, pretenses.

Some of the Brothers, more or less, smoked tobacco. It was "frowned upon." Yet, it was cool, as long as it wasn't done on masjid property. Saadiq and I would, literally, pray for the women of our dreams. Having Muslim wives, was a topic, we often talked about. I too wanted a Muslim woman. I wanted a pious, humbled, God-fearing woman. It would've been hard, without a Muslim Sister, who didn't understands, I thought. The masjid was, considerably, 24/7, so I would stay, for hours. I'd read Quran and Hadiths, (related sayings and actions of Prophet Muhammad).

I'd spend the night, sometimes. It was an open door policy, at all times, except for, after last night prayer. I was scared for my transportation, though. Before I knew it, the "adhan" or call for prayer was made. It was enchanting. Quickly, Brothers rose, washed, and stood for prayer.

Meanwhile, at VCU, Mr. Jones paired the class into groups. It was for a term paper. I had the distinct pleasure, and honor, of being paired up, with Lissa. We tried our best, to do a report on Marcus Garvey. One would think, she was my "boo" or girlfriend. We spent a lot of time together. She was the nicest girl, ever. We, quickly, became good friends, as we tweaked here and there, on our upcoming paper. I couldn't help, but be, affected by her.

Lissa was, undeniably, pretty. With her, not having a car, I had the privilege, of taking her home. She didn't seem to mind, I was unfit. Just as I, seemingly, didn't mind her being a little prejudice.

As part of my Social Work training, I interned at Byrd Community House, on Cherry Street, near campus. It was during an after-school program. School buses would valet park, behind the building. I was, happily, looking forward to working with the children. We did various things with the kids. We'd feed them snacks, and help them with their homework. We would take them on the playground, or play games inside, if the weather didn't permit. With vengeance, the children would sometimes act up. After stern patience, they would calm down. It was great, being in the vicinity of so many children.

"Hi, Marco…hi, Marco," they would say, passing me by.

It was sweet. It was nice. I definitely, caught the bug, for wanting a career with children. I'm sure, the other volunteers felt the same. I was young at heart, so I thought, perfect match. I couldn't wait, to see the children's warm smiles, and bright faces. It was good, getting a kid, a cup of water. As silly, as that may sound, that's how my heart felt. I got a whiff, of seeing what it was like, to be innocent, and young again. It made me think, having children of my very own, someday.

Islam, clearly, was the best thing to ever happen to me. I wanted to expand my horizons. I was interested, to meet other Muslims, from other races, and other places. Let's just say, it wasn't by accident, I started to go to Masjid Ar-Rahman, on Hull Street, as well. Actually, it was at a fish market store, owned by two Arab brothers, Fatih and Ali. They were Egyptian. It was on the bottom floor. The masjid was small, and located over the store's second floor. I was comfortable with a small place, because it was more intimate, and personable. They made great, fried fish sandwiches.

"Ali! Ali," they would shout, whenever, I bolted through the door.

Shaykh Muhammad was the imam. He was from Egypt too. He always wore a white turban, white beard, and a white robe. He was glad to see me too. They bequeathed me, with all the, brotherly, love they could muster.

Some of the African-American Muslims would complain, Arabs "looked down on us." It was as though, they thought, we weren't "real" Muslims, or didn't know Arabic, for that matter. I didn't see, or feel that, at all. They treated me nice. I didn't have a complex, I'm proud to say. At Masjid Ar-Rahman, they gave me a new, thick Quran, to have. Since, I was a "new Shahadah," or recent, Muslim convert.

There was the time, I was working at Old Country Buffet. It was, predominantly, Vietnamese workers, with heavy accents, who worked there. Those, who weren't Asian, ridiculed and made fun of them. I felt there was nothing comedic, or funny about it. I saw human beings, who deserved to be respected. I thought, it was, completely, unfair. I committed myself, to make the Asians feel comfortable. I refused to aggravate them or be bitter towards them.

"You're special," an Asian waitress said to me.

I took it all in stride. However, when she said that to me, I was floating on air. Somehow, I wanted to make a difference. Perhaps, I was.

Rajaee, from Masjidullah, introduced me to his friend. She was a woman, he was dating. Her name was Wanda. She had pretty eyes. I was smitten. I could gaze into them for hours. She had a nice, caramel complexion. Wanda was the type, to ask for an alimony check, after a divorce. What I liked about her, she wasn't typical girl from the block. She was a little conceded. She had the nicest, telephone voice, I have ever heard. It was smooth as aloe. To be, perfectly, blunt, she would give all the details of the guys she was seeing. She could be, brutally, honest. We would talk for hours. I was having a bonanza of a time. So much confidential information. The genie was, definitely, out the bottle.

I enjoyed meeting Muslims, from all over the world. Some were from different parts of the country. I liked the fact, we took our shoes off, before we entered the prayer area. I liked, when we sat in a circle, making decisions on behalf of the community, voicing our opinions. It was all new to me, but it felt great to be involved. My brain consented to everything. It didn't hurt I saw a few Sisters at the masjid, who I wanted to get to know better. Brothers, who were a little more established, financially, with their own place, were, quickly, married off. I'd see the guys, happily, married with children.

It made me feel, like an ant on a mole hill. I was green with envy. As usual, I wasn't "getting the girl" it felt. It was as though, someone gave me a dirty bucket to clean, while everyone else was outside, enjoying the weather.

There were times, I'd hear remarks about Jews. Particularly, about the Jewish occupation, or apartheid in Palestine. I didn't understand. I felt confused, in a corner. I knew, racism was forbidden in Islam. I knew, I didn't want to hear derogatory comments, which I heard from the Nation of Islam.

"That's anti-Semitic," I blurted out.

With candor, a Brother counseled me, about the Zionist army and Jewish settlers. I knew little, if anything about it. I was naïve about the Middle East conflict or situation. Yet, I knew, racism, bigotry and prejudice wasn't Islam.

"Ali, call the adhan," someone encouraged.

It was time for prayer. They wanted me to take a crack at it. I was, absolutely, terrified. The adhan was a loud proclamation for prayer. It was an art form. I didn't want to mess up. Next, I carried myself outside, unto the porch. I had little credibility, and no experience. I stood before the world. I aspired to call it, with all the compassion, I could muster. Needless to say, I was nervous. I couldn't be more nervous, as if a crocodile was standing, right before me. I assumed the position. My index fingers were thrust into both ears, which made both arms outstretched.

"Allahu Akbar. Allahu Akbar. Allahu Akbar. Allahu Akbar."

"Ash-hadu en laa illaha ill Allah. Ash-hadu en laa illaha ill Allah."

"Ash-hadu anna Muhammad ar-Rasul Allah. Ash-hadu anna Muhammad ar-Rasul Allah."

"Haya alas Salah. Haya alas Salah."

"Haya alal Falah. Haya alal Falah."

"Allahu Akbar. Allahu Akbar."

"Laa illaha ill Allah."

Which means…

"God is Great. God is Great. God is Great. God is Great.

I testify, there is no deity, worthy of worship, except God. I testify, there is no deity, worthy of worship, except God.

I testify, Muhammad is the Messenger of God. I testify, Muhammad is the Messenger of God.

Come to Prayer. Come to Prayer.

Come to Success. Come to Success.

God is Great. God is Great.

There is no deity, worthy of worship, except God."

I called the adhan, with a certain loudness, and proudness. I was no longer, using my appearance, or weight as a crutch. I became another person, when I called it. I was in atonement, with Who was in charge. The Muslims seemed, pleasantly, surprised. They said, I had a good, strong voice.

"You sounded like you were from overseas," said Shaheed.

"Like the Sudan," said Saadiq, which was a huge compliment, coming from him.

"Beautiful," I also heard.

(Wow). It felt like it was the first time, I did anything right. I felt cultivated. I felt attractive. The chemistry was just right. They all seemed to enjoy what I did. I was, currently, one of their champion adhan callers. I was, instantly, made the "muadhan." Not for all the tea in China, would I have given it up. I was happy to do it. I would have cut my right arm to do it. Such an honor. Once, the imam's wife laughed with joy, when I called the adhan. In spite of my, normally, soft-spoken voice, it became strong. I'd cast all doubt away. It was a duty, I couldn't be more proud of.

It was like wiping dandruff, off my shirt collar. Quickly, I sold my gold jewelry to Jefferson Pawn. It was a total rip off, but that wasn't important. It was like a badge of shame, I wanted to get rid of.

I was no longer tagging along with Mel, to gay clubs. However, I was still wearing my hair relaxed. I wasn't ready, to ban it, just yet. As though in an unwritten rule, I knew it wasn't "natural" so it'll, eventually, have to go.

I then, readily, decapitated everything in my life, which wasn't Islam. My weakness, however, was still women. I just, barely, had my foot in the door, as a new convert. I hoisted myself up, with the best of them. I looked the part. I was doing, nearly, everything I was "supposed" to do. I listened to cassette tapes. I went to meetings. I read Muslim compositions. I wore my crown or kufi. I had the notion to change my name, legally, to. Ali Muhammad.

Thanksgiving 1994, I was a complete moron at our dinner. Mel lead the thanksgiving prayer. Unbeknownst, to how I'd feel, he ended the prayer with, "In the name of Jesus," which was offense to someone like me, who believed it should be "In God's Name" instead. I ruined dinner, with every degenerate thing, I could think of, about Christianity. I was, essentially, going off, with every word. It, gradually, made my family cry. I denounced everything that wasn't Islam. My family exchanged looks, looking on, as I became unraveled.

In a much happier time that year, there was a Christmas celebration. (No, I didn't go off). It was at the daycare center, where I volunteered. There were Christmas songs. Christmas decorations, and gifts under the

# ISLAM

tree. Children were everywhere. The only thing missing, angels descending from heaven. It was my last day as a volunteer. I was grateful for the exposure or experience at Byrd House. Santa Clause, finally made his way, towards the children, baring gifts. They responded with glee. Santa Clause fabric suit was red as hemoglobin.

Before I left the building, and being a faded memory, I was giving an envelope. When I got home, it was a card, with a handful of children's signatures. I was touched. I could've cried.

I felt bad, as a Muslim, I wasn't to celebrate Christmas, so I was told. Of course, when I was a kid, I could wait for the new fallen snow. I couldn't wait for us to open the many, different presents. Coincidentally, I felt horrible, at not buying anything, for the family. They said, they understood.

In 1995, I had a large assortment of kufi caps. Different colors and styles. I didn't want to be wearing "the same old one." That's boring. I kept in step, with Masjid Ar-Rahman and Shaykh Muhammad. Five or six of us, would pile into a car or van. We'd, heartedly, go to various masjids, throughout Virginia and North Carolina. Shaykh Muhammad wanted to spread the message of Islam, far and wide. I was okay with that. I feasted my eyes on Muslims of every race, background and heritage there was. Muslim or Arab-owned stores would offer us, free food or drinks, for our act of service. We would, quickly, decline their generosity. We wasn't encouraging people, to gain anything from them.

"We're not here, to judge you, Brother," we would often say. "We just want, a few minutes of your time.

Meanwhile, we were pretending, we didn't notice their lottery tickets, alcoholic beverages and pork products. All were unacceptable in Islam. We'd be in dressed, in our best Muslim garb. We'd invite them, to their own local masjid. Shaykh Muhammad would ask us to go hither and thither. We"d, openly, display that Muslims were in the area. The work, and the weekends were a flash in the pan. It all ended so quickly. When all was said and done, we'd put honey, or sour cream on our pita bread. That, along with tuna fish and rice. Of course, tea.

Sure, I was long distance from home, but I was flooded with emotion and brotherhood. I didn't mind, being away from the daily churn and burn.

It felt great to gone, for a few days. It was like pulling the plug, out of the socket. No distractions. Religion was on my mind all weekend. Reality was right around the corner. I was being spoiled, with so much friendliness and generosity. I was sad, when we hurried to Richmond. I knew too well, the drama of everyday life. I wanted to cry, like a melting icicle. I was dumbfounded, when the fortitude of Islam wasn't around me. I tried my best. I'd illustrate, what on earth we did, to my mother.

I'd keep up what was going on. With implicitly, I went to Masjidullah. Whenever I went there, I stuck to Saadiq like plastic. Occasionally, I would frolic to Masjid Bilal, or Islamic Center of Virginia.

I'd go, whenever possible, to the functions. I saw Shaykh Abdullah Hakim Quick. He was a renown Islamic historian. Incidentally, I met Jamil Abdullah Al-Amin. He was, formally, known as H. Rap Brown. He was a famous Black Panther emancipator, in the 1960's. I went to hear him speak. He was promoting his book, "Revolution by the Book." I listened to, an empowering lecture, by the imam, Warith Deen Muhammad. He was the son of Elijah Muhammad, who founded the Nation of Islam. He was, especially, sponsored by Masjid Bilal.

I continued, in my secret garden of conversations, with Wanda. I was infatuated with. Her favorite singer was Prince also. Yet, we were mortal enemies when it came to Islam. She felt Islam was oppressive towards women. I begged to differ. I couldn't convince her otherwise.

*VCU Graduate*

*SEASON 10, EPISODE 11*

# Criminal Justice

I WAS STILL enrolled at VCU. My counselor advised me about my grade point average. It was something like a 2.2, which needed to be a 2.5, to continue as a Social Work major. I had the choice of taking electives, to bring it up. Also, I could change my major, to something else.

I talked to Lissa about it. She had a beautiful, long neck, like a giraffe. Her major was Criminal Justice. I could switch to Criminal Justice, with no problem, despite my current average. So I did. I began to see, the law as a great way, to make a living. Regardless of my estranged father, I was inspired. I wanted to do my best. I had every intent, to go into the field, being all I could be.

Somehow, Snow, who I met, years earlier, gave my phone number, to a buddy of hers. Her name was Donna. She was, currently, serving time in jail. I didn't have a problem with it. We must've used every method possible, over the phone, without being too specific. She liked the fact, I was going to school. She liked, I wasn't into the street life. I accepted, she once used her body, for drugs.

So, when she, finally, got out of jail, we got together. I ate Pizza Hut with her children. We migrated to a hotel. We made a connection, holding, caressing. I kept my car keys, in my pocket. (I'm no fool). Eventually, I fell asleep. In the middle of the night, she sneaked off, to a nearby neighborhood, to score to drugs.

I woke up, alone, in an empty bed. Apparently, she grabbed my jacket. I juggled, whether or not to leave Donna. I was embarrassed, she stole my coat. I decided, to stay until check-out time, to get my money's worth. Before long, she walked in, apologizing. She relapsed, her first day out. I didn't want another partner in crime.

Admittedly, she was cute. We patched things up. Yet, I didn't kid myself. She'd ask for a ride, food, or money, which I hated to do. (I didn't want to be used). Sometimes, we napped under the moonlight. We got together, on other occasions.

I was working at Royal Bakery, at the time. It was, predominantly, Muslim workers. I knew them all, from the masjid. The bakery made bread, particularly, pita bread.

I enjoyed my Criminal Justice classes. However, I was getting tired of school, and wanted to finish. Quitting wasn't an option. I had plenty of assignments. I was moved to tears, learning about the penitentiary system. I'd read about landmark courthouse decisions. I'd study about the murky waters of law enforcement and lawyers. I had great instructors. One of my teachers was a former FBI agent. Another was a current, presiding judge. He was Judge Robinson, who was an advocate of firearms. I could have laughed, how out of touch they were. Especially, when it came to the mindset of what disenfranchised people feel. Particularly, being wrongfully treated, accustomed and accused.

Leaving nothing to the imagination, one of my classes was invited to the local, county jail. I saw legions of mostly, Black faces. I wasn't sure how to act, or what was next. Most of the inmates were in there, for narcotics, I heard. I admired their willingness, to persevere through their hard time. I'd be nearsighted, if I did notice the importance of keys, locks, thick, steel doors, thick glass windows. As a human, I had a license to feel. I was somewhat nervous. Yet, I didn't want to be of judgement.

I thought it was, highly, unlikely I'd work in a prison. Let alone, be an officer, carrying a loaded, nickel-plated gun. Looking at the bigger picture, I was willing to try. I knew I was against terrorists, bad people, gangs, who put people in pine, wooden boxes. It was located, somewhere in my heart. I had a nose, for wanting to help people. I wanted to plant my feet in the law. I wanted to look justice in the face. I was following the footsteps of my father, and I realized it.

At the time, the guys from the neighborhood, were, practically, non-existent. Except, for the Brothers, I knew from the masjid. I hung unto

# CRIMINAL JUSTICE

Islam, for dear life. Eventually, I plowed my way into different homes. I visited Dr. Ismail. He had multiple wives. I went to Abu Bakr's home. He was straightforward. I spent time Ali, from Botswana. He was a handyman.

I was loyal, to my new way of life. During our annual visit to South Carolina, I told the family there, about me, becoming Muslim. (Boy, was I in for a surprise). They asked me, obnoxiously, weird, rude and disrespectful questions.

"You can't drink, no more?"

"You can't eat pork, no more?"

"Why did you change your heritage? Your parents didn't raise you Muslim," said Baby.

It was like peeling the skin off a polecat. I was explaining what Islam was, and wasn't. I had the luxury of hearing sarcastic remarks. It was a drop in the ocean, no matter how hard I tried. I wanted to show the family, I was still "the same, old Marco," they knew and loved. It was of no use.

How could I ever forget, when we decided, to go to Taco Bell? I was appalled, but I kept my cool. Before I get ahead of myself, let me explain. We went to the drive through. I ordered my usual, personal favorite, Mexican Pizza. My cousin, Fist took his hand, reached into my food, and started eating my food. He was, obviously, being disrespectful, because I was Muslim. My Mexican Pizza was important. It was the pain I felt.

I remembered a Hadith or saying from Prophet Muhammad (peace be upon him). "The strong man is the one who can wrestle, but it is the one who can control himself when he is angry."

I stayed as optimistic as possible. I needed a pasture of patience, due to the amount of horse manure that was being thrown at me. I tried to explain, I wasn't a terrorist, an extremist, or fundamentalist. If anything, I resented those kinds of people. I told them, I was "orthodox," or believed in the original idea of Islam. It was like talking to a brick wall.

I was, thoroughly, heartbroken. So much so, I told my mother and aunt North, what Fist did.

"How could you let him, do that to you?" they cried.

"He is not a believer whose stomach is filled while his neighbor goes hungry," I quoted from the Prophet (peace be upon him), putting his words into practice.

However, I didn't eat. None at all, for myself. My food was being ripped out of the container, before my eyes. (Because I'm Muslim). I considered it, a test from God. Outwardly, I pretended to be tough as nails. Inside, I was being condemned. I was a building, ready to crumble, at so much condescending attitude. I never would've guessed, how my family members would be, in beloved South Carolina. I was overwhelmed, with all the compassion I had. It was the drama. It was the tears. I cried and felt horrible pain. I was hoping for the best, but I prepared for the worst.

My maternal grandma, Maggie, developed glaucoma. Eventually, she went blind. She developed dementia. Eventually, she had Alzheimer's disease. Helping her was like taking a stab in the dark. She seemed saturated in confusion, not knowing which way to turn. It was hard, seeing her helpless. She always took care of herself. She was strong as any young stallion, in her day. We all took our stations, and took our turns to do what we could. We took her to prying doctors. With grandma under a stethoscope, the most we could do, was make her life as comfortable as possible.

It was like punching a whole, in a screen door, when grandma had to live with us. We wrestled with the constant running into furniture, or her being disoriented. The stork came early, if you will. My mother, suddenly, had to put everything on hold. She searched for medical accommodations. The house wasn't the same. We, quickly, had to secure and make it safe. We all to go to either work, or school. We'd often hear a thud, in the middle of the night, which startled us. Grandma was walking throughout the house, not knowing where she was. Not to mention, she couldn't see, where she was going. It was like sinking into quicksand.

I continued to be submerged in Islam. In front of the believers, anyway. Once, I raced to Abu Bakr's house to watch "The Message" movie. It was a September, like any other. Yet, it was my first time watching that. Nothing prepared me, what I was in store for. When I saw "The Message," I was railroaded, with raw emotion. Especially, watching historical figures, serving God, in Islam's early stages. However, there wasn't any actual depictions, or images, of Prophet Muhammad (peace be upon him).

Though, the film was based on his life.

My heart suggested tears. So, my eyes cried. Personally, I was proud to see the Bilal character become Islam's first muadhan. I had goosebumps, when a Black man, who was a former slave, called the people to prayer. My soul rattled with feeling, because I too, was a muadhan. It was a shattering moment, because a lot of people didn't know about the religion. Not anyone I knew, anyway. Instead of people's misconstrued, misunderstood, and misinterpreted nonsense.

My tears fell again, during the movie, at the Prophet's last sermon, on Mount Arafat. He was, clearly, against racism, prejudice, and discrimination. He, overwhelmingly, welcomed brotherhood of all people. During the movie's closing credits, there was an intertwining of different adhans, throughout the world. Actual Muslims, not actors, were viewed praying, as the film ended. I could've been knocked down, with a feather, at that moment. It was so beautiful.

Shortly, thereafter, the family and I went to annual Second Street Festival. I thought, I was a changed man. I was no longerI was no longer, taking my frustrations out, on the family. The sidewalks was filled Afrocentric art, jewelry, and food. There was singing and dancing. People were enjoying the laidback atmosphere.

Suddenly, I realized, there was an Indian Festival that day too. It wasn't too far away. It was within walking distance. I just, recently, saw the "Ghandi" movie. It was about Mahatma Ghandi, who liberated India from the British. He protested, with nonviolence. I had respect, for such a man. He was once a prominent lawyer. He ditched the business suit, for a very basic, poorer attire. I admired that. He advocated civil disobedience. He was synonymous with peace.

I asked, we go to the Indian Festival. I loved India. The people are beautiful. Open as refrigerator, my immediate family agreed. I was wearing my white kufi, of all things. It wasn't exactly, "Sir, may I take your hat?" hospitality, but I was comfortable. The dancing was well-rehearsed. On stage, were pretty women, who seemed to have drank, skim milk, all of their lives. Some people were drinking tea at neighboring tables. Others tried on clothes. We were the only Black people, in the entire building.

Seemingly, our presence didn't matter. The Indian people at the festival were relaxed as sleep. It was nice to see a culture being themselves. They were enjoying each other's company.

Monday, October 16, 1995, many Black men were going to the Million Man March. It was sponsored by Louis Farrakhan, and the Nation of Islam. Undoubtedly, it was the biggest event, in Farrakhan's career. People were going by bus, plane, train, or taxicab. Imams in Richmond, were, emphatically, against it. Particularly, the imams were saying, we shouldn't go, because Farrakhan doesn't teach, true Islam.

I slumped in my chair, not knowing what to do. I was under a microscope. I didn't want the folks in South Carolina to think, I had anything to do with the Nation of Islam. Especially, with how they treated me, that summer, about becoming Muslim, months earlier. Surely, they would ask. So, I didn't attend the rally. I was worried about, "what someone would think."

I had a ride to go. Actually, several Brothers, from the masjid, invited me, to go with them. I regretted not going. (I know what I believe in). I too wanted to be involved, in Washington, D.C.

Like smoke in the wind, I tried to block it out. I asked Lissa out to a movie, that day. We saw, "Dead Presidents" movie. That night, I watched Farrakhan's speech on tv. Of course, it wasn't the same as, actually, being there. Like a person snoring, what sense did it make now?

As time went on, I continued to go with Shaykh Muhammad, in unknown territory, with limited amount of resources. We felt, we had a job to do. Retain people's ears. To spread the message of Islam, with whoever cared to listen. Sometimes, we didn't have a clue, what the people were going to be like. We didn't know, what it was going to be like, in another masjid, until we got there. Our reward, we wanted in Paradise.

Wetting his whistle, Shaykh Muhammad would encourage fellow Africans and Arabs, to strive, into being better Muslims. He would speak, unthreateningly, yet confident. He was, elderly, but full of vigor. His personality was good. He was very wise, but engaging. He encouraged us all, to do something different, and be involved. Lastly , he wanted us to be a part of the life, we declared we lived. Putting a spin on things, Shaykh

## CRIMINAL JUSTICE

Muhammad would sometimes, "write people's name down," on a piece of paper. It was a "promise" in that, they too, would strive, and do the work.

January, 1996. I was asked to come inside the imam's office. Shaykh Muhammad of Masjidullah, introduced me to Khadijah. (Whoa). She was from Senegal. She was wearing a white hijab, head covering. She was beautiful! She looked "serious business." I could tell, she was nobody's fool. (Is she for me)? Everyone knew, I was looking for a wife. She looked as though, she could've ran track and field. I was careful, not to say or do anything stupid.

Of course, Shaykh Muhammad was from Ghana. Not to be confused, with the one from Egypt. He explained what was going on. He wanted me to help Khadijah in her transition to VCU. She was studying to be a doctor, a pharmacist.

Apparently, Khadijah needed a "Green card." She needed to work. We would both save our money, to get our own place, by the end of the year. So, he could then, marry us. (Wow).

We were to file for a marriage license, at the city hall. We would all, simply, sign the paperwork, as though the wedding took place. The plan was for Shaykh Muhammad to, eventually, marry us, in an actual Muslim ceremony. Yes! Like a lion in the bush, I was game! I've waited my whole life for this.

Khadijah and I became good friends, in spite of it all. As it turned out, she was quite a party girl. She loved to dance. She loved music. She was, finally, free from her conservative father. She was no longer with her abusive ex-husband. She was, currently, living with her cousin, Ibrahim. She was under enormous pressure, to do well in school. She often studied. I took her to VCU, whenever possible. She was very smart. She, definitely, had scruples.

Surprisingly, she didn't, normally, wear a hijab. Not unless, she was at the masjid, or praying. My family didn't know I was "married." Besides, Khadijah and I felt, it was "just on paper." Shaykh Muhammad didn't "actually" marry us, we told ourselves. It was a secret, because it didn't happen, yet.

I confided in Khadijah my idea of, possibly, going into law enforcement.

My thing was to get well-versed in Criminal Justice. Finish my education. Get my degree. That way, I wouldn't have any problems, getting a great job, someday.

I virtually, called or visited Khadijah, nearly, everyday. I had volumes of homework, assignments. Yet, I wanted to be near her, though we weren't "really married." Donna would tell me, there's only one thing, I cared about.

Besides Khadijah, I hung out with other Africans as well. Ali (Paul) would be busy fixing things, working on someone's car, plumbing, or working on people's house hold appliances. We would often talk about getting wives, or meeting women. Oddly, he was married, with two children. He had a boy and girl.

Eventually, Ali and I went to strip clubs together, as quiet as kept. It was the Paper Moon or the Red Inn. Coincidentally, as Muslims, we'd order only a grape soda. (We didn't drink). However, on stage, the women's clothes and accessories, quickly, came off. They would be dancing "bucket naked" or "butt-ball naked." (You decide).

We'd ride through south side, or north side, looking for action. We'd go on dark streets and alleys. We were living a lie. It was "double agent style." We would be, in complete compliance, around fellow Brothers. We were straight as a new, tire alignment. They knew nothing. Praying in the masjid, by day. Frequently, going to the strip bar at night. We'd go as much as a biscuit, being dipped in gravy.

I felt bloated as usual. I wanted my comrade, Khadijah. Yet, we'd, simply, hold hands. (My idea). She had the prettiest, almond skin. It was "shinny," if you will.

She looked great, in her blue jeans. She had pretty hands. However, she would hold me off of her. She would control me, religiously, by saying we "weren't married." She had a certain boldness, or tenacity about her. She was focused, strictly, on being a doctor someday. Obviously, not doing anything sensual with me. I liked her. So, I stuck around. However, it was hard times. Yet, we went to the same masjid, listening to the imam, who introduced us.

A few followers wanted to boycott, the Arab-owned convenient store, across the street, from the masjid. Rumor had it, they were Muslim, selling pork and beer. Needless to say, they didn't go out of business or anything. (Maybe we should've invited them to prayer).

It was my second year as a Muslim. Time flew like a breeze. As many as the constellations were, in the sky, I needed money. I anticipated the familiar faces, I would see, working at the nearby Burger King. It was part-time on the weekends. It was a dead end job, with irate customers. I was in my grease stained uniform, flipping burgers. Suddenly, my father walked into the restaurant. I couldn't believe it! I dropped my spatula to greet him.

"You doing alright?" my father said to me, on the other side of the counter.

My brunette-headed manager didn't have a clue, who the man was, in relation to me. It felt like I crawled from under a rock, looking at my earthly past. After that, I applied the necessary pressure on the broiled burgers, with custom-made condiments, or conditions on each one. "Hold that mayo." That sort of thing. Of course, my day wasn't the same, after seeing my father.

Incidentally, I met a young lady, named Ladeva. I called her by her middle name, Renae. Accidentally, she dialed my glow-in-the-dark pager. (We didn't have cell phones). Naturally, I called, to see who it was. We didn't know each other, but we talked on the phone. Before you know it, we became friends. Eventually, she invited me over. She was short in stature. She was deformed, on the left side of her body. She walked with a limp. Yet, it didn't matter to me. Whenever I went to her apartment, we sat on the couch. Renae would cuddle in my arms.

Usually, she would ask for food, if I was coming over. Particularly, she wanted Chinese food. She reminded me of Donna, doing that. (I didn't want to be used). So, sometimes, I would oblige her. Sometimes, I wouldn't. It depended, if I was in a giving mood or not.

Straight as an arrow, I was in front of Khadijah. She didn't know, I was seeing other womenfolk too. I didn't want her to get the wrong idea. I was, merely, friends with them. She continued her creative dance steps. She introduced me to African cuisine, like fish heads. (I'm not eating no fish head). She introduced me to African singers, such as Youssou N'Dour, who was from Senegal also. It was, astonishingly, beautiful. A wonderful cultural experience, which I knew little about. Surprisingly, Khadijah and her cousin liked White singers as well. Celine Dion and Elton John.

There were times, I was crushed. I wanted a Muslim wife, more than anything. I waited for Khadijah, like a lost puppy. Other times, I wanted her like the atomic dog.

Under a charcoal colored sky, I would "make myself" go to the masjid. I started to not go. Actually, not as much. Alone, I would, hardly, pray at all. Whenever I was praying at home, it was becoming less and less. I was starting to feel uneasy, being "made" or asked to wear a kufi, for promotional purposes.

"Brother, where's your kufi at?" I'd hear, if I dared to not wear it that day.

I noticed Muslims, from other continents, like Africa, didn't, necessarily, wear a kufi, all the time. Let alone, dress in traditional, Islamic attire, all the time. I would tell myself, the African-American Muslims at the masjid, had an "attitude." I thought, they were being "extra" with it. I looked for any excuse, not to go. I started to see them as acting "too serious." In my mind, they were becoming less cheesy, as they used to be. I wasn't being, entirely, myself. It was the wrong chimney. I was acting like a disgruntled customer, who was avoiding the employees of the store. They all seemed to be happily married. So, I wanted to eat Chinese food, using chopsticks, with ladies I knew.

"Damn," I'd tell myself, wondering what I was doing at the masjid sometimes.

I was just going through the motions. I wasn't "feeling it" any longer. I was, seemingly, mad at bacon. I struggled with my heart broken. I was hurt and felt confused. The pain and my frustrations felt horrible. I was embarrassed. I cried. I felt like I needed a little bit, more attention from Khadijah. I felt like a fool. I felt like a kid, who wasn't allowed, to play with his favorite toy. I was scared for my life. I didn't want a life of loneliness and despair. I was a lion, who wasn't going to get his prey. I wasn't sure, if she wanted the imam to marry us anymore.

Also, I juggled with identifying myself, and myself as, who I was. Was I "Muslim" enough? (I wasn't praying all my prayers). Was I "Black" enough? (Color didn't matter to me). Was I "American" enough? (I love America).

"I'm Muslim, but I don't practice," I would introduce myself as, to nonbelievers.

Putting myself in a certain category, I would only pray, whenever I was at the masjid. My new religion had a great launch. Now, it was getting further and further away from me.

Malik was still my hair barber. He was tall as any grandfather clock. He also made security decisions, on behalf of the masjid. He even wore a long trench coat, seemingly, for the affect.

In 1996, I was, definitely, Khadijah's personal escort. I wanted children with her. I would throw hints. Eventually, the walls evaporated. I didn't bite. I wasn't so bad after all. I thought, we made a cute couple. She wanted to be a doctor in pharmacy. I wanted to work, in the criminal law field somehow. Our common denominator was Islam.

Apparently, she was fond of her new independence. Khadijah was, exhaustingly, clever. She wasn't inviting me, to go to clubs with her. (Why)? However, there were happier times. I'd buy her lingerie. We'd go grocery shopping, practically holding hands. We would both, hold onto the same carrier basket, the store offered.

I'd give her a ride to INS (Immigration and Naturalization Services). It was located in Norfolk. They, suddenly, wanted an interview with her. She was nervous. Especially, with her now, as my "lawfully, wedded wife." It was all an act. It was important, we kept our same story straight. I was, supposedly, "living with her" then. We were, desperately, trying not to expose our "lie." Obviously, they wanted to know, we were together, for all the right reasons. Besides, my family liked her.

Rashida had a job at Head Start Daycare. I was no longer, giving her money. I hung out with her, from time to time. Things were different. I was, happily, showing her, I was a Muslim, myself now. I gave her one of my Qurans, that was handed to me, when I was a new convert. Somehow, I was still wrapped around her little finger. I think, I fell in love with her, every time I saw her. Despite her breaking my heart, I was still, completely, there for her.

She was adamant of us remaining friends. Sometimes, I'd pick Rashida up, with most of her belongings. It was whenever her husband kicked her out of the house. (Yes, husband now). The very one, who showed me, the video tape of them "getting it in." I learned to get over it. I overlooked her faults. We had many heart-to-heart talks. Especially, on why she was staying, with a guy like that.

Once, Rashida met Khadijah. It was by happenstance. Khadijah needed a ride from her job at CVS drugstore. I just so happens, to be with Rashida at the time. It was nice, hearing them speak French to each other. I loved it. (It was sexy).

It was 1997. My mother, usually, filed my taxes, on my behalf. Especially, since she was an accountant. Due to my tax return that year, I finally, confessed to my mother, about my legal, married status. My mama declined, because she didn't want to be responsible, for taxes, outside of family.

Other things came crashing down. Khadijah said, her cousin, Ibrahim, who she was living with, was raping her. Needless to say, I was shocked and appalled. I was furious!

"He raped me," she said, which sounded, suspiciously, like something Rashida would say. "He said, he'll tell INS on me, if I didn't do what he wanted."

I wanted to tear the guy apart. I wanted to make fertilizer out of him, and throw him to the pigs. Rape is the most heinous crime, a person can do, to another human being. I was yelling and screaming, to the top of my lungs, because I was so hurt. Someone called the police, because I was so loud. Khadijah discouraged me from doing anything to him. She said, the guy wasn't worth it. Finally, I agreed, she was right.

Khadijah needed a place to stay. So, I asked my mother, if she could stay with us. Just for a little awhile, until we can get our own place. I was glad, she was with me, safe and sound.

She was somewhat disgruntled the next day. We were, suddenly, thrown together, trying to get a firm grip on the emergency situation. She had no where to go. We had the task of looking for an apartment. We needed something safe, but affordable. Our problem was the size of a hippopotamus. Khadijah and I went to see the apartments all week. I was a moth to the flame. I could've lived anywhere, but I wanted her to be happy. She needed a place, she could call home. I wanted to help her dissolve all her anxieties. I wanted her to float on air, while I paid all the bills.

"Just be my wife," I would say to her.

She, finally, settled on the apartments, on north side. They were beside a cheap motel, on Chamberlane Avenue. It was dizzy with flies. Prostitution ran like scolded dogs. The women were hunting up and down, the street for potential people to go with. Drug dealers drafted in the drugs. Yet, it was a chance to live with Khadijah. Looking at the forecast then, it was worth it. I wanted us to be the ultimate, dynamic duo. In spite of, what anyone at the masjid, had anything to say about it. I wanted to go forward, and put the ugly thing of her cousin behind me. It (She didn't press charges).

It was the first time, I moved out, on my own. I was 26-years-old. Tears illuminated, in my mother's eyes. Of course, it earned my empathy and full attention. I asked her, what was wrong.

"I've always known, you'd leave here, for a woman," she said, frankly.

At the point, I nearly, changed my mind. Khadijah was the woman I cared about. She was already, on the edge, of going into a frenzy.

"I'll never leave you, mama. This will always be my home," I said.

I was almost crying myself. So, without further ado, I left the nest. Things at the apartment, were frivolous at first. Somehow, I was hoping the neighborhood would improve. Oh, how I longed for the days of elementary school. Life seemed so much simpler then. No worries, no bills. I fumigated our apartment without incense. I wanted it to be, as comfortable as possible. I thought it was great, Khadijah and I had our own, little, exclusive spot. However, she turned out to be, fussy about this, and that. The way she talked to me, was inconsistent, from earlier. Especially, with how I helped her, with no other place to go. I began to feel used.

It was a hot, "Indian summer" that year. I imitated Africans, from the masjid, wearing sandals and baggy slacks. I wore sandals all the time growing up. Typically, when I visited South Carolina, where nearly, everyone wore sandals or flip flops.

"It's in your genes, Marco! It's in your genes," my maternal grandma said, when I once had a huge hangover there.

She was referring to my grandfather, who was known to have a drinking problem. I thought about that, whenever I wanted a drink.

I needed financial stability. So, I applied for Wackenhut. It was a security job, on the weekends. My mother was between jobs herself. Her and I worked at the new, home décor store, Garden Ridge. We stocked the shelves, before its Grand Opening.

It seemed like endless hours, when I worked security, at the warehouse parking lot. It was very boring, but easy money. All I had to do was, strategically, sit in my car. Occasionally, I'd show my face or patrol every once in a while. I listened to a small, portable radio. I'd read or do puzzles. I may have took a nap or two, while I was supposed to watch the parking lot.

I'll never forget, the enormous amount of respect, I seemingly, got from the warehouse employees. One day, I decided to grab a soda, inside the employee's break room. Stiff as the gingerbread man, they all stared at me. (Did I do that)? It gave me pride, what my security job could do to people. Stop and take notice! I liked the idea, my uniform allowed people to wave at me. Total strangers, suddenly, waving at little, old me. Yes!

Things got intense back at the apartment. For a lack of a better word, it was horrible. It was like tiptoeing through a meteor shower. Khadijah would, hardly, spend any time with me. Half the time, I didn't have a clue, where she was, or who she was with. I had my suspicions. I'd pace the floor. It was intimidating, wondering, where in the hell, she was at, this time. Sometimes, she'd disappear all night. Other times, she was gone for days. Needless to say, I was irritated with her. I was paying the rent, all the bills. She would only jeer at me. As though I'm trying to control her, or tell her what to do.

I couldn't believe, she behaved the way she did. I felt, she was taking me for a joke. I wasn't going to take it any longer. I wasn't going to keep quiet about it. What hurt me, I wasn't invited to the party. She'd continue to justify her actions, with the "not married" stuff. I felt compelled to start, or at least try, to date other people. It was a kick in the ass, being stood up, and she lived with me. I was in a crime-ridden, dangerous area, for her, and I was often, all alone.

I went over to my mother's house, as often as I could. I was miserable at mine. I was unhappy. Also, I was too embarrassed, to tell my mother, what was going on. I knew she wanted, the best for me, and this, certainly, wasn't it. I was having nosebleeds, from the anxiety. My nose once bleed, while I was at Masjid Rahman.

I saw a flyer, jammed in mama's front door. It was a picture of the martial artist Bruce Lee. That caught my attention. It was a Kung-fu class, teaching the Wing Chun style. Wing Chun was, actually, a woman who mastered Kung-fu. Bruce Lee learned it. So, I joined the classes for awhile. However, it became boring, learning the same, hand fighting techniques, over and over. I wanted to get into the nitty gritty stuff, like in the movies.

I was feeling secluded. I just wanted, a good woman in my life. Was that too much to ask? Khadijah wore the leopard-designed scarf I bought her. Yet, it wasn't enough. I thought, I should've joined the Navy. At least, I would've traveled around the world. Possibly, met someone else.

Once, Joe gave me his stance, I was in school too long.

"All those years, you could've been a doctor by now," he said to me.

I thought, that was rude. It hurt my feelings. Little did he know, I "started over" when I went to VCU, after J Sargeant Reynolds. I didn't give up, on school.

I talked the Major, supervisor, at Wackenhut. I wanted a better location to work. Something morning and full-time. Something exciting. I was bored, sitting in the backseat of my car all day. He assigned me to NationsBank. It was an office building downtown. It was a 24-story high rise. The place was filled with lawyers and bankers. They seemed likable and nice. I enjoyed the cushy, corporate atmosphere. It was a welcomed change. My uniform was a dark blues sports jacket, navy blue tie, and gray slacks. Pleasant as a Sunday picnic, I'd stroll the office floors.

Because of my problems with Khadijah, the liquor bottle was calling me. The lack of trust, was a bit much. However, I stayed the course. I nodded my head, in the right direction. I was stressed, as plain as the pimple on my face. I loaned myself to watch tv, alone. Sometimes, the tv was watching me, as I slept on the couch. I didn't know, exactly, what was going on. I knew it wasn't right. I was a man, without a plan. I just, simply, wanted a wholesome, loving relationship. That was something, which I never had. I refused, to give up on love. (Was I a nuisance)?

I'd get on my computer, to chitchat with anonymous strangers. Politicking my blues away. I'd go into various chat rooms on AOL (America On Line). My favorite was the Ebony and Ivory Room.

Khadijah and I would, constantly, argue, fuss and fight.

"Motherfucker!" I called her one night, during a heated argument.

She then smacked me. I didn't do anything to her back. Maybe my comment was obliged or justified. Her, in her twin-sized bed. Me, in mine. We were, more or less, like roommates, sharing an apartment. She, obviously, wasn't ready for marriage. She only cared about her future occupation as a doctor. I was, merely, the means to get there.

With her pompous attitude, I wasn't the maid. So, I did very little Spring cleaning. I was nothing more than a train porter, keeping the place running. I was there, to keep the lights on. That's how it felt anyway. Khadijah didn't seem to care. At that point, I didn't either. The only one, who seemed to love me for me, was my mother. It didn't take an optician, recommending eyeglasses, to see our "marriage" was, indefinitely, postponed. Luther Vandross said it best, "A house is not a home." Many nights, I cried. I was the orphan nobody wanted. It was, powerfully, an emotional time.

Meanwhile, I marveled at my younger brother and sister, going out, with lots of friends, having fun. My father, still wasn't in my life. Ordinarily, I'd drown my troubles, by listening to my melodies of music. I wanted my stupid situation with Khadijah to be over. I wanted to get in charge of my life.

For a little while, one of Khadijah's personal friends stayed with us, on the weekends. I said okay, when she told me, her friend was also Muslim. She had long Senegalese, twisted braids.

Later on, I found out, Khadijah lied. Her friend wasn't Muslim after all. She knew, I couldn't say no, to a fellow Muslim, who needed help.

On a lighter note, my security job at the bank, gave the privilege of escorting the bank tellers. I'd meet them on the lobby, inside the bank. Then I would walk with them, to their bank's vault. They would carry huge sums of money. It was great, being a deterrent, for the bad guys. It was an honor. I was the only thing, which stood in the way, between potential criminals. Not to mention, the security cameras. I would've died, to protect the innocent. I loved it.

Sure, I only made breadcrumbs, but I liked being a security guard. Calling off work was, hardly, an option. Often, Captain Green would place me, at the Information Desk, in the lobby. That was our post as well. I'd answer questions or give directions, with a smile. There were so many, pretty women, in skirts and high heels. I couldn't resist, a glance or two.

If I had to fill-in for someone, during the evening, I'd do silly things. I'd steal pieces of candy, off someone's desk. Nobody would be around. I had the keys, to all the doors. Of course, I knew where all the security cameras were.

Sometimes, I'd lay around or nap, in their prosperous and luxurious board room. It was located on the top floor. It had creepy, life-size pictures of former bank presidents, hanging from the wall. I assumed, they were all dead. It seemed, they were staring at me, watching my every move. Every now and then, I was brazen to cut a tv show on, in someone's office. I was bored, so sue me.

My fellow coworkers thought our Ms. Kearny was a real prude. However, she was, especially, nice to me. She treated me like I was her son, at work. She reviewed herself, and the security job, a little "too seriously."

With an eye to the sky, and ear to the ground, I was only a push button away. My hand-held walkie talkie was always handy. It was fun, walking throughout the building, here and there.

My security job was in the heart of downtown, Main Street, of Richmond. I wouldn't dare risk, letting the American flag, touch the ground. I raised it on the flagpole, every morning. I had zero military duty, but it was an honor.

Bike messengers would drop off packages at the front desk, and I would sign it. I would also monitor the lobby bank, for potential scum of the earth. I'd also, watch the armed guards, bringing money in, or out, unto armored trucks.

My only qualm, with the job, was the attitude, of some of the other security guards. I loathed the sarcasm and arrogance. I saw security as protecting people. I was keeping them from harm's way. It was sacred.

"Martin, you bring something to the job," said Captain Green. "I think you'll be great, working in corrections."

"You think so?" I said.

"I know so!"

Captain Green was once, a correctional officer herself. It wasn't a question of what, I wanted to do with the rest of my life. It was a matter of how, I would get there. I couldn't save the world, but I wanted to do my small part.

One of my professors at VCU, assigned us to meet at the local police department. It was no snickering matter. It was the very spot, my father used to work. That is, before his massive heart attacks, which put him into early retirement. It was a "field" trip, at best. We all listened to the satire or rhetoric of what it was like to be a cop on the street.

We all took turns, riding around in actual police cars, with the officers. I was soiled with disappointment. The officer, we were riding with, said my neighborhood was a White neighborhood. Little did he know, I was from the very neighborhood, he was said, was mostly White. Black people can't have nice houses, or upscale neighborhood? (I should've said something). I grew up in that predominantly, Black neighborhood. If not all-Black.

Somehow, I wanted to be a police officer too. I wanted to try out for it. There I was, going over the ramp, not knowing what was on the other side. Because of my education, I felt souped up, or prepared for it. I was a rat, going for the big cheese. To me, at that time, nothing was more noble than locking up criminals. I had a personal vendetta, with people, who hurt people.

I could've screamed, when I aced the written exam, for Chesterfield and Henrico law enforcement agencies. However, I did awful, when it came to the actual moment of the physical exam. It didn't require any reading or reasoning, just endurance and stamina. I was becoming loose at the seams. I was tangled unto a spiderweb, not knowing which direction to go into. My college graduation was around the corner. I had no idea, or job prospects. I was on pin needles or worried, who would receive and hire me.

By the end of the year, it was no secret, my so-called spouse left me. She, simply, packed all her belongings in her car, while I was gone. No goodbyes. (Sounds familiar)? My mother recommended, I spend the night at her house, rather than being by myself. So, I did. I didn't want to be in that apartment anymore. My heart wasn't for sell. I squinted my last tear, over a woman, who didn't want me. Soon, I was felt redeemed, I was separated from her. I was a man, slowly, climbing his own staircase.

I decided, to try to serve God better. I was starving for attention, from Him. I regretted the shabby things I did. I became stern with making my prayer. I relied on Him, more than ever. I was tired of being tired. I was weary of the sharks out there. They were using me, like a local convenient store. I was remitting myself, back into the fold of Islam. I was shifting gears. I was trying. I didn't want to be a stranger anymore, at the masjid. I wanted to repent, for coming up short. I strutted around the believers, as much as possible.

It was sublime. I felt great, I told myself. I wanted to get the "ball and chain" of being, actually, married to Khadijah off of me. I didn't waste any time, seeking a divorce lawyer. Yet, I lacked a substantial amount of money, for the lawyer to do the right thing.

My tongue was left out to dry. Nobody wanted to waltz, but I was okay.

"Allah will suffice," I'd tell myself.

I wasn't the type, to throw the towel into the ring. I believe in love. I didn't want to give up on love, and romance. I wanted to compliment a woman's smile. I wanted to be with someone, who enjoyed watching a sunrise. I didn't want to transgress backwards. I didn't want to accept, just anything. Let alone, from the first woman that hopped along. I wanted to, someday, be wed. I supposed, to a Muslim. Not necessarily, from the same tribe or color I belong to.

I was proud of myself. I didn't need help, paying the rent or bills. I was, hardly, at the apartment. It was a smack in the face, just being there. It wasn't the same, without Khadijah being there. We got the apartment for us. Now, there was "no us." I surrendered all my time, at my security guard job, or at my mother's house . I was longing, for a wholesome environment. I put on a brave front. Underneath the smile, my heart was strained. I was in constant turmoil. I wanted to come inside, from the outside wind. I took a fall, but I wanted to, swiftly, get up. I opened up my umbrella. I was trying to withstand the rain, people gave me.

Synchronizing my time, I made a conscientious decision to worship. I was tired of being the nail, being hit on the head. My understanding, obviously, was working. I was doing, what I was doing, in the dark, only to find, I was wrinkled, in daylight.

My love life seemed, completely, unfair. I had so much love to give. However, I had no one, actually, to give it to. I would have walked yards. I would've drove miles, to see my special love.

I wanted a tattoo. Something just for me. I wanted one for years. Yet, under Islam, it was frowned upon. You don't know, how many times, I saw skin and thought it was cool. I couldn't tell the Brothers at the masjid. I thought, it was somehow unreasonable. I wasn't allowed to express myself, with my body. Allah knows best.

*SEASON 11, EPISODE 12*

# Girl Scout Cookies

"ALI, YOU KNOW I'm not married to Mustapha anymore, right?" said the other Khadijah, from the masjid.

Not to be confused with the African one, I was "married" to. This particular Khadijah was, clearly, American.

The year was 1998. My eyes, quickly, zigzagging across her. (Was she flirting with me)? I was in Aladdin's Pizza. I was with a couple of Muslim Brothers. We frequented Aladdin's because they didn't sell pork on their pizza.

"American" Khadijah told me, all about her failure of a marriage. She told me, about her little landlord problem. (No money for the rent). She was upright. She was outspoken. She always wore Islamic garb. She was submissive in a hijab. We exchanged phone numbers.

I couldn't wait to call her. Especially, since the African princess moved out the apartment. I explained to "American" Khadijah, the terrible ordeal. The pain, I went through, with her friend. She told me how, Mustapha wasn't so "hot in the cot." I found out, he hardly, spent any quality time with her. He spent most of time at the masjid, neglecting her. Thankfully, she took a liking to me. She said, I was cute.

For a variety of obvious reasons, I visited Khadijah's apartment. We gossiped about the masjid, and some of the people who went there. She had a figure like the rapper/ actress Queen Latifah. She had a great sense of humor. I bought the food. We prayed together. We seemed very compatible. She said, I could spend the night, considering it was getting late. One thing led to another.

I often wore a kufi, wherever I went then. "American" Khadijah wore threads, which covered her, from head to toe. Yet, we were two consenting adults, enjoying each other's company. It felt viable. It was great to be alive. Also, we were waiting for a thunderbolt, sort of speak. We weren't married, but we were seeing each other. Some would say, we should've known better. Finally, I was doing what the "African" Khadijah wouldn't let me do. I was being virile. I was being a man. Things were tight. Not to mention, I was in violation.

"American" Khadijah said she liked big men. I most, certainly, wasn't the athletic type. I wasn't bringing in an abundant amount of money. We showed our fondness for each other, by wearing matching colored outfits. We both loved Islam, however imperfect we both were. We believed in being ourselves, above all else. To be, perfectly, frank, "American" Khadijah could be sometimes, brutally honest. It could leave a bitter taste in your mouth. I was glad, she was in my life. She had the aurora of a new day.

I loved her apartment. I loved the view, from her living room and bedroom. Tips of the tops of trees blocked the view, which gave it privacy. "American" Khadijah didn't have a job. So, her kitchen cabinets were quite empty. She adopted by eating rice, and canned food. Her food was food donations, from the masjid. I'd be at her place, all afternoon.

She admitted, she couldn't have a baby, because she got her Fallopian tubes tied. Starting a family was what I wanted, eventually. I wanted children, but she couldn't. Yet, she was agreeable. I saw myself "going bald," growing old, and laughing with her. I liked her carnal humor. Like me, "American" Khadijah gave up alcohol, when she decided to be a Muslim.

One day, I prepared a small banquet in my apartment. A blind man could've saw, with cataracts, how much we enjoyed each other's company. It wasn't at all planned, what I wanted to say. I knew, I had to say something. It was like eating something, very spicy.

"Khadijah, I want us to get together," I said, as though breaking the sound barrier.

I was laying it all out, on the table.

"You want us to get to married?" she said.

I gave a two cent nod. I was nodding my head "yes."

## GIRL SCOUT COOKIES

"...I accept."

As always then, I shared, whatever I was up to, with my mother. Bare in mind, I only started speaking with "American" Khadijah a few weeks prior. Also, in Islam, there's not a "boyfriend, girlfriend" thing.

"Do you love her? Do you even know this woman?" pleaded my mother, Etta.

I tried to explain to her, it's a welcomed change for the better.

"I trust Islam, Mama," I said to her.

I took amnesty in the idea. I thought, "American" Khadijah and I, had a beautiful beginning. She announced our wedding plans at the masjid. In hopes of stopping any gossiping chatter, about us going out, and not being wed, yet.

I asked Mustapha, her former husband, was it okay with him. I wanted to see, if he had any hard feelings about it. Such behavior was below his character. He was more humble than a child, with a new Raggedy Ann doll. He gave me his blessing.

Eventually, I decided to introduce "American" Khadijah to my family. That was important to me. My secret elopement with "African" Khadijah was a sham. That was a joke, but this was the real thing. Never mind I was still, legally, married to her. However, in Islam it is, perfectly, okay to have two, three or four wives. Besides, I was hoping for a divorce soon. I had steady income, with a bird's eye view, at the bank high rise building. So, I was set. Sweet as cinnamon, my family, seemingly, liked her. They got along great. Things were happening fast, but my mother liked her anyway.

I needed the cash. I accepted another school loan. Also, I wanted to fulfill a religious obligation of offering a potential spouse, something of value. I went beyond the call of duty. "American" Khadijah clapped for joy at my offering. She needed the cash. Especially, for her rent due. We felt we were grown, and didn't, necessarily, need an imam as a chaperone or go-between. I gave my $1000 dowry to her, personally. "Tax free."

Working up an appetite, I took "American" Khadijah and the family to Old Country Buffet in Chesterfield. In the blink of an eye, she had them laughing. She responded on how dry the food tasted. She swore to never visit their restaurant again. Our wedding was, approximately, less than a month away. I blotted out the notion, we were moving too quickly. She wanted to be wife, regardless of it being "legally binding" or on paper.

"American" Khadijah talked me into taking her to Halalco. It was located in Falls Church. We wanted to look, especially, special for our big day. It was an Islamic bookstore, which sold everything. They had plenty of catalog options for books, Muslim attire, cassette tapes, you name it. In our travels, we got lost, trying to find the store. Finally, we arrived at night. We wanted to get a wedding outfit, which said "Boom!" Something which begged for compliments. I even wanted the perfect oil or smell-good, as asinine as that may sound.

There was no bowing out now. No more combustion of a secret life. Question was, was she going to breach our unwritten contract, someday. I believed, everything was going to be alright. Not only, from the comments she made, but the communication we did. I was planning to move all of my belongings into her apartment. Particularly, with me liking her place so much. I was enchanted, with the fact, "American" Khadijah covered herself in modesty, wherever she went. She would only present herself or show her beauty to me. I felt compelled, to do right by her.

I went to Virginia Commonwealth University as a full-time student. I worked full-time as a security officer. There was little room for anything else. I compressed my studying, into an hour or two, before an actual exam. I was at a disadvantage, doing that, and I knew it. I was sick of going to school. I wanted it to be over with. I wanted to hide in a cave sometimes.

As a Muslim, death no longer disturbed me. The Brothers shared with me, there was Paradise on the other side. It was much more decent than this, worldly, life. However, I wasn't in a hurry to die, to get there.

Brothers like Saadiq, quickly, sent me their congratulations, on my upcoming wedding. That meant a lot, coming from him. Doctor Ismail, the latest imam then, offered to cook the food for my wedding day.

One day, my mouth dropped to the floor. "American" Khadijah admitted to him, were together, intimately, already. With that, Doctor Ismail called off the wedding, the whole thing. He was her "wali" or designated chaperone. I wasn't sure, if she felt guilty or convicted, but he knew, everything. Abu Bakr, earnestly, came to my aide. He had all sorts of advice. He took it upon himself, to speak to the imam, on my behalf.

"The marriage is off!" I was told.

"He can't do that," drummed Abu Bakr.

It echoed support from other believers as well. My good name was now tarnished. My reputation was contaminated. In a perfect world, people would've forgotten about it, and moved on. Two consenting adults, but it was neither. The embarrassment was "American" Khadijah's. She was hurt. No denying that. Elegantly, I kept my head up. I was only human. I felt bad for her. She wasn't given a cooperative tone or smile. Her value as a woman was, seemingly, depreciated. An elopement was out of the question. Meanwhile, our matching white and gold wedding outfits were collecting dust.

With a desire to rebel, I called the imam, to give him a piece of my mind. I've been to Doctor Ismail's place many times. Especially, for the pay-per-view boxing events. We cheered on Mike Tyson, because he was now, a fellow Muslim. The imam was like a cousin to me. Yet, I was determined to show him, he was wrong. I pleaded with him, to change his mind. I was going to go crazy, if I wasn't allowed, to marry "American" Khadijah. The imam and I got into a heated debate. I devoted all my energy, into what I once had with my "intended" wife. I wanted it back. However, he came at me with patronizing comments. It was a crime, the way we argued, back and forth.

"Are you threatening me?" I said to him, with a dictation which took years to master.

I made a list, in my mind, of what I would do, should worst came to worst. Hanging up the phone, I cruised into self-pity. My eyes dilated, from so much crying. I didn't want to return, to being a lonesome guy again. My heart was in my handcuffs. I thought it was the most disagreeable, erroneous thing, to keep two people away from each other. "American" Khadijah and I wanted to be together. I was being thrown out of a car, unto a curb. I continued to go to the masjid. She stopped going. I didn't use curse words at that point, so I used as my euphemisms. As many as I could find.

I began to examine my life, for what it was. It was like a freight train, making haste, in the middle of the night. I made an executive decision.

I decided to forget about it, and move on with my life. I met a fun woman, with fringe benefits. It was fun, while it lasted. I was "American" Khadijah's eyes and ears, as she stayed away from the community.

"What the hell was she thinking about?" I said, to myself.

(Why did she tell anyone our personal business)? She still had the money, I gave her. I was full of frustration. I was like a hedgehog, demanding what was, rightfully, mine. I gave "American" Khadijah the $1000, on the condition, we were getting married.

I talked to Doctor Ismail about my refund. He was after all, her "wali," respectfully. He said the money was, reportedly, gone, spent. I didn't know, what type of game she was playing, but I was, highly, disappointed.

One faithful day, the imam came to his senses, after reading the Holy Quran. He had a change of heart. He said, we could get married. The damage was already done. I blamed him, for breaking us up, in the first place. "American" Khadijah's reply wasn't anything, I wanted to hear. I hated to hear it, like I hate hospitals.

"I can't marry you," she said.

My heart stopped. Especially, after all the trouble we went through, to plead our case. Not to mention, we got together before marriage. Arguably, more so, we should've been allowed to marry.

"Why not?" I said, looking a gift horse in the mouth.

"Because, I have a drug problem. I don't want to do that," said cried.

It was so humiliating. I sealed the fence in my brain. I didn't want to not to hear, what I just heard.

"Khadijah, we can get you help," I said, swallowing my pride.

My hypothesis was, it was a little late, to hide behind the fig leaf now. Her goblins got the best of her.

After that, things became unbearable. "American" Khadijah would do unbelievable things. She'd call me on the phone, letting me know how drunk she was. She'd tell me, she's been with another guy. I was under fire, with more and more calls from her. It only proved, what an idiot I was. It was a dark time. It was blacker than Gothic. I felt, completely, used and immobilized. Soon, "American" Khadijah fizzled out my life. I grappled with the idea. I never heard from her again.

## GIRL SCOUT COOKIES

My mother felt, the whole thing was impetuous or rushed anyway. Yet, she respected my wishes. The fling I had, with "American" Khadijah was a mere thing or flicker, but it grieved me anyhow. I was under the impression, I should fast, on Monday and Thursday, until I got a wife. That only made me feel flushed. I couldn't believe, I was at the drawing board again. Eventually, I told myself, she couldn't have any children. Perhaps, it was best anyway. Already, I was missing her hardy laugh, "Ha! Ha! Ha!" I missed the way, she communicated. She was the life of the party. However, we were, no more.

I was, formally, becoming a hammerhead at work. I smiled less, despite my new independence. I was a fragment of a being, which wanted to belong to someone's heart. I searched the internet on the computer, for happiness. I was still hoping, for that special individual.

Then there's the day, which changed my life forever.

"Excuse me, sir. Would you like, to buy some Girl Scout Cookies, for my daughter?"

Her name was Mary. She seemed to pop out of nowhere. She came into my life, when I couldn't feel any less inferior. I was desperate, but not serious. We lived in the same apartment complex. We made light conversation on the spot.

"Yeah, okay," I said.

After I finished dumping trash, I picked out a few Girl Scout Cookies. I hopped into my automobile, and drove to my mother's house. I have never spoken to Mary, before I ordered the cookies. She assured me, she'd call me, when the items came in.

My first impression of Mary, "She must go to church." She was well-mannered, and soft-spoken. She walked a fine line. She had a wonderful "inside voice." When I ordered, what I ordered, I thought nothing of it.

My livelihood at the bank, became monotone, if not boring. I wanted to do something interesting or intense, and intellectual. It was my last semester at VCU. I wanted to put my brain to more use, than foot patrol in someone's bank building.

I must've mailed, through the US Postal Service, dozens of resumes, to different, local law firms. I was inquiring for interviews. I thought, maybe,

# BEHOLD

I could be a paralegal. (Why not)? I loved the law. I liked lawyer shows. However, that didn't amount to a hill of beans. Especially, without a job, to do it with. The idea of a law firm was, simply, irresistible. I had to try. I wanted to work alongside lawyers. I'd settle for law enforcement. So, I lunged forward with the applications. I resented criminals. I detested crime.

Perhaps, that's why, I'll never forget, when I got off work. It was 6:00 am. Unassuming, I returned to my apartment. Someone broke in! It looked like a disaster area. Apparently, somebody threw something, through the bedroom window. The front door was wide open. Whoever did it, could've been still there. I went inside anyway. My things were thrown on the floor. I should've walked away, and called the police. The first thing I did, call my mama. I wanted to punch the perpetrators in the jaw. I wanted to cry, but I wouldn't give the thieves the satisfaction. Magnanimously, they only took my .25 caliber handgun. It was silver with white pearl handle-grip. Also my beloved VCR was gone. Eventually, I called the police, to tell them about the mere two missing items.

I felt, completely, violated. It was no longer my sanctuary, at that point. Feeling, totally, uncomfortable, I moved out my apartment, that very day. I grabbed a few things, day after day, but I wouldn't spend the time the night. What happened was ugly. It was malice. Naturally, I just wanted to get the hell out of there, and never return. Judging from the looks of things, whoever it was, knew exactly, what they wanted and where. I had a creeping suspicion, it was "American" Khadijah. I couldn't prove it, but I knew she was behind the break-in. The police officer, who finally, did show up for the report, didn't seem to care much either. I vowed, to never move into a crime-infested area again.

Marriage became the last thing on my mind, as I moved back into my mother's house. Being alone was nothing new. I sank my fangs deeper into the computer monitor. My screen name was "Playa Playaa." Online, I met Jennifer. She was White. We were a perfect match. She didn't have to send me a nipple shot or picture, in order for me to like her. She treated me like a king. She would call me, long distance, at work. It felt like, I knew her all my life. We were soulmates. Not to mention, she was having boyfriend-trouble.

## GIRL SCOUT COOKIES

Remarkably, Jennifer and I had the same thoughts, at the same time. We finished each other's sentences. It may seemed novice, but we, instantly, fell in love. Quickly, I got used to the idea. My heart was laminated, with hope, once again. Love was no longer a metaphor. Love songs were no longer, small bits and pieces, I happened to hear on the radio. The larynx in my throat, longed to say her name. The computer was, simply, the "middle man." No doubt, she'd make a fine wife. She obtained my every thought. My eyes leaked with joy. I kept my feelings to myself, from other people. I didn't want people to think, my mind was turning into mincemeat. Especially, with a woman, I have never met.

From the security office, my coworkers would hand me the phone.

"It's Jennifer," they would say.

However, like all mirages, which come and go, mine came to an end as well. Somehow, the boyfriend stopped her from contacting me. He opposed me, and relinquished Jennifer and I's reliable network of feelings.

March 1998, I asked my landlord, if I could, somehow, break my lease. I only got a resounding or reprimanded "No." So, my mother and I removed more of my things, from the apartment, over time. Yet, I was still obligated, to pay to pay the rent. Going back to the apartment was hard. It was like, taking a splinter out of a finger. It was something which had to be done.

Then I got a phone call, in the hallowed out, empty, "used to be" living room. It was Mary, letting me know, the Girl Scout Cookies orders were in. They were ready to be picked up.

Like a shepherd boy, I staggered over Mary's apartment, later on. She had a personality I liked. She was 10 years older than me. She had an old-fashioned, motherly way, which drew me in. I wanted to "window shop" her, or get to know her better. So, I met Mary, for a dinner date. We sat around her dining room table. We watched reruns of the Jerry Seingfield show. Meanwhile, her blue lightbulb hung from the ceiling, which gave it a "grown folk" or mature, after hours feel. I bought us some Chinese food. Surprisingly, I was comfortable and not rigid. Behind the closed curtains, we talked for hours.

"You got somebody?" I asked her.

"I got a friend," Mary said.

Of all the rotten luck, I thought. She got a man. Her voluptuous silhouette was breathtaking. Especially, under the blue light. Mary's stock and trade, or bread and butter, was being a caretaker for the elderly. From the looks of things, she didn't, seemingly, make a lot of money. I was, usually, broke too. Particularly, with all the money going to bills, or rent, for the apartment. It was our first date. It was a perfect night. Nothing seemed to sabotaged it. Certain thoughts shouted in me. Yet, I remained a gentleman.

The following Wednesday, we agreed to meet again. I told her about Islam. I told her about my salary, among other things. Mary, finally, told me about the skeleton in the closet, or elephant in the room. Her name was Carolyn.

"She's the lesbian, not me," said Mary, believing in her stronghold on men.

The sarcasm came much later. We laughed. We talked about any subject, under the sun. Some would say, we had a slothful way, enjoying each other's company.

"Are you attracted to women?" I asked.

I wanted to see what turned her on. Mary said, "No." She lit scented candles, which gave a smell of a succession of flowers. She didn't, necessarily, have a scrapbook of family pictures. There was none. The only family she had, was her 12-year-old daughter, Toya. She was so adorable. I was afraid someone would snatch her up, for their very own. That's how smitten I was with her.

Like a sunburn, Mary was, emotionally, scarred. She didn't know her father. She was an only child. Her mother abandoned her, at the tender age of 13. She was living with grandmother after that. I thought, that was a crummy thing to do. I was told, the few family she did have in Richmond, had little to do with her. Socially, she didn't seem to have many friends. I didn't have many myself, at that moment. Except the few females I knew, and the Muslims at the masjid. Carolyn supplied all of her needs. For the last eight years, taking her to the store, and what have you.

We both lived secluded lives, up until that point. Pathetically, the solitaire game wasn't an option. Mary's eyes seized upon the new, '96 black

# GIRL SCOUT COOKIES

Dodge Stratus I bought. (It was new to me). I felt sorry her, whenever she would cry about her severed family ties.

At her job, Mary would page me. Usually, I'd call her from the 24th floor of NationsBank. I'd whisper sweet nothings in her ear. It was like having a suspended sentence over my head. I could, hardly, wait until the next time we met in her apartment. Occasionally, I'd take her to our favorite Chinese restaurant. The female owner would refer to me as, "gentleman."

"Where's Gentleman?" the lady would ask, in her heavy accent, to Mary, if I wasn't around.

Mary was without a car. I'd drive her to the movies. I'd take her to the store, or whatever she wanted to go. One night, I must've had her out too long.

"Where have you been?" said Carolyn to Mary.

She was about to have a spasm. Mary and her were having an argument. It was a lover's spat, over me. My palms were getting sweaty. It turning into something, quite serious. From spending time together, we were developing symptoms of love. It was great. We could be ourselves.

"What if you get pregnant?" I said.

"If I get pregnant, I get pregnant," Mary said.

That was music to my ears. There was a gulp in my throat. It was nervousness, yet happiness. Having a baby, at 27-years-old was, perfectly, fine with me. (I wasn't getting any younger). It was pleasure. It was pain. Mary, seemingly, had visions of a house, two cars and a white picket fence. It was a pure feeling. We cuddled, which gave it balance. As a rule, I had to leave before one o'clock a.m. I wasn't allowed, to spend the entire night over there. (Go figure).

Things became grim after that. Eventually, the mask came off. Mary had a quaint, little way of thinking I was gay. Somehow, for some reason, she thought I was "on the low."

"You, probably, don't want me, or any other woman!" she said, hanging the phone up on me.

(What)? I was on post, at the information desk, at work. So, I couldn't, outwardly, react. I was crushed. I absolutely, love women. I'm very attracted to women. I'm not attracted to men. (Are you kidding me)? I cried, like a baby, when I got the chance. It was the most absurd thing, I have ever heard. I tried to wipe the tears from eyes, before any clients in the building saw me. It was no use. Tears kept coming, no matter how hard I tried.

   I thought Mary liked me. I thought we were having a good time. I thought we were getting to know each other. I decided to call my sister from work. I needed someone to talk to.

   "You know you're not like that! Don't worry about it," Drika said, trying to stop me from crying.

   Mary and I had so much in common. We both didn't have our fathers in our lives. We were both hurt by that. Soon, she called. She apologized. Reluctantly, I accepted her apology.

   Yet again, Mary had the idea, I must've been gay. Especially, when it came to one of my oldest friends, from my old neighborhood, Gerry. She would, actually, act jealous, when it came to him. As though something was going on, between him and I. Every blue moon, we'd hang out, or catch up, with what's going on in our lives. Rather, I wanted to be on my own, than take what she was offering. It was unbelievable. However, she kept pleasing me. I was going to quit our relationship, if I heard another damn possible "gay" thing, directed at me. The nerve of her! Claiming to be something, I was not. (Why would I waste my time, with a woman, if I wasn't into women)? I was flabbergasted. With her thinking, somehow, I had "tendencies," brought me so much pain. "Hurt" didn't give it justice. She didn't consider, she was in a lesbian relationship herself, all those years?

   My Islam was, practically, thrown out the window. My religious life wasn't parallel with my love life. It's a wonder, I didn't start eating pork. (I was doing everything else). I spent all my free time, chasing behind Mary. I took her to the park, or wherever, I thought she should be.

   I was still on post, at the bank, at that moment. Graduate school, or going for a Master's degree was out of the question. I was "tired" of school.

   Mary told me, in a raspberry jam voice, she was pregnant. I was the father. I couldn't have been more happier. However, my family held out their reservations. Especially, for a woman, I hardly, knew. So, I felt alone, welcoming my child into the world. I reached out to the mother-to-be, as much as I could. Because of my father, I certainly, didn't want to abandon her.

I guessed, because of her turmoil past, gave me the hardest time. We kept arguing. The police precinct was, merely, a phone call away. We rebutted each other's statements. Ready or not, the sound of the pitter-patter small feet was soon coming. Despite it all, I gave Mary preferential treatment. I would take her to Community Pride grocery store. She was on "Section 8" and used food stamps coupons. She would often keep me in the car. In hopes, nobody would recognize her, with me.

"Why I can't, go in there with you?" I would say, noting how peculiar it was.

"I don't want anyone to laugh at, the one I love," Mary said, who obviously, was intimidated by people's opinion. "That would hurt me."

"Fuck them people!" I said, in recovery. "I ain't worried about them!"

It was okay to be with her, privately. God forbid, if prevailing eyes, should see us together. I didn't get it or understood. It helped refined my thinking. I'm alright with me, if nobody else is. I didn't care what people had to say, at that point in my life.

The people at the masjid were less than perfect, but there was dialogue. It was the one and only place, where I could, fully, release my honest sentiments about Islam. At the masjid, I was permitted to be a Muslim. As opposed, to hearing Mary's persecuting remarks, against me. She made everything, a personal attack, against her. I paid the masjid, whenever I could.

Mary and I never addressed each other as "boyfriend" or "girlfriend." We didn't do labels. Yet, that's, exactly, what we were. However, she tactfully, avoided being apart of one of the most important days of my life. I invited her to my VCU graduation. She declined. (Somebody may laugh, I supposed). It was the day I received my Criminal Justice degree, from Virginia Commonwealth University. It was a long time coming. Like a true warrior, I didn't let her absence, get my spirit down.

It was 1998. I was about to graduate! I put up a brave front, but I was terrified. I was tangled in emotions. I cried and cried at my college graduation. Resistance was futile. Perhaps, because I didn't have a father around. Maybe, because I worked so hard for it. I was thinking of Mary's miscarriage, which also, gave me a tumultuous turn of events. Not to mention, anxiety. We were already standing on a weak foundation to begin with.

Ted Turner, who owned TNT, CNN, and a host of other cable networks, gave the commencement address, at my graduation. However, I had a bitter taste in my mouth. (Don't get me wrong). Walking across the stage was a huge accomplishment. Yet, it felt "uncharitable." I had no idea, what my welfare or job was going to be. I didn't know, what I was going to do with myself. I didn't have a great career, waiting for me, in the wings.

As far as I knew, my college degree was a tease, on a piece of paper. It didn't guarantee anything. A job, was the underlining question. At the Criminal Justice school, graduation class, I was in a sea of White people. A telltale sign sign was, there was me, and only one other Black guy. "Beggars can't be choosers," I thought to myself.

I wanted to unearth whatever job, I could get, in my field. I knew, it was going to be hard. I was willing to try. I must've went on, 10 different interviews. In unison, they all told me, "No." Some didn't bother to answer back.

Feeling I had enough gumption, and wits about me, I applied for the Henrico County Sheriff Department. The job interviewer, who was doing the hiring, seemingly, tested my voice. Apparently, I didn't have what it took, to work in a jail.

"If a fight broke out, and you wanted the inmates to go to their cells, how would you tell them?" said the interviewer, along with a panel of potential supervisors.

I imagined myself, in a world of shit.

"Um, I'd tell the inmates, 'Go up in your cells?"

"Yes, but how would you tell them?"

The man, wrapped my answer, with his tongue. Obviously, he wanted me to exert myself, more. Needless to say, I was offended. It was though my voice wasn't "strong" enough. Of course, I didn't get the job. So, the vacancy remained open. With me, anyway.

## GIRL SCOUT COOKIES

I got on the phone. I made call-backs. I walked the pavement. I mailed resumes. It seemed like a thousand doors, slammed in my face. I felt like a controlled variable, which was left alone. My job search was going slower than a YIELD sign.

I needed an occupation. Criminal Justice was something, I really, wanted. My heart throbbed, when Pamunkey Regional Jail, in Hanover County, wanted a job interview with me. I was going for the counselor position. I parked my vehicle near the front entrance. I was in a suit and tie. I was nervous as hell. I didn't know what to expect. I didn't know, if the inmates would be walking around in zebra-stripes, or what. I wanted to make a difference. It was a young hustler's life. I had a ticklish, butterfly feeling as I waited to be interviewed. It was like waiting for the verdict to be read.

Finally, I tiptoed in the office to meet a man in a vest. I could tell he was bullheaded. I could tell, he was the type, to not tolerate any nonsense. I used style. I was wanting to help. I relied on my vocabulary. I was willing to transfer. Especially, from what I was doing, to a better job. After the job interview, I vowed to a better Muslim, if I could get that counseling job.

I trembled with anticipation. However, after a few weeks, it was a "No." It was another wake-up call. I refused to give up. I was like an aardvark, in a search of any ant, I could find.

Meanwhile, Mary was apprehensive, being around my family. I bended over backwards, trying to make her comfortable. She insisted my family didn't like her. Particularly, she didn't like Drika.

"I want you to honor me," Mary said, hinting at wanting to be my wife.

I abided my time. I wasn't sure, if I wanted to marry someone, who didn't like my sister. Especially, if she hasn't done anything to her. My family was on their annual trip, in South Carolina. Mary and I spent a few days at my mother's house, alone.

"I'll think about it," I said, thinking things were solved.

*C.O.*

*SEASON 12, EPISODE 13*

# Correctional Officer

MARY WOULD LAY in my arms, which put me in a bind. Carolyn, who may or may not have been in her house, was still around. She would accentuate her stake in their relationship. She would go on errands for her. She would fix or replace things around the house.

Yet, Carolyn was nice to me. She'd buy me anything I wanted, from the store. Mary would, accurately, act one way with me. She'd act another way, around her friend.

If I could sum it into words, Mary was the assertive or controlling one, when it came to her friend. Carolyn and I both blended for her affections. It was a friendly conversation or competition, for the same woman.

Once, Mary made Carolyn and I dinner. I was trying to hold onto, the little Islam, I had left. I didn't drink. Nor did I have any beer, as they did. Yet, I was tempted.

Mary jeered at the way, I sat. She didn't like the way, I held my cup.

"You act like a woman!" Mary said to me, in comparison to her lesbian friend, Carolyn.

I was devastated by that. I took action. I kicked over the drinking bar. I felt that was the problem, in the first place. I was ready to go. I had enough.

Next thing I know, Mary started, physically, attacking me. She was scratching me. She was biting me. My mind blotted out the "never hit a woman" thing. I protected myself. I defended myself. I pushed her off of me. I hit her off of me. My heart was adjourned. My shirt and face was covered in my blood. Carolyn was put to the test. She tried to break it up. However, I was a boat, heading up stream. It was full steam ahead.

"You want to fight? I like to fight!" I said, taking my shirt off for the

Main Event. "I'm tired of this shit!"

Evidently, Mary's next door neighbor called the authorities. I pleaded my case to the police. I told them, she starting hitting me. I was, merely, getting her off of me. They saw how, her apartment was a complete mess. With me, being a big, Black man, they arrested me. I was in handcuffs. I was in utter disbelief. I was in bondage.

The police arrested me, saying I was the "primary aggressor." They charged me with "assault and battery." Not only that, Mary made them aware, I was a security officer, for NationsBank. She was hoping, I'd lose my job over the incident.

The police threw smirks at each other. They saw the cuts on my face. I was bleeding, from all the scratches. They took it as "self-defense" by Mary, I suppose. I was thrown in the Richmond Police van, as though, I was nothing. I was on the borderline of going crazy, in the van. I was, completely, scared. I didn't know what to expect. I was riding, isolated, in the darkness. I couldn't see, where I was going. I didn't what I was coming to.

I prayed to Allah. I screamed in Arabic. I yelled praises to Allah. I groaned in humiliation. I recited every small chapter I knew, from the Holy Quran.

"Aah!" I cried in the holding area, of the dark van.

I was a quiet, shy guy from Henrico County. What was I doing there? I blamed Mary's damn alcohol consumption. With my hands behind my back, I ached with agony inside. Putting on the brakes, the police took me to the hospital. I was examined by the doctor at MCV. Because of the cuts, I had to get a tetanus shot. I was bandaged up.

I was placed in a holding cell, at the city lock-up. I soon said words, I'll never forget.

"Mama, I'm in jail." I said, with my one phone call.

It was going to be a few hours, before I was bailed out. The sheriff deputy lady, sitting behind the counter kept laughing at me. Obviously, she thought it was funny, a woman got the best of me. As though, just desserts. No cared, if Mary started attacking me. It was in the middle of the might. So, most of the guys, in the holding cell, were sleeping. Along with me, awaiting arraignment or bail.

Mary's put-downs wasn't worth it anymore. I looked like an armature fighter, wrapped in face bandages. Within the blink of an eye, I was reduced, to being viewed as a common criminal. My soul amped up with heartbreak.

"What are you in for?" the other inmates wanted to know.

After careful consideration, the guys in jail told me, I had nothing to worry about. They said, the judge will, probably, drop the charges. Especially, since it was my first offense. Finally, a deputy barged in, with his brown uniform. I was informed, I could go home.

My mother gave me a long speech. She said, I don't need a woman, who doesn't believe in me. Also, I needed to iron my clothes. There was the preliminary hearing, set at 9 a.m., the next morning.

"Why do you keep talking to her?" Mama said. "All she does is hurt you! All she does is hurt you!"

Thinking of what Mary was, sleep was nonexistent. It was, hardly, a buffer that night. I tossed and turned, what was left of it anyway.

The sun, rudely, announced itself. It was time, before I knew it. The sunbeams made me sick. It felt like a hungover. The thought of me, possibly, going to jail, made me lose oxygen. Bedridden, I decided to make myself busy. Boy, was I nervous. I was an apostle, who often delayed his prayers. I buzzed, with remorse.

My sister suggested, I wear the bandages to court. In order for the judge, to see what, I went through. Drika took pictures, of all the scratches on my face. Especially, for when I went to court.

I was certain, the judge, whoever it was, was going to be in cahoots, with the police. I was sure, they would not be hearing, my side of the story. The climate in the courtroom was very courteous, I must say. The judge presiding, was none other than Judge Robinson. My professor from VCU. He looked like he consumed too many calories. I wasn't sure, if he remembered me, from his class. Yet, there he was. The man with the clout.

"Damn," Judge Robinson looked, as though he wanted to say. "What the hell happened to you?"

I was feeling crafty. It looked like I had dealings with a cannibal or something. He set a court date, for a couple of months away. It gave me a chance, to retain a lawyer. I was going to need one. Mary was driving me nuts. She was always creating problems, for herself and I.

Like close-caption tv, I lowered my standards, with reputable law firms. They were expensive. Money was scarce. It all went to my apartment bills.

I applied for a correctional officer job. I felt I was overqualified. Walking around in someone's cold, unfriendly, prison wasn't exactly, the career move, I wanted to make. It wasn't what I was looking for, but nobody, seemingly, wanted to take a chance on me.

Besides, working for the Department of Corrections, had something to do with the law. Needless to say, I was worried about a conviction. It would have crippled my chances, in working in the field of law. I was facing a misdemeanor. My possible jail time carried up to a year. It would have put my life on hold. My pursuit of happiness would've been in a coma.

A privately-owned security company wanted to hire me, but that would've been eating crow. I wanted benefits. I wanted possible promotions. I had a job interview, at a juvenile correctional center. Evidently, they curveball my application in the trash.

I noticed an ad, in the newspaper. It was for Powhatan Correctional Center. They were having a coming-of-age job fair, during the weekend. I got, completely lost, trying to find it. Luckily, they were having interviews, at the prison, the following weekend as well.

Major Barksdale made it, abundantly clear, being a correctional officer wasn't for everyone. It was as though, he was saving us from a catastrophe, or making a mistake. I communicated as best I could. I told him about my college curriculum. It gave me a cavalry of knowledge, of the penal system. I told him Captain Green at Wackenhut didn't have any complaints either. I was on the cutting-edge. I was, absolutely, the last one, being interviewed that day.

Doing damage control, as usual, my mother paid for my legal fees. The lawyer, who was rented for $500, didn't see my case as much of a challenge.

It was a combination of things. I had so much on my mind. At the moment, I wasn't talking to Mary. I was missing, Toya, who was like a daughter to me. My lawyer assured Judge Robinson, my relationship with Mary was over. Robinson dropped the charges.

"Congratulations," said the lawyer, we hired to help. "Stay away from her."

I should've been chin-checked for considering it. I wanted to shuffle the deck, by giving Mary, another chance. She was, after all, a good-looking woman. Eventually, I could no longer contain myself. I got in deeper and deeper with her. My family was shocked. I told them, I forgave her, after the trial.

As far as my "deen" or religious life was concerned, there wasn't any. I was nothing more, more than a degenerate churchgoer. I became, what was known as a "Jummuah Muslim." That's a Muslim, who only shows up, for the weekly, Friday congregational prayer. I deluded myself, thinking I was a weak Muslim. I loved cars and women.

I wanted to show Mary, how "manly" I could be. I traded my slacks and sandals, for jeans and sneakers. I ditched the kufi, even though she seemed to like it. I was helping her, smoke her marijuana. I'd borrow a cigarette or two. I started cursing. I began drinking beer. It was, definitely, something the "Sunni" denomination was against. I was a classic case, not being myself.

Carolyn was still hanging around. She admitted Mary could use counseling. Especially, with all the depredation going on.

"I wish you would stop, acting so damn ghetto!" I said to Mary.

I had a desert thirst of resentment.

"You like this ghetto pussy!" drilled Mary.

She would say or do things, to even the score. It was as though, the world owed her. The details were hard to come by, as I watched her get drunk. Mary was a great, devoted mother. Yet, she would dump her frustrations on me. It was execution-style.

It was the atomic bomb, each time, she would hate on Drika. She assumed, my sister was telling me what to do. That was, totally, ludicrous. I felt miserable and misunderstood. I didn't know, what she expected from me. It was hard to digest. I had little idea, what a woman wanted in a man.

Carolyn, on the other hand, was great. She was easygoing. She'd always express diplomacy, whenever I was near. Never idle, she would continue to fix things, around the house. I wasn't the wiser.

Winning her affections, I would kiss and hold Mary's extremities, as much as I could. Particularly, when Carolyn wasn't around.

However, Mary would disband or pull away, from me, if Carolyn was near. That was like eggs, being thrown in my face. I knew something was still, probably, going on, between those two. I didn't have any facts. At my discretion, I would leave cassette tapes, books or electronic devices at her house. Letting my guard fall, the only time I didn't feel dislocated from her, was when we were together.

I got a phone call, from Powhatan Correctional Center. I got the job! Of course, I was saying farewell, to my position at NationsBank. I was so excited.

Being a correctional officer was a chance to prove myself. I didn't want to abuse my power. I wasn't the fault-finding type. I saw my employment as a distinguished endeavor, on my future resume. It was, presumingly, going to give me a lot of feedback.

A correctional officer was a good investment, I thought. So, I quickly enlisted for training. I wanted those, who didn't believe in me, or didn't give me a job, to be fertilizer. I was a John Dow. Yet, I had the eye of the tiger. I had the heart of a lion. I feared no man. I wanted to be in the trenches, working along side other officers. I felt blessed, to have my feet in the door. I was grateful, for the equal opportunity.

My dream of a filmmaker, getting a hold of one of my books, was put on hold. Mary was pressuring me, to make her my spouse.

Starting out, I was a a trainee. I couldn't wait, to try my hand, with the prison-issue firearms. I wanted to be like the rest of the guys, cool and casual with the inmates. The working hours were long and draining, et cetera. However, I was fixated on the bigger picture. I was using my prison guard experience as a stepping stone. It wasn't, exactly, rocket science or complicated. I didn't plan, to be there forever. I wanted bigger and better things. I became buddies, with a fellow trainee, Akinwande. His parents were from Africa.

Some of the inmates were flat-out rude. Others were getting on my nerves. Many were loud as an Hawaiian welcoming party.

"Martin, get a real job," some inmates, would sometimes say.

I didn't know, whatever that meant. It was great, learning how to use handcuffs. We were taught in the M-Building, which was the Segregation ward. The sergeants, lieutenants, and captains warned us. They warned us during our daily muster, and uniform inspection. Inmates, convicts or felons were not to be trusted. They taught us, the inmates were sure to take flight. It was our job, to keep them locked up.

There were so many grim faces. I let myself emphasize with the inmates. We all mistakes, I thought. I was a nice guy. The inmates would let me hear their problems, despite all the shouting.

In the cell-blocks, C-1 and C-2, holes were in the glass windows. Inmates threw trash on the floor, for the heck of it. Flies were everywhere. There were leafs of paperwork to do. The floor was sticky as glue.

The inmates at Powhatan would do foolhardy things, to get our attention. Their goal, seemingly, was to spew as much misery on us, as they could think of.

For much of my training, we covered a lot of ground, quickly. Sometimes, I'd be under a watchful eye of a veteran officer. They had brass keys, attached to their hips, which was a privilege. On our lunch break, the inmates piled on a hill of beans, and other items. The food was bland or not all that good. There was nowhere to hide. Supervisors called us trainees, here and there, to do menial tasks.

I learned early on, I was around a different caliber of people, than I was used to. There was a very thin line, between inmate and C.O. My coworkers, and the people, we were asked to watch over, cussed just as much. Every other word was the F-bomb. My coworkers didn't have any grace or tack. They acted just as "ghetto," if not more than the inmates. The radio, hitched to our sides, were blaring. I took pointers, on how to be a good C.O.

I often found myself, feeling lonely. I didn't fit in. Especially, with the White guys, who lived in the western, rural part of Virginia. I was given the grand tour, like anyone else. Apparently, they thought, I didn't have what it takes. Powhatan Correctional Center was an old prison. It was a hole in the wall, but I was determined, to do a great job.

The veteran officers told us, not to fraternize with the inmates. We most certainly, weren't to tell them, personal things about our lives. Yet, they didn't listen, to their own advice. However, I thought it was great, to be honest. The inmates were human beings, after all.

"I ain't scared," I would tell myself.

I began as Super-cop. I was ready, for anything and everything. It was refreshing, how the other officers were relaxed. Eventually, I let my hair down and relaxed too. Remarkably, the female C.O.'s would often grin in Akinwande's direction. It would give him something to hope for. He was a rookie, like me. He practically, had groupies, willing to let him have his way with them. Full of himself, he would tell me some of his guiltless pleasures, with our coworkers.

I, on the other hand, needed a hug. I realized, my coworkers were full of crap. They thought it was silly, I'd hang with a social misfit, dweeb, who I'll call Hunt. I refused to mock him, or make fun of him. Sure, he wasn't gallant. He had a hard time. Yet, he was trying. His hair was messy as unrehearsed church hymns. His breath smelled like garlic. However, he was a human being. He was our coworker. I gave him a hand, whenever I could. Helping people was my "calling."

There was a lot of standing around. We waited, for our next assignment. We were told, when we could go. Working in a prison, there was always something to do. We would get the ice, while the inmates were on lockdown.

Methodically, the trainees were like gazelles. We were ready to jump, at a moment's call. If we got into trouble, such as not knowing to do, an inmate always knew what was happening. I remained my mannered, polite self. I refused to change. That was more harmonious for me.

For a "bar-check," we would, spontaneously, go into the cells. We were checking the windows and bars, for possible escape attempts. Naked pictures of women were plastered everywhere in the cell. It left little to the imagination.

With the the extra cash coming in, I became immune to Mary's arguing and any self-doubts. Finally, I had a real job. It was a "manly" job. I wasn't making enough, to buy a Mercedes, but I was getting a taste of the limelight.

Wearing that prison guard uniform, made me feel proud. I felt important. I was doing something meaningful. A lot of people would've been nervous, to do what I was doing. Yet, I refused to be a jerk, with those convicted people.

Liposuction was out of the question. However, I did want to lose weight. Maybe, I wanted to impress Mary. I was scared to smoke a join, along with her. There was the possibility, random drug test. Meanwhile, I still had an absentee father.

To make thing, even juicier, Mary was pregnant. I couldn't be happier. I daydreamed of our baby, working for the justice system. Better yet, the military. In any case, I was certain, our baby was going to be beautiful. Beyond the incrustation of Mary's heart, she was a great mother. I wanted to keep, my end of the bargain. I wanted to be a great father.

Mary didn't want to know, the sex of the baby, until after it was born. So, I didn't know, if we were having a boy or a girl. He could be a perfect gentleman. She could be a pretty princess, for all I knew. I just wanted a healthy baby, regardless. I knew for certain, I didn't want to raise, a loudmouth, dishonest, dice-shooting, cop killer.

I wanted nothing more, a dear, sweet baby. I wanted to sing lullabies. I wanted an industrial son, or daughter, who had a knack for math.

However, I was hoping I'd have a son, who'd eventually, be a chick-magnet for all the young ladies.. If I had a son, I wanted to give him a glorious Muslim name. I was stuck on the Arabic name "Jibreel," after the archangel Gabriel.

At any rate, I tried to make the best of it. I'd tell my mother, the good news, who was practically, Mary's daughter-in-law at the time. I wanted to buy all sorts of things, for the expected baby. Yet, my money was, constantly, being inserted into envelopes. Due, largely, to bills. I was a maniac, for trying to make things work. My fatherly instincts kicked in, immediately. No kid of mine was going to be a laughing stock, if I could help it.

However, considering how Mary marched over my heart. My mother

BEHOLD

took the news, rather well. I intended, on being the best, damn father there was. I was willing to do, whatever it took, to stay on top.

Speaking of names, I wanted to give the baby my last name, Martin. Though I wasn't married, it wasn't important to me. I wanted to lace my child, with as much of my family as possible. Nothing was going to make me leave my child's side, I thought.

I was a matador for the name "Aaliyah," should she be a girl. I was a fan of the R&B singer, Aaliyah. Plus, the Muslims referred to me as "Ali." It made sense. Mary wasn't going for it. We decided, she would name the baby, if she was a girl. I'd name the boy.

Living a lie, my credit card was maxed out. I took Mary and Toya to see the Beloved movie. It was starring Oprah Winfrey and British actress, Thandie Newton. It was a great movie about a ghost, and the darkness of slavery.

"How about the name, Thandie, if it's a girl," said Mary, not letting up.

"That's cute," I said. "I like it.

Especially, after my infatuation of women, with British accents. I wanted to name our daughter after Aaliyah, like the Muslim women, who visited Makkah. Yet, it was a no-win situation.

I wasn't the type of guy, who ruled his woman, with an iron fist. I was clad in open-mindedness. I allowed Mary a license to be herself. It was a no-judgment zone. With, hardly, any melodrama, I wanted to spell "Thandie" as "Tande." It was a nod, after our beloved singer, Sade, which her name ended, as in "-de." The name "Sade" was a "No" too. I tried. Also, she was British, like the actor, Thandie Newton.

It felt like an Israeli without a home, to call his own. Things were, slowly, coming to light. Eventually, I wanted to move back into my own place.

Thankfully, Mary gave up the menthol cigarettes. It was a necessity, while she was carrying our child. Her pregnancy, by me, made it extra special was. I was the one, who finally, got her pregnant, 12 years after Toya. Her former lover, Carolyn, took care of her.

I, on the other hand, was always out. I was on the run, trying to make ends meet. I was like a bike messenger. I was overworked and underpaid.

## CORRECTIONAL OFFICER

Having a baby gave me a dose of reality. However, it was a feeling of "lucky me." Being a new father was like being on newly, discovered land. Yet, it was already founded land. I was nervous. I knew, I had to quickly, get over that. To put it mildly, fatherhood felt wonderful. It was nirvana. It was a sacred pact, I've always wanted. It was unconditional love, which was mine to give.

I was getting a better feel, on what it takes to be a correctional officer. Powhatan Correctional Center sent us trainees, on a week-long course, at Deep Meadows Correctional Center.

"Work smarter, not smarter," repeated the instructor.

It was in his monologue on work ethics. We were now, the proud, next generation of prison guards. I nearly, went pale, when I saw the assistant warden at DMCC. He happened to be, one of my former instructors at VCU. Somehow, my pride apprehended me. I didn't reveal to anyone, I graduated from college. Ironically, I was, slightly, embarrassed. Especially, since it didn't take a degree to work there. I'd avoid eye contact with him. I'd hope he didn't recognize me. Besides, I didn't want to appear any different, than I already was.

We spent long hours, in the trailer, for our training. Everyone prayed for an early dismissal. Being from different correctional institutions, we peeled out of that classroom, like a supernova. However, during class, the sergeant made it, abundantly, clear. It was paramount, to get the count of inmates, right. Also, we learned, how mobilize ourselves, in case of a fire. We learned, how to nurse first-aide. We were taught, the proper way, to carry a gun. I couldn't wait, to finally, hold one. I felt obligated, to pass my written tests, with flying colors.

"Whatever you do, do not open that gate!" said the instructor, in his monologue of a riot-situation. "I don't care, if it's the Warden, and they say, they're going to kill him!"

The class occupied us, with a patchwork of worse-case scenarios. It taught us work morale. We were to stay on the offensive. We were to never, be a pawn, in an inmate's game.

I was motivated. I was a new dog, being taught old tricks. I had a peculiar feeling, it was much easier said than done. I felt, being a correctional officer was my one shot, to get it right. For me, everything was pending on how well I did, in that prison. Yet, it gave me nerves of steel. It was like, I was in a municipal court, being judged and observed, on my every move. Working for the DOC was my opportunity of a lifetime. It could have open doors, for something else.

The cows moaned in a non-orderly, fashion. Periodically, I was reminded, the prison sat in a rural area. It was, namely, in a diary farm.

I didn't have a ring for Mary. She was too persistent. She snickered at me, as a man. She treated me as though, I was a "down-low" person or not "out of the closet." (Why would I waste my time)? Naturally, it made us have our arguments. I tried to dissuade her, as much as I could, but it was no use. She had this silly idea about me. Also, her attitude, more or less, "What have you done for me lately?"

It was the year 1999. Things were getting rampant. Mary was, physically, getting bigger. Ready or not, the baby was coming. Sometimes, I'd get a rare glimpse into her pregnancy. It was like a quick ear piercing, of what it was like for her, in early stages of motherhood.

It didn't matter to me, Mary was getting as big as a pincushion. The problem was Carolyn. She acted like her talent agent. She was always there. She was always around. She was always pitching in to help. Like the Nutty Professor, I didn't stand a chance. I didn't recant. I didn't complain. I didn't project anything, like I'd be a bad father.

I just, simply, wanted to Mary and I to conduct our own private affairs, without Carolyn around. The "midwife" act was getting old.

I had the propensity to do swell. Being a correctional officer made me feel redeemed. Especially, with White people waving at me. Usually, they would say "Hi," whenever, I was in my prison guard uniform. However, I knew full well, it was the clothes. if I wasn't in a police-looking uniform, they'd likely, clutch their pocketbooks, and wouldn't say a word.

I was plotting my steps at work. I would often see fellow Muslims praying. They'd stand rigid, reciting Quran, or prostrating to the floor, as usual. They had no idea, I was a believer too.

A non-smoking dorm pod, like D-8, had more Muslims than others. I allowed myself, to be unnoticed. I wanted to introduce myself to the brothers. I decided to wait. Besides, I hardly, prayed myself. I was like a someone, who only came inside, when it rained. I was nervous to tell the believers. Perhaps, they would only see me as "the police." Maybe, they would, publicly, scrutinize me. I didn't know.

Eventually, I relinquished my fears. I made nice, with some of the Muslims. Some of the them looked bloody mean. During one of my rendezvous as a C.O. I had a plan. I would volunteer, to post myself at the inmates' Friday congregational prayer, "Jumuah." Purposely, I too, wanted to listen in on the "khutbah" or sermon. Especially, since I was missing the prayer service myself, on the outside. Of course, I grew, exponentially, involved hearing the inmates' imam.

However, I was an officer in training. So, I kept my composure. I kept my distance. Needless to say, I didn't pray along side the inmates. I was supposed to be "watching them."

There's not enough postage stamps, to describe how humiliated I felt, with Mary. With her, I felt like a putz. She shot my self-esteem to hell. More importantly, I let her. My job treated me more seriously, than she did. It gave me the respect, I badly needed. Sure, I had reservations. Obviously, it wasn't working out between us. I wanted to meet someone else, but who?

I was only a paycheck away from poverty. Powhatan sent us trainees to Lunenburg Correctional Center. It was an hour and a half drive away. Apparently, we needed to work out the quirks. It was a two-week course we had to do. It was on a fairly new, big, respectable place. It was the preamble of things, yet to come.

After the grand tour of the prison, the trainees were, practically, ushered to the administration building for classes. Obviously, Lunenburg had female inmates working there, from a woman's prison. They were cleaning administration offices and their bathrooms. My coworkers, simply, nodded and wave. I too, nodded and wave.

I could no longer contain myself. I did the most unpredictable thing. There was a female inmate, I had my eyes on. She was a beautiful, Black woman. She was a quiet as a rabbit. We kept making eye contact at each other. Everything I learned about "not fraternizing with the inmates" went into reverse. It was well-known, officers doing so, could get fired. It wasn't rubbish. Yet, every time I looked at her, my heart would beat against my rib cage.

Every night, I had dreams about her. She was no ordinary R&B chick. How could something so wrong, feel so right? Everyday at work, the woman, apparently, from New York would select me with her eyes. The staff, who worked there had no idea. I dared not, tell anything to anyone. I feared, they would send me up the river, packing. She was am inmate, sure. She could have sold her body, to the highest bidder, for all I knew. I didn't care. My feelings had one thing, lead to another. With a snowball effect, I rolled out a small piece of paper.

Dropping to the floor, it had my name, address and phone number on it. Quickly, she put it away. I had desires of giving her a normal life. I wanted to take her to soft ball games. I wanted to give her roses. I wanted to serve her the love, she never had. I wanted to be someone, she always wanted.

My mind roved around, from place to place. Meanwhile, the sergeant at Lunenburg taught us this and that. Among other things, he taught us about the misconceptions of inmates. We applied CPR tactics.

"These people will switch on their mother, if it will give them less jail time," he said.

He was dissolving the snitching rumor, inmates don't tell.

"Don't lie. Be a man of your word. Always be the same," he would also tell us.

The relationship between an officer and an inmate is hard to sew up, once the trust has been broken. I imagined a world of soulless human beings. Eventually, I was going to be in charge of them. As a rule, I was taught, inmates feel no shame. We were taught to be "firm but fair." We were taught, how to write infractions or "charges." It was like a spanking, which could make their lives miserable.

Running his mouth further, the instructor would tell us self-righteousness things. Coming out of his shell, he'd forget about the speck, which was, probably, in his own eye. It was a lot of sanctimonious crap. It was too shocking for words, some of the things inmates do. Spilling the beans, the sergeant warned us about, all the homosexuality, which goes on in prison.

We worked on a salmon-colored dummy man, for CPR training. We were taught, the things we should or shouldn't do. I think, us trainees, did splendid. We were like children in a sandbox. We were shushing each other, for a chance in the spotlight. The food they served us, was great, by the way. Satire was always in sight. It forced me, to have a little spunk about myself.

Tipping the scale in my favor, my "girlfriend" from work called me, when I got home. It was like a careful game of Simon Says. Especially, since DOC could have easily traced the call, I thought. Just by taking to her, I was putting my job on the table. Every evening, the inmate would phone me, right on schedule. She allowed me to sip, from the wine of infidelity.

It wasn't like, I had a stampede of women, chasing after me. I did what, I felt I had to do. I wanted to feel appreciated. Even if, I had to search for love, on my personal computer. With that being said, I became an avid internet user. I wasn't keeping score, but with my screen name as "Playa Playaa." Clearly, the women seem to like "bad boys." Not the shy, quiet type. I met plenty of women, online. They'd tell me, what was under their skimpy clothes. It left little to the imagination. I was a "rock star." On the computer, that is. I wanted my steak, and eat it too.

My slogan must've been, "What you got on?" Not to stereotype, but White women were, categorically, more open or freakier. Yet, I didn't want someone narrow or small-minded. I was looking for someone, who could, mentally, stimulate me.

I wasn't made out of stone. However, I had the task of letting the female inmate go. It was too close, for comfort. In a sick, twisted way, I was in charge of her. Being that I was a DOC employee, it was insane. So, after a few weeks, I closed the door on our relationship. I never opened it again. I was the trap, and she was the bait.

The academy, for the correctional officers, was just as straightforward. For four weeks, we were endured with military-style training. I absolutely, loved the marching.

"Your left! Your left! Your left, right, left!" demanded the drill instructor, while we were in the ranks, for every step we take.

I was apart of Company 1-A. We had a reputation to protect. It could also be stressful at times. Yet, it was important to be a team. I tried my best. I did my part.

"Left face! Right face! About face!" barked the drill instructor, in which direction to stroll.

There were also, tender moments too, as we trucked into the chow hall, for our lunch break. At Lunenburg Correctional Center, it was great stumbling upon nicely, prepared food.

"Left flank! Right flank!" barked the drill instructor, during our exhibition practice steps.

On home territory, I would tell my mama, how much I enjoyed the marching. I was starting to believe in myself. I was becoming the little tugboat that could. "I think I can..I think I can."

The subjects at the correctional academy were more, physically, demanding. Thankfully, the teachers' attitude was, "Just do the best you can do."

All the cadets would take turns. For example, we'd all get a total experience, with the stun guns. It was in that moment, my heart, nearly, reached my throat. It was like being bound in twine. I didn't have a choice. I wasn't going anywhere.

It was, seemingly, torture being stunned, with electric riot shields. Also, we were stunned on the flesh, with stun guns. It hurt, like you wouldn't believe. The point was to put us all in the same boat with the inmates. The captains wanted us, to somehow, feel what inmates go through. In the event, if there was a riot.

As though that wasn't enough, we were chocking on tear gas. My heart thumped. The instructors would pepper spray, near our eyes, at the gun range. Actually, we had the task of walking through the tear gas. I needed all the support I could get. My eyes were shut tight. I was bending over in agony. Quickly, I surrendered, under a tin, water faucet. Being bombarded with tear gas, took its toll. My stomach felt like it was going to explode, with all the coughing. There were swatches of spit and snot.

I toasted with anxiety. I was under a time watch. The instructors took value, in teaching us how to lock, load and fire .45 revolvers. We were taught how to, properly, use M-15's. We learned about buckshot shotguns. We were assimilated snipers, from atop a high rise. We had to "shoot at targets" below. We were given this enormous opportunity. I was proud, I was a prison guard.

"Halt!" I would say, syncing my aim.

POW! POW! The bullets would torpedo into nothingness.

Letting lose, everyone was trying to keep up. We learned self-defense tactics. We learned proper exercise. It was part of the tour. In the grand scheme of things, we had to do it. We were to meet force, with equal force. We had to learn how to, quickly, use restraint, if being under attack.

Can I run a mile? That was the question. From the starting point, I had to run a mile, in order to graduate from the academy. It was the final trademark, of all who went there. It was a required test, to show we were physically fit.

"Just do your best," dangled the instructor, with our reality.

In order to run, I had to transfer myself. I had to reach, into the depths of my very soul. It was an unwritten policy of mine, to never quit. So, I didn't. Unfortunately, the academy no longer allowed families at the graduation, at the time.

It was like a shot in the arm. It was important, I get my own place again, before the baby was born. Wholeheartedly, I wanted my child to know, I was an independent man. I went the usual route, to look for an apartment.

I landed at Seven Gables, formerly known as Jarrett. It was, merely, a willow tree distance away from my mother's house. The rent was $450, a wop, with two bedrooms. It had a washer and dryer. I was sold. It was a sale, I couldn't refuse. Also, I excited the place was close to my mama's house.

Yet, I had conflicting emotions. I didn't want to, necessarily, live alone. I knew it was something, which needed to be done. I still had my wits about me. The central air conditioning, in my new apartment, was beautiful. The air blowing through the vents, gave me goosebumps. I didn't have many words, with my neighbors. Just an occasional, friendly wave, nod or smile.

However, I did my best, to make things worthwhile with Mary. She was a bull in a china shop. Still, I viewed her as the mother of my child. I forgave all the wrong she done. I wanted to move along.

I was a state employee. As a new employee, I was given the "creepy hours." I worked from midnight to 8 o'clock in the morning. It was a slow way to earn money, but it paid the bills.

"I don't like it," many of us would complain.

The prison was quiet as a mouse, by the time, I was on duty. The "villains" would be in their cells. They would be in their rack, sound asleep. I was a guppie, surrounded by sharks. Before I was a correctional officer, I lived in a bubble. I wasn't from the streets. I lived a sheltered life. Somehow, my supervisors, seemingly, had a vote of confidence in me.

Occasionally, I'd drink coffee, while fighting to stay awake. I nearly, wore a hole in the bottom of my shoes. Many routine rounds, from all the walking up and down the aisle. The sergeants, lieutenants and captains would be in the Watch Commander's office. Often, they'd be laughing, or telling dirty jokes.

Regardless of Mary, I couldn't be, but so "on the low," as she treated me. I was working with convicted murderers, rapists, robbers, thieves and liars. I worked along side, drug dealers and drug users. I started to develop a cocky, westernized attitude. Whimpering wasn't allowed.

May 2, 1999 was a day I'll never forget. I was tired as hell. I just got off of work. I noticed a phone call on the caller ID. It was from Chippenham Hospital.

Mary just gave birth to our baby girl. It was one of the best days of my life. Kandi was so beautiful. She was better than any architectural design, man could come up with.

I was proud. I had a biological daughter of my very own. Dreeka and my mother hopped aboard in the car. We were on our way to the hospital. Mel was at work, at Capital One.

"I don't like your sister," Mary would say, without a just cause.

Needless to say, my new daughter was important to me. I wanted

Dreeka be there, to welcome her niece to the world. Every dime I made went to my apartment. I had to pay the bills. I was broke, as usual. I didn't want to be blackballed. Certainly, I didn't want to be seen as a father, who didn't care. I didn't want to walk in the hospital room, empty-handed. I bought. So, I bought a small pot of flowers, out of the hospital gift shop. I was all I could afford. I was absorbed, into my heart, and my soul of emotions.

Dreeka was the one, who actually, bought Kandi a balloon. My mother, incidentally, didn't have any money either.

I was in awe, seeing my daughter, for the first time. I was blinded with love. Quickly, claiming her, I put Kandi in my arms. Everyone assisted me.

"As-Salaamu alaikum," I whispered in Kandi's ear.

Kandi was so cute. With Mary having the toll of just giving birth, we decided not to stay long in the hospital. Her body needed rest. My daughter was following her lead. The hospital was willing to release them, in a couple of days.

I was happy as can be. I was also hungry. We got Toya some food from Mc Donalds. Thanks to Dreeka. I was a proud father. I was ready. I couldn't wait, to change my daughter's boo-boo for the first time.

Behind closed doors, my family advised me, to get a DNA, blood test on Kandi and I. Automatically, I got defensive.

"I trust Mary," I said.

I won't bore you, with the details. Eventually, I agreed confirmation was better than uncertainty. The next afternoon, I went to Chippenham Hospital. Everyone was awoke. Mary was eating out of a bowl.

"You got a strong daddy, Kandi," Mary said.

It was pointless to resist. I had to pick up my daughter up. Carefully, I held her back. I made up my mind, I wouldn't use corporal punishment on her. I wouldn't spank her. That idea was alien to me. Especially, after the physical abuse, I went through, with my father.

I wanted to go to the highest balcony. I wanted a gentle breeze. I wanted the lowest valley. I wanted to shout my daughter's name.

I put my bills on hold. I took money, out of my checking account, and found a baby store. Ambitiously, I got things I needed. The hospital passed the baton to me, sort of speak. By law, they said, I needed to get a car-seat. So, they could release Mary from the hospital.

Like a bat out of hell, we finally, left Chippenham Hospital. Carolyn was like a guardian angel. As usual, she wasn't too far behind. Against my better judgement, I was like a teddy bear, dipped in soy sauce. I had the pleasure, or burden, of being with Mary. She often brought out the worst in me. She thought the worst of me. Yet, I was trying to make things work, for the sake of our newborn daughter.

Almost anonymously, Carolyn would beetle her way near. She wanted to make sure, Mary was comfortable. With a sweated brow, and busty, she was the family friend. Kandi was sweet as syrup. Bells seem to ring, whenever I was around the baby.

"I'm your daddy," I would say to her.

I'd search Kandi's eyes for approval. It was a very special time. Mary and I figured out, child support, without court involvement. I'd give her $75 every two weeks, whenever I got paid. If I could describe my my time with Mary. It was like a biscuit, which came with gravy. Good, but sloppy.

I canned some of my earned vacation time. I drove Mary, Kandi and Toya to South Carolina. I wanted them to meet my family. Everyone knew my daughter's mother had a temper. I felt bygones should be bygones. Especially, with our baby involved. What kind of critter would I be, if I didn't abide my heart?

Gathering our collectibles, we stayed at a nearby La Quinta hotel. I felt it was crucial, I bring my new made-family to a nice hotel. I wanted us to have fun. I wanted a carnival atmosphere. I was bursting with excitement, on the thought of Kandi, meeting my grandparents. Toya could have all the chocolate fudge, she wanted. I wanted to spoil her too.

I didn't have much cash, as usual. However, I tried to be as commendable as I possibly, could. I didn't use curse words, around the children. I'd catch myself, being protective of my little, compact family. At the time, we weren't married. Yet, I wanted my clones of myself. I was Muslim. Yet, I dared to be compliant.

We were having a dandy ol' time. Soon, I took the girls to my maternal side of the family. Ceremoniously, I gave my grandma, my daughter to hold. Kandi was, merely, three months old. Conceptually, my grandma was blind, due to glaucoma. She couldn't remember day-to-day, thanks to Alzheimer's disease. However, it was important to me, she be around "my family."

Mary, on the other hand, preferred to sit by herself. A bunch of people, from my mother's side of the family, was there. My aunt North, with cousin Nikki. There was my uncle Reggie, with his wife. My aunt Cedel. My cousin Cissy. They were all trying to decide, the plan for that day. Especially, on when, how long, and what time to pick up the kids, from the swimming pool.

Somehow, Mary conjectured, as usual, she was out of place. She sulked in my car, as though she ran out of cheddar. Her patience was wearing thin. After all was said and done, I couldn't understand why.

"Maybe, you should be with your girl,"Cedel said to me.

To cool things off, I took Mary to my paternal side of the family. Obviously, she didn't like my sister. Dreeka tagged along anyhow. We had an united front. Yet, I didn't want my child's mother to defeat my sense of purpose in South Carolina. I wanted us to be a family.

"Don't bring your Richmond ghetto shit down here!" I told Mary.

I was letting her know, how childish she was acting. In the middle of my grandparents' driveway, my sister and Dreeka got into a heated argument. Mary wasn't content with that. Later, she stormed in our grandparents' house after us, to continue.

"If y'all got something to say, say it to my face!" Mary said, with tears streaking down her face.

I nearly, flopped to the floor, I was so embarrassed. It was the most unconventional way to have an argument. I thought of my poor grandparents. They didn't suffer from dementia. However, I felt they were accessible to a heart attack.

Mary would point to my father's picture, in his police uniform.

"That's your grandfather, Kandi! That's your grandfather," she enunciated, when she was on better speaking terms.

I'd hated to admit it. I was proud, my father wasn't an ordinary civilian.

Though we haven't corresponded to each other, in years, at that point. I was living in my father's shadows. However, I was glad, I was deputized as a correctional officer. It struck a cord in me. I'd often wonder, if my father and I would ever encounter each other, ever again. I desired a relationship with him. Even if it meant, putting our hatchets away. I wanted to, for the sake of my child.

I was smothered in bad memories. I was determined, not to give Kandi the same, crummy relationship I had, with my father. My mother, as it turns out, was my number one supporter. I gave her credit. She was always there for me.

At our hotel, Mary said, I let my family "dictate" me. Other words, telling me what to do. Of course, it wasn't true. No one was "telling me what to do." I don't mind sound advice, or opinion. She was behaving as eclectic as ever. It was supposed to be our summer vacation. She was ruining it.

"I don't know about us," Mary said to me. "You ain't man enough for me."

It was yet, another stab at my manhood, coming from her. My eyeballs dilated in disbelief. I couldn't believe the words, I was hearing. Naturally, I became upset. She then picked up the clothing iron, threateningly. As though she was going to strike me with it.

"Hit me!" I dared Mary. "Hit me!"

I was in her face, giving her the opportunity, to hit me with the iron. I was tired of her wild antics. I was tired of Mary, hinting I had "gay tendencies." I was fed up, with her treating me, as though I was less than a man. I was ready for war. I was ready to protect myself. To think, this was the woman, who gave me a child, a couple of months ago.

Supposedly, seeing the flame in my eyes, Mary eventually, put the iron down. She dissed me further. She also implied, I was nothing. She attacked me, with her sharp claws. She scratched my chest again. Like an elephant, it was something, I'll never forget.

I remembered to block my face. Unlike the first altercation Mary and I got in. I smacked her, in self-defense. It wasn't something I was proud of.

"I'm calling the police," Mary said.

She reached for the hotel's phone. Quickly, I unplugged the telephone. I was thick as a cucumber. I wrestled her body to the bed. I felt obliged, to somehow calm her down.

"I'm sorry, Mary. I'm sorry," I said, sweeping her off her feet.

Putting it another way, I catered to Mary's insecurities. Especially, during other family festivities. It was a distorted relationship, en route to nowhere. Fifty percent of the time, Mary was indecisive, whether I was a man or a mouse. Undoubtedly, it was mentally abusive. What we had, was anything, but environmental friendly.

Finally, I went my cousin Baby's house. He had pit bulldogs chained to old car equipment, in the backyard. Apparently, he was a firm believer, at the end of the day, drinking a nice, cold beer. Who was I, to criticize?

I decided to drink some too. With my cousin around, I gave myself permission to drink myself flat. Mary was a party pooper, if I ever saw one. She would always flip things around. She was often paranoid, as though we were talking about her.

South Carolina was worth the drive, after all. Besides the drama queen, things were excellent. Antonio met us at the La Quinta hotel, where we were staying. My father fathered him, before I was born. We didn't grow up together, but we were family. Suddenly, my blues went away. There was, hardly, a dry eye in the place. My brother and I hugged each other. We got to know each other again.

"We need to promise to always stay in touch," Antonio exerted.

I couldn't agree more. Also, I was embarrassed. I was probably, fatter than he remembered. It didn't matter, Antonio once had a drug habit. He spent time in jail. Child support was expensive. I was glad to see him. With his foot in the door, he lended me his ear. I filled him in, on what I was doing, for the last few years. Surprisingly, Mary didn't have a temper. Looking at my brother was like looking in the mirror. We had the same forehead. We shared the same skin complexion.

Antonio agreed to meet with us, the day before, we leave for Richmond. We formed a bond. A grade higher anyhow. We hoarded food at IHOP.

Not long afterwards, Mary said she was pregnant, again. She was looking foxy as ever.

"Already?" Toya said, trying to grapple with the idea.

I put everything on hold. I applauded her with emotional support. I was willing to kiss, every freckle, on Mary's body. I treated her like Greek mythology. When everyone, finally, cleared the room, I got on one blended-knee. Honorably, I kissed Mary's stomach. I was welcoming my second child. The friction was then fiction. It was gone. The meat gristle she, usually, gave me to chew on was over, as far as I was concerned.

I told my family the good news. With another baby on the way, they were horrified. They were frustrated for me. They thought it was going to be hard, to take care of two kids, on a prison guard's salary. Children were cute creatures. However, they required lots of money. They needed plenty of grub. Yet, I reassured my family, not to worry. "Everything was going to be alright."

With joint-custody of Kandi, I'd visit her on my days off. I'd take her to my mother's house. Mary was sure to lose her hourglass figure, but it didn't matter to me.

One night, when I took Kandi home, to her mother's house, I found myself in a misunderstanding. From the look on my face, Mary somehow thought, my family was unhappy, about her pregnancy. Simply put, I was merely contemplating on the future newborn. I just wanted a healthy human being.

Like a fortune teller, Mary was always trying to read something, which wasn't there. As a result, she would be hurtful and panic-stricken. I spent half the night explaining, "It's not like that." I mentioned, it was just so "sudden" and so "soon," that's all. I knew how fragile Mary's relationship was with my family. I told her, I had her back, no matter.

I was hyped up for work. However, I'd often my mama for gas money. Lieutenant Barnett placed me anywhere handy. The inmates were crafty at making me comfortable. I didn't believe in being rude, to get my point across. In my experience, the White inmates would often strike up a conversation. They treated me like gold. Yet, the Black inmates, for the most part, harbored me as a traitor to the Black race.

I was, certainly, no night owl. It has hard, trying to stay up, all night. The lieutenant had a genius move, to check up on us. in the middle of the night, he would flash his high-beamer lights at us, working the towers. The officer, working the tower, would have to show his alertness, by flashing his flashlight back at him. Naturally, I dozed off. I was in a harvest of reprimands.

"The tower is our last line of defense," Barnett said about my security breach.

It was intimidating, I could lose my job, over that. Graciously, the prison warden gave me a three-day suspension, without pay. He could've fired me. I considered myself "lucky."

I was impartial. I met a woman named Johnson. She was a fellow coworker. We became good friends at work. We'd call each other on the prison's landline, throughout the night. Others saw her as a crazy, country girl. I saw her with a good heart.

Several times, she would meet me, at my place. We'd heal each other's wounds. We'd often complain, about our probable "significant other." I would, slyly, tell Johnson, I cared about her. We had no strings attached.

It reminded me, when I had a small fling with Lambert, when I was a security officer at NationsBank. It wasn't worth the ink, to write home about.

Gerry decided, he'll be godfather to Kandi, should something happen to me. Every now and then, him and his brother Cal, would come out of hiding and seek me.

However, it was incompatible at times. Gerry would Bible-quote at me. It wasn't like me, to argue my truth. I didn't want to debate. Obviously, he thought Muslims were nothing more, than political goons, who traditionally, stood on their hind legs, five times a day. The arguments we had, about religion, didn't help. It didn't get us anywhere or understanding.

"It seems to me, they're just following tradition," said Gerry, after I took him to visit Masjidullah, during prayer.

Discreetly, I'd often take Mary to my apartment. I never gave her a key. As loony as it may sound, I wanted to spend some quality time with her. Especially, with more of my children on the way. We were like lovebirds, in the middle of a flame. She knitted my clothes. She fixed me lunch. She inherited my children. Meanwhile, my Quran collected dust, while I thought of myself as a love machine.

"You act like a woman," Mary projected to me.

Once again, she was projecting her own sexual insecurities on me. Has she forgotten, when I met her, she was in an affair, with another woman? I was stunned.

Obviously, it was said, to get me upset. It worked too. It was yet, another disrespectful thing, coming from her. I didn't lack integrity. Our baby, Kandi was in my arms. I stormed out of my living room. I walked away. I didn't want her in my sight. I didn't want to be near her. To make matters worse, Mary started to, physically, attack me. I was inside my hallway. I was holding the baby. I put our child down on the floor. She was crying. I was getting my attacker off of me.

Mary headed for my back door. I grabbed the back of her shirt, ripping it.

"Where are you going? You've got a baby here!" I said.

"You keep her! My baby at home," Mary said, referring to her oldest daughter, Toya.

Pregnant, and starting to show, Mary slipped and fell. I played no instrumental role, in her downfall. It all happened so fast. A lasso wouldn't have caught her.

"Help! Someone call the police," Mary said, in hopes of a neighbor would hear her, through my apartment's thin walls.

When she got on her feet, she had a smirk on her face. I was about to get in trouble.

"Okay," said another lady, reassuringly, on the top floor above me.

Not again, I thought. Mary had every intention, on getting me locked up. I feared for my new career. It meant so much to me. I had a responsibility to uphold.

"Officer, he's a correctional officer! His gun is in the bedroom," warned Mary, to the responding police officer.

"Where's the gun?" he asked, intermingling into our affairs.

I didn't want him mislead, than he already, probably, was. I told him, our prison issued weapons were kept at work, which was true. However, I really did have my own personal gun. My gray .9mm handgun was a

Smith and Weston. It was hid near my bed.

Marijuana wasn't around or alcohol. I didn't know why, the sudden statement or outburst from Mary. I was an introvert, who decided, to come out of his shell. I loved women. I adored women. I didn't act like a woman. I wasn't gay. Nor did I want to be.

I tried to explain to the cop. I wasn't the type of guy, to muscle my will on women. I didn't believe in hitting women. Especially, if she said something, I disagreed with. I watched my father, who was physically abusive with my mother. I didn't want to be, anything, like that. Yet, there I was, explaining myself, again. I wasn't hitting her. She attacked me. I was leery. I was mucked in frustration.

Mary saw my situation hanging in a balance. It was, totally, invigorating for her. She wasn't the least bit lenient or cared. My life was a cookie, crumbling apart. After all, she was a materialistic girl, in a materialistic world. I was never in jail, or a compromising position, until I met her.

I told the arresting officer, "She hit me first." However, when he looked at her torn shirt, somehow, my story became irrelevant. I was in a pair of "lucky" Levi's jeans. I was amazed. The police officer believed Mary's lies. It was as though, he was about to receive The Medal of Honor. Apparently, he thought, he was doing something for the greater good.

Once again, I was in a pair of handcuffs. I was in police custody. I was heading to the jungle. A lightbulb came on in my head. "If you're Black, you're assumed guilty." I was sure to be prosecuted. A melody of hit songs were being played on the police car's radio.

I was a little jittery. Yet, I knew not to get out of line. Silently, I prayed to Allah. I asked for His Mercy. I asked for tranquility.

After a list of formalities, such as having my pictures taken, and fingerprints with the jail, I made my "one phone call."

"Mama, I'm in jail," I said.

I was, yet again, in a familiar metamorphosis of sorrow. My mother sounded like she wanted to jump through the phone. I was loaded with remorse. I waited for her, in a cell, to be bailed out. I was in a microcosm of criminals. Screams and yells were off the meter. I jutted myself to sleep. I was trying to drown out the unnecessary noise. I searched for any logic

I could find. Meanwhile, Mary threw me away like spoiled milk, and was safe at home.

I kept my contact with Mary, at a bare minimum. We made contact with each other, less as possible. We had a new perspective, what we were.

My visitation was like clockwork. On every other day, on my days off, I would pick up Kandi, from her mother's house. She allowed me to pass as the child's father. Mary would leave our daughter, in a child seat, on the floor, without us facing each other.

It was indescribable. Mary would, actually, be in another room, as though she didn't trust me, not to hit her. She was the one, physically abusive to me. Not the other way around. I was harmless as a neutered dog. Sadly, it was the path that was laid out before me.

Make no mistake about it. Mary and I went on like this, for months. She blamed me. I blamed her. It was the most obscure thing, I ever had to go through.

It was "payday" going to court. It felt like a lynching. Everyone in the courtroom spoke in a quieter voice. It was a lower octave than usual.

I hired the same law firm, which represented me, the year before. Especially, since I was again attacked, by the same person. Being petty, Mary and I were, really, at odds with each other.

I was, more than willing, to take a polygraph test. Yet, I knew it would be inadmissible in court. "She started it." In light of things, that was what, I wanted to prove. My lawyer informed the court, I was an officer, for the state pen.

The commonwealth prosecutor, as well as Mary, painted me as a monster, who assaulted a pregnant woman. No one seemed to care, initially, she was hitting me. I was getting her off of me. Yet, she was carrying my unborn child. Lies were hard at work.

"Just perfect," I thought. "They're going to throw the book at me."

I was mortified. I wished I invested in savings bonds. My lawyer doodled something down on paper. The judge reached his decision. I perked up, despite the amount of opportunities, I didn't want to lose. Personally, I wanted to get it over with. I was tired of my name being dragged through the mud.

"I find the defendant guilty," the judge said, ordinarily. "With twelve months suspended, pending he stays out of trouble for a year."

It was pretty nice, not going to jail. I was coated with relief. I was smelling the musk of freedom. Like orthopedic shoes, I promised myself to straighten up. I wanted to fly right. In that moment, Mary was phlegm, as far as I was concerned. I thought, I never wanted to be involved with her again.

"Also," said the judge, being problematic. "I'm ordering him to Anger Management class."

"My, my," I thought.

I didn't think, I had an anger problem. I thought, it was outrageous. I had a bone to pick, with the judge. However, I wiped the nape of my neck, and learned the class was something, I had to accept. Besides, being frustrated gets you nowhere.

Without a woman's touch, my apartment was a pigpen. Whenever I wasn't working at the prison, I was trying to get much needed sleep. I'd often hear my neighbors, from above, carrying on. I had needs too. I'd wonder what, voluptuous Mary was up to. It was pitiful. The more I felt, she would've got on my nerves, the more I wanted her in my apartment.

I was planting my feet even deeper. My purpose, pay Mary, our agreed upon child support, and leave. Our relationship was appalling, at best. I thought, at the time, she wasn't exactly Playmate of the Year, but she was the mother of my children.

All the same, our eyes met. Before I knew it, we were doing this and that. I couldn't believe, I was being with her again. It was like something out a paperback, romance novel, without the romance. Being stupid was second to none. However, it was great, not having to wait, necessarily, on the porch anymore. The last thing I wanted, being disrespected and being disappointed. I didn't want to take anymore crap either. Like a politician, I wanted to get along.

I couldn't wait to buy Kandi ponies, when she got older. I wanted to place a quarter, under her pillow, when she lost a tooth. The same way, the tooth fairy did me. I wanted to get ride of life's nasty, little rumors. I wanted to rid the world of bad people, and whatever evil things it had to offer. I merely, wanted the best for her.

*SEASON 13, EPISODE 14*

# Misunderstood

NOT THAT IT was important, I was supposed to be watching the area, from the prison watchtower. I fell asleep again, like a slab of wet cement. It was another quid pro quo situation. Again, my supervisors wanted to ring my neck. They gave me five suspended "days on the street," without pay. I was grateful, I had a post to come back to. They have me a script, and I was sticking to it.

It was year, 2000. There was so many theories, about unknown possibilities. Such as banks accounts, deleting funds, or defaults to zero. Despite the "Y2K scare," 2000 came in, like a racehorse. I roared with excitement. The power was still on. Houses were still in order. It was an exciting time. It was like going from rags to riches. I was having the time of my life. That evening I spent a moment with Mary. I was searching for romance, regardless of our peculiar arrangement. Being with her, seemed the only time, she wasn't a Rottweiler, hurting my feelings.

At any rate, I'd rub Mary's stomach. I was in anticipation of our new arrival. It would been, utterly, preposterous, to think I wasn't ready, or didn't want the baby. My fatherhood wits was razor sharp.

"Look, mommy!" Toya said.

On a whim, I surprised my ladies with a poster of Paris, France. It was a delightful picture of the Eiffel Tower. In the realm of things, it was a perfectly, pink sky, which glorified the way the Paris is. However, it was a poster I bought, years prior. I thought it better to share the picture of Paris. Rather that, than have it collect dust, in the corner of the house somewhere.

"I want to name it Paris, if it's a girl," Mary said.

I gave a nod of consent. Never in recent history, have I heard of anything, more appropriate. I couldn't agree on a more prettier name. "Paris" felt safe. It felt nice.

Kandi, however, kept us busier than a firecracker. She was a priority. I wanted to record, every cute moment.

I gave my salutations to the world. I was in the process of being a father of two. I looked at the universe, through rose-colored lenses. A superstitious person would've knocked on wood. I was proud. There was nothing wrong with my manhood. I had Kandi. I had another baby coming. It was back to back.

I refused to throw in the towel, regarding my job. To me, I was in the business of protecting lives. I made so many hospital runs. I'd be in the back of an ambulance, escorting an inmate. I've seen plenty of guys in prison, having seizures. They'd drop, helplessly, to the floor. I'd elevate their heads, while calling for a nurse.

There were plenty of fire drills. Once, I had to had to help evacuate a cell block. Apparently, someone set a person's cell on fire. The prison population was, predominantly, Black. I rejoiced at the chance to help someone. What a scandalous way to be, right?

Whether it was a boy or girl, I wanted them to know my truth. I planned to teach my children about Islam. Not in a deliberate, forceful or intrusive manner, but if they had any questions, I was more than willing to answer. I wasn't perfect. However, I wanted to be the best example, I could possibly be.

I was going to make it my earnest, to see to it, that my kids get a scholarship. I wanted to protect my children, at all cost. I wanted to teach them, about the beauty of the Orient, or East Asia. I wanted to show them, the scoundrel lie of racism.

I didn't want them to be prudes or superficial. Yet, I wanted them to believe in themselves. Sure, as an author, I wanted to write scrolls, and have them published for people to enjoy. I wanted my children to be President someday. I had every reason to believe, I'd always be there for them.

I wanted to be punctual in their lives. I wanted to take responsibility.

BEHOLD

For my children, I wanted to take the edge off of life. I wanted them to go out into the world, in the pursuit of happiness. With the thought of two babies, I retook my life, more seriously. I was a self-aware person, awaiting the birth of his second child.

It was like standing at the bottom, looking to the top of an ancient pyramid. I had the enormous feeling, something great, yet to come. Another innocent child coming was reviving my spirits. However, I was somewhat sad. I wasn't married to their mother. I wanted to spend time with my children.

It was April 15$^{th}$. Also known as Tax Day, some would say. I wasn't available at the time of my daughter's birth. Unbeknownst to me, while I was at work. I wasn't there again, much like I was with Kandi. That left a sour taste in my mouth.

Her name was Paris. The baby's birth was a success. I was all set to go to Chippenham hospital. Mel was work himself. Drika didn't want to go, for obvious reasons. Mary didn't like her. So, my mother and I, alone, went. We welcomed my second child to the world.

I couldn't wait to see the sparkles in Paris' eyes. Suffering the fact, I didn't have any money, my mother and I went straight to Mary's hospital room. I couldn't afford, a ballon or anything, from the gift shop, at the time.

Paris was so beautiful. Seeing her, I wanted to shack up with her mother. Our baby was a spectacle for all to see. It made me feel stupendous. I felt fruitful inside. She was in wonderful shape. Carefully, I picked her up, as though she was spineless or frail.

Disconcerting, Paris didn't cry, like her sister, Kandi, did. She was motionless. She was suppressed, lethargic. I wished I had a bottle of something, to celebrate with. I tried to hide my fears, I thought something was, terribly, wrong with the baby. I sputtered, on the outside, with pride. Yet, I was panicked, on the inside. I wondered, was I the only one, who noticed it.

Carolyn, of course, was there. For moral support, I suppose. Kandi was hopping around. Toya's smile spread from ear to ear. Mary was under the hospital sheets, like it was it was no sweat off her brow. We were a small band of happy folks.

I wanted to showcase Paris, to the world. I wanted to lift her to the heavens, like I did Kandi.

"Behold, Paris, the only thing greater than yourself."

On the way home, from the hospital, my mother noticed how quiet I was. It was as though something was bothering me.

"What's wrong, Marco?" she said to me.

I wanted to squash it, but Paris' grandmother, finally, swiveled it out of me.

"I think something's wrong with Paris," I admitted. "She just laid there."

Paris was beautiful. She was sleek as any Siamese cat. However, she was stiff as stage fright.

"Yes, I noticed it," my mother said.

She coached me, everything was going to be alright. Her support was enough to comfort me. Summertime was right around the corner.

Maria admitted, she didn't want to go, to my annual pilgrimage, to South Carolina. Not with my family and I anyway. I wasn't lowering my standards. I wanted to go. Yet, I wasn't exactly, comfortable taking two babies, to South Carolina, all by myself. It was nearly, an eight hour drive. Not to mention, food, traffic, or having to use the bathroom.

So without further ado, I decided to take, just Kandi with me, when the time came. Simply, because she was the oldest. It certainly, wasn't out of favoritism. Besides, I didn't want Mary performing "Tae Kwon Do" on me, if she thought someone was talking about her. I didn't think it was a sin. It didn't feel right, taking two, small children across state lines, alone. I was in the neighborhood of thinking, newborns belong with their mother. There was no magic talisman or argument. There was no rush to judgement. Mary seemed to understand my decision.

Drika, absolutely, couldn't have been happier about the babies. She would, actually, rush to see them, on her hour lunch break.

After a seven year stint behind bars, Hassan was home. What else, for selling drugs. I told him about Mary's temper tantrums. I mentioned the problems we had. He promised to hook me up with a skirt.

"I want a White girl," I said, feeling like the Stetson Man.

I was fed up with attitude. I was tired of drama. I wanted something, refreshingly, different.

Before I knew it, Hassan was introducing me to a young, blonde, White woman. Her name was Lauren. She was great. I tattled all my business to her. She was more wonderful than a sleigh ride. She was young. It was fun.

More importantly, Lauren didn't judge me. She didn't make me feel like crap. She didn't treat me like I was something, I wasn't. She certainly, didn't assume I had "gay tendencies." She didn't act as though, I was an "in the closet" gay person, unlike Mary.

Nor did Lauren look at me, occasionally, and say, "I don't see it anymore," as my children's mother would say to me, as if the gayness dissipated. It felt great, not being treated as a possible gay person, because I wasn't. I was being myself. I wasn't being second-guessed. I was grateful.

Also, Lauren wasn't embarrassed to be seen with me in public, like Mary. That meant a lot too. I wasn't treated like some grotesque, overweight beast, in which all would stare and laugh at. So, I appreciated that from her. I stuck with her like glue.

Lauren's parents didn't like Black guys. So, she stipulated, I pick her up, at the end of her street. I was a teddy bear with her. She was only twenty-years-old. I was twenty-nine.

I bought us the beer. I bought us the marijuana. She kindly, wrapped the weed in cigar paper, for us to smoke. We'd stop somewhere, to get high. We slothfully, drank our Tequiza, which quickly, became my favorite alcoholic drink.

It was so nice, being with someone, who didn't have temperaments, all the damn time. It didn't matter, if Lauren was 9 years younger than me. She made me feel young. She allowed me to enjoy myself.

Whenever I was off from work, I'd take both of my children, to my mother's house. Often, I was alone, awaiting for her, to come home after work. I didn't mind, changing my daughters diapers, however smelly. It went along with the territory. I certainly, didn't mind Kandi's relentless strands of whining and crying. I only censored her, when she about to get into something, and possibly, hurt herself.

Mary, once cried, when she saw me place Paris into her baby car seat. I made darn sure, she was secure in it. Evidently, she was moved, with my love of the children.

When it was Kandi's one-year-old birthday, I wanted to capture the moment. I got professional, photographer snapshots at JC Penny's. My daughter took the pictures in stride. It was the least I could do. I wanted to do the same, with both children, the following year.

Meanwhile, Lauren was really, starting to grow on me. We called each other, everyday. I was soaked in gratitude. She struck me as a real friend. We saw each other, often. I felt thawed around her. The world didn't seem as cold. Finally, I was starting to come out of my shell, and enjoy who I was.

I was tired of being taken for granted, by so many people. My heart was sold to the highest bidder. Yet, I didn't want to settle for anything less, any longer. I simply, wanted to be respected and accepted. It was all I wanted, and ever hoped for.

Lauren didn't make me feel stupid. She introduced me to her friends. Of course, they were potheads too. They were cool. We sat around, playing music. We were high as birds. I was submissive to Lauren's beckon call. She made me comfortable. I wanted to wet my whistle, maybe kiss her.

The following weekend, Mary and I threw a party, for Kandi's birthday. All kids, under 3 feet, were invited. I insisted in some James Brown music. I was exposing my love for old school music. Everything was going rather well.

Kandi had plenty of presents, cake and ice cream. My family chose not to show, on account of Mary's relentless, animosity towards them.

However, Paris was in her crib, lying perfectly, still. It was like, a deep, coma-like sleep.

"What's wrong with her?" a neighbor's child, who was from across the street, asked.

She was peeping in on Paris.

"She's okay," said Mary, with her hips on her side.

Undoubtedly, Mary was in denial. Paris rarely, opened her eye. She didn't move. Let alone, cry for food. Out of earshot, away from everyone else, I added more weight to the situation.

"Maybe we should take Paris, to the doctor," I said to Mary.

"If you think something is wrong with her, you take her to the doctor then," said Mary.

Obviously, she was offended. It was as though, I was saying, she was a bad mother. In a vicious cycle of hindsight 20/20, I should have went to the doctor. I would have gave anything, to hear Paris wail, to the top of her lungs. I wish, I thought she was normal.

"Well, some babies are different," my family said, letting me know, not to worry.

With Mary, it was the tip of the iceberg. Especially, when it came to Paris and I. Once, in an highly, unlikely situation, I dropped Kandi and Paris off, at their mother's house. Rushing out, I made the mistake of kissing Kandi goodnight, but not Paris.

"Aren't you going to say goodbye, to your other daughter?" whipped out Mary, as I headed to the door.

"You didn't give me a chance, Mary," I said, in my defense.

I kissed Paris. I was embarrassed. I certainly, didn't mean anything by it. I love my children, equally. Yet, Mary, of course, made a big deal about it. When it was just, the three of us together, Kandi, Paris and I, it was beautiful.

"Kiss Paris, Kandi. Kiss Paris," I'd say, which I got from Toya.

Kandi would do, just that. She'd kiss her younger sister's cheek, at my request. I didn't know, which was cuter. Seeing my daughter, kiss my other daughter on the cheek, or watching her trying to walk.

Meanwhile, I was a fool for Lauren. She didn't make me do anything, I didn't want to do. However, it's a wonder, I didn't get in a car wreck, from all the drinking, while driving. I started smoking, Black and Mild cigars. It was delightful. Not to mention, plenty of marijuana.

Lauren was from a upscale, west end neighborhood. Yet, I could barely, keep my little apartment together. I was in it, to win it. In a toss up, I'd let it be known to her, I wanted her. She made excuses. She said, she recently, broke up with her boyfriend. She wasn't trying to get serious with anyone, then. She just wanted to have fun. We were friends. I was upbeat about it. I was cool with that. I thought it was wise, to just be with a woman, I really like. So, I accepted it, rather than being alone, without her. Besides, we were both potheads. We searched upwind, like wolves for our next hit of weed.

What was really, tragic? Hassan used our friendship, to try to get a piece from Mary. It happened once, while I was at work. She told me so. I was so hurt. What's more, I should have known, how transparent he was. My evaluation of him was at an all-time low. I stopped hanging with him, after that.

I wrapped myself around family, and the other people I knew. I traveled here and there with Lauren.

We went to a couple of movies. We went to an all-you-can-eat. It was a Chinese food buffet. Eventually, her parents wanted to meet me. I was flattered. I was fascinated. Considering, I was Black. Her parents thought, I was respectable, enough to meet. That felt good.

Mary and I were actually, getting along great, at that point. It seemed the verbs and pronouns, we had for each other, were of yesteryear. We were finally, acting like co-parents. It was a small triumph, which mattered a lot. I'd loosen her bra, while we listened to the trumpets of our favorite slow songs. We became vigilantes, having fun. We did what we did best. She no longer treated me like a virus. It seemed our relationship made a complete turnaround. Things were taking a chance. It was Russian Roulette, without the vodka. Sure, she had a jealous twit. Once, she spotted a beer, bottle cap in my apartment. She never saw me drink before, and knew I wasn't alone. She gave me an ultimatum, forcing me to take her home. However, after enough walking and talking Mary through it, we became somewhat, compatible again.

Whenever I would meet someone on a social, get-to-know basis, I'd admit to them, "I'm Muslim, but I don't practice." I wanted to be comfortable. I wanted them to be comfortable.

Not to mention, I had in my apartment, Arabic calligraphy pictures. I had a picture of the holy Kaaba, which is in Makkah, Saudi Arabia. I had a picture of the mosque in Medina, Saudi Arabia, on my wall. Also, there was a drawing of the mosque in Jerusalem. I had prayer rugs. I had "kufi" or skull caps. I'd burn incense. Occasionally, I'd buy baked, bean pies from Brothers, after Friday prayers. I certainly, wasn't embarrassed to be Muslim.

However, I wasn't performing my prayers, regularly. I was getting high on marijuana. I was drinking beer. I was dating women. I wasn't married. All of which, was a "no-no" in Islam.

I didn't want to give Islam, the beautiful religion, a bad name. Especially, by seemingly, being a hypocrite, or "not real." Also, I knew people were so misinformed about Islam. Particularly, the terrorism, extremism, fundamentalism, and any other "ism" wrongly, attached to it.

Personally, I was becoming tired of hearing anti-American rhetoric, by some. I wasn't a no-nonsense, stoic guy for Islam, like a few. That wasn't me.

Usually, I didn't dress up in Middle Eastern traditional garb. Unless, it was a special occasion, like Friday prayer, which was seldom. Perhaps, for our two annual, celebratory Eid prayers, which was hardly.

I didn't wear a big beard. Nor did I want to. I didn't read a few Islamic books, and self-appoint myself, in "importance" or "holiness." I wanted to be myself.

I wasn't perfect. I certainly, didn't pretend I was. Nor did I want to be. Seemingly, prayers were becoming empty rituals. The Brothers, at the masjid, would warn me to pray, but it was no use. No one else cared, outside the community, if I prayed or not. Honestly, I wasn't giving to charity. I didn't do anything right. I drank beer, like it was water. I was colored in with "dunyah" or worldly things.

It was May 26, 2000. It was, seemingly, a Friday like any other. I picked up my children, from Maria's house. It was one o'clock as usual. Carolyn was there, to give me the baby bottles, pacifiers and the like. I placed Kandi and Paris in the back seat of my car, as I normally, would.

So, I made a complete, about-face to my mother's house. I stopped at Burger King. I wanted to get a bite to eat. Meanwhile, I was still, the son of a father, who I have heard from in years. At any rate, I didn't get one of those new, fangled Blitz ice creams. A Double Whopper was perfectly, abundant for me.

# MISUNDERSTOOD

I just got off work. I didn't get any sleep. Yet, being with my two kids, was never too much to ask. I put Paris' blue milk bottle in my mother's refrigerator. I was in good company. I took us to the den. After I finished my food, I assumed myself on the couch. I looked at tv, getting some rest.

I remembered the conversations my mother and I had about Paris. She as well, noticed Paris' eyes would roll to the back of her head.

Sometimes I'd boldly, give Paris a small pinch, to try to get some kind of reaction out of her. I desperately, wanted her to look at me, her father.

Every four hours, I'd feed the baby. With Paris' last feeding at noon, 3:30 I decided to get the bottle ready. Nearly, 4:00, I was attacked with worry, about her well-being. Nevertheless, Kandi was ripping and running, while her sister, just laid there, without peeping a sound.

I was naïve. I shook Paris to make her well. To make things worst, her body went limp. I put my head to her chest, to check for breathing. I felt I ought, to put my finger under her nose, to check for breathing. It was extremely, shallow. Detecting something was wrong, Kandi started to cry. We both started to panic. Nearly, nauseous, I remembered CPR training. It was available to me as a security officer at NationsBank. Also, as a correctional officer at Powhatan Correctional Center. I was scared. Apparently, it wasn't working.

I blamed myself. I thought something was wrong with Paris. I was only trying to, with the shaking. I didn't have any intent to harm her. My first thought, was to call her mother. From my heart, I felt Mary should be the first to know. I panicked.

"Something's wrong with Paris," I said to her on the phone.

Death was the farthest thing from my mind. I could hear Toya crying. She was getting hysterical, on the other end of the phone.

"What's wrong, mama?" babbled Toya.

"Paris is gone," Mary said, automatically.

I heard more confusion, more hurt.

"Call 911, Marco," said Mary.

Stunned, I did just that. Shocked, I called 911, immediately. I tried to remain calm. Especially, as my training taught me, in times of crisis. The emergency dispatch agent gave me a backwash of questions and suggestions. Brick by brick, step by step, she walked me through it.

"Shake the baby," said the dispatcher. "See if you can get a response."

"I did," I said.

With the dispatcher's instructions, again I checked Paris for air. I again, checked for air. Again, I got nothing. My heart formed into a tight ball. That is, before it broke in two.

Before I knew it, the paramedics were there. I was in total shock. I was numb. It was the most awkward situation. I could hardly, speak. I could scarcely, express myself. At least 20 people were in my mother's living room. It was the EMS, the police. Outside, there was an ambulance. There was a fire truck, police squad cars. All of which, was there for my little baby.

My entire world, the only bubble I knew, just popped. I had so many plans for Paris. I wanted to teach her the alphabet. I wanted to show her farm animals, a petting zoo. Yet, I was sitting helpless on the floor, with Kandi in my arms. We just cried.

I could hear some of the civil servants, complain about a strong smell. Also, the somewhat, sticky floor of my mother's recently, finished floors.

"We got a pulse! We got a pulse!" said the paramedic, which gave us all hope.

"Go! Go! Go!" the medic said.

Everyone bullied their way out of my mother's house. We were all rushing to the hospital, VCU Medical Center.

An eyebrow, from a paramedic was raised, when I ran to look for my shoes. Normally, in the house, I was in socks. Also, I grabbed baby baubles, I may need. Kandi and I hopped in. The ambulance was burning rubber. Emergency personnel was busy logging things down.

I alerted Mary and my mother, to meet me downtown, at the hospital. My heart skipped a beat, as the loud sirens rang. I wanted to burst my head through the window. I couldn't believe what was happening.

Paris was in the back of the ambulance, fighting for her life. Little did I know, it was the quiet before the storm. It was something, I'll never forget.

Finally, we quickly, ran to the operating room. It was the last place on earth, I wanted to have been. With nothing to hide, I told the doctors everything that happen. I had nothing to fear, with the social workers. Nor with the police, namely Detective Norris.

When Mary, Carolyn and Toya arrived at the hospital, they were obviously, detached from me. It was like a draft from the Antarctic. Nobody was talking, or had anything to do with to me. It felt like snow in Southern California. We were in the waiting room. I wanted to be anywhere, but there.

I put my best foot forward. I picked up Kandi, in order for us to be near her sister, Paris. I couldn't just sit still, wondering what was going on. Mary continued to sulk and wait in the waiting room.

"At least somebody cares about her," I heard the nurse say, shifting her eyes towards me.

I wasn't looking for any applause. I was simply, a guy wanting to be near his precious daughter. I didn't want Paris to be alone. Also, a little bird told me, Mary didn't want to see our daughter like that.

Detective Norris gave me his business card, along with a board of other questions. I was filled with agony. Of course, he was looking for someone to blame. I answered every important thing he wanted to know. As far as I knew, I was considered a panicked father. I continued to wait for my Paris to make a comeback.

"She stopped breathing," I said, knowing how skeptical and fickle people can be.

When my mother arrived, she gave me a banquet of love and understanding. She was the main one, beside myself, who also noticed how lethargic Paris was.

I gave myself permission to grieve. I cruised into second gear, second-guessing myself. Every cell in my body regretted what I did. I racked every compartment in my brain. Did I accidentally, hurt an innocent baby? Was she actually, normal and okay? Did the more I tried to help, the more I was hurting her? Did I misunderstood?

203

*CHAPTER 14, PART 15*

# Jailbird

IT WAS THE cultivating feeling within me. I wasn't going to leave Paris' bedside. I stayed in the hospital, without Mary, for hours. I wasn't going anywhere, until the doctors told me, she was going to be certifiably, okay.

My demeanor was a composite of calmness. I struggled to accept God's Will. I cupped my hands in prayer. I relied on my religious convictions. I was quiet, before the storm. It wasn't, I didn't care. It wasn't, I didn't show any remorse.

I asked the doctors to inform me, on any signs of change, on Paris' condition. A hospital counselor was sent, to talk to me. To hold my hand, sort of speak. It was a dark and gloomy night. Paris' hospital charts showed, no signs of physical or sexual abuse. Only that, she was shaken.

"She has 'Accidental Shaken Baby Syndrome'," said Paris' doctor.

Those were her exact words. I was devastated, to say the least. Mary, on the other hand, decided to confine herself at home. She personally, didn't check to see, how our daughter was doing at the hospital.

I was anything, but a deadbeat dad. My family was there for support. We were trying to prepare ourselves for Paris' possible demise. My quest for a wife and kids, seemed to decay, before my very eyes. My head and chin was hung down in guilt. I blamed myself for shaking her. I didn't blame anyone else. I only knew what I did. It was my fault.

"Why?" I constantly, asked myself. "Why did I shake her?"

I was crying. I was sniffing. I needed a decongestant. Eating chow was the last thing on my mind. I deferred my very existence. I considered myself, "a fat, piece of shit," who hurt his baby. I went in circles, knowing it was not intentional.

"Mama, you saw how she was. I didn't mean to hurt her."

In our conversations, we went to the deli, to block some of the pain. The cafeteria at the hospital was clammed tight with doctors, nurses and families. It was nice to see my family. My mother, brother and sister on one accord. We all was there, to see Paris get well. She was on life support. The doctors were telling us, she had little brain activity.

None of the doctors, seemingly, expected any foul play. As far as I could tell, they didn't think any criminal activity went on. I was a father, who thought something was wrong with his child, when maybe, it wasn't.

My mother insisted, I spend the night at her house. The little sleep, I did get, was filled with demons. I searched for clearance. I searched for answers.

It was the worse Friday. It was the worse day, I ever had. Consequently, I had no idea, I would one day be depicted as man, who didn't care, or didn't show remorse about his child. Not to mention, being viewed as hurting her, on purpose, because I didn't want her.

The next day, Mary was like a bump on a log. She was so counterproductive. I tried to get her to go to the hospital with me. She insisted on staying home. So, Paris was in fact, deprived of her mother's presence. I wanted a united front, as parents, with our child. I was disappointed. Yet, I knew, like charcoal, people burn in different ways.

I wasn't the one, sitting cowardly, on the sidelines. I was watching and waiting for the outcome, beside our child. Anything else, I would've done was despicable to me.

I racked my brain on what I could've done, differently. I went over what happened. The life support machine was merely, pumping air. The highly skilled doctors couldn't help. In my thinking, I felt somebody from Paris' family should be there with her.

"If Toya was laying up in a hospital, would Mary stay home?" Mama wondered.

"I don't think so," I pondered.

At any rate, Paris' condition worsen. Toya met us at the hospital, with some of her fellow church members. Her and I were once a dynamic duo. She was a well-mannered teenager. She was never rude or temperamental towards me. She didn't use slang or colloquialisms. By the looks of her, one may think she was Creole. She was an honor roll student. She spoke in a soft-spoken dialect.

We prayed for a miracle. We prayed Paris wouldn't die. My lips quivered at the sight of a doctor's white, lab coat near her. She was diminishing, before our very eyes. It affected me, greatly. To me, it wasn't fair. My life felt like, one, huge diss, which seemed to last forever. I wasn't a fan of hospitals.

The doctor said, we should think about disconnecting Paris' life support. I had the duty of running it by her mother, who was acting like, some sort of elitist. It all happened so fast.

I cried at my mother's house. It was my place of refuge.

"I killed her!" I cried in disgust. "Aah!"

I wanted to break up something. I flipped over the dining room table, which knocked it to the floor. My family was there, seeing my surge of frustration.

"Stop, Marco!" my mama said, fearfully. "This isn't helping Paris!"

My family hugged me. They told me, it wasn't my fault. It was an accident.

"We're going to get through this," Mama said, spelling out her support.

I was looking, for some type of closure. I went to the local 7-11. I wanted to get a pack of Newport cigarettes. I wanted some beer. At that point, I didn't care. I wanted to calm my nerves.

I was in pain. I was in agony. I was shocked. My heart was screaming. My brain was crying. My body was laughing at me. It didn't want to move. My eyes were hurting. I felt like a jerk. Instantly, I became a chain smoker. One would think, I'd smoke regularly, for years.

"Marco, you don't smoke. This isn't you," my family said, worried about my state of mind.

Lauren, single White female, felt sorry for me. She lended me support. It didn't make sense, to go to our nightly, getting-high sessions, but there I was. Self-pity, I was. I didn't trust myself, not to do something stupid.

I gave my sister, my gun to hold. I entered into a deep depression. I was so sorry about what happen. I was so remorseful. I was so regretful.

Suicide was seemingly, the prize. I figured it was the least I could do, for hurting an innocent baby. Finally, I had a cool head. It was the most ironic thing. I always loved children. How could this happen?

Sunday, May 28, 2000, Mary and I decided. The decent thing to do, was to take Paris off of life-support. Should the occasion call for it. We didn't want Paris to suffer. It was absolutely, the most hardest decision I ever had to make.

I never pictured myself, dealing with the possibility, of the death of my child. I found myself in an uncomfortable, uncharted territory. It was the saddest time of my life.

I spent some time with Paris' mother. We put our differences aside. Once, Drika bought us all fish dinners, from Long John Silvers. There wasn't a hint of trouble, as Mary ate her entrée. It was a nice, family get-together. There wasn't any shadiness going on.

In our downtime, inside, we knew. We all had a very emotional day, the next day, to pull the plug. Essentially, letting our daughter go. I was trying, to be strong for the family. I tried to carry my head, held high, for them. I was free to dream, Paris would be in a better place.

Evidently, I had to accept, a long life for Paris wasn't meant to be. She was our Spring flower, who was just that. She was here, for a Springtime, literally. Her short six weeks life, came and went, as a morning dew drop.

It was Monday, May 29, 2000. Mary, as usual, stayed home, like a check in the mail. I thought, it was only proper, Paris' parents be together, at a time like this. She was coming off of life support. Her last day with us.

So, without the fluorescent lights of VCU Medical Center, I quietly, stayed with her. Our relationship was stuck as duck tape. I made the best of it. Underneath the hurt, we talked about everything, except what was happening at 2 o'clock pm at the hospital. It was hard to explain. Just the two of us finally, alone. My mother, brother and sister was at the hospital, representing me. Carolyn and Toya was there, for Mary. Tande, our truth, represented us, as a couple. Paris externalized my hopes, of being a real family man. That, I will never forget.

Tuesday, May 30, 2000, my family and I had the fortitude of making all the funeral arrangements. Mary, who went against the grain, did nothing constructive. Getting her to participate was like, taking a garden hoe, and hitting hard earth. She wasn't going in.

I had the week off. It allowed me, to pick up the broken fragments of my heart. I remembered a beautiful cemetery, if there's such a thing. I'd pass by it everyday, to and fro work. Somehow, whenever I went to my jail job, I wanted to be able to pass by the graveyard. I wanted to have the satisfaction of being nearby Paris, on my way to work. She wouldn't be "alone" or isolated.

I was grateful, Gerry came over to the house, to pay his respects. I was free, to feel blessed Paris was born and in our lives.

However, I wasn't exactly, green or new, to how Muslim funerals go. I gave the Manning funeral home, specific instructions. They weren't to give Paris embalming fluid. A Muslim would be there, to wash and pray over the body. I gave Sheik Muhammad, from Egypt, the honor.

I was anything, but a hoodlum. I had many a fried fish dinner, at the masjid. Especially, at Ali's and Fatih's "A and F Seafood" market. Their store was conveniently, below Masjid Ar-Rahman. I often excused their rough edges. Especially, with their sometimes blunt, Egyptian ways. They spoke their mind. Yet, they all had an unyielding, undeniable faith in Islam. I trusted Sheik Muhammad, to let him once, pat me on the head.

"Ali is a boy," he once said, about me.

I didn't take offense. I took it such as he was noting my innocent, boyish charm. Whether Sheik Muhammad actually, did what I asked, at the funeral home or not, I don't know.

Mary and I were of two different faiths. She wanted the minister, from Toya's church, to preside at the funeral as well. I was fine with that, if Sheik Muhammad was.

My family paid, all of the funeral expenses. I had the sole responsibility, of picking out a gravesite plot. I alone, chose the type of wording on the headstone. I picked through the depiction of angles, flowers, etc.

I spotted a groovy, little horse. Actually , it was a unicorn. I thought it was playfully, perfect for my special, little girl's headstone. I nearly, cried with excitement for it. I guaranteed the assistant lady at the cemetery, we'll take it. Yet, I wanted to make sure, it was okay, with Mary. Especially, before things were finalized.

At Mary's house, I told her all the options we could get, for Paris' headstone. Also, I happen to mention, I saw examples of parents' names, on headstones, for their deceased children.

"How about we get the one, with our names on it?" Mary said, finally, putting in input.

"Let's just get it, with Paris' name on it," I suggested.

At the time, Mary didn't seem to have a problem with that. She certainly, didn't have a problem, allowing my family and I to make all of the funeral arrangements. We had the "whole boat to ourselves." She was on a humbug, keeping away from it all. I wouldn't say, I was glad.

Meanwhile, I was still smoking, pretty heavily. I was going about town, making the final touches. We needed things, such as flowers and an outfit.

Wednesday, May 31, 2000, the most unimaginable thing happened.

"Daddy wants to know, can he come to the funeral?" Drika said.

This was coming from the man, who shut me out of his life, for the last 13 years. I had to think about it. What kind of game was when playing? Was I hallucinating? What's the worst can happen?

"Yeah, he can come," I said.

I thought what a gathering it would make. When it came to Kandi and Toya, I did whatever, to make myself handy, man. I didn't want to be idle. I didn't want to fix my mind on the tragic thing which happened to Paris.

Thursday, June 1, 2000, in general, was very hard. Especially, knowing my daughter's funeral was the next day. Little did I know, I would one day have my back against the wall. Unbeknownst to me, I'd be fighting against an illegitimate claim.

At any rate, I was physically, tired from a lack of sleep. My headaches hatched spats of immeasurable pain. I had a ghostly, walk due to my headache. I sounded like, I had a speech impediment. I hardly, felt like talking. It was the worst moment of my entire life.

I lived like a heathen. I was impolite to myself and others, who had to smell me. I hadn't taken a bath in two days. I smoked, Black and Mild cigars, like it was nobody's business. I was in a global nuclear war, within myself. I was going through hell, blaming myself. I hated myself, for Paris' death.

"What the hell was I thinking? Why didn't I just let her be?" I said to myself.

"Some father I turned out to be," I thought to myself.

I saw myself as a pig, going here and there. I was always messing things up. I loved Paris, ever since her conception. My golden child was no more, and it was all my fault.

Lauren wanted to go out, and get high. I was inconsolable. Marijuana and beer wasn't going to bring my daughter back. So, I wasn't hip about it. I had a permanent dent in my heart. I had a lot to think about.

Friday, June 2, 2000 was a week later, after the accident. Of course, I was a remorseful individual for my daughter's funeral. I was dressed in a Muslim, white kufi (skullcap). I had on a dark, grey gown. Typically, Middle Eastern origin. I had on a black and white checkered scarf, draped over my neck. The kind they wear in Palestine. I had on black, dress shoes. Normally, I didn't necessarily, dress like that. However, I wanted to show my utmost respect for my deceased daughter.

It was a clear, beautiful morning. I was surrounded by kinfolk. I wanted happier times. I wanted anything, but this dreadful moment. It didn't take an expert to see, I was "Dad" knocking on heaven's door myself.

I was no longer, mad and cursing. I was influenced by my mother, to remain calm. She grabbed my hand, which mailed some of my anxiety away. Before I knew it, the limousine was parked in front of my mother's house. My family and I all piled in. We headed for Mary's house.

Kandi was cute as a ladybug. My family and I was layered in our best attire. Mary and Toya was questionably, in Summer sun dresses. Carolyn, her former lover, landed in linen, best suited for her.

I was a man, without a solution. I was feeling totally, helpless. I reached out to hold Mary's hand. She was hesitant, like a latecomer. She marked the event, as though I was being phony. Ordinarily, I didn't show my affections with a lady, in front of my family.

The limo was sure, to be at the funeral home soon. I tried to relax. Especially, knowing masses of people would be there.

I prayed. Sheik Muhammad had to be there. I asked him to commence the funeral, by giving the eulogy. He wasn't exactly, thrilled about sharing the podium at an "interfaith" funeral.

"Do it for me! You'll be there for me!" I said, trying to get the imam to reconsider.

Paris' body was in an immaculate pink and white coffin. Supposedly, as a man, I tried to stay strong. I didn't have a leg to stand on. I cried, the minute I got near our baby's closed casket.

The family was ushered to a back room. Toya's minister wanted to say a few words of prayer. He asked me about Sheik Muhammad. Obviously, he wasn't there yet. The reverend allowed me to pray, the way I know.

Then my father walked in. Instantly, I ran up to hug him. Quickly, I forgave and forgot, every mean thing I ever said about him. Mel seemingly, did the same. I introduced my father to a picture of Paris. He also met his other grandchild, Kandi, for the first time. Of course, there was Mary and Toya. Drika stood by his side.

Without Sheik Muhammad's presence, it was less than perfect. I didn't hold it against him. I sat meditating, in the funeral home's church-like pews. I was thinking about Paris. Involuntarily, my tears fell. Sitting directly, beside me, Mary did nothing to console me. The reverend took his place on the pulpit.

"Is Sheik Muhammad here?" said the Christian man.

He was taking the liberty to show respect. Looking around, the imam was not. He was personally, invited by me. The memorandum was nice, if I must say so myself. Paris was irretrievably, gone but not forgotten. It was a celebration of Paris' short life. I was proud. It was my blood, which flowed through her veins.

Eventually, the pastor asked us, the family, to say a few things. I was too hurt to speak. Feeling urged, Mary's long-lost relatives said a few words. It was hard to fathom, an itty bitty person, who looked like me, was in that box.

Afterwards, we all met outside in the funeral home's parking lot. There was haunting words of encouragement. Soon, all the cars lined up. The funeral hearse was in the middle of the row. It was a very grim sight.

I wanted to eat crow. My little girl, who once milled around, was now on a peaceful journey. Kandi buried her earlobe in my chest.

I was in the minority, who knew the least, little about Islam. I did such as I did, in the two Muslim funerals, I attended before. I personally, helped bury the Brothers, by shoveling ground, back onto their graves. It was an honor. So, I made it my business, to do the same for Paris.

I wished I had a lollipop to give Kandi. At the gravesite, I made it known, I wanted to be the first to put earth on Paris' final resting place. My chest felt like it was on fire. After more tears, more fears, more words, more prayers, I kneeled down to pick up some ground. I hauled it on the small coffin, with love.

I was lopsided with grief. Especially, with my misuse. The only time I saw Mary cry, was when we were alone at her house. She openly, cried in my arms.

"Oh, Marco," is what she said, hugging me, crying.

My father went his separate way, after the funeral. We all went to Mary's house for the repast, or a nibble to eat. I was at an all-time low. However, I felt it was important, to be the liaison for the family.

Normally, I'd be broke as a joke. All my money, usually, was poured into rent and bills. Yet, on this particular day, I wanted Paris' family to finally, have some money. Maybe, to do something special we wanted to do, after the funeral. So, I took every cent, out of my checking account. I was going to use the money I had, set aside for rent, to have it for us.

"Toya, it's whatever you want to do! You want to go to Captain George's or Kings Dominion? I got it!" I said proudly.

I was open-minded. I was with a fist full of money. It was ours, for the taking. It was for whatever, the family wanted to do or go. My intentions were pure. I certainly, wasn't trying to show off, or brag about the unpaid rent money. Of course, it wasn't because, I didn't have any remorse. I simply, wanted to assure Paris' family, we could do something nice later, should we want to.

Mary was a phantom, waiting in the wings. Everyone exchanged lots of hugs and smooches. I had the option of changing into a pair of jeans, so I did. Across the board, I drank and smoked. I was destroying my organs even further. Picking my brain, I wasn't mad at God. I was upset with myself.

I tried to see, if Mary was okay. She was quiet as a mouse. However, oh so quiet. She didn't want any help, we tried to give her. The family said their goodbyes, promising her, if she needs anything, let them know.

Another chilling affect, Detective Norris saw me again. It was at my apartment, the next week. Seeing him at my door, turned my heart into mulch. He wore the same-looking outfit, I seen him in before. I wasn't expecting, any company to come by.

He asked me, was I going somewhere? Untidy, by the looks of things. I took his insinuation, as though I was planning "a run for it." It was his job to be cynical. It was my job to stay out of trouble. My pipe dreams of being a great father were obviously, put on hold. I cut my music off, to accommodate him. Naturally, the detective wanted to go over, what happened at my mama's house.

He said, he wanted to "help me," if I told him what happened. I had nothing to hide. So, I told him, yet again, about shaking the baby. Also, I knew, if I asked for a lawyer, or be noncompliance, I'd likely, be arrested on the spot. I was buying time.

Did I shake my baby too hard? Yes. Did I want my baby to die? No. For me, I shook a lethargic baby. For him, a baby was now dead.

I couldn't remember, the exact time, when the incident took place. I told the detective, it happened around 3:30 pm, give or take. Whereas he told me, I actually, made the 911 Emergency call at 4:01 pm. He took what I said, using my uncertain timeline, against me.

I could tell, the man wanted to put me, in an overpopulated jail. I could tell I was "late," as they say. I knew, there wasn't a chance in hell, he'd simply, believe me. I thought something was wrong with Paris. Talking during my interrogation was like talking to a brick wall. So, I told him, I primarily, noticed the baby wasn't getting any oxygen. It was an actual fact.

"If I were you, I'd get myself a good lawyer," Detective Norris said, with pleasure.

When he finally, left my apartment, of course I wasn't okay. What the hell did he mean by that? I wondered. The doctors at the hospital didn't treat me indifferently. Why now? What was being said?

The next day, a woman from Social Services, came to see me. The social worker was pretty. She looked like she belonged in a beauty pageant. Right away, the lady wanted to plunge into what happened that tragic day. Evidently, Mary told her something negative about me.

Seemingly, the social worker's mind was already. I tried to explain how Mary was usually, paranoid, insecure, and jealous. However, it was pointless to continue.

"You think, I'd let a child stay with someone, who wasn't safe?" she said, which apparently, hit a nerve.

"I don't know," I said, as though she knew something, I didn't.

"Well, I wouldn't," said the social worker.

Was it a parable? My life was turning into a game of Polo. I didn't know the rules. The woman didn't have any children of her own, only a niece, I found out. Somehow, things weren't looking up to par.

"You can't go over to your children's house anymore. Nor see their mother," the woman warned. "Not until The Department has finished its investigation."

She said it, as though it was for the better. She said it, as though she, herself had moral excellence. My heart nearly, stopped. I was like a particular, model citizen, up until that point. For God's sake, I majored in Criminal Justice at VCU. I currently, worked for a prison. I voted during election time.

"What? I need to see my daughter! Why can't I go over there?"

I was positively, heartbroken. I just lost one daughter. Now this? The union my family and I had, kept me grounded. We made urgent phone calls to Social Services. We demanded to speak to a supervisor. I couldn't get a straight answer from anybody.

No longer passive, the family and I went to the office building, downtown. The lady, who interviewed me absolutely, refused to see us. Not until, I calmed down anyway.

I was suddenly, being treated like a suspect. I didn't know who, or where it was coming from. I felt like the world was closing in on me. It was enough, to make me go back, smoking marijuana.

Obviously, the detective, Norris, wanted to pin something on me. My father personally, took me to meet David Baugh. He was an attorney, my father knew.

"I sure wish, I could've been there for you all these years. I wish things could've been different," said my father, as though he wanted to pat me on the back.

The lawyer had an impressive resume, as well as a gold earring in his ear. He looked more like a city slicker, than a Black guy, who practiced law. That's what impressed me, about him. He was being himself. He was was going against the establishment. He was going against the grain, if you will. My father, who knew a lot of people highly, recommended him.

David Baugh made national headlines, on the news. He once represented the KKK, though he was Black man himself. Also, he had a client, who was an alleged terrorist, who bombed an US Embassy in Kenya.

My father was there for support, nudging me on. I couldn't believe, my father and I was actually, at peace with each other. We made a great "father and son" team.

Paris being here, brought us together. At last, after so many years, I was face to face with my father.

"Paris did this," I thought, knowing her death wasn't in vain.

"Well, you're looking at a charge of Involuntary Manslaughter," said David Baugh.

He said it precisely, as though preparing me for the worst. An oasis of emotions came over me. I was no criminal. Yet, there I was, being pegged as one. It was weird, boarding up my defense.

"Being that you don't have a felony record, I can get it where you'll only have to do a year and a half," Baugh said.

My life, as though he could fix it. I figured, a year and a half was a long time. However, I was willing to accept responsibility somehow. Before I left his office, Baugh was the lawyer I wanted. He also had another thing to say.

"Stay away from her!" said Baugh.

It was the second time, a lawyer told me that. Obsessed, upset, I did what I was asked. I was penned with so many questions and concerns. I told my mother about the lawyer, with a gram of hope. Baugh presented himself a little arrogantly, but that could be good. If I had to go to court, I wanted him.

I was stressed out. I was starting to feel old. I was worn out. I had intentions to help my daughter. Yet, everything went terribly, wrong. I was a little pretentious, but I was trying to help. None the less, my life never felt so, offshore. I was permitting myself to feel. I was in the prime season of my life. I was hanging in the balance. I was staring destiny in the face.

I didn't know, if I was going to jail or not. I wanted to go to The Omni hotel, and stay there. Things were, unsure. Uncertainty, filled my life. I was no longer, a private citizen. The law, I took an oath to, as a correctional officer, was now breathing down my neck. Eventually, I prodded back to back to work. It was business as usual. Things were the same, but different, after my daughter's funeral.

"Martin, if there's anything I can do, let me know," I'd hear from coworkers.

"I'm sorry to hear that," others would tell me.

"What happened?" some would say.

"My daughter stopped breathing," I'd say, in the abridged version.

I spared myself, to not go into the details. I felt stupid. I wasn't allowed, to be more supportive of Mary and the children. However, I was going along with the program. Obviously, it was a classic case of "divide and conquer."

The detective, with his police savvy, wanted me to stay away. The social worker, promoting a "safe" environment asked me to stay away. The lawyer, who I wanted to retain, said stay away.

I couldn't move, if I wanted to. I was stiff as a scarecrow. I proposed to see Mary anyway, but my family didn't think it was a good idea. I could only imagine, what was going through her mind, with me suddenly, not showing up. It didn't take a rocket scientist, to know she would likely, think I didn't care. With me out of the picture, it seemingly, appeared I had no remorse. Nothing was further from the truth.

Was I a good Muslim? No. Was I Muslim? Yes.

# JAILBIRD

I remained professional on the job. I perished the thought of me, someday being an inmate myself. I continued to scramble for answers. I tried to wrap my head around what happened to Paris. I'd go through their belongings, as normal, during a "random shakedown." I still received the usually, sore-looks from the inmates. Publicly, I moved on. I did my job.

I'd yell,"Chow!" when it was time to eat in the Chow Hall, or dining area. I'd say,"Pill Call!" when it was time for them, to take their daily medication, administered by the nurse. I'd holler, "Lock Down!"when the Warden decided, it was time to isolate the inmates from general population, for possible contraband.

The inmates would still shuffle their feet, whenever I asked them to do something. My personal favorite at the time, Puffballs, in the vending machine, had their same taste.

I smoked my usual Black and Mild cigars. Also, I smoked Kool cigarettes, without resistance. Sometimes, I still had the duty of being secluded, in a watchtower, waiting for the sun to come up. While checking cells, bars, doors and locks, I still wished for Chinese food, at my favorite Chinese restaurant. Better still, I wanted to hang out with my daughter somewhere. The only one child, I had left.

The inmates were still pushy as ever. They were still living in the glory days of the past. Many were in retrospect of what they did. Some bragged about what they use to do. A few relished what they had, when they were on the street. It was evident, life moves on, despite a death in the family. No matter how rude life can be. Being a prison guard had its rewards. Especially, if someone had seniority.

A month and a half passed, before I knew what I was facing. Incidentally, a little bird told me, the prosecution was going to require itself to a grand jury. In order to see, if it had enough evidence to go forward. It ripped at my very soul, I wasn't allowed to be there, in my defense. To me, that in of itself, was a major setback. You're guilty, until you can prove yourself innocent.

"No news is good news," I would sometimes say. "If we didn't hear anything by now, maybe they're going to drop it."

I was hoping for something radical. The whole thing rocked my world.

BEHOLD

The waiting, the suspense. I was more nervous than Shaggy from Scooby Doo.

At work, the rain hid my tears. My police-looking, correctional officer uniform, coated my fears. On the job, I continued to randomly, spotlight the roofs with a sharpen eye, if I had tower duty. I still tighten up, with a "Yes, sir," whenever higher rank or supervisor was around.

The inmates, the roughnecks, blamed their amount of time on the skin they were in. As usual, I tried to rationalize, the absolute rubble I was in. Day by day, my freedom was getting short.

I reached out, to my father. I was glad, I was his son again. Rather than be treated like an afterthought, or distant "relative." However, I used to feel, "I was his son," but I wasn't "his family." The American justice system was trying its best, to chew me out.

"Be reasonable. You're not going to jail," I'd tell myself.

Meanwhile, I was driving my black Dodge Stratus. I wished I could afford a black Saab. I knew what was on the sideline waiting for me. I hoarded as much quality time, as I could possibly, get from my mother. She reciprocated my sadness with only a quiet, loving presence. It certainly, was enough for me.

I was missing Mary, despite her paranoia. I wanted to be with her, regardless of her misguided attitude towards me. In spite of common sense, I was seemingly, a glutton for punishment. She thought I was "secretly" gay or "in the closet." It was insulting. It was deplorable. Mostly, she couldn't shake that feeling. Sometimes, she did. Many would've ran from her, but I stayed. Obviously, I didn't want to be alone. I was desperate. I wanted to be dating a woman. So, I endured the mishaps and misgivings. Every sign and advice told me, "No." The recreation we had was put on hold. The most I could do was sleep it off, or listen to love songs.

As I waited for a possible indictment, which could be any day, I went to South Carolina. It was a planned vacation week, during Independence Day. I wanted to hear my paternal grandma speak. Desperately, I wanted to let my mind go. I needed to take it easy.

"Sorry, to hear about your daughter," my family, down South would say.

# JAILBIRD

I wanted to be a better servant of God. I really did. At the time, I was in a "I'm Muslim, but I don't practice," theme. I wanted, like hell, to rise above my situation. Like thievery in the night, my cousins and I went to a strip club. The Diamond was an all-nude strip joint, located in Greenville, South Carolina. My cousins thought it would be a great way lift my spirit. Baby, Jonathan, Fist and I brought our own alcohol. We each held a six-pack of beer. The women tossed and turned. Whimsically, they danced to the music on stage. I felt like Superman.

I knew there were people in Virginia, who wanted nothing better to do. They wanted to lock me up, and throw away the key. I was making the best of it. The strip club was a springboard. I needed to bounce back. Surely, time was ticking away, which was bringing jail closer and closer.

The naked women made me squeal with excitement. It was nice getting my mind off of things. I let down my heavy load.

Over the next few days, the heavy drinking sustained me. The moon was a constant timekeeper. The alcohol had a way of fighting off a staircase of emotion.

My grandmother made the family sweetbread. Tirelessly, she would cook and clean. She used old-fashioned standards. My paternal grandma was the symbol of a matriarch. Meanwhile, my granddaddy ate and watched Tv shows. He tolerated little disturbance.

I wanted my life to be stationary. I wanted to stay right there, in South Carolina. For the accident I made, I wanted to put it on my tab. I'd pay for it for later, sort of speak. Like Dr. King, I knew eventually, I was going to the promised land. I was on a mountain top, looking at me legal problems below.

I couldn't have stayed a better time, to be with my mother's and father's side of the family. The support I got from them couldn't have been more tailored made. Being in South Carolina always had a special way with me. It kept me in touch with my childhood.

I remembered playing stickball in the street. I wished, I was a taller boy. I remembered the traces of firecracker gunpowder on my fingers. As a child, I'd feel cocky, I was from a more northern state, such as Virginia.

I'd bring loads of cassette tapes for my cousins to try out. I'd trail behind, to see what kind of mess I could get myself into. When it was a storm brewing outside, my grandfather would cut off, all the power in the house. Which meant, no running fan, tv on, or talking on the phone.

I remember, old ladies riding a taxi cab, to get here and there. I remember my uncle Clearance, who worked on cars, namely transmissions.

There was a strategy of me getting on a telephone, asking Baby to take me somewhere. There were the conferences Kenn and I would have, when he was alive, on which scary movie to watch.

The best job, which Anderson had to offer, was working at a factory mill, in those days. South Carolina gave me precious memories of going bowling. I was trying to get a strike.

I nearly, broke my neck, trying to roller skate, at the nearest roller skating rink. My parent's hometown was my temporary home from home, during the summer break.

I was a temperamental, trickster, chubby kid. I wanted things to be on my terms. If not, I'd pout like a trumpet player. The South had its own contemporary style. It was a testimony to its trust in God.

Having to go back to work soon, I had to drive myself back to Virginia. My car flew on the highway, without turbulence. Yet, I was. No vice. It was just me, yanking myself up the road. Little did I know, I saw certain family members alive, for the last time.

I imagined Paris over and over. I was in slow motion in my mind. A turtle couldn't have been more slower. It felt like vinegar. It couldn't have been more sour. On the highway, I felt burned. It was like a heavy yolk was placed around my neck. I had no idea. I didn't know how, I was being typecast by the prosecution.

I was a visionary. I had yet to find true love. Like a maniac, I played a Mariah Carey song over and over. It was a bit much, but this was different. It was a great song called, "Butterfly." I played it so many times. The lyrics were, "Spread your wings and fly." It was telling me to be brave, in other words.

I didn't have any tissues, to wad my face. Especially, from all the tears, which were coming down. There on the highway, alone, in my car, I knew, I had to be brave. When I finally, got to my apartment, I called my mother. She was still in South Carolina. I wanted to let her know, I was okay. I made it, safely. Wham! It hit me. I was in Richmond, Virginia feeling all alone. I felt like, I was sitting under a pine tree. Rather, the tree was sitting on me.

*CHAPTER 15, PART 16*

# Capital Murder

IT WAS JULY 14, 2000. It was a Friday morning. A day like any other. I had to work at Powhatan Correctional Center, later on that night.

I received a phone call.

"Hello," I said.

"Mr. Martin, I've been trying to reach you all week. I heard, you were vacationing in South Carolina," Detective Norris said.

He said it as though I may have been trying to escape or "on the run." I thought to myself. There's only source, he could've got that information from, Mary. I never told him, I have family there. Let alone, know anyone, anywhere in South Carolina.

"Yeah?"

"There's a warrant for your arrest," he said. "You've been charged with Capital Murder."

He sounded glad, the gig was up. It was a slap in the face. It was a kick below the belt. Unequivocally, I was in pain.

"What?" I said, not believing my ears.

"You either turn yourself in, or they're going to arrest you at the prison. Your choice," Norris said.

I was completely, dumbfounded. I didn't want to be arrested at my job.

"The mother said, you meant to do it," said the police detective, about Mary.

SHE SAID, I MEANT TO DO IT? I was completely, shocked. Then again, I shouldn't have been. He was going in for the kill. Immediately, I called my mother. It was a long-distance call. Suddenly, with my change of plans, she was on her way back to Virginia.

I didn't want to be wearisome, but I called my father. Unmistakably, one way or another, I was headed for jail. My father was quickly, on his way over to me. He was nearest kin, distance-wise.

"Son, this is the hardest thing, I ever had to do," said my father.

It was only scratching the surface. He was nearly, in tears himself. He personally, took the task of wheelbarrowing me, in his red, pickup truck. He drove me to the county jail. It was a place, he himself, once locked up alleged criminals.

Truth be told, I was scared out of my mind. Whizzing down the highway, with my father, I didn't know what to expect. Nothing my father said or did was able to uplift me. Wide as the sky, I was sorry, for the mess I made. I was sorry, I met Mary.

"Shawn," said Norris. "I didn't know he was your son."

The detective said it, as though it might've helped matters. I embraced the wind on my face. I didn't know, if it might be the last time, I'd feel for awhile. I was taken to the Booking and Baggage area. Of course, there were vacancies. As I was being processed, it seemed all a blur. I was still in shock. I could not believe, what I was charged with.

I cried and cried. I could not make myself stop. I was losing all my wits about me. In vain, the nurse quickly, checked me, to see if I was okay. It's a wonder, I didn't pass out. I was rushed to a psychiatrist. She asked me, did I have thoughts of killing myself.

"Sometimes," I said.

I was being honest about my depressive, fat-shaming teenage years. Also, not knowing, the oppressive outcome of a future trial.

The woman tried her best, to settle me down.

"Give me a chaplain!" I demanded. "I want a chaplain!" I cried.

I needed God. I needed to speak to a man of God. I didn't care about his faith. As long as he had faith in God, I could work from that. I was hoping, I'd get myself a Holy Quran.

Next, I was placed, in isolation. The jailers affectionately, called it "The Rubber Room." It was a soft padded cell, under "suicide watch."

I was stripped completely, naked. I was forced to wear, only a blue Velcro vest, which barely, reached my knees. No privacy. A camera studied my every move. The walls were seemingly, see-through plexiglass. If I had to use the bathroom, I had to work with merely, a hole, in the middle of the floor. It was not only embarrassing. It was humiliating. I was absolutely, trapped in that room.

My mouth was dry, from all the prayers, I made. I wrestled with my very sanity. I was trying, not to go insane, about the unknown.

Capital Murder? Me? I was faced with two counts. I was charged with Capital Murder and First Degree Murder. It was crazy. I tried my best to make sense of it all. It was a badge of shame. I sat in the padded room, butt-naked. The commonwealth attorneys actually, made me a candidate for the death penalty. I could've served life in prison. I didn't know which was worst.

Obviously, Mary gave them a case to use against me. My children's mother threw me under the bus. Perhaps, in a process of elimination. My heart was pounding. I was caged like an animal.

Being on suicide watch gave me plenty of time to think. I was in full access to reevaluate my life. Everything was happening so fast. It seemed like only yesterday, I was having a ball. I was having the time of my life. Then suddenly, everything, I knew and loved was snatched away from me. There I was, totally, alone. I was isolated from the world. Yes, I was boo-hoo over a Capital Murder charge. I fell into an abyss. I was in and out of sleep. I must have thought of everything, I ever said. I thought of the last thing, the detective said, in front of my father.

"Did the baby cry?" said Norris, before I was placed under arrest. "That could really help us."

Help who? Help him? Help the prosecution? Help me? It was insulting my intelligence. No, Paris did not cry. I didn't shake her, because I wanted to sleep. No, I wasn't angry at her mother. I shook her, because I was tired of seeing her lethargic and NOT CRYING. I wish she did cry. If she did, I was thinking, I wouldn't be in the predicament I was in. However, it gave me something to think about.

"No," I hesitated, feeling the detective was up to his old police tactics and tricks again.

Mere words cannot describe the humiliation. It was sheer degradation, being locked up. I wondered, whether or not, I was going to be harassed. I couldn't trust the deputies, or anyone for that matter. I witnessed, certain correctional officers, treat the inmates at my former job, horrible.

I became nothing more than a number, and expected to identify myself with it. Suddenly, I became a nobody. I was being viewed as a barbarian. One would think, I was a career criminal, to my oppressors.

Day after day, in that "Rubber Room," I was being held accountable, for something I didn't mean to do. Basically, I felt carsick, from sitting on my ass all day.

Once, a kitchen worker, a fellow inmate, slid some food inside my tray slot. He took a look at me, through the glass. He could tell, I wasn't exactly, having "a day at the beach."

"You're okay," he said causally, with approval.

He meant, I didn't need to be in that particular, suicidal area. There was no denying it. It was the most conversation I had in days.

"Stay strong, Black man," said the man, in his kitchen whites.

He didn't know it, but what he said meant a lot. I finally, beckoned a sheriff deputy, to let me use the phone. I was sick of dull moment, after dull moment. I promised the deputy, I'd be on my best behavior. He was standing right beside me, to censure me, should I say something crazy. It was an affirmative. Yet, the other deputies surrounded me, should I do something foolish.

"Mama," I cried. "They charged me with..."

I could hardly, continue. As soon as I heard my mother's voice, I cried like a baby. The charges, and the overzealous prosecution, was grinding into my soul. I felt insulted. I was agitated. It was heart-wrenching.

"Don't cry, Marco," said my cousin Nikki.

With the sound of my tears, it forced her to cry herself.

For the betterment of three days, I was kept in isolation. I was finally, chaperoned to the psychiatrist. He wasn't a bastard, after all. He said, I was okay. He didn't prescribe any pills. We chatted for a few minutes. So, he elevated me to "population" status.

I was a bit nervous. I wished, I was still in my father's red Ford truck. Being with the other inmates, I assumed there was going to be attitude, blasphemy, and God knows what. There wasn't any birds chirping, where I was going. I prayed, my experience as a prison guard would hopefully, give me the wherewithal I needed.

Before I was taken to the bloodcurdling, concrete jungle upstairs, I had to make a Pit Stop. I was summoned to the counselor. She went over my job chronology. She saw, I was a correctional officer. Being that my ancestors was "law enforcement," it made me blush.

Under the circumstances, she asked me, was there something she should do? Such as a home-arrest ankle monitor. I was sort of flattered, they were willing to take safety precautions, on my behalf.

"I'm okay," I said.

Then a bomb dropped on me. It was clear. I was now, "an inmate." I was on the other side of the fence. Without an apology from anybody, I was seeing how the other half lives. It felt like, society gave me its foot up the ass. I was now considered a scumbag, a lowlife. I was another statistic. Another young, Black man in jail.

Gone was the 1990's friendly, family atmosphere of the mosques. Gone was the familiar faces, I knew and loved. No one knew me. No one cared.

For a lack of a better word, I was disappointed. What was to become of me? I had no idea, what to expect. I wasn't sure, if I'd ever see a woman's cleavage ever again. I wanted to write a new diary.

Walking on "The Boulevard" or main hallway was enough to be a life-altering experience, in of itself. There was yelling. There was screaming. Many closed minds of chaos and confusion.

Every eye captured me, as I walked into Pod 226. I was assigned to Cell 6. More disappointment. I had the distinct pleasure of sleeping, with my mattress on the cold, cemented floor. Meanwhile, my two other cell mates were already snuggled in their metal bunkbeds. First come, first served, supposedly.

Being in jail was nothing to brag about. I wanted to clobber someone over the head myself. Others did just that. So many fights, quick tempers. Without thinking, the correctional officer in me tried to break up fights. I was quick as an Arabian horse. If I had a coin, for every argument I heard,

I'd be a rich man. I could've got hurt. I could've been killed. Somehow, I wanted to show my fellow inmates, there was a better way. We were all in this boat, together. Some guys had massive arms. Some were willing to cross the bridge, whenever they got to it.

Most of the men, in the county jail, were black. That's a fact. Because of the central air-conditioning, it wasn't hot. There weren't any roaches. Thank God. Many inmates laughed and joked through their situation. Some slept their problems away. Some were comedians at the card table. Despite their reality, others had aspirations of doing better. A few wanted their own businesses, when they get out of jail. A handful bucked or were disgruntled at any common mistake or mishap.

I was fresh off the street, sort of speak. I straddled to be a nice and friendly guy. I had an education. I had a meaningful job. I was no bum, dumb, or came from the slum.

"You want a Reese's Peanut Butter Cup? Two for one," said Stanley.

Mmm. It was my favorite. I'd have to give him two back, with the price of one. He was running a "store box" hustle, obviously. Interestingly, he notice, I was a newcomer to the penal system. I didn't have anything, so I took his offer. I should've been burned at the stake. I was desperate. I was hungry.

I was depressed, like anyone else. Yet, I tried not to show it. To spice things up, I'd watch a few card games. I'd watch card players argue and butt heads. I concurred with many "aviators" who liked to get high sometimes.

Overall, I felt bad. I couldn't wait for my day in court. I would have the chance, to confront my accusers. I was a bachelor, now labeled a murderer. Consequently, I thought of every legal loophole, I could think of. I was going to fight my case, or die trying, literally.

"If it's war they want, it's war they get!" I thought to myself.

I was told, my lawyer wanted to see me downstairs. What lawyer? As soon as I took one look at those dinky eyes of his, I knew I was in trouble.

"Oh, hell naw!" I thought.

I could already tell. Collins was seemingly, an evader, a plea bargainer, who wasn't going to do much in my defense. He was set to be my court appointed lawyer. I didn't know that at the time.

"I appreciate it, but my family already got me a lawyer," I said to Collins, not allowing him to continue.

I didn't know exactly, how. I felt my family was going to retain David Baugh, "a real attorney." He was the one I wanted to ride a convoy with. Of course, this wasn't the case. As usual, I called my mother, daily. This time, I called my father as well.

"Yeah, that's your lawyer," he said. "I know him. He's good."

My father was referring to Collins, not Baugh. I felt cremated. I was stuck with the cornball, not the flashy lawyer. I was floored. Unfortunately, with a high-profile case like mine, my parents couldn't afford a great high-profile lawyer. I was infected with helplessness.

I was locked in my cell, like another day in the office. My roommate, Mike, had some questions for me. After all, jail was more than "three hots and a cot." People sometimes, become buddies, friends, or acquaintances.

"Marco, you don't seem like the type of dude, who'll get into trouble. What are you in here for?" he said, finally.

I took it as a compliment. However, I was most displeased. I had a lot of things, I wanted to get off of my chest. Besides, I had nothing to hide. Yet, I knew what I was about to disclose, could cause an explosion. Not to mention, if Mike didn't believe me.

I knew early on, even though I may have been around true murderers, rapists, armed robbers, thieves, liars, drug dealers, and drug dealers, they "didn't play that." Especially, when it came to innocent children. Many of them had children of their own. After a few minutes, Mike knew my reasoning for being there.

"Man, that's fucked up, they got you in here for that! You ain't mean to do that shit!" Mike said. "I think the babysitter, at your baby's mama house, did it."

My other roommate was known simply, as "Wood." Usually, he kept his distance. He took time, out of his busy schedule, from reading the Bible, to know what was going on. He had a crappy attitude. He slept all day. He was in and out of jail, most of his adult life. Also, he had a bad habit of nose diving in heroin.

"We got another one!" Wood said.

He was saying that about me. With that, he was informing the whole tier. I had somewhat, a similar case, to another fellow inmate. Woodrow was a dope fiend, a crack head, a late-forties, faceless criminal in the penal system. He made me want to scream. However, I kept my cool.

"What did her mama say? That's the most important thing," said Mike.

"She knows it was an accident," I lied.

Mary gave the assistant commonwealth attorneys, their entire case. Everything they thought they knew about me, centered on what she told them. The whole docket of everything, I ever did with her. As far as I knew, she was on their side. I knew it in my soul. When her and I got into it, her nails ripped into my skin, like falcon talons. Surely, she didn't mention that, while painting herself as the perfect mother.

My visitation days were Sundays and Tuesdays. On a hard-to-hear anything phone, behind thick glass, the sheriff deputies timed us for approximately, 30 minutes.

Once my father dropped a jewel, which I didn't forget. It sparked something in me. It put me hard at work.

"Marco, I want you to write those stories, you used to write, when you were younger," he said.

So, I did just that. I got a blank, composition book. I got my hands on a dictionary. I wrote and wrote, until my heart's content. I wrote, like it was nobody's business. Words and ideas poured out of me. I'd write during tv show commercials. I'd put my writing down, to enjoy the show, only to pick it again during break.

I nearly, forgot how creative writing gave me a sense of purpose. It's been so long, since I did any writing. It was like being reacquainted again, with a long-lost friend. I wrote poems. I wrote short stories. After I became discouraged, because a book publisher wanted money upfront, I just stopped. My ambition was lost. Now it was found. I founded me again.

It never dawn on me, my father still remembered. Especially, after 13 years of no communication. My father reminded me, through my writing, I can be whoever, I want to be. I could go, wherever I wanted to go. I could "escape" and live out, all my fantasies. It sounded great! Also, he told me about Charles S. Dutton. He was an accomplished actor. He was once in prison for murder, and overcame it.

Not long after, David Baugh paid me an unexpected visit. He was sure to cross all the T's and dot the I's. However, not as my lawyer. Doubtlessly, he was the best man for the job.

"I thought about your case and I couldn't sleep. So, how are you doing?" he asked.

My upcoming trial was one string, my father couldn't pull. Wiping the crust out of my eye, I thanked Baugh, for coming down, in the middle of the night to see.

Like a summer draft, which breezed in, Doctor Ismail said his door was always open for me. I called him often. Being the imam of Masjidullaah, he assured me, it was a test from Allah. It was that sort of thing. Feeling fragile, I'd also call Brother Abu Bakr.

It was all, so ironic. I never thought, in my wildest dreams, I'd be in jail. It was a cup, I thought, I'd never drink from. Yet, it was no dress rehearsal. It was the real thing. Ghetto guys were firm in their ways. I was set in mine.

My former life was cut up. It was torn to shreds. Held against my will, I was forced to browse among the criminal minded. Whether I liked it or not. I was a fish out of water. I was out of my element. Almost daily, there was a fist fight. Should an inquiring mind wanted to know.

Trying to beat another dull moment, the inmates would file in line, for the library or canteen. I longed to be behind the dashboard of my car again. I missed my freedom. I was dying inside. Especially, knowing, I was fingerprinted downstairs, for Capital Murder. One thing I knew for certain, I did not want my daughter dead. Going from grief to jail was like jumping, out of the frying pan, into the fire. Being around a bunch of no-good people didn't make things easier.

I had a fit, when I found out, some of my food items were missing. I knew it was no other than my roommate, Mike. I felt so deceived. It wasn't my fault, my parents were economically, okay. Rather than flap my mouth, and get my ass into trouble, I learned to be patient. Sure, he creeped into my bag, when I wasn't around. Not getting into, a fight with him, was a feat in of itself. Flexing my social skills, I asked "Pops" to hold my canteen bag in his cell. Gratefully, he agreed. Problem solved.

By definition, the food at the jail, which they served us as deplorable. Often, the inmates in my pod elected to send the food back, if it was too cold.

Once, I flopped my tray down on the table. Then I proceeded to get something to drink. Of course, there were limited places to sit. I was about to eat from my tray. A young guy, Glenn stood over me, in an immaculate display of wanting to fight me. In a fluke or misunderstanding, Glenn happen to put his tray beside mine. He actually, thought I was eating from his tray.

I lost it. The quiet demure I had was gone.

"You think I'm going to steal your food? This nasty ass tray?" I amplified. "Sit down, boy! Sit down!"

Next, I got up. I went to my cell and slammed the door behind me. It's a good thing, Glenn didn't follow me, as mad as I was. Frustrated, there's no telling what I would've done. I sat in my spot and cried. I couldn't believe, I almost got into a fight. I was in a crypt. I hated it. I forced myself to relax and take it easy.

I was a descendant of slaves. It was as though, they rose from the grave. I felt a small glimpse of what it must've have felt like. Formally, I was indicted as a "destroyer of life." My entire being knew the difference. It was the biggest fight of my life. It was though I was fighting the Devil himself. I was pissed. I was framed. I was thrown under the bus, by the woman who gave me two babies. I was going to the Law Library. I had a lot of work to do.

The "Penthouse" was an empty room upstairs. It overlooked the pod. Once, I was lounging with my White counterparts. Looking through the large, glass window, I could still hear the relentless screaming and shouting. I made my final dialysis on the subject.

"Look at these people! They're animals!" I said.

I was sick of the toxic yelling. The prison slang made me feel like I was frozen in a time warp. It was difficult to fit in with the other Black people it seemed. I wasn't from the streets. Nor did I want to be.

Being in charge of inmates, as a correctional officer, was one thing.

231

I wasn't living with them. Actually, being an inmate myself was quite another.

I held unto my childhood memories. I was secretly, proud of my VCU achievement. Anything to keep my sanity. I needed to remember, being an incarcerated person wasn't always my condition. I could remember, many years prior, when it was Easter holiday. I'd give me younger brother, Mel, "frogs" by pinching his arm.

For fulfillment, I'd read Star Trek books and horror novels, to pass the time. I'd read Stephen King. I'd read Deen Koontz.

Sometimes, I'd grab a Donald Goines book. His stuff was usually, about pimps, players, prostitution and high rollers. Inner City life became interesting to read about. I liked Goines' writing style. Yet, I thought Black people deserved more than the ruthless killer stereotypes.

I wanted to write about the Black middle class. Especially, Black people, who didn't necessarily, commit crimes. I could understood characters working hard, struggle, and being financially, independent. I wanted to write about a Black person, who had to work twice as hard in corporate America.

I wanted to write about a Black woman, who wore furs to her Historical Society Dinner parties. People were unsure of her Blackness.

Perhaps, I wanted to write about a Black man, who was gainfully, employed. He was holding on to his cheating ways. However, he was searching for inner peace. He wanted a woman, he always wanted, despite his marriage. She was a recently, divorced woman. She had to sell her precious, and not so many pleasant memories at her own Garage Sale.

With my father's encouragement, he created a "monster" in me. I couldn't put the pen down. I wanted to show the world, not all Black people are from the housing projects. Not everyone was under homicide investigation. "No man is an island." So, I wanted to portray Black people as a thriving community, like anyone else. I wanted the world to see, Black people have the same goals, hope and dreams, as everyone else. Some of us go to Ivy League schools.

I wanted to write. I needed to write. I was literally, stripped of everything, except my mind. It was all I had left. Also, it was in my genes, which I got from my mother. She used to write her family really, long, detailed letters.

My lawyer was no slice of heaven either. However, he was great friends with the assistant commonwealth attorney, Deglau. Collins would give me the inside scoop. Especially, what the prosecution was planning next. Plenty of times, I walked into the courtroom, because my attorney filed a motion. Sometimes, I'd walk in, with the two of them laughing their heads off. My gracious host dropped a bomb on me.

"They said, they got witnesses saying, you're going around the jail admitting you didn't want your child," Collins said to me.

Nothing could be further from the truth. I did not say that. I did not feel like that. Nobody would tell a bunch a hardened criminals, however, fathers in jail, he didn't want their child.

"That's a lie! I ain't say nothing like that!"

Obviously, I thought it was some jealous fool, trying to get a gift of reduced time. I wanted to howl to the moon. It was outrageous. It was a mockery of my character.

"I have a list, with ten names on it. Let me know, if you recognize the names," said my lawyer.

With a lump in my throat, my heart skipped a beat.

"No…uh-uh…nope," I said, as he read the names.

I was starting to feel hopeful, at the unfamiliar people. It was nearly, humorous. Especially, if that was all the prosecution had. I couldn't wait to meet the judge.

"It's the EMS people then," said my attorney, with thick glass between us.

The paramedics? It was worse than electric shock. Somehow, they looked upon me, as though I didn't care, or showed remorse over my child? Was it because of what Mary said to any ear, who would listen? This was the thanks I get? I was confused. I absolutely, wanted a jury trial. I didn't want to go to the courtroom, with only one person deciding my fate. Namely, a judge, or bench trial.

When I told my family, I thought the whole thing was hysterical. I had to keep in mind, I was a good person. Only an idiot would think I didn't want my child. I not only demanded respect, but I gave it. I illustrated kindness to all who knew me. Everything, I worked so hard for, was flipped in an instance.

That's not the worst of it. My maternal grandma, Maggie, passed away, after a couple of months of my incarceration. It was Labor Day weekend. She lived her final days in California, with me uncle Reggie. My grandma was a modest woman. She suffered from blindness and Alzheimer's.

When my mother gave me the news in the visit room, I dropped the phone. It felt like gravity was kicked out from under me. The pearls she left behind. The thing I remember, most from her, was fortitude. She was strong. One would think, she was made of iron. She was independent. Yet, inside she was soft as a lamb. She knew a lot about plants and flowers. She had a small garden.

Before she put into the ground, in her final resting place, I had one request. I asked the family, to dedicate a song, from The Color Purple movie, "Maybe God is Trying to Tell You Something," at the funeral.

When I was a little boy, my grandma was quick, to spank me across her lap. She was stern but fair. However, my cousin Carl led the eulogy. I was told, he said some harsh words. It was upsetting. He implied, our grandma didn't attend church. Supposedly, like she should have. Why the judgement, was anyone's guess.

I had a lot of work to do. I had a lot of decisions to make. The alarming part, I wasn't around many Latinos, until I was locked up. I could only guess, why they weren't in the corporate office.

Sometimes, I'd lay down and I'd have a "Aha!" moment. I was determined to learn, all I could about my case. Like a hammer to the head, I didn't belong there.

I was conducting myself in orderly, fashion. I went to the Islamic Service at the jail. It was more or less, a class being held on Saturday morning. Though it was only a handful of Muslims in attendance. Yet, it gave me a leg to stand on. They weren't the type of people normally, I'd hang around. I wanted to make the most of it. I figured, they were in an infant stage or new converts of Islam. The imam was an inmate, like the rest of us. He'd let us read along with him from the Quran.

I wanted to pray. However, I was hard on myself. I didn't want the infrared, added attention. I didn't want the vulnerability. I didn't know what kind of libido was lurking in there. I didn't who I could trust. I didn't know, whether or not, I should bend over, or prostrate to the floor, in prayer. It haunted me. I was in jail. I needed God, more than ever. I was Muslim. Prayer was something we did. Yet, I wasn't comfortable doing it. Especially, in front of non-Muslims. Being in that environment was no easy cruise. Anything was subjected to happen, at any given time. Islam was my life, despite my imperfections. Somehow, I wanted to work my five daily prayers in. I really did.

Shaheed was our spiritual leader. He was headstrong. He wrote the chaplain and the sheriff. We needed to have our Jumuah, Friday prayer, religious service. We didn't think it was fair, other religious groups could have their service on Sundays, but offer us nothing. It was heavy.

The administration handed us an excuse. We were stalled, because we didn't have an outside sponsor. Linguistically speaking, we didn't have any help in sight. Yet, we held our integrity. Literally, we were waiting for a hero, from the street, to walk through the county jail doors.

Interestingly, Malik's name, who I knew from the masjid, kept coming up. I was amazed, under lock and key, he was practically, a penitentiary legend. He was known to visit and support Muslim inmates.

It wasn't before long, when a Brother, nicknamed Duck, came along. Rumor had it, he was a certified paralegal. He threatened to get the American Civil Liberties Union on Sheriff Wade. We were being denied our Friday service.

Eventually, the Muslims were granted congregational worship for Friday, and Friday only at 2:00 pm. Everything was laid on the table. We were partially satisfied, while letting our Saturday class go.

The chaplain, was who many thought of as Lucifer. He had a method of marking out, in the English translation, within the Al-Fatihah. It was the (parentheses) interpretation of not "wanting to be in His Wrath, such as the Jews, or go astray, such as the Christians." It was the Opening, or first chapter of the Quran. The chaplain denied, he had anything to do with it. Yet, it was crossed out with every copy, he gave us. The Muslims in the jail wanted to punish him. However, we couldn't prove it.

Nationwide seemingly, a lot of Muslims felt America treated us like we were all radicals, all wrong, and so different. Many thought we were all viewed, in the same way, as would-be terrorists or out-of-touch extremists. Islam is a religion. It's not Mafia, or organized crime syndicate. Hardly, anyone trusted the media. Especially, if It was a pattern of mistrust and misunderstanding from them. Nearly, all the believers in jail believed in this conspiracy theory. Such as the administration was against Muslims. Not to mention, in their attempt to destroy Islam.

I maintained my loyalty to the religion. However, I neighed in frustration. It was the "Penitentiary Islam" version, I had a problem with. It was the unpleasantness and street mentality. More importantly, it was the malice backbiting.

Whenever, I spotted a so-called Brother, the feeling wasn't neutral. I wasn't comfortable, to put it, delicately. I wasn't in the state penitentiary, and already, the rough edges were getting to me.

Clearly, the special bond of brotherhood, between believers wasn't there. It was unlike the believers I've known at the masjid. They were rough around the edges, sort of speak.

I wrestled with the idea of humble, laidback, easygoing Muslims on the street. In comparison, to the stern, stoic, judgmental, incarcerated Muslims. The Muslims in jail isolated themselves. Yet, they were just as loud. They'd curse just as anyone else. It made me numb inside. Especially, because I knew we were supposed to be inviting, helpful, nice, comfortable and relaxed.

With no one to talk to, or give me a pep talk, things seemed bleak. I moaned to myself in misery. I saw no difference, in the Muslims' behavior, and the non-Muslims in there. Only in their looks, books and beliefs. It was the only thing, which seemed to matter to them. The no-nonsense projection wasn't me.

"Where's the love? Where's the compassion?" I'd ask myself.

My faith plummeted. I know, nobody's perfect. Some of those guys were as blatant as a well-lit marque, for a movie premiere. It wasn't normal. It wasn't what I was used to. I was perplexed. I didn't know who to trust.

Masterfully, I didn't notify my mother, too much, of how bad I felt. Sure, I was pesky. I was calling her collect, everyday, discussing the case. I didn't want her to worry.

I no longer wanted to be Mary's doormat. I knew her phone number. I refused to call. Especially, after she told the prosecution, I meant to do "intentional hurt" to our baby.

A lot of inmates were poor as peasants. It may explain why some were so damn mean. Some were robbing and stealing from each other.

Going to recreation, outside or inside the gymnasium was once a week. It was an hour and a half event. I played a little volleyball. It wasn't exactly, a photo op moment, but I participated. Many inmates would meet to talk about, the obvious, their cases.

Every other word, which dripped out people's mouths were "shit" or "motherfucker." It drove me nuts. I learned quickly, not to meddle in folk's affairs. If I saw something officially, I didn't see it. Too many questions, could get a person pinned against the wall.

I was mesmerized, how many canteen items, it took to grease palms, for one cigarette. I wasn't made of stone. Smoking everyday, then suddenly, having to stop, was enough to piss anyone off. Pulling a few tricks out of their sleeves, some inmates, who were on work-release, would overcharge for cigarettes. I was placed in a tough spot. I'd pay for a roll-up. Someone else would be on the lookout, for a possible sheriff deputy, making his, or her rounds. An inmate would often warn, "Five-0," if one should appear. That would force us to be smooth operators.

With no woman around, I had to get used to the idea. It was toxic. I had a lot of things on my mind. The few ladies I knew, became a blur. I was a squirrel in a nutshell. It was difficult.

Jail was confrontational. I was on Planet Pluto. The inmates slayed me, how they treated each other. I wasn't trying to win a popularity contest. Yet, I'd mix with folks. I was trying to be a "people person." I'd say hello to everyone. I didn't want to be an antisocial. I certainly, didn't want to send the wrong message, like I'm better than. Some gave themselves another outlook on life. With others, street life was all they knew, or aspire to be.

# BEHOLD

I'd walk the middle path. I didn't act hard, but I wasn't soft either. I minded my own business. I stayed to myself. I flew under the radar. It seemed to work. People seemingly, respected me, for being a nice guy. I was being myself, without the false pretenses.

I wished I had a polygraph. I can't tell you, how many times, I heard, "I didn't do it." Particularly, from an older guy, who went by the name of Shaft. He was a "jailhouse lawyer," who operated at every angle, to get back at the system. He'd write grievance after grievance. His Afrocentric ways were a little overbearing. However, he was popular with the inmates, who needed help with their legal work.

Shaft was charged with First Degree Murder. He was no monk. Yet, his knowledge of the law overshadowed that. Him and I talked daily.

I possessed a little know-how myself, as a VCU graduate. Guys would ask me, to write on their behalf, a Sentence Reduction, to the judge. I was happy to do so. "The world is your oyster," so I gave it a try. Besides, it was my way of sticking it to the system, who didn't care about us. I was helping to "check and balance" a fair trial for the underdog.

I missed smoking pot. I missed being with my family. I wanted to be with people, who actually, loved and cared about me. I missed playing my Prince music. I missed being around praiseworthy Muslims. I missed my movies. I missed being around law-abiding citizens. I missed regular, everyday-people. Instead, I was stuck in an unnatural environment. It was filled with pandemonium.

The thing I had to remember most, I was destined to be there. I believed in fate. I accepted God's Will. Yet, I was sitting in jail, charged by its definition, with "premeditated murder."

I took the time, to push other cases, paperwork and loopholes, I found in the law library, at my lawyer. I was fighting for my freedom. He looked at it as though it was irrelevant.

"You don't have to try to convince me," said Collins. "I believe you."

So, in other words, my sermon was being preached to the choir. The lawyer acted as though, he was preserving his talents for the courtroom. I wasn't a remote control. I wasn't something, you can turn on and off on a dime. I needed to talk about my case. 70 times, I had to.

My depression varied from day to day. Paris' accident replayed in my mind, over and over. My shaking of her was viewed again and again. I was down, not out. As far as I was concerned, jail was a primitive gesture. The pain of my daughter was no match. Prison paled in comparison. I did what I did, what I thought was needed of me. I wanted to help, not hurt.

"If only, she'd been more active," I'd say, blaming myself.

I resolved what could've been. I didn't know where my ship was going. I didn't know how long, I was going to be on it. I wanted to be productive. I was strictly, thinking about "good time," should I happen to get time. I entered my name on a short list, for the "Trustee" pod. My life was prohibited. However, I wanted to do something to vamp it up.

I shriveled up at the thought. Especially, at the amount of years I was facing. I had no idea, what kind of proof the commonwealth attorneys was going to use. To win the case, I assumed they were going to throw everything, but the kitchen sink. I didn't know whose side, Mary was going to be on. The prosecution was sure to rig the trial to their advantage, but how?

It became perfectly, clear to me, regardless of my educational status. Despite being a former employee, of a correctional institution, I was nothing but a "nigger" to the folks, who threw me in jail.

I felt silly, having Collins as my attorney. I felt, he didn't give a damn. My family couldn't afford to provide me with a paid one.

"You've got a good lawyer," some inmates said, thinking I should just, let it ride.

"Man, tell the judge, you want another lawyer. Collins some shit," said others, letting me know, I was with a real sinkhole.

I was surrounded with sociopaths. Many inmates didn't know their roots. A few didn't know, who their father was. Some could sketch a drawing, as good as any artist. A lot of guys were proud of the bullets they shot, in a roundabout way. I knew a few, who wouldn't hesitate to slash a neck, if someone was blocking their path.

The jail was purged with rude sentiments. A slip of the tongue could be punitive. Some ran their mouths, a mile a minute. Some smacked their lips, about nothing. Others had nothing to do, but complain, such as how the laundry wasn't coming back clean. Many laid in bed all day.

Apparently, it was their refuge. However, I was smooth. I was social. Yet, I trusted no one.

"He be messing with boys," a gay slur, I'd often hear, about a possible sway of someone.

I was amazed. It was so homophobic in jail. Many were fearful of someone stereotypically, being gay. I flinched, whenever I heard someone utter the word, "faggot." It was appalling. I hated that word. I didn't understand, why so many men in jail, who apparently, liked women, was concerned about someone else liking men. I didn't care what someone else was into. It didn't have anything to do with me. I just knew what I liked, which was women. That's what mattered to me.

My brother was gay. I had two uncles, who were gay. I wasn't thrilled about the idea, but I moved on. They had their life. I had mine. I didn't hate anyone. I just wanted "salaam." I wanted peace. I didn't want to be a snob or anything.

What made me feel great, no one suspected me, of being gay, unlike Mary did. The caliber of people, from the hood, treated me as a regular guy. I was socially acceptable, which was nice, in of itself. My question, if people in jail could see I wasn't gay, why couldn't Mary?

Don't get me wrong, a lot of inmates were radical as Satan himself. However, on a solo effort, I raked in more and more associates. I thought it was important, to build bridges, not walls. I was an open wound. I didn't know what tomorrow was going to bring. I heard so many rumors of how many people were raped in state penitentiary.

Call me a "scatterbrain," but when I was a correctional officer, I didn't notice any sexual misconduct from the inmates. Nor did I want to. Everyone seemed to give everyone their space. I thought that was crafty.

On occasion, I'd voice to my court-appointed attorney, how I wanted my case to go. There were so many points, I wanted to make. I wanted my mother to get on the witness stand. Obviously, she could testify how lethargic Paris was. I wasn't making things up.

"She'll just fuck things up," Collins said to me.

Needless to say, with his lack of professional courtesy, and direct insult to my mother, I wanted to curse the man out. Yet, I didn't want to sabotage my case, with the lawyer, even further. Collins thought of getting a blood specialist on my behalf, to speak about Paris' state of being. Eventually, he declined the idea.

What a sphere. What a world I was in. I didn't feel, I had to go into the courtroom, with a bluff anyway. The truth was on my side, right? It was a sea of confusion. Despite all the crap, I had to go through, there was truth.

More than anything, I wanted to be home. I wanted to be reclining on my mother's couch, where it all began. While at the county jail, I didn't have anything to hide. I had no secrets. My life was an open book, sort of speak. I wanted people to see, the injustice being done to me. Accident, yes. Murder, no.

The only television in the pod, was usually, stuck on sports. For the first time, I was interested to know, what was going on with current events. Especially, in the outside world. So, I began reading the newspaper. Between television segments or commercials, someone might turn the tv channel. In hopes, to catching a spunky music video, or nice looking woman, here and there. I saw so many arguments, over that one-eye monster.

"Fuck that tv! I'll pour water on that shit!" someone would say, flexing his bravado muscles.

The TV set was a self-regulating machine in of itself. Touching the tv was taking matters into your own hands. There were plenty of times, I'd be watching a show, and I'd get a reminder, I'm not at home. Someone would turn the channel, without asking. It was rude. It was no consideration. It made me squirm in my seat, but it wasn't worth it.

"Sports rule," I'd often hear from inmates, in their regulation, before things went further.

So, I'd do what any sensible person would do. I became somewhat of an avid book reader. I'd read a book or magazine to steal time. It was a lot safer and less complicated.

I had stars in my eyes, when the deputy finally, told me to pack up. I was approved for the Trustee program. In theory, I needed all the help I could get, to come home sooner. Rumor had it, it'll increase "good time."

I had an unshakable faith in Allah. However, I didn't want to stay in prison, any longer than I had to. I didn't want to spend years in that place, as nothing but inmate number. I didn't want to be another, so-called thing-amajig, wearing prison blues, day in and day out.

The Trustee pod was better than general population. Yet, my cellmate was like a stepbrother, in the way. Eventually, I wanted to get my own cell, like everyone else.

I was assigned the "houseman" job. I exchanged my tan scrubs for noticeably, navy blue ones. I had the privilege of gathering trash. I'd hear the uproar from inmates, if they felt the showers weren't clean enough. I had the stigma of moping the floors. I had to clean tables. I mostly, thrusted the broom aimlessly, trying to make myself look useful.

I had a peculiarly, weird roommate, Michael. He usually, gave me stoic tidings. He wanted to sleep with me. He was a drug dealer. He was a vagabond, at best. I assumed he was only joking. Yet, time and time again, it was an issue. I had to let him know, I wasn't that type of guy.

A couple of times, he grabbed my ass. He wanted to see my reaction. I refused to sink to his level, and street brawl with him. I didn't want to anything violent. Especially, with the so-called scales of justice tilted even further. Despite as blind as that may sound.

In my bed, I was stripped down to my underwear. I didn't know, if he was going to try anything or what. Eventually, Michael toned it down. Also, I made sure, I wasn't standing directly, in front of him, with my back turned.

Studying Islam became more and more, on the top of my list. I sought the victory. I wanted to subdue the trials and tribulations. Many were laid out in front of me. It was either study, or watch football teams, trying to score a touchdown.

At any rate, the loudness was violating my quiet time. Eventually, I began to cheer for Tampa Bay Buccaneers, for the first time. It was the color red, pirate mascot, the pirate flag, embraced with swords, for me. "When in Rome.."

Sometimes, I had a one-time mind. The Quran was vital to me, none the less. I was tired of the suffering. I was sick of the bad transition between people. So, I vented, like everyone else, at some of the games. Sports became a great opportunity to escape.

Without another Muslim leader in sight, I assumed myself as imam, for the county jail. I wasn't fishing. However, when Shaheed was transferred to another facility, someone had to do it. I wasn't looking for the imam position. Yet, I did feel, I was best man for the job, at the time. I wanted to help supervise the affairs, on behalf of the Muslim community. Besides, no one else was willing, or volunteered to do it.

It was the chance of a lifetime. Being an imam was an honor. I felt great. I felt taller than a tree. Being the imam, gave me the whopping task, of carrying the message of Islam, to the people. With years of experience, I didn't have to guess how things went. I was completely, nervous as to make a mistake. Of course, there were a million other places I rather be. However, nothing was more important than making sure guys at the jail had a firm grasp of what Islam is, and isn't.

As imam, I didn't want to sound shallow. Not with books. Certainly, not with attitude or attire. I didn't want Muslims being betrayed as troublemakers. I simply, wanted to get the wax out of people's ears. I wanted the truth to sweep them away.

Sure, I wanted to be home. I wanted to soak in a tub. I wanted to wear weatherproof Timberland boots, like anyone else. Yet, I had a job to do. I had the responsibility of being empathetic, and bringing people to God's Word.

When it was my turn to give the Friday prayer service, I didn't have time to be shy. Well, let's just say, all my little insecurities went out the window. I was on a mission. I put it all on the table. It was nothing sweet. I was brave. Therefore, my voice was louder. As I was looking out into the small congregation, they seemed to be taking what I was saying well. I would notice typical nods of approval. I had their undivided attention. I didn't whitewash anything.

Besides, it wasn't about me. It was about Allah. At the end of the "khutbah" or sermon, my eyes were damp with tears. I was filled with pride. After the prayer, some of the guys walked up to me. I didn't know what to expect.

"That was a good khutbah!" one said, without debate.

It was humbling. It was a wildflower blooming. It wasn't, "Darn, I'm the leader." It was, "Wow, I'm the leader." It all balanced out. Being the imam allowed me to spread my wings. I truly, felt like it was my calling. It wasn't about how much I could memorize. It wasn't about "being smart." I was coming from the heart.

In the pod, a buddy of mine let me know, I had a weak court case. I appreciated his honesty.

"When's the last time, you talked to your daughter's mother?" he said.

It was months. Not since Paris' funeral.

"Oh, forget her! She's the one, who told the police, I meant to do it!" I said.

He let me know, there's no way, I'd be able to function in that courtroom, without her. He didn't think it was a good idea, to be in withdrawal, or not speaking with Mary. Not to mention, I was following the lawyer's council.

"Man, you need to get on that telephone, and make her understand, from you, on what happened!" said he, who shall remain priceless for the advice.

Even if I wanted to talk to her, there was a block on the phone.

"You need to write her then!" said Charles.

I didn't know what to say, let alone write. I didn't know where to begin.

"Man, I'll write it. Just copy it down," he said.

Charles assured me, it would work. It had to work. I had to try. I was facing a Capital Murder charge, for God's sake. If not, I was a dead man. The only thing, Mary had a tendency of taking things the wrong way. I didn't know, how fixed her mind was made up about me. So, I was a little worried. The wrong word could backfire. One letter for that matter. It could terminate me, forever.

Day after day, I was in anticipation for Mary's mail. On a prayer, I hoped she would realize. There's no way, in the universe, I'd try to hurt my child. I'd slit my wrist, before I'd try to hurt a child.

Finally, from the context of what Mary was saying, I think she believed me. Like the Quran says, there's a barrier between fresh water and salt water. Her letter was palatable to my eyes. It was the 11th hour. Maybe her and I were on the same team. Maybe I gained some yardage with her. It was hard to tell. One thing for certain, I didn't know.

"You've got to communicate with her," smiled Charles, when Mary wrote me.

I was a zombie. I was a dead man walking. I was sick of the melodrama. My sister, Drika wrote a response letter to Mary, on my behalf. I simply, copied it.

I was taken aback, by the lack of progress I was making. Every bone in my body tingled, whenever I was summoned to court. My attorney filed several motions.

He wanted the two assistant commonwealth attorneys be removed, because of both of their seventh-month pregnancies. Due to the nature of my trial, it would be prejudicial. DENIED.

Collins filed a motion, for the removal of another prosecution's cheap tactic of prejudicing the jury. They wanted to use against me, a picture snapshot of Paris' gravesite. DENIED.

I was insulted with that one. How dare they go my daughter's grave! That is sacred ground! They had the audacity, to use the image of my child's headstone, to use against me.

Court was horrific. I lost the ability to breathe at times. Collins asked Judge Hammond, if the bailiffs would take the handcuffs off me, before I entered the courtroom. It could've been upsetting to a jury, thinking I was "dangerous man." APPROVAL.

Suddenly, it hit me, like a cannonball. I was fighting Capital Murder inside a courtroom. I was literally, fighting what Mary told those prosecution folks.

Being around a self-absorbed, lead assistant, commonwealth attorney, like Deglau drove me bananas. She told captivating lies to a fairly, new-appointed judge. She walked Judge Hammond through her first Capital Murder trial. She led all the so-called evidence to the judge. Such as what was acceptable for my case. It was a Barnum and Bailey circus.

Somehow, I had to show, I was a caring father. Especially, to a bunch of people, who didn't know me. Sometimes, I wished I never met Mary.

I felt my lawyer was a real bastard. He probably, only cascaded, with the money the state was paying him. Somehow, I had to show, I always played an active role in my children's lives.

Deglau was no beanpole. Anyone could look at her, and her assistant, and see they were nearly, full term. How was this fair? She was still pretty. Surely, she would get catcalls from the men. Yet, rumor had it, she was going to say or do, whatever it took to get a conviction. Despite it all, I never regretted being Paris' father. It was a covenant, I happily, took.

Thanksgiving and Christmas in jail, an adventure in itself. Instead of spending time with my family, I had to endure the belching and farting from certified criminals. It was with people, who couldn't care less about me. That alone, made me feel numb. I was thinking, I could possibly, never walk down the avenue again. It made me want to argue. The thought of never seeing a woman again, made me want to cause a riot.

I wanted to dive for cover. How could those prosecutors be so blind? I made a mental check list. Everything I did was accounted for…and that's not all. My mother was a potential witness for my defense. However, unless she was summoned into the courtroom, she wasn't allowed to see how things were going. It was so bizarre. The judge, the prosecutors, and my lawyer, were talking about my child, as though I wasn't there. That amazed me.

"Why, that lying (beep)," I would think.

I couldn't help but think, the commonwealth attorneys were coming down, so hard on me, was because of my chocolate skin. Amping my feelings even further, what else was I to think? It didn't take a lot to see, my case was accidental. Regardless of Mary's figment of her imagination. It was a drag. I was on a boat, without a paddle. A storm of lies could've went anywhere.

All of this, I thought, because Mary blamed Madrika. Apparently, for not seeing her romantically, any longer. She felt my sister was telling me what to do. Of course, it wasn't true. I was sick of the physical abuse, and the mental madness. I was tired of being labeled something I wasn't. I was done with fighting for my dignity.

Going to trial was the most horrific experience, I ever been through.

It was sheer torture. My family assured me, I wasn't alone. I was not in a class by myself.

"People are wrongly, accused all the time," I'd hear.

I was treated like I was the Antichrist. Deglau wanted nothing more, to give me life. A life of boredom. It was a hostile climate, and I was the trophy for the taking.

In that moment, I wanted a shot of bourbon. If course, there was none around. I didn't believe in lucky charms, or lucky four-leaf clovers anymore. Nor did I praise name-brand clothes. Yet, I did have the odd feeling, "The truth would set me free." So help me God.

Though I had flat feet, bad arch support, I began to stand for prayer, like I did before. I could hear the other inmates laughing under their breath, but it didn't mattered.

I called my mama. I needed a friendly, ear. I didn't need an army. I just needed one person, on the jury, to believe in me. That would give me the bridge, I needed to cross. Otherwise, I was going to be in permanent comatose.

*CHAPTER 16, PART 17*

# The Trial

"I NEED YOU, Allah. I need You, ASAP," I thought.

It was Wednesday, February 21, 2001. The deputies in their crisp, brown uniforms escorted me out, to their command post, the courtroom. I was in handcuffs. They held me by the arm. It wasn't necessarily, assertive. However, it let me know, I didn't have a choice in the matter. I was bugging out, inside. Yet, I acted cool as a cucumber, which was a good thing. I didn't eat anything, because I would've thrown up.

"Gee, why did I have to go through this?" I thought.

The deputies were in compliance with my lawyer's wishes. They took my handcuffs off. I certainly, wasn't going to attack anyone. I was bushed. I was tired. I didn't get an ounce of sleep, the night before. As I continued to my seat, automatically, every eye was on me.

I couldn't remember everything Deglau was saying. I do remember buzzwords from her, such as "murderer" and "no remorse." None the less, it felt great to be around "normal people," my so-called peers on the jury, who probably, owned condos.

I was wearing a gray suit. I had on a gray tie. It was nice to get away, from the occasional cunning ways, of the criminal offense environment.

One lady, a possible juror, started to cry. So, naturally, she excused from serving on the jury. It was a time-consuming process. Finally, after a long question-and-answer session, my jury was made.

"You've got a lot of Black people on your jury. That's good," said Collins, congratulating me.

It was five Blacks, to be exact.

"Yes, sir," I said.

# THE TRIAL

Considering what I was up against, I placed on my table, a pocket-sized Noble Quran, a pen, and paper. I kept my diplomacy. I did what my mother said, about giving eye-contact.

"Marco, I want you to look the jury, in the eyes, okay?" she said.

Growing up, I could be terribly, shy at times. Judge Hammond contained her courtroom decorum. It was eerie, how the prosecution led her along the way.

"Unbelievable," I thought.

The prosecution executed a contrived and discriminatory opening statements. That was to be expected. What I didn't like was them practically, calling me a "disloyal father." More lies from the two, very pregnant, coordinating women. It was the ugliest lie, I ever heard. I wasn't allowed to express myself. So, all I could do was silently, cry.

It was so hard, hearing about Paris' corpse. I never disagreed what happened. I didn't dispute, it was my fault. Despite the forensics, it was an accident. Over and over again, the judge stopped everything. She'd counsel the adversarial commonwealth attorneys out of the jury's earshot.

It was very distinguished, I must say. Everyone remained professional. I did my part, by being the perfect gentleman. Unbeknownst to me, the local media was there, writing stuff down.

"Ladies and gentlemen, you will hear the facts of the case, from Mr. Martin himself," said Collins, giving me the courtesy I needed.

The prosecution had everyone's undivided attention. I was made to be to the fall guy, from the jump. Apparently, they thought of themselves as crafty. Perhaps, they felt they were good-doers, by putting me behind bars.

The prosecutors said, they weren't necessarily, seeking the Death Penalty.

"Yeah, right," I thought.

The commonwealth attorneys said, I didn't care about my baby. Nothing could be further from the truth. They painted me as "not remorseful." To them, I was a horrible creature, a monster. The door to my eyes opened with more tears, listening to the fault, I caused. I cried again and again.

My father was on the front row, hearing every crisp word. He was the only family member allowed to be there, during the testimony of the police officers and the ambulance personnel. Especially, since he wasn't in my life, on the day of questioning. I had nothing to do, but listen, for the time being. I had nothing, but doves in my heart for Paris.

How dare they imply, I didn't feel any pain! I looked at the crowd, to see how well they were raking it all in. It was incredibly, painful.

One of the first witnesses for the commonwealth was Detective T. Norris. He too vented, I didn't show any signs of remorse. Obviously, he was trying to crystallize that crap, into the minds of the jury. I prayed, the jury wasn't going to drink in that mess.

For cross examination, my lawyer got up from our table, as though he was a friend of mine.

"Detective, have you ever met my client, before the incident?" Collins said, curling his lip.

"No," said the detective.

"Then, how do you know, he wasn't remorseful then?"

Exactly. What a dope. Norris filtered out something about me, not cutting up, "when my daughter was in the hospital." The detective wormed his way, through other follow-up questions. Of course, which dumped even more crap on me. I was on fire. I was a bomb, ready to explode.

"Damn," I thought.

I was eager, to get on the witness stand. Somehow, I had to fix the countless lies. I could tell, the jury was eating it up. I wanted to be a fly on the wall. I wanted to listen to the their thoughts, and correct them. I was a flat footed prison guard. What did I know? Yet, I was the one, who stood by Paris' deathbed. Surely, I was the one going up the river, not Mary. I didn't decidedly, take flight, at the first sign of trouble.

I longed for Christmas eggnog, flowers, deer meat. Anything to keep my mind off one possibly, electroshocked future. The prosecution was calling me a liar. While the jury was in recess, I wished Deglau would shut her flytrap.

The prosecution called in Mary. She took the stand, with black leather pants and a tight white blouse. Her hair was amber. Possibly, she had Deglau fooled. She was proof how delusional their case was.

# THE TRIAL

When Mary took the stand, all eyes were on her. There wasn't an empty chair to be found in the courtroom. Obviously, spectators wanted to see what Paris' mother had to say. My forehead was beaded with sweat. Especially, with her testimony. She was key to my survival.

Actually, there was lady, who sponsored Mary. In case, she cried, broke down, and denounced me before the world. She was a shoulder to cry on.

Here comes my end, the assistant commonwealth attorneys seem to think.

"Please state your name, to the court,"Deglau said, as part of her formality.

I became depressed. Especially, because of the hot mess I was in. I didn't know what Mary was liable to say. However, I noticed Mary giving me delicate looks. Maybe, I wasn't such a troll after all.

The prosecution frowned. Apparently, they didn't detect the animosity, they anticipated. It was refreshing to say the least.

"What day was Paris born?" Mary was asked.

"April 15$^{th}$?" she said, looking at me, while asking for conformation. "2000."

I nodded my head, with a smile, from the defendant's table. She was actually, making me out, to be a devoted father. The whole thing wasn't totally, a smooth escalator ride, to be honest. The prosecution was trying their luck. They were itching for a scratch.

Deglau forced fed questions at Mary. Assuming, it made me look bad. I was fuming mad. Especially, at what the prosecution was trying to do. I'd glance at the digital clock, on the clerk's desk, to my left. I could see, what time of the evening it was. I thought I was going to blow a fuse. The commonwealth attorneys had the audacity to ask misleading questions.

"Was Mr. Martin planning to leave his daughter Paris behind, while taking his older daughter Tande to South Carolina?"

Of course, I wasn't comfortable, taking both of my babies. South Carolina was an 8-hour drive, considering food and gas. It would've been a one-year-old, and an infant, by myself, due to my work schedule. Mary didn't want to go at the time. It never happened. Yet, it was brought up in court.

She had no choice, but to answer the question. She was under oath.

"Yes," Mary said, without explaining why.

"Is it true that Mr. Martin did not want his name, as one of the parents, on her headstone?"

"What the hell does that have to do with anything?" I thought.

It was simply, a choice. It was an option. I decided to let Paris have, just her name, on the headstone. Nothing more, nothing less.

It's a good thing my attorney fought to keep out, I actually, hit Mary. It was in self-defense, while she was pregnant and attacked me. I could see where Deglau was going with this. Again, she had no choice, but to answer.

"Yes, but I think it was because, he felt guilty about what happened," she Mary.

She'd inadvertently, look at me, to see how she doing. For what it was worth, Mary was doing great. However, it was too little, too late. Initially, she gave the prosecution my arrest, or the garter belt they needed.

"Did Mr. Martin flash your oldest daughter Toya money, bragging that he could take her to Red Lobster, Captain George's, or Kings Dominion, the day of the funeral?"

The family was grieving. I was grieving. It was just an idea. I simply, wanted Toya to know, we could do whatever she wanted. It was a private moment of good intentions. It was innocent of hidden agendas or ulterior motives. It didn't happen. Yet, it was brought up to the jury.

"Yes," answered Mary.

I could only imagine how it sounded, and made me look, to the jury. I wanted the best for us, as Paris' family, the day of the funeral. I wondered, what the judge was thinking, about all of this.

I love children. That's the irony of it all. The thing that stuck out the most, from Mary's testimony, was when I was at her house. There, she told me the good news, of her being pregnant again, with Paris. She had a certain, loving gaze in her eyes, when she told the story. It was good my lawyer talked to her, before trial.

"When I told Marco, I was pregnant, he got one knee, kissed my stomach, and made love to me," Mary said.

# THE TRIAL

Sweet as honey, right?

"But when he brought the girls back from his mother's house, he had a headache. I could tell something was wrong."

"No, Mary!" I thought.

The jury would think my mother and I had issues, with her having another baby. My mother's only concern was "affordability," so soon after Kandi.

"You may be excused," said Judge Hammond, when they were finished, with their questions for Mary.

I gave Mary a gentle look, as if to say, "Thanks anyway."

The prosecution hoarded more of our precious time. It was more courtroom jargon than I could stand. Especially, bringing in the next witness. Deglau, I was willing to bet, drove a Jaguar.

Next, Carolyn was brought in to take the witness stand. I didn't get her. She was that clingy friend of Mary's, who wouldn't go away. She sat, with a stern look on her face. My smile for her quickly, vanished. I didn't know what to expect.

"Did Mr. Martin bring a balloon to the hospital, when Kandi was born?" said Deglau.

"Yes," replied Carolyn.

"What did Mr. Martin bring to the hospital, when his other daughter Paris was born?"

"Nothing," said Carolyn as though, I was a real jerk.

"Oh, my God!" I thought.

A damn ballon? The jury was going to hate me. Actually, I didn't have any money, at the time. I rushed to the hospital, after work, to see Paris for the first time. It didn't occur to me, to stop by the gift shop. I wasn't keeping score.

Again, my sister was the one, who bought the ballon and flowers, for Kandi's new birth at the hospital. Drika didn't accompany me, at my second daughter's birth. At that point, she didn't like Mary, for all the miserable things, she put me through.

"Is everyone on gin and juice, and forgot to tell me, the big man sitting at the defendant's table? Was this some type of joke?" I thought.

253

My late grandmother, who had glaucoma, came to mind. It was getting hard, to hear all the rhetoric, pointing towards me, in the courtroom. I wished, she was still around. What would she say, if she knew a jury was judging me, for something, I didn't mean to do? She'd probably, curse those glutton attorneys out, whose only motive was to get a conviction of me, by any means necessary.

My court case was nothing, but unsubstantiated hype. It was a bunch of bull crap. It's like, I was a Black man, trying to catch a cab, in New York City. The paramedics also seemed to be pulling my coat. They too, alluded to the repetitive idea of "didn't show any remorse. Obviously, it was their icing on the cake.

Was I dreaming? I wanted somebody, to pinch me on the hand, to make sure I wasn't . I couldn't believe the stuff, I was hearing. It was so bogus, I had to question myself, whether I was a good person or not.

The jury was stiff as igloos. Some were looking at me, as though I was possibly, a child-killer. Especially, for not having the grace of calling 911, first. I never would have imagined, informing Mary about Paris initially, would've had a jury forming an opinion about me. Seemingly, that alone, got me in so much trouble.

How could I be so naïve? I wasn't immune from making a mistake. I was in a life or death situation. The prosecution made it seem, there was criminal intent.

I made a tragic mistake. I should've went to the doctor. I simply, buckled under the pressure. I was tired of seeing Paris lethargic. That's all that was.

I was definitely, in an Ancient Greek or Roman Empire atmosphere. There was Paris' doctor and other medical experts. The state medical examiner nurtured Deglau's claims even further. The odds of surviving was stacked against me.

Paris' doctor was not necessarily, lashing out. She said the baby was shaken, with "no signs of being abused." Another medical expert drilled it along, by saying my baby suffered Shaken Baby Syndrome. Also, in that she was shaken with "moderate to severe force."

The state medical examiner, who did the autopsy, had the impression

# THE TRIAL

Paris was healthy and breathing, when she was shaken.

It felt like a lance was stuck in my heart. I made the biggest mistake of my life. At any route, my inalienable rights were largely, going down the toilet.

When court was adjourned for the day, I felt like all the air was sucked out of me. I was a guinea pig, for a lack of a better word. Back on the cell block, I went into the incognito mode. I wasn't wanting to talk about it.

"How did it go?" inmates would ask me.

Of course, it would launch me back inside the courtroom.

"It went okay," I'd lie.

Actually, I was scared to death. I was tossing and turning, trying to sleep. It was virtually, impossible. I held myself, in a incubational fetal position. Especially, with not knowing, what's going to happen to me.

Thursday, February 22, 2001. It didn't matter, I was the leader of the Muslim community, held at the jail. I didn't particularly, like weaves and fake hairpieces either. Yet, I was going to the courtroom. That day was a little different. It was finally, my turn to speak, in front of the jury. However, I was leaving everything in Allah's Hands.

When my attorney called me to the stand, I felt inebriated. I leisurely, walked to the stand. I was nervous as though, I was about to sing a karaoke song. It was the fight of my life, as "loco" as it was. Watching my father sit across the room brought harmony to the situation. It let me know, I wasn't alone. I was going against the grain of salt. Especially, with a people, who wore a smile and a passion to say anything about me, they damn well pleased. Before I spoke, I thought about the trivial things my lawyer and I been through together.

"Let me be the lawyer and you be the client," he once said to me.

It pissed me off, whereas I was only trying to help him, help me. Shedding light on the subject, Collins said the prosecution mentioned, I made the infamous 911 call at 4:01 pm. Not around 3:30 pm, as I originally, guessed. Deglau was sure to use that little, bit of information against me.

"I want you talk, just like did, when you made the call," said Collins. "Stay calm. Don't let them get to you."

255

My lawyer wanted the jury to hear my soft, speaking voice and usual demeanor. My father also gave me advice.

"Don't say, 'Uhm.' Don't say, 'You know.' Don't get mad, when you get on the stand," said my father.

I thought, I was ready. I was prepared for any slime, which was to come my way. Everyone was staring at me. I prayed, I wasn't institutionalized. I didn't want to notice, the nice shade of lipstick, on the pretty ladies. I had to somehow, hem up inside, what was happening to me.

"Please state your name for the court."

"My name is Marco Martin, Paris' father," I said, while looking at all the piercing, intense faces.

My liver was bubbling. I felt like, I was going to implode.

"What do you do for a living?" my attorney said.

"I'm a correctional officer," I said.

I wished, I would have said, I was working at Powhatan Correctional Center as well. I wanted to leave and finally, go home. I was at a loss for words, when I saw my brother, Mel siting in the audience. I wanted normalcy again. I wanted to help my mother pay bills. I wanted to win. I simply, had to. Anything else would have been intolerable. I was on the lookout for any loopholes, I could find.

I attempted to tell my side of the story. I went step by step. I was without the tit-for-tat, coming from the two pregnant, assistant commonwealth attorneys.

Deglau looked at me as though, I was some, sort of demented person, or a carrier for a deadly, disease. I glanced at the nameless faces of the jury. Obviously, they were listening for any patches or holes, I had to say. The only thing I had to work with was me. I was my only defense. I wanted for me to be as intellectually, sound as possible. I needed to be natural. I spotted Deglau jotting things down. Inexplicably, she'd twist my words, to make me her pawn later.

"I was broke!" I wanted to scream, about why I didn't have balloons at Paris' newly, arrival at the hospital.

Lack of BALLOONS were used against me, in a court of law. However, my lawyer stayed away from asking me about "the balloon thing."

# THE TRIAL

"I wasn't trying to show off!" I wanted to yell, to explain how I showed Toya, we could do whatever she wanted to do.

MY RENT MONEY which was merely, suggested by me, to give to Toya, was used against me, in a court of law. Yet, Collins stayed away from asking me about "the flashing money" incident.

I saw my brother, Mel moving his neck in disappointment at the prosecutors. He was quietly, demanding an apology, for what I was going through.

My whole life seemed, I was a magnet for trouble. This day was no different. I was a humble guy, who loved all music. What in the world was I doing in a courtroom?

"I am now going to play the 911 tape," said Collins.

He was hoping, it would penetrate through the lies, for the jury. With Kandi crying on the audio tape, it was hard to hear, what I was saying.

"I WANT YOU TO SHAKE THE BABY, to see if you can get a response," said the emergency dispatcher to me.

"I did," I heard myself say on the recording.

Hearing that, Mel ran out of the courtroom, crying.

"Order!" Judge Hammond said, hitting the courtroom gavel. "Order! I will not have anyone running in the courtroom."

However, I wondered, how much of a percentage of the jury wanted me to receive a life sentence? How many possibly, wanted me to get a death sentence?

I prayed, sympathy was nourished inside their minds. How many thought I was a nit-wit? How many thought, I deserved to be punished? With my peripheral pain and anxiety, I couldn't tell.

Deglau finally, manifested her very pregnant self in front of me. She aligned herself, only a few feet where I was. She had the persona of a hard-driven mare. Her lovely, assistant looked on. Possibly, Norwegian descent.

It was time for me, to put the petal to the metal. Thanks to my lawyer, I knew what the prosecution was going to insinuate, for the "time gap," and use it utterly, against me.

"Mr. Martin," said Deglau. "What time did you make the 911 call?"

"I don't know the exact time," I pointed out. "Around 3:30, 4:00 o'clock."

257

The look on Deglau's face was priceless! Her eyes grew tight, with her philosophical misperception of me. My answer was a perfect match to what I was saying all along. Nursing her ego, she was under the impression, I waited 30 minutes, without doing anything.

Physically, Deglau went into maximum overdrive. Obviously, waddling and holding her back, much like a pregnant woman would. The optics were purely, mechanical manipulation. It was a spectacle for the jury to see motherhood. Meanwhile, I was portrayed as a man who shook his baby.

I was asked about other things which occurred that Friday, fateful day. The prosecution could not wait to throw me out with the trash. I couldn't help but wonder. Was it the melanin in my skin? Why didn't the commonwealth accept my plea deal? I was willing to plea to Involuntary Manslaughter.

"How hard did you shake the baby?" said Deglau, pitching me a fastball.

I didn't write anything down. Yet, I remembered everything, which was being mentioned.

"I used moderate to severe force," I said, by using their doctor's exact words.

That too, caught the prosecution by surprise. I was spoiling their ingenious plan, to make me look bad. Somehow, I had to clean up this mess. I didn't want to sound calculating.

"How many times?" Deglau wanted to know.

"Three."

It was the one time, I was unsure about my answer. Everything was a play on words. Deglau billed me as a monster. My attorney was MIA. She took the opportunity to make things look worst. She plowed her seeds deeper. She wanted me to share with the jury exactly, how.

"Will you demonstrate for us?"

"Like this," I said, with my mind, a mile out into space.

I shook my arms, as though Paris was in my hands. It was one of the hardest thing, I ever had to do. I had no choice, but to do it. I had to shake my hands, in order to show the people, I panicked. I thought something was wrong with my baby.

# THE TRIAL

On that podium, I felt like crap. It was me against the world. Anyhow, I became upset. How dare they say, I didn't care! How dare they imply, I didn't show any remorse! My heart cried for mine.

"I shook her. Not to kill her. Not to hurt her. I shook her, to save her. To retrieve her," I quickly, interjected.

Little did I know, what I said would be a sound-bite for the local newspaper. It was my policy to stay strong, in front of Deglau. I didn't want to give her the satisfaction of seeing me cry. I couldn't hold it. "Was I missing something" I asked myself.

Paris was my begotten daughter, who was ousted from this world. Someday, I wanted to see her as a cheerleader, with a pom-pom, like her older sister, Toya. She was captain of the cheerleader squad. Perhaps, I wanted Paris to spend time with her grandparents. Yet, she was gone now.

I told them, I tried CPR, with the help of the 911 dispatcher. Like a heat-seeking missile from the offset, the prosecution vilified my statements. Particularly, with me learning CPR, during my correctional officer training, from the academy. More importantly, the prosecution knew, I wasn't lying. At least, not I received training. With mockery, Deglau wanted me to explain on the stand, what exactly, I did to help Paris overall.

Drawing them a picture, I said how, I checked for breathing. I put my finger under Paris' nose. I breathed into her mouth, and such. It was awhile since, I held a security post. The prosecution looked at me as though, I was a piece of mold or something.

"Mr. Martin, you said, you checked your daughter's wrist for a pulse," Deglau said, in a sarcastic tone. "Shouldn't you check the inner thigh?"

"I did the best, I could!" I said, boosted with emotion.

I was going nuclear inside. The nerve of her! As though, I didn't "sound" panicked enough. As if, I didn't do enough!

"No more questions, Your Honor," said the commonwealth attorney, which sent me packing.

I was my only defense. I was the only witness for the defense. When things hit the fan, I didn't know what to expect. I was floored with morality. I cried more, which made myself pale. I hoped for the best, predicting the worse.

"He's lying!" said Deglau, while looking at me.

She said it to her motley crew, when the jury left out of the courtroom. I was weary. I tried not to pant or panic. I thought of my family. I couldn't believe, I was going to jail over a balloon! I was trying to prepare myself. I was proud, I gave it my best.

Even though my name was dragged through the mud, I'll never forget a certain jury member. It was the Black nurse lady. She quietly, nodded at me, as though she understood. That let me know, I was normal. What happened to me, could've happened to anybody.

I was under enormous pressure to do great. Despite the amount of ammunition, the commonwealth was shooting at me.

"Every second counts," I said, repeating the words from my CPR training, when I was once on the stand.

I wasn't fuzzy with the details. I remembered everything, as though it was yesterday. Did I pass or fail? That was the question. The clerk typing everything, seemed to understand my situation too.

I felt, I should have got one of those, fresh out of law school, pro bono lawyers, respectfully. I'm sure, Collins thought he did proficiently, well.

After court was adjourned, I went to my cell. I wanted to retaliate. I wanted to shove something. I projected in my mind, whether or not the jury believed me. I called my father for a review, on how I did.

"I wish you didn't get mad," he said, shutting any shred of hope I had, down.

My mother thought, I did properly, enough. Regardless of the flavor, or temperamental discussion about me.

"Either way, they would have said something about it," she said, being insightful. "If you were calm, they would have said, you didn't care and showed no remorse. If you were mad, they would have said, you're potentially, violent. Either way, you couldn't win."

My mother said, it was good, I told the jury, about my CPR training. I was taught, to remain calm, in life-threatening situations. Especially, when I made the 911 call. She let me know, I did right. It was simple as that.

I made so many personal prayers, provocations, supplications to Allah. I knew, I was going up the river. Question was, for how long?

# THE TRIAL

"Pray for me," I'd ask of people, whether or not they were believers.

Yes, I was scared. The inmates and their public opinion seemed to be on my side. I certainly, didn't want to be there. I wanted to try rollerblading. I wanted to soak my skin in the sun again. I wanted to pump up, my old Kenwood stereo. I wanted to meet sleazy women on purpose. I wanted to fish on a rowboat, with my father. I wanted to be sloppy as I wanted to be.

However, I was puzzled. I grunted with sarcasm. I was tired of being around quarreling people. Also, I was sad. Things went slow as a snail. The jury's verdict was the next day. Yet, with the quickness, I wanted to jury's decision to come. If I never saw another sporting event on tv, in jail, it would be too soon.

It was like wishing for snow in April. Naturally, I promised an inmate, if by chance, they let me go home, he could have everything, in my canteen bag.

"You need to pray for me then," I reminded him, as part of the deal.

I wanted to meet a young lady and mate like rabbits. I wanted to be at Virginia Beach. I wanted to let the sand run through my toes. I wanted to be in touch with Mary's softer side. I thought of river rafting on the James River. I wanted to be in South Carolina, the upcoming Saturday, somehow. I wanted to be anywhere, doing anything, except be there, in jail.

Friday, February 23, 2001. It was like ramming a steel rod, deeper, further, into my heart. It was possibly, the day of "acquittal." Maybe, it was the day of being "found guilty." I wished I was home, eating fried scallops. I could hear every sound, which was going on in the courtroom.

Mary made a rare appearance. Our girls was there. All my immediate family was there. It felt like the first day of school. I was nervous as hell. Not a dry eye was spared.

It was the day of courtroom closing arguments. It was the day of the verdict. It stung worse than a scorpion's tail. I had to sit there, and listen to more crap from Deglau. She insisted, I didn't care about my own daughter. I was frustrated, in the same way, I wore my same suit, three days in a row. All I could do was cry. I wondered, what the guy in specs (my lawyer) was going to say to counter all that. Things were getting real screwy. My head was spinning.

"Maybe she cried," lied Deglau.

She implied, all I cared about was getting sleep, after my 12-hour shift, at the prison. It was another damn lie. Her reconnaissance would say anything, to get my conviction. I sprouted more tears. I was frustrated. The prosecution redevelopment of me wouldn't sway. She told the jury, to not let my crying "fool" them. Nothing could be further from the truth. She implied, I was crying, because I was "scared" of prison. It wasn't so. Yet, I actually, worked in a prison. Not to mention, for nearly, two years.

I sputtered with grief over the loss of my daughter. I sought refuge in Allah. Only He could save me now. The odds were stacked against me. The treacherous lies reinforced me to a courtroom. I could only imagine what lengthy sentence, I was going to get. It stank like a septic tank. The filthy unknown.

Relieving M. Deglau from her courthouse duty, I could tell her assistant didn't believe, all the stuff her mentor was saying about me. I could tell, she wanted to cry, right along with me. She was practically, stuttering at times.

It was clear, I was going to serve time. Collins started his closing statements. He mention, I was not "the renegade father," the commonwealth wanted everyone to believe. Somehow, my attorney had to clean up the sewer plant I was in. Apparently, he thought of himself as a clever, stealth fighter jet. Hearing my cry, made him cry as well.

"He's actually, crying," I thought, in amazement.

"Did he shake his baby too hard? Hell yes! Did he want his baby to die? Hell no!" Collins shamelessly, said.

Seemingly, the jury was sterile to any excuse, I may have had. They sat there, stone-faced, as though reserved, in some sort of impenetrable shell. It couldn't have stung any worse. Ray Charles could see it was an accident. Next, I watched my attorney wipe a tear from his eye. He then gulped a cup of water. It got me thinking.

"Maybe, Collins wasn't such a stooge after all," I thought.

Only time could tell. Finally, the jury was ventured out of the courtroom, to deliberate on my Capital Murder trial. I was straining to make sense of it all.

# THE TRIAL

The juror, who nodded in approval at me, was excused. Also, another Black lady was excused. Actually, 14 jurors listened to my case. 2 were alternates. So, now it was the finalized 12 people in all, to decide my fate. I wanted some tobacco.

I was trying to digest my possible time. I was made to wait, and wait, in a holding cell. After I ate my lunch, if you can call it that, I stretched myself out on the bench. The air seemed to weigh tons. I daydreamed about my family. I viewed over every gathering, I could think of. I tried to be strong. Yet, I was so torn apart inside. I was on the verge of a nervous breakdown. My sister, Drika was simply, stunned this was happening to me. I was just a much a tourist, as she was.

One day, I was at my mother's house. One moment changed my life, forever. Before I knew it, I was thrown in jail. I would trade my life for Paris, in a second. I thought of myself as a fat, piece of shit for shaking her too hard. I missed my sweet, little girl. I'll forever know she looked like me. I missed her dark, tropical skin.

After five and a half hours of waiting, I was transferred to the courtroom. The rest of my life was being decided. I was fully awake. The verdict was in. My generic brand lawyer was trapped beside me. I was at war, within myself. I was supercharged. I was stressed out. I was watchful of my mother, at the same time.

"Will the defendant, please rise," Judge Hammond said, like she was supposed to.

It felt like triple bypass, heart surgery. I was weak in the knees. The sheriff deputies surrounded me. Apparently, in case, I lunged towards the judge. I didn't want to hurt anyone. I wanted some weed, at that point.

"No sweat," I tried to tell myself.

However, my lips were quivering. I glanced at the jury foreman.

"We the jury, of sound mind, find the defendant, Marco Lance Martin, guilty of murder, in the second degree," he said.

It's no wonder, there was a White juror, who looked at me, the way he did. He gave me a mean eye.

"No!" Mary cried, running out of the courtroom.

I was quickly, swished out of the room. So, for the jury to recommend a sentence. Things were turning ugly. It was the beginning of the end.

" I ain't going out, like no wimp. Damn that Shaking Baby Syndrome," I told myself.

The more, I thought about it, the more it was getting under my skin.

"Let me see my lawyer!" I demanded, to the deputies.

I had a twinkle in my eye. It was a wholesome, good as time as any, to want justice. I needed to see what was going on. Collins came to my holding cell. He was apologizing. He was making tacky excuses for why we lost.

"I ain't no murderer!" I said. "It was an accident! I thought, she wasn't breathing right!"

It was like a UFO sighting. I knew, there was nothing he could really, do about it. My attorney was blaming himself.

"It's okay. You did good," I said to Collins, offering him to take the guilt off.

Under his advisement, he said I had 21 days to file an appeal. I was so wired, with weird thoughts. The time, I was facing was unimaginable. I didn't have a gram. I didn't have a clue. I didn't know what I was going to do. In a blink of an eye, my life changed forever.

"How can they do this to people's lives?" I asked myself.

My VCU graduation tassel obviously, didn't mean squat. I was the underdog. However, from research in the law library, second degree homicide was 5 to 40 years.

After awhile, the jury reached their "amount of time" decision. What was my punishment? I was in a world of shit, and I knew it. Eventually, I was escorted back to my seat. I was scared for my underwear.

"...Fifteen years," revealed the jury foreman.

Somehow, I was relieved. It wasn't exactly, a life sentence. It could've been worse. Needless to say, my family took it hard.

"You came out lucky," Collins said, practically, congratulating me.

It was still wrong. Gingerly, I smiled at my family. I gave them a thumb's up. I was okay. Looking at my daughter, I knew one day, I'd have a lot of explaining to do. It wasn't the amount of years, which terrorized me. It was the question, held in the air. I was officially, being labeled a murderer. It was sure to be a drag, for the rest of my life.

On the phone, I thanked my family, for all their love and support. The unknown factor stressed me out. I didn't know whether or not, the judge was going to go with the jury's recommendation. It was merely, a suggestion, after all. Of course, the judge had the final say so. I didn't want to go there, or think about it, but my life was in the air. My life was up for grabs.

I spent a third of my time, wishing I was a fly on the jury's window sill. I wanted to listen in, on the jury's deliberations. What were they thinking?

My mother threw a writing campaign together. She wanted everyone I knew, to write Judge Hammond on my behalf, for the sentence hearing. She wanted the judge to know usual, good things about me. In hopes of a leaner sentence. It was as though, I was out in the rainstorm, waiting for a thunderbolt to strike. It was a tight rope, without a net. My only defense was hoping, I didn't fall.

Tuesday, May 1st, 2001.

"So, I think the jury had before it, as clear a picture, as they could get. It's just that it's a sad picture. And, I'm impressed by these letters, submitted on Mr. Martin's behalf. And, I know most of them describe Mr. Martin as a shy person and a gentle person. And, that is totally, inconsistent with the injuries that were described by the medical examiner," said Judge Hammond. "And, I am very reluctant to supplant the jury's role and substitute my judgement, for the jury was already done. But, I am impressed by the support for Mr. Martin. And, I can only say, that he's still a young man. And, he should be able to overcome this."

Pause.

"Mr. Martin, can you stand up? Is there anything you'd like to say?" she said.

"Yes, ma'am," I said, with the many notes, I wrote down.

"Go ahead," said the court.

"I would like to say that, I'm sorry. I'm just real emotional," I declared, with the paper in my hand rattling.

"Take your time."

"Well, as a young boy, I grew up in a very loving, caring and sheltered environment. At that time, my life was filled with many toys and imagination. I then became a proud member of the Cub Scouts of America. It was where, I was taught to love God, honor my country, help and respect our neighbors. Their writings and teachings are very much instilled in my life today.

When I was a teenager, I had so many aspirations and dreams of what I wanted to be, when I grew up. I dreamt of being a writer or a poet. I wanted to write material that would touch people's lives. Maybe, open their hearts.

But at the same time, I've always had a profound respect for law enforcement, and the American military. Especially, after my father, who was a Marine in the Vietnam War. Later, he became a police officer for the City of Richmond. Afterwards, it was the Henrico Police.

I too, wanted to join the military, to fight for my country. Naturally, and and needless to say, I too, wanted to become a police officer. So, I could protect the innocent, fight drugs and crime, to the best of my ability.

As a law abiding citizen, I wanted to help my community. I wanted to help, lift my community, for a better tomorrow. Call me a patriot, but my heart was, and still is, with the military and law enforcement.

After high school, I became a security officer for NationsBank. However, at the same time, I wanted to be a police officer.

Also, I wanted to work with children. I love children. I love seeing their innocent faces, and playing with them. The whole world can be against you. Yet, seeing a child's smile or hearing a baby laugh, makes it all worthwhile.

I went to Virginia Commonwealth University in 1993. I was a Social Work major. I wanted to dedicate my life to helping children, in whatever way I could. During my years in college, one semester I volunteered at The Byrd House Community Center. It was a daycare center, in the "Fan area." I loved giving the children snacks. I'd help them with their homework. I'd take them to the playground.

As the saying goes, "Help the children and let them lead the way." That's fine, but my passion was law enforcement. It was still calling me. During my third year at VCU, I finally, changed my major to Criminal Justice.

# THE TRIAL

After my college graduation in 1998, I desperately, wanted a job in the legal profession. I applied at various law firms, for a paralegal position. Also, I applied for a employment at Richmond, Henrico, and Hanover, Police or Sheriff. Respectfully, I aced the Henrico Police written exam. I failed miserably, the physical exam. I also had a job interview, here, for Henrico Sheriff Deputy. I was denied. Yet, I didn't give up. I was determined, to get my foot in the door, to law enforcement. I went to various juvenile centers, and adult correctional centers. For some reason, I wasn't hired.

Powhatan Correctional Center was the only institution, which took a chance on me. That was one of the proudest moments in my life. I was proud to be a correctional officer. I was finally, doing my small part, to protect society from criminals.

Anybody, who knows me, knows how much family and children mean to me. The happiest day in my life was when I became a father. I'm bold enough to say, there's nobody on earth more proud, to be a daddy, more than me. I'm a daddy, and very proud of it.

I was going to teach my two children, to love God, honor their country, and respect their neighbors. I had so many hopes and dreams, for my two children. Anybody, who knows me, knows I'm a big kid at heart. I couldn't wait until my two children got older. So, I could take them to the circus. I couldn't wait to take them to the Virginia State Fair, the movies, to the park, or anywhere else, fun. My mission was to be the best daddy in the world.

I was going to teach my children, about the religion of Islam. The true religion of Islam. I couldn't wait, to buy babies clothes, school clothes. I was going to buy the best tennis shoes, money can buy. I couldn't wait to be an overprotective father. Especially, when they go out, on dates, and to the prom.

I was going to encourage my children to either join the military, or go to college. And, to hold…"

"Maybe you shouldn't read, what somebody else wrote," said Collins.

He noticed, I was going from handwritten words to typed. Obviously, I asked my mother to type it up. I'm the one who actually, wrote what I was saying. I was highly, insulted.

"No, sir. I wrote all this myself," I said, wanting to continue.

I couldn't believe the nerve of him.

"I've been convicted of second degree murder. It implies, by Virginia statue, I committed a willful, deliberate act of malicious intent, of a reckless nature, and a disregard for life. I beg to differ.

The commonwealth told the jury, I didn't want my own child. This is not true. The commonwealth went as far as to lead the jury to believe, I loved one child, more than the other. This also, is not true. I loved my children equally, and unconditionally.

The commonwealth told the jury, when my oldest daughter, Kandi, was born, I bought her balloons and flowers. Yet, when Paris was born, I didn't buy her anything. If somebody would have asked me on the stand, I would have told them, I didn't have any money at the time. I simply, went straight to the hospital, to welcome the birth of Paris.

The commonwealth told the jury, I wanted to leave my child, Paris, behind. Meanwhile, I planned to take only my other child, Kandi, on a trip to South Carolina. If somebody would have asked me, I would have told them, on the stand, I certainly, didn't think it was safe. Especially, taking two infant babies, alone, on an eight-hour drive, on the the highway, by myself.

The commonwealth told the jury, I shook my baby, because she was crying, after spending many hours crying. So, I could get back to sleep. Again, another untruth. There's absolutely, no proof or evidence of this.

I would never have slept, if Paris "did not cry." Paris was a baby, who slept all the time. Anybody, who saw her, knew about that, including Paris' mother.

The commonwealth's own witness testified, some babies sleep, 20 hours or more, a day. Obviously, Paris was one of them. She was not crying that day. Just as she never did. It was my fear, I realized. Like I said on the stand, I shook her, not out of malice. Not to hurt her, or kill her, but to save her, to retrieve her.

The commonwealth told the judge, my baby's mother had to tell me, "Go, get the baby." As if, she was in another room. This is not true. My

# THE TRIAL

baby was with me, the whole time. I was on the phone.

The commonwealth told the the judge, I did not tell the truth about the polyurethane on the floor. My mother was going to be called as a potential witness. She was going to verify my statement. The commonwealth did no investigation to determine, whether the polyurethane was a factor, in Paris' death or not. We will never know for certain, one way or the other.

The commonwealth told the jury, I waited 30 minutes, to call 911 emergency. Another untruth. Their own subpoenaed witness, Carolyn, told the jury. When I called my children's mother, and from the time they called me back, the paramedics were there, at the house, within 10 minutes. I called 911 emergency, IMMEDIATELY.

The commonwealth told the jury, I did not tell the EMS people, or the police investigator, Norris, I shook my baby, initially. There were at least 25 people in the house. I don't know what, I told each, and everyone of them. Why didn't the commonwealth summon them all together, rather than a few? I know, I told some of them.

The first person, I talked to was a 911 dispatcher. I told her specifically, after she told me to shake my baby. I hid nothing from her. I had nothing to hide. I did nothing wrong. I told everybody, everything.

The commonwealth told the jury, I didn't want my name as a father on Paris' headstone. Since when, did not having a family member, also mentioned on the headstone, become a crime? If someone would have asked me, I would have told them, I wanted Paris to have her own identity, on her own headstone.

She was only with us for a very short time. I wanted her to have something, which was just hers. This is not a crime.

What the commonwealth failed to tell the jury is, my children's mother, Mary, believes in my innocence. Also, she knows, I didn't purposely, or intentionally, harm my own baby.

The commonwealth said, I could cry for myself, but I couldn't cry for Paris. You can mock my tears. You can try to belittle my feelings. I know in my heart, the pain, I have suffered, due to losing my daughter.

Again, I say, I had absolutely, no intention of harming my own baby. That was a complete, and total, accident on my part. I will live with this, for the rest of my life.

I would like to take this opportunity to thank Allah, my family and friends, for all their love and support. Thank you."

"Thank you, Mr. Martin," said Judge K. Hammond.

"Your honor, may I speak, please?" said my mother.

"Ma'am, please, no…no, ma'am," said an identified court official.

"The court will impose the sentence, that was chosen by the jury. I sentence the defendant to serve 15 years in the Department of Corrections. The defendant is remanded."

"Thank you, judge," said C. Collins.

I wasn't about to go off. The bald deputy got ahold of me. I wasn't going to make dash for it. I was only 29-years-old. I was missing my car.

"As-Salaamu alaikum," I heard someone say to me.

To my wonderful surprise, it was Brother Saadiq, Brother Abu Bakr, and Brother Mustapha. They were sitting in the courtroom. They too, strove for Paradise, an everlasting, peaceful abode. They didn't care about bank cards, or that sort of thing. I waved my pocket-size Quran in the air. I wanted to let them know, I'd be alright.

"I have Islam," I signaled to them.

"Allahu akbar…Allahu akbar," I heard Brother Saadiq say, who taught me about Islam in the first place.

It was that day. Then and there, I made up my mind. I no longer wanted to be a carnivore. At that moment, I wanted to be a vegetarian. I've always wanted to try it. So, being sentenced to 15 years gave me the audacity to do it.

I kept my high-esteem. However, it was no barbecue picnic for my mother. Outside of the courtroom, in the lobby area, my mother cried and screamed. She felt she let me down. Particularly, for not having enough money, for a better defense.

Thank God, Tuesday was also my visitation day. My family was in a climate of sadness and despair.

"15 years? They gave you 15 years," cried my brother and sister.

I simply, smiled and remained calm.

"I'm okay," I reassured them. "Don't cry. I need you to stay strong for mama."

# THE TRIAL

My mother, who always went to bat for me, did "Catch-22."

"It could have been worse," I said.

I had an ache in my heart, seeing her like that.

"It could have been better too," she said.

My father was great. He kept my spirits up. We laughed. We joked.

"Marco, you were railroaded. Son, there's no way, you were going home. Not with two pregnant, White females, and a White female judge."

Mary was in the visitation room too. I could tell, she was under the pressure of being a single mom. It was only befitting, my daughter Kandi was there. Toya was there.

Carolyn also rose to the occasion. She always demonstrated southern bell charm to me. Under the circumstance, she was actually, being an advocate of mine.

From the start, in the cell block, guys were telling me, the judge was going to go with the jury's recommendation of 15 years. There were so many jailhouse charlatans around. So, I guess they were right.

Afterwards my bid, or jail experience, became harder. For example, I appointed Bilal as "Amir" or a community leader. Obviously, he was ambitious for a position, if not my imam position. He was chin-checked, by a couple of our guests, at our Friday religious service. While I was giving the "khutbah" or sermon, a few of the non-Muslim guys were talking among themselves. Sure, it was rude. Obviously, our weekly meeting was a way to get out of their respective pods, and meet. Somehow, they didn't know any better, but I kept going. Apparently, Bilal had a bone to pick with those being rude, and talking during the service.

"Excuse me, Imam, but I have something to say," said Bilal, interrupting me, in the middle of my monologue. "This is Islam! This is my life, which I take very seriously! There's no talking during the khutbah! Anybody, who doesn't like it, we can go to the bathroom, right now. So, I can put your ass in the hospital! I'll shit down your throat!"

Suddenly, the guys, who were having their conversations, rushed over to where Bilal was sitting. It was chaos. Fists were flying. Chairs in the air. Blood was everywhere. I was caught off guard. It happened so fast.

The good thing, nobody laid a finger on me. Maybe, it was because, I

271

was the "Muslim preacher" they listened to every week. Like the Bionic Man, I got the hell out of there. Deputies came out of nowhere. Eventually, they broke it up.

Blood was all on my clothes. That fight gave me the chills. It wasn't okay, seeing Black people act that way.

"There're only coming to Jumuah, to get out of the pod," Bilal would say, pointing out the obvious.

That may have been, but it wasn't my concern. There were merely, three to five actual Muslims. There were approximately, 20 guests or non-Muslims. Perhaps, they were curious about Islam. If they wanted to disguise themselves as "getting out of the pod," it was okay with me. Allah knows the heart. However, from a bird's eye view, they all seemed interested in what I was saying. Some nodded their heads in approval. Others listen quietly. Yet, they were there, in the same room I was.

The next day, I received a "kite" or discreet letter from Bilal. Also, it was signed by Abdul Raheem. It was calling for my immediate resignation. Particularly, because I didn't jump in the fight, to help. I was in choppy waters, without a paddle. My small congregation lost faith in me. It was "jihad," or struggle, man. I was blindsided. A bloodbath during Jumuah or Friday prayer was the last thing, I expected.

I was forced, to be around a certain caliber of people. It was a world, I wasn't use to. Whatever the case was, it was no Cinderella story. It gave me ample time, to think about what happened. With Bilal, along with Abdul Raheem, my assistant Imam gone, I had some explaining to do. I had an alibi, and I was sticking to it. Meanwhile, they were in "the hole" or segregation for a few days, for fighting.

"They came in so fast," I said, meaning the sheriff deputies.

I wasn't Mr. Cool. I wasn't Mr. Tough Guy. I thought of myself as being civilized. I was amazed by things a teenager would like, science fiction, superheroes. I wasn't from the streets. Nor did I have to claw my way through the ghetto. I didn't have an angle. I wasn't about fighting people all the time. What did I know?

I thought Sheriff Wade was going to cancel Jumuah services, all together. The chaplain had a long talk with me. Things had to be different.

# THE TRIAL

Unlike before, people had to sign a registrar, whenever they walked into service. Apparently, someone stole my Nobel Quran, during the fight. I wasn't upset. I just hoped, they'd read it.

As usual, I gave the khutbah, the following Friday. However, after prayer, the four of us Muslims, had a vote. We all doodled on a piece of paper, whether or not, I should stay on as the imam. Of course, Bilal and Abdul Raheem voted "No." They wanted to clip my wings. Meanwhile, another Brother and I voted. Naturally, I voted for me to stay on. The vote was two votes, against me. Two votes, for me. Clearly, I could see what was happening. I wasn't born yesterday.

So, I decided to take a chunk out of my leadership. I figured, Bilal and I could alternate every other week. I assumed, that's what he wanted all along anyway.

"Hope he's happy," I thought.

At any rate, it was a compromise. I wasn't about to go, tit-for-tat. I didn't want to do the blaming game. I didn't see the point of pointing fingers. I just wanted "to bowl" when it was my turn, until I got transferred to Department of Corrections.

Years prior, my Black History professor at VCU, Norrece T. Jones Jr, suggested I look in the Yellow Pages, for Muslims, other than The Nation of Islam. Especially, when I confided in him, I had a problem with NOI's ideology of white people, despite my decided Malcom X paper. Unbeknownst to him and I, looking in that phone book, changed my life forever. I never knew one day, it would be like this.

Whenever it was Bilal's turn to speak, it became very intensive for me. At every appearance, he would say something, in reference to people killing their babies. Obviously, it was out of spite for me.

When he did so, I kept my composure. I kept a brave front. I was cool and collected, as though he wasn't saying anything directly, pertaining to me. Of course, he was.

Fellow inmates would tell me, Department of Corrections was a breeze. Others would say, my time would come and go so fast. Particularly, when I got some music and a tv.

"Marco, you're going to be alright," said Ron, who did jail time before. "You're Black. You're Muslim. Muslims stick together in prison. Muslims run the prison."

"Yeah, right," I thought, thinking about Bilal.

Little did I know, it was my prelude of some the Muslims, in the penitentiary, yet to come. However, I met so many talented fellow inmates. People, who could have been artists, architects. Some verbal skills, to go into broadcasting. Others had the creativity for a clothing designer. Yet, there were also, the obscene comments, the disappointments. It was brutal. A thief had the audacity, to steal from my magazines, when I was in the trustee pod.

There was the time, a buddy and I had a few words. Aaliyah, the R&B singer, died in a plane accident. I first saw it on MTV News. I was a fan. Naturally, I was sad about it. I had all her albums. I loved her music.

"I can't believe she's dead," I said.

"How can you say that?" he said. "Look at what you did!…Look at at what you did!"

He said that, referring to my case. At the time, I didn't keep it a secret. I felt, I didn't have anything to hide.

"What?" I cried.

I stood up. I got in his face. I was going to punish him. I wanted to make him burn. Especially, for implying such insulting words to me.

I was concerned for Paris' well-being. That's what happened. Every atom in me wanted to explode. Before any fists or licks could be exchanged, the deputies were busy, breaking the two of us, away from each other. I was taken away, like any other convict.

"Naw, naw! He don't be saying that shit!" I said.

It was typical other stuff, one says when they're about to fight someone. According to the jail bylaws, I was thrown in "isolation." The guys beside me, in their own cells, conjured up conversations between themselves.

I actually, had fun in my stay there. I automatically, laughed at anything funny. Our meals were calculated, at the same time, everyday. I was in constant awe of the human spirit. Particularly, in our ability to adapt. I was like a camel. I became content with my situation. I laid back. I waited for canteen, and other conventional things. Eventually, my charge was dropped. I was free to go back to general population.

*CHAPTER 17, PART 18*

# Inmate Number 298601

TUESDAY, SEPTEMBER 11, 2001. It was "9/11," as it was commonly called. Words cannot copy, how it felt inside. It was the most disorderly day in American history. I was placed in pod 220. I hoped, it was only temporary. I corroborated a request form, to get back in the trustee pod.

9/11 felt, something like Judgement Day. New York City was being made to disrobe. Right before our very eyes.

"AMERICA UNDER ATTACK ," the news headlines read.

Distracted, I thought the first plane, which flew into the first Twin Tower, was an accident. I thought, the plane's computer system failed, somehow. However, when I witnessed the second plane fly directly, into the other World Trade Center building, I knew.

"That's no accident," I thought.

"They're saying Muslims did it," I heard someone say, about the tragic news.

That's not Islam. I was disgusted, anyone would hurt innocent people like that. Thousands of people in Manhattan were running for their lives. My heart ran with them. People were heading for cover. Others inside the Twin Towers let themselves fall to their deaths, rather than burn in the fiery inferno. Many were helpless, hundreds of feet above ground.

I called my mother, and family, to see what was cranking out there, in the real world. A third plane shafted itself into the Pentagon, on Virginia soil. Another airplane was dragged heroically, into the ground, in Pennsylvania.

I was fascinated by the country's patriotism. American flags were flown everywhere. I wanted badly, to show Muslims are not terrorists. Nor is it remotely, acceptable in Islam. Extra security on the street didn't hurt matters either.

"AMERICA IS AT WAR," read another news headline.

I wanted to be in free society, more than ever. I wanted to show the world, it is possible to love Islam, and love America too. Especially, with all its inalienable rights, freedoms and privileges, unlike any other country in the world.

My throat was stuck, hearing about all the senseless deaths and destruction. I too, wanted to downplay the misconception, Muslims were outcasts, criminals or murderers. I thought, I was going to faint. I wanted to show America, Muslims could be tolerant of people. Particularly, those who wore crucifixes, for example.

9/11 was a sucker punch in the jaw. I wanted to show…no, needed to tell, not all Muslims in Islam, believe in a distorted racial view, or baseless, violent, political agenda. My feet were behind thick steel bars. My hands may have been in handcuffs. Seemingly, there was nothing, I could do. However, my heart screamed. I knew, differently.

The media claimed Osama Bin Laden was behind the terrorist organization's driver seat. America wanted to fight back. America wanted answers.

Melvin was a guy, I went to high school with. He was one of my cellmates at the jail. It was great, being with someone, who didn't curse all the damn time. He was a born-again Christian. He didn't have a dual personality, like some of the inmates. During high school, he was on the basketball team. The girls adored him. Ironically, he was financially, stripped, a crackhead, in the same cell with me. He was once a "chick magnet." I couldn't believe my eyes. I'm sure, he felt the same about me. I was a quiet, shy guy during high school. It's funny, how life surprises you.

"Pack your shit!" said the deputy, waking me up, four o'clock in the morning.

It was Friday. It was a few days after 9/11. I was getting shipped. I was being transferred to a other facility. I was in the first thing smoking. It wasn't exactly, a Great Dane, Greyhound bus ride. Yet, it was okay. I was in the backseat of a sheriff deputy' car. My hands were in handcuffs, behind my back. Much to my delight, my eardrums got a chance to listen to the radio.

From the highway, the sign read Mechlenburg Correctional Center. It was a receiving unit, which flagged us down. Driving in the dark, it was finally, daylight. I was nervous. I didn't know what to expect. I could hear the echo of inmates. They were calling for each other loudly, in the distance. The prison was merely, a stone's throw from North Carolina's border.

I had to worm myself, in a burgundy jumpsuit, according to my building's assigned color. I went with all the new arrivals. I was around a bunch of people, from all over the state. An education didn't seem to matter. A lot of guys flirted with the female correctional officers. I declined from touching bad behavior.

I had to wait days, before I could get an access code, to call my mother. It was going to be days, before a letter would reach he. Particularly, to let her know, where I actually, was located. It was two weeks, before I was allowed a visit. So, it felt like an elephant was walking, all over me. I knew my mother was going to be worried sick.

Through the fog of inmates, on the recreation area, my heart leaped. I spotted some Muslims. They were praying outside, no less.

"There's no deity, but Allah," I said to myself.

My smile was a symbol of pride. Suddenly, I didn't feel so alone anymore. I had on cheap, Velcro, strap-on sneakers on my feet. I went to arrange my assigned locker.

Getting the dust bunnies out, my cellmate and I sprayed, and cleaned our cell. I thought of Mary. What was going on behind that forehead of hers?

I had to wait, before I could get my hands on a radio, of my own. I stalled time, by reading my Quran. Initially, I didn't have any food. I merely, had deodorant, and other small, miscellaneous things Mechlenburg gave us.

"Where would I be sent, after Mechlenburg?" I thought.

My enigma was fitting in. It was only, a temporary place, until I was classified, and sent on my merry way. For pity's sake, I didn't want to go to Powhatan Correctional Center. I was deputized there. I certainly, didn't want to be a prisoner there.

Throughout the weekend, I watched Muslims ensemble for prayer. I couldn't wait to introduce myself. I too, wanted to be in the foxhole with them. My building's supervisors insisted, our recreation was only with new intakes, like ourselves. So, I'd have to wait. I visualized myself around good brothers. I felt so lonely, and feeble without them.

My cellmate simply, went by the letter "O." He'd usually, brag about all the drug money he once made. The cars he had. The women he had. We were from two different worlds. Also, he would piss on the floor, near the toilet. Apparently, he didn't want me there. It was a ploy for me, to request a cell change. I wasn't equip, or prepared to deal with so much foolishness. Yet, with patience, I dealt with it. I couldn't wait, until the following Friday. So, I could finally, go to Jumuah prayer.

"Why do I get all the messed up cellmates?" I asked, dialing in to Heaven.

Next, my so-called "celly" started to throw, smart aleck comments, towards me. It was one after another. What kind of fruit basket did he take me for? Finally, I couldn't take it anymore.

"Look!" I said. "Your boys and your guns ain't in here! I'll fuck you up!"

I was ready. I wasn't playing either. I was sick of his "ghetto shit." Because I wasn't from the housing projects like him, he took me as fundamentally, weaker. "O" was a lot nicer to me after that. He began telling me stories of his everlasting love, for his future wife.

Soon, I was assigned to Building 5. Their color code was beige. So, I had to exchange my burgundy jumpsuit for a beige one. My new pod was okay. Except, I was galvanized by the cigarette smoke. I claimed a spot in the dayroom, to watch tv. I felt like, I inhaled exhaust fumes. It smelled like gas. From time to time, I engaged in conversation.

"What are you in for?" someone would ask.

I didn't want to make the same mistake again. I didn't think it was good, telling people my case anymore. Especially, after I almost got into a fight over it.

"It's hard to talk about," I'd say.

It was true. It was extremely, hard seeing babies on tv. My precious gem, Paris, was gone. All I had, to show for it, was a 15-year sentence. Perhaps, only 13 years, with "good time."

"Martin," said the C/O. "You have a visit."

I couldn't go fast enough. My family was the center of my life. My mother's house was approximately, an hour and a half drive, from where I was. I was glad to get away, from my hostile environment.

My heart sprouted, like a geyser. Particularly, when I saw my mother and sister in the visitation room. I nearly, knocked down tables and chairs to get to them. It was over a year. I could physically, touch them. I hugged them, without a thick glass between us.

I felt like a human being again. I was looking at them, in my beige jumpsuit. I was nearly, in tears. I wanted to cry. Finally, I was sitting in front of the woman, who gave birth to me. Also, my sister, who I wished could find someone decent in her life. It was nice, getting a glimpse of family life again. It was better than all the therapy, money could buy.

The following weekend, my family visited me. My father accompanied them, this time. Hugging him, almost made me cry.

"You can do it," he said.

He believed, I was going to be alright. I've always wanted to be a G-Man. I've always wanted to work for the government, somehow. Politics was something, I always idealized. It was instilled in me, from an early age, to vote. Particularly, since I was in kindergarten, I'd watch my parents go to the voting polls. I wanted to be just like my father, and be a policeman. Yet, look at me now.

I felt higher than helium, seeing my family. The only thing, which cut like a knife, was the fact my brother, Mel, wasn't there. Mending Mel's and my father's relationship together was something, I'd have to work on. I said it to myself, making a mental note of it.

It gave me goosebumps, to see my parents together, in the same room. It felt immaculate.

"I don't eat meat," I said.

I reminded them of my new, self-imposed diet, when they went to the

BEHOLD

vending machine, to purchase me something to eat. Gradually, I became used to Mechlenburg. However, I had to pass the weekly inspections, from the C/O's. We had to stand in a line, hands raised, palms down.

"Need to shave," I'd hear.

"Cut your fingernails," they'd say.

It was humiliating, to say the least. Especially, being treated like a 2-bit criminal, by the staff. It was hard, not to things personally, when they personally, made it hard.

I tried to get a grasp, on the Muslim brotherhood, at the prison. I made a plausible effort to fit in. We were a small group of guys. Being that, Mechlenburg was a receiving unit, one of us was always being transferred to another facility. We would pray directly, onto the green grass. Meanwhile, the sun was beaming on our backs.

"Ali, call the adhan," asked the imam.

"Okay, but it's been awhile," I said, being bashful.

I made the call for prayer. Loud and proud, as I normally, do. Anything else wouldn't be proper, as far as I was concerned. I must have made a lasting impression. Soon after, I became the community's "muadhan" or prayer caller. It was like, earning grits at the breakfast table.

"Man, you should hear this Brother call the adhan!" the imam said about me, to the other Brothers.

There was a thing which bothered me the most. When certain Brothers would be with their non-Muslim buddies, they wouldn't say the Islamic greeting of "As-Salaamu Alaikum." They would rather act like, "they didn't see me." Some would walk by, pretending to be so heavily, engaged in conversation. That should have been against the law. I considered it, so rude and fake. Islam is a complete way of life. I wasn't about to be shy about it. It was disappointing. A leaf could've knocked me over. I wished, I had a piece of chewing gum. I'd talk to Muslims, who actually, did "Salaam" me, regardless of who, they were walking with. I couldn't understand, why certain Brothers acted "indecisive."

"That's because, they ain't living right," said Abdullah.

He gave me leeway. He knew about the gambling. Some were not making their prayers. I then took it all in stride, or not to take, personally.

My counselor looked more like a gypsy woman, with indiscriminate, thick glasses. She raised my custody to Level 3.

"What happened?" she asked out of curiosity.

It was none of her business, but there I was, telling her. It drove me half-crazy, but I told her. A penny for her thoughts. I told my counselor, how I innately, thought something was wrong with my baby. However, it gave the prosecution leverage to charge me, with second-degree murder. I wished, I had a handkerchief handy. She looked as though she wanted to cry.

I was inflamed. It was a lie, which got me in prison. I tried to not have a harden heart about it. I exhibited a light disposition. I knew, deep inside, I was a has-been. I used to be, free as a bird. I used to have a real job, relationships, responsibilities. The innumerable times, I cried, under bed sheets. The many days, months, years lined ahead. The pain and suffering gave me insight. Yet, I made a mental note of the things, I should be thankful for.

Once, before the Brothers and I were about to pray, bump our heads, they had a question for me. I didn't know, what on earth was going on. Especially, from the way they were looking at me.

"Ali, are you gay?" said the imam, surrounding me with the community.

I loathed that question. I was shocked, more than anything.

"No, of course not," I said, on the edge of my seat. "Why do you say that?"

"People say, this gay guy kissed you, in the visiting room."

I nearly, forgot how homophobic people in jail were. The slightest thing could be taken out of context, misconstrued and mistakenly, thought of as "homosexual."

"That was my brother," I corrected them. "He kissed me on the cheek, before saying goodbye."

Not that it was anyone's business. I shouldn't have needed to explain myself. My biological brother, Mel, can kiss me on the cheek, if he wanted to. I'm not gay. I never was.

For all intents and purposes, the Muslims were no longer "bumps on a log." Seemingly, they wanted to jam me up, if I were to say the wrong thing. Like smoking herb, homosexuality was very taboo in Islam. I'm very much, attracted to women, not men. Despite any haphazard, silly rumor going around, in an all-male environment, like prison. It could put someone in permanent intermission.

That wasn't the half of it. I wasn't out of the woods, yet. Mary would write me letters as though, I was hiding something from her. She implied, without any women around, I was bound to "go gay." It was nonsense. It was insulting. It was stereotypical. Also, she was concerned, with her being 10 years older than me. She thought perhaps, I wouldn't want her, when I get out of prison.

I was an introvert. I usually, stayed to myself. I didn't want any problems. I didn't want any issues. I'd write Mary, lovely letters. I wanted nothing more, than to be with her, at that time.

In the visitation room, Mary spent quarter, after quarter, on me for the vending machines. Only to violate me in a letter, when she got home.

"Didn't we just have lunch together, or what?" I'd ask myself, reading what I couldn't believe.

Mary did the unthinkable. She had the audacity, to send me a certain flyer in the mail. It was from a "Down Low" seminar, she attended to. It was sponsored by DL King.

I hobbled with hurt. I was floored. The pain was irreversible. She actually, went to that place. She really, took the time, to hear about "secret" gay, alternative lifestyles. To see, if there was a "homosexual" hint, or "gay" clue about me, on my behalf. I was so upset, I ripped up the brochure, peed on it, and flushed it down the toilet. I was disgusted. Mary acted like, I was "possibly gay," when I first met her. A lot of agonizing pain came back to mind.

I'm not saying, I'm the most macho man in the world, but damn. All I thought about was women, and this is the thanks, I get? Mentally, I put it in italics, highlighted, in bold letters…

"For the last time, I am not gay!" I said to myself.

At that point, I wanted a Magnum malt liquor. Amazingly, Mary still wanted me to "honor her" in marriage.

I had a buddy at Mechlenburg, named Dallas. He was a huge football fan. He was a Black guy, who always hung with White guys. He loved his tobacco. He didn't particularly, care for the other Blacks there.

"Then why do you hang around me?" I asked Dallas.

"Because you're from the suburbs," he said.

He let me know, I acted "different" from the usual guys, especially from the projects. In turn, I complained to him, about some of the Muslims, in the penitentiary.

"They're so…"

"Rough edged," said Dallas, finishing my sentence for me.

He always got on me, about my supposedly, lifestyle.

"You say you're Muslim, but you don't pray. Why don't you pray?" Dallas asked.

Good question. So, by January 1, 2002, I had my New Year's resolution. I made up my mind, to pray the prescribed five prayers. It felt great, making my prayers again. My cellmate at the time was horrible. He'd have the window open, letting the cold air in. Even he was taking me more seriously, with my starting to perform my prayers. Prayer was a jewel after all. Somehow, I managed to make it work.

For years, I wanted a tattoo. For years, I didn't get one. Mel and Drika had plenty of ink done.

"It's against my religion," I'd say.

There was a fellow inmate in the pod, doing tattoos. He drew a beautiful, Asian dragon, which caught my eye. I was tempted. So, before I knew it, I was decidedly, in his cell. My right arm was stiff as a mannequin, letting him get it done. Of course, it was against Islam. Nonetheless, I thought it looked great.

The dragon on my arm, served as a reminder, of the year 2000. According to the Chinese calendar, it was the Year of the Dragon. It was notably, the year my baby, Paris was born. Also, 2000 was the year, I lost her. I went to jail, and it became the worst year of my life.

Feeling I should've known better, I kept my tattoo covered. I felt somewhat guilty, because of religious beliefs. Though I wasn't perfect.

I had the houseman job, scrubbing the floors. It amazed me, how much phlegm was on it. The pay certainly, wasn't a heck of a whole lot.

Occasionally, it gave me some of the items I needed. The snacks I purchased were anything, but nutritious.

My mother paid 15 THOUSAND DOLLARS, for my appeal. She retained M. Morchower. He was one of the most prestigious lawyers in the area. According to his reputation, he was one of the best, money could buy.

My court appeal made some valid points. Yet, it was denied. With the appeal court denying my appeal, it felt like the American justice system was picking its nose at me. I felt obsolete. Especially, with my earlier court case "already decided." It made me pig out, or eat, even more. I was stressed and depressed. The only time, I didn't feel so badly, was when I was in prayer. It was meditation. It was medicine, if not for a few minutes. "God is Greater," it said.

I bought me a cassette tape player, in October. It also had a radio component. Remarkably, it picked up Kiss 99.3 / 105.7 FM, a Richmond radio station. It played "Today's R&B Hits and Classic Soul." It was a welcomed taste of home. I was pinned to the headphones, whenever I'd hear any Richmond news. That old school music drowned out the loud pricks. It melted away my problems. My "Walk-Man" or cassette tape player was officially, my new best friend.

In the pitch darkness, I asked Allah, "Why?" I needed His Mercy. My mind would run Olympic marathons.

"Pack it up," said the C/O to me.

It meant, I was being transferred, tomorrow, to another "plantation." My state identification number was 298601. It was metaphysically, assigned to me. So, off I went. The fellow inmate I rode with, oozed with complaints. We were on our way to Augusta Correctional Center. It was a 2-hour drive or more, for my family, just to get there. The scenery was beautiful. The mountains served as wonderful, tall things.

Augusta was in the northwestern part of Virginia. In of itself, it was very oppressive- looking. Particularly, with the heavy-duty doors, fences, and bar wire everywhere. The C/O's were plump and expected our arrival. In the middle of a farm, it seemed. Cows were all around. They weren't dairy, or the kind for the milk. These cows were for slaughter.

The prison was bleak. Ordinarily, it was filled with redneck prison guards, who were quick to point us in the right direction. After a series of events, we were sent to medical. The nurse warned us, not to be late for pill line.

I met a lot of guys, with a lot of time. Blame it on politics. I conducted myself in a non- assuming manner. Whenever the guards let us out for recreation, I balanced my time with lifting weights.

My cellmate JB's was "okay." Sex was all, he ever talked about. However, being in a cell gave a person, a sense of privacy, except for pooh-pooh.

"I have to use the bathroom," I practically, had to say.

That statement alone, would force him out of the cell, and vice-versa. I'd sit in the dayroom and chat with someone. During other outtakes, I'd write in continuation, my short stories. I'd write during commercial breaks. I'd write to keep my mind busy. I was still, dreaming my dream, of being a published writer someday. It was still important.

Jumuah or Friday prayer was somewhat moderate. We were in a gym, with a rug spread out on the floor. We made do, with what we had.

"Takbir!" someone would encourage, after our congregational prayer.

"Allahu Akbar!" replied the congregation, with enthusiasm, which meant "God is Greater."

My only concern, or disappointment was seeing Brothers having to posture like bodyguards, throughout the service. Of course, I spoke up about it. It wasn't our way, at the mosques. Clearly, I thought it sent the wrong message. It reminded me of The Nation of Islam, which I opposed, spiritually.

"That's the 'sherif staff'," I'd hear. "Something could happen, at any moment."

I didn't like it, but I was overruled. We were in a hostile environment, it was explained.

"You have to hear this Brother call the adhan!" said Abdullah. "I'm telling you."

He was the same one, I met at Mechlenburg. I was flattered about his pow-wow about me. I was only doing what, I felt needed to be done, when I chanted out loud, the call to prayer.

It took a few weeks, before I was finally, able to move to the non-smoking pod. I was still a relatively, new arrival to Augusta. Some of the Muslims gave me this monstrous look, when I moved into my new area. I couldn't understand, "Why?" I was up the stream, without a paddle. What precious thing did I do, wrong? It wasn't the cheerful, humble faces at the mosques, I was used to.

Checking me out, the following morning, I'd get the same, mean looks. It was the same attitude. I found it appalling. It felt like a gang initiation. More so, than being around fellow believers, or so-called religious people. If I gave the Muslim greeting, "As-Salaamu Alaikum," it wasn't in their best interest to say it back. The Brothers looked as though, they were ready for a pre-emotive strike, on anyone who wasn't Muslim. Especially, if they weren't sure, if someone "proclaimed" to be Muslim, only for their protection. Their distrust, of the "mountaineer" correctional officers, was obvious. I didn't fit the typical, penitentiary profile. I was, more or less, a paperweight, until I could prove myself to them.

Later, my voice became the only prerequisite I needed. I became the muezzin, when the one we had suddenly, stepped down. On Fridays, I'd perch myself in the middle of the front row. When it was time, the imam, Yahya would give me the cue. I was happy to give my presumptuous call, to all the believers.

My cellmate was Derrick. He was younger, slightly muscular. He was great. He was the best cellmate, I ever had. He wasn't weird, or treat me like, I was "different." We talked about everything. We laughed. We shared food, if the other didn't have. It was genius. A priest couldn't get more, mutual respect. Sometimes, he would pray, alongside with me. He was even considering being Muslim.

Time was passing fast. Before I knew it, Derrick was looking to be, on his way home. Before he left, he promised me, he wouldn't go back to selling drugs.

Shedding light on the subject, I became close with another, Abdul-Raheem. If I wasn't at his cell, he was at mine. It was better than taking a nap. He took pride, in once being a truck driver. He had traveled all over the country. Our path was both Islam. So, we talked about it much. He seemed to be a good judge of character. He said, he could tell, I didn't have any hidden agendas. He didn't think, there was anything "sneaky" about me.

"You're just looking for a friend," Abdul-Raheem said to me.

At the county jail, I was simply, Marco. At Mechlenburg receiving unit, I was called "Big." At Augusta, I insisted on being called "Ali." The name which was given to me by the Muslims, years prior.

Occasionally, Abdul-Raheem would confide in me, what he was in prison for.

"I killed somebody," he admitted to me.

I was getting nauseous, just thinking about it. However, I played it off, like it didn't bother me. He was a master manipulator of the law. He stayed in the law library, working on his appeal, himself.

Abdul-Raheem was formerly, on death row, he told me. He was able to get his sentence reduced, to Life instead. He often talked about his children, a girl and some boys. He grew up, poor, on a farm. He was handy, with a sewing needle. He made a point of improvising.

I wasn't trying to peek inside Abdul-Raheem's case. Yet, I heard him say, he was in prison for rape. It was something he said, he didn't commit.

The Muslims were constantly, trying to get me to work out. Abdullah was one, who discreetly, thought I should wear a trash bag, to increase my sweating. He wanted me to run with him, promising how much weight I'd lose. Making excuses, I didn't feel like it. So, one day during lunch, I nestled beside Abdullah at the table. He was an elderly. He didn't bite his tongue.

"I tried to get Ali to run with me, but he don't want to do nothing! Oh lazy ass!" said Abdullah.

My self-respect was pinned to the wall. The inequity of it all nibbled at me.

"I'm tired of this 'penitentiary Islam' bullshit!" I said it, for all persons to hear.

I was sick of the street protein, which was forced down my ears. We were brought up on "community charges." Especially, for "arguing with a Brother, in a public place." Our punishment, or prize, was for us to both speak, before Friday prayer on "The Importance of Brotherhood." Afterwards, Abdullah and I hugged. We apologized.

Brotherhood was always permanently, in my mind. Brothers said, I sounded good on the microphone. On the podium, I wasn't shy or a prude. Something would come over me. It reminded me, when I gave the sermon once, at Mechlenburg. The guys seem to really, dig it.

Mary and I would pucker up, whenever she came to visit me. I got over the rotten "possible gay" thing, she accused me of. Meaning, the "On the Down Low" brochure I received, when I was at the receiving unit.

Once, when Toya visited me, Mary accused me of having a "hard on" for her daughter. I had no such thing. It was in a letter I got, after I thought, we all had a great visit. Needless to say, I was devastated.

Immediately, I called Toya on the phone. I was hurt. I was crying.

"Don't cry, Marco," said Toya. "I know it's not true."

"I wanted you to hear it from me. Toya, you know I would never, ever do something like that! I adore you," I said to the young lady, who I wished was my own daughter.

At any rate, Mary was exercising. She was getting noticeably, slender. I couldn't help but wonder, whether to not, there was another man in the picture. Was he wearing a rubber? Was he making her, his love-slave? Did he serve her, like I did? Without a smidgen of proof, I learned to let it go. I just had an inkling. It was a feeling I had. I saw no use, in crying over spilt milk. So, I did what any rusty-butt person in jail would do. I asked her, to marry me.

Meanwhile, Abdul-Raheem snarled, how the new Muslim convert in his cell, stopped praying. He was threatening his celly, to leave. Sooner or later, someone was bound to hit the deck. The celly moved out for safekeeping. With Derrick now home, I put a request form in, to move to Abdul-Raheem's cell.

We got along great. So, I saw no reason, not to. I was clueless. Boy, was I in for a treat. Abdul-Raheem would always backbite, so-and-so.

"That nigga don't know what he's talking about!" he'd say.

"Faggot!" he'd say, if the C/O in the operating booth, didn't open our cell door fast enough.

"Wench!" he'd say, if she happen to be a female C/O.

And, my personal favorite...

"Slut!" he'd say, making my skin crawl.

I kept quiet. I didn't want to argue. Yet, I knew the stuff he was spewing wasn't our way. I simply, wanted to give my salutations, and keep it going. With the amount of time Abdul-Raheem was facing, I tried to understand. I dealt with his solar flares. I had to endure his bittersweetness.

Saturday, November 23, 2002. The anticipation of waiting was grueling. I had the task of getting everything approved. Mary and I were finally, getting married. By the same Pastor Drew, who commenced Paris' funeral. I was so nervous. My heart felt like it was on a racetrack. Should I go full throttle? Do I need a pit stop? How many miles will it go?

"Do you love her?" Mama asked, knowing I can't lie to her.

"I love her mama," I said.

Was I going insane? Mary was the same one, who told those prosecution folks, I meant to hurt my baby. She gave them the case, "no remorse" and didn't care.

"I forgive her mama," I said, as though it was the Muslim thing to do. I had the feeling of a sonic boom in my chest.

"As long as you love her, you have my blessing," Mama said.

I swore Abdul-Raheem to secrecy, because it was a "Christian wedding." I wanted an imam. Particularly, from the mosque, to perform our wedding. However, Mary acted as though, she couldn't get an imam for us. So, it was beyond my control.

Adul-Raheem seemingly, understood. I reassured him, I wanted to renew our wedding vows, at the mosque, when I get out of prison. Save the fact, he was a sourpuss, he wasn't so bad, after all.

Yet, he would often rant, how he hated "faggots." I'd cringe inside whenever he said it. Especially, with the stuff I had to go through with Mary. All in which, I found scandalous, because gay people were the last thing on my mind. The thought of gays sparked so much hatred and venom in him. Whereas, I couldn't care less.

Abdul-Raheem was rather, proud of the fact, I went to school. I was speechless, at all the razzle-dazzle he made about it. Overall, it took courage, to be around somebody like him, who was so prone to violence. My head would spin, at all his cussing and fussing. Particularly, about Jews. What was I to do?

I was due for a reality check. I'd lovingly, rub my white gold, wedding band finger. The fellow inmate, who took visitation pictures of the wedding, spoke about it to the Muslims. Needless to say, they weren't receptive of it. Adding salt to injury, they said, "It wasn't valid," or "It didn't count," because the marriage wasn't done by an imam. I never read anywhere, a wedding has to be done necessarily, by an imam. Just a trustworthy person, an accepted dowry, and witnesses. I didn't care what the Muslims had to say. I loved Mary. I was heading to our wedding vows. For better, or worse. I was in my usual "inmate blues" clothes. She was in a beautiful dress. It was cloaked in white, African attire, along with a white turban.

Our marriage gave Mary, an extra spring in her step. On her visits, she'd be dressed in Muslim garb, from head to toe. It was out of respect for my faith. She had inclinations, to learn about Islam. It was a possibility, she was becoming Muslim herself. However, we'd recount our old arguments, private moments, my trial. You name it.

"If I knew, I was going to jail, over some balloons, I would have stolen the motherfuckers," I once said.

The jury didn't hear squat. Especially, my side of the story, I'd remind her. I'd ridicule the greedy prosecutors. Mary ADMITTED, she put me in prison, from what she lead them to believe. I knew, what I had done. Yet, I was well-aware, she had a lot to do with "the case." Though she was my wife, the person, who was responsible for misleading Deglau, was sitting right in front of me. Holding her hand, I gave her regal, queen treatment, anyhow.

With our daughter Kandi, I made the most of it. I loved to play with her. I was holding her, in such high regards. I'd read children stories to her. It'll rejuvenate my own love, for a good story. My daughter and I were inseparable.

However, I was a ward of the state. Of course I knew, it wasn't going to always remain that way. I was away from my family. I wasn't going to always be behind thick, steel bars. Yet, it managed to work itself out, into a hurtful feeling, all the same.

"It could've been worse," I'd say, while repaying my debt to a shady society.

Sometimes, I'd look at Mary, and wonder, what was going on, in that brain of hers. By this time, she was printing me crazy letters. They would be in first person, as though they written by Paris herself. She was blaming me, for her death. I too, shared grief over our lost daughter, but that wasn't fair. Instead of stirring up something, why couldn't she see that I too, was fried, dyed and laid to the side?

## CHAPTER 18, PART 19

# Residue

IT WAS 2003. That's how I felt. I felt like cheap residue, from another failed marriage. Mary left me. I told her about a dream of mine. I wanted my wife and child, to be in the same house, I grew up in. I wanted my child to go to the same public school system I went to.

Everything stopped in its tracks, after a few months in the marriage. Mary suddenly, wanted to move into my mother's house, along with Kandi and Toya. She wrote me a letter, wanting me to run the idea to my mother. Considering how my wife had an obsessive, deep hatred, for my sister, my mother's response was "No." Especially, with me having to serve prison time. I had 10 YEARS remaining.

So, Mary was took it as a huge insult. With that, she closed shop on our marriage. The rug was lifted from beneath me. She stopped writing me. She stopped visiting me. Consequently, it made Kandi and I strangers. I'd write my daughter letters, but to no avail. I didn't get a response, or a card.

It was surreal. I was out of touch, with the family I made. Mary was on strike, like I needed a cold shower. I quit wearing my wedding band. I was confused. I had questions. What was the point? What did I do? What would make her revoke, what I thought her and I had? I thought she loved me.

My siblings assured me, it was for the best. Mary didn't have any strudels anyway, they wanted to say. It was a very emotional ride. I took it as a sign from God. Such as, not to get mixed up with a woman, who would stir my heart with so much controversy. My mind was racing. It went around and around.

My wedding ring was the so-called token of our love. I wanted to throw it in the trash, like my marriage was. I sincerely, loved my wife. So, I didn't. Be as it may, what she did wasn't normal.

I roasted with anguished, not being able to see Kandi. I wrote letter after letter, to Mary. In that, I was her father, and have right to see my daughter. Yet, no such luck. I even took the romantic correspondent approach, to see if that would work. It didn't. I was a kicked rock. Days which turned into weeks skipped by. It was a lot of nothing.

"I wish, I never met her!" I sulked.

Meanwhile, my cellmate, Abdul-Raheem was always talking about, his glory days of trucking, on the superhighway. Once, I forgot exactly, what we were mad at each other about. However, he was trying my patience. It happened to be a cold night. He decided to open the windows. Doing so, he let a wealth of cold air in. It didn't take long, like a laugh over dinner, to see he was being funny. During Abdul-Raheem's triumph of making me cold, I attempted to get some sleep.

"Penitentiary Muslims," I said, under my breath.

I was feeling the weight of the world, on my shoulders. Oh, shit! He heard me. Suspended on the top bunk bed, Abdul-Raheem jumped down. Especially, with him breathing hard. I was in a world of trouble.

"Get up," he said.

He was making it perfectly, clear he wanted to whale on me. He actually, killed somebody. I sweated under pressure. He was a real murderer. I panicked. I panted.

"He ain't in here, for nothing," I thought.

It felt like a ton of bricks, were on top of me. He was grabbing at me. I whirled around, my leg away from him. I was sure, to get a swollen eye.

"I'm really sorry, okay?" I pleaded.

Miraculously, things turned for the better. I totally, buckled under that wicked face of his. From then on, no matter what, I learned to keep it to myself. It didn't matter, how plastic some of the Muslims were. I twitted tears, under the covers. I cried like a baby, knowing this guy could've killed me.

Afterwards, Abdul-Raheem continued to be a windbag, over his adventures about his six year stint in the US Army. What I wouldn't give, for a piece of chewy, caramel taffy. The usual sounds of him burping, and farting, was a bit much. However, I learned to keep quiet. The all-in fun, wisecracking relationship we once had, was no more. I no longer "talked" to him. He once wanted to fight me. I was his so-called friend. That changed me. I merely, nodded or gave him one-word answers. We both liked Asian and White women. It didn't matter anymore.

When Abdul-Raheem wasn't throwing a temper tantrum at the "bias media," or bashing Christians for their beliefs, he was sleep. For which, I was grateful.

"You're an extremist," I'd playfully say.

On the other hand, I didn't work any job at Augusta Correctional Center. I refused to be a houseman or clean anyone's nasty shower.

Tee-hee. There were hardly, any women at the prison, to undress with my eyes. I looked at pretty, girly magazines, every chance I got.

As usual, Abdul-Raheem was losing his temper. Also, there was another time, when he wanted to fight. My mother was regularly, the sole person sending me money, for canteen. So, going to "the store" was nothing new. I went week after week. He rarely, went.

"Don't hate," I said to him, jokingly.

Again, Abdul-Raheem wanted to put his tentacles on me. I unloaded more apologies. It led to more distrust of him. If I was a gambling man, I'd bet my VCU graduation tassel, he'd sneak into my locker, to see what I was actually, locked for.

"I know you're a cop," Abdul-Raheem would say to me. "I know what you're in for."

That was his way of torturing me, as though discreetly, knowing something about me, which others did not.. It wasn't the only time, a so-called Brother, wanted to scuffle with me.

"I never met somebody, like you," Latin would say.

He was a fellow Richmond native. This was coming from the same person, who wanted to fight on our first day of the holy month of Ramadan. Finally, breaking our fast, I was still eating. Meanwhile, Latif hurriedly, wanted to commence the prayer. After we made "salat" or prayer, I admonished him, for rushing me to pray. Particularly, after a long day of fasting, with no food or water.

"Get a room!" Latif said.

He was challenging me to a duel, in an unoccupied cell. The Brothers stopped it, before it reached that point. Still, I was hurt, by the thought of yet, another Muslim wanting to fight me.

Joey, a short, Caucasian guy, confided in me, he wasn't Muslim anymore. Especially, with no one pressuring him to pray a certain way. No one was deciding, what he was allowed to read any longer. The Christians there, weren't as theatrical, he assured me.

It wasn't long, before I started hanging around my good friend, Jay. He was from my area. Through him, I was exposed to more, and more Christians. He loved to sing. He joined the church choir.

The Christians made me feel comfortable. They invited me to their meals. They invited me, to sit with them. They invited me to their church meetings, which I declined. It was all good. They reminded me of my own upbringing. They were humble, mild-mannered and middle-class. They were unlike the belligerent, ghetto boys, I had to endure. They weren't like the judgmental, no-nonsense, grim Brothers, I had to be around with, at Augusta. However, the Muslims had a real problem with it though.

"You're always around those Christians," they'd say to me.

Yet, those same Brothers were free to talk to, and hang, with whoever they wanted. It was a double standard.

"They don't believe, like we believe," I'd hear. "You'd rather be around them, than being around us."

Allah knew my intentions. I simply, valued people like Hassan, who treated me, fairly. He too was a used-to-be Muslim. Yet, I liked his manners. I liked his conduct.

"You're not a homeboy," Joey would say quietly, to me.

I could tell, he wasn't that fond of Black people, but he seemed to like me. Also, that was his way of showing me, I was "different" from the other Muslims.

It should have been a crime, hanging around Jay. He was a former deejay. He was a bouncer in a club. I was determined to be with, who I wanted to be around. I refused to be intimidated or "look the part."

"I don't care, what somebody's religion is," I'd refute.

That was my verdict, and I was sticking to it. By this time, I lost my position as the Muslim community's muezzin or prayer caller. Due to me, "trading the pork on my tray, for some cookies." I didn't see the harm, in getting something in place of it.

Losing my position, in the Muslim community, made me feel, some kind of way. However, seeing I, alone was liable for my actions, I no longer toiled with the idea. I learned to accept things, as they were. I felt like a Viking, sitting in the back row, not being able to do, what I do best.

Watching Ameen calling the Adhan for prayer, was like pulling teeth. Getting a visual, of someone else calling it, was hard enough. It was totally, obvious, he didn't have the voice for it. Giving me brownie points, a lot of the Brothers felt Yahya, our imam, should give me, my job back.

I could do without the vulgarity. I longed to me be profanity-free. I wanted to be around peace-loving people. The Christians happened to be, on the same trail I was, it seemed. Not in beliefs, but in deeds.

I wasn't nearly, about to walk out, on Islam. Certainly, some Muslims thought I was. I wasn't about to transfer myself to another religion. I didn't necessarily, want to go another facility. I was feeling, the Muslims.

However, many of the Muslims there, had a warped sense of what it is, to be a Muslim. I was sick of it. Weekly, Yahya would go over versus in the Quran, against slander, backbiting, being sarcastic, being suspicious of fellow believers. Yet, it seemed to fall on death ears. I was in the middle of a desert. I longed for water. I searched for my soul. I wanted my comfort zone.

I was taken aback, by the lack of true brotherhood. Yet, I had the gall, to do what I wanted to.

"You act like a Christian," Jay would say, which was complimenting me.

When my pregnant cousin, Tameka, died in a car accident, it was hard. All I could do, from my prison cell was send her mother, my first-cousin, a card.

When my uncle Joe died, from AIDS-related pneumonia, I was

devastated. He was gay. So, across the board, I made a point, of not telling Abdul-Raheem. Out of respect for my uncle, I didn't. It was for his memory, regardless of his homosexuality.

I didn't want to give Abdul-Raheem the pleasure to now know, a gay person, was now dead. I was fed up, with his overbearing, homophobic anything. I didn't tell anyone, for that matter. Especially, in prison, that my uncle died. I suffered in silence.

Jay was finally, assigned to the kitchen worker's pod. I began hanging around Black Man. He was cleaner than a Baptist preacher, in a new car. His clothes were always ironed. His shoes were always shining. Black Man taught a Black History class, to anyone who cared to listen. The classes were called, "Knowledge." I couldn't help but be, impressed by him. He seemed to take his surroundings, with a grain of salt.

More importantly, Black Man respected me. He thought of himself, as an honorary member of The Nation of Islam. Though, he was not. He was my accomplice. Particularly, when it came to sneaking a peek, at nude women magazines. He was not a follower of any organized religion. Nor did he apologize, for his sexuality. Neither did I.

Like anyone, I enjoyed a good cat fight on the Springer show. Apparently, that was okay with Black Man. He wasn't there to judge me. I loved my watching Charmed. It was a tv show about three, pretty witches, using their powers, and helping innocent people. Seemingly, there was nothing wrong with that, as far as he was concerned. He wasn't self-righteous, like the others I knew.

Black Man showed me, the light of my problems. He showed me, the beautiful spirit, I possessed inside. His cell was next to mine. So, we always visited each other.

"Ali," he would say, phoning me over.

I was addicted to Black Man's humor. I liked his straightforwardness. It was the beginning of a good friendship. Jay was cool. However, with Black Man, we talked on an intellectual level. He helped me, with low self-esteem.

"I want to help people," said Black Man.

He made it his life's mission, to serve others. Somehow, that resonated with me. I too wanted to be inspirational and happy.

I was feeling stupid, with my "wife" Mary gone. She out of the picture, and wouldn't return any of my letters. I haven't seen her, or our daughter, since Father's Day 2003.

Black Man introduced spiritual, yoga lessons to me. He received them monthly, in the mail. It changed my perspective on everything. Especially, what I was going through. It was an instant love affair, with the teachings. The lessons taught me, to love myself. It gave me the best advice. For example, not to chase a mate, in order for me to be happy. As soon as I finished reading one, I quickly, wanted the next lesson.

I was open-minded. I wasn't the type, to put all my eggs in the same basket. Islam was still, the shining armor, I wore. However, the yoga lessons made me walk on air. It contained such beautiful words. It was a love boat. It showed me, my connection to God, and all fellow human beings.

On October 21$^{st}$, I mailed a birthday card to Mary. There was no reply, no nothing. This was coming from the same woman, who used to call Asian people "chinks." Especially, when I first met her.

Allah knows best. My mind went blank. For all I knew, she was teaching Kandi to hate me or something. Numerous times, I blamed myself for being bloated. I felt completely, helpless.

My National Geographic circulation was nice. Yet, it was nothing. Particularly, without an all-American girl to share it with.

Every blue moon, Mary would torture me in a letter. She'd write about some guy she met, named Burt. She told me, he was great with the children. She mention that, as though that would somehow, soften the blow. In her usual glamour, she still refused to visit me for dialog.

"Bull!" my mother said, "She's playing with your mind again."

What made things worse, Mary was actually, driving my car. I gave it to her, as a Christmas present, the year we got married. I gave her the keys, the title. She had everything. She was the type of woman, who waited on Publisher's Clearinghouse Sweepstakes.

What was her angle? I thought of her, as a gold digger, at best. I sent her the first, four books, I wrote in the penitentiary. I named them, "Loot," "Bone," "Three," and "Judge Not." As the proud, new owner of my automobile, Mary refused to give me my stories back.

"You gave those books to me," she'd say.

It made me clamp down on my studies, even further. My five inch tv became my movie theater. I'd keep myself in the cell all day. Mary had the body of a glass, Classic Cocoa-Cola bottle. I was missing that. The space I gave her was of no use. I couldn't help, but think about the times we shared.

"I like your body," I'd tell her.

It got my wheels spinning. However, I refused to let one, bad apple spoil the bunch. I needed a break. All the cologne-wearing in the world wasn't going to bring her back. I didn't apt to do anything crazy. I regretted, I decided to make Mary my bride, in the first place. Deep down inside, I knew there was no coming back from that. Yet, she was wearing my last name. I just wanted to forget the whole thing. As far as I was concerned, she was a heartbreaker, who didn't know the word "commitment."

All I had to show for it was a "Dear John" letter. It was life, imitating art. I was anything, but bubbly inside.

I confided to Jay, I used to work for the Department of Corrections myself. I asked him, not to say anything. I was in a place of bull-headed people. Dozens of times, inmates would ask me, what kind of work, I used to do. I'd keep my composure. I'd lie and say, I worked in a warehouse. I was uncertain, how they'd react to the truth. It was an assumption. Yet, I seen so many inmates get burnt with charges, caving in their chances for good-time. I didn't want to be attacked, over a misunderstanding.

Abdul-Raheem, who acted, more or less, like The Butcher of Baghdad, was confirmed with another institutional charge again. Especially, for typing personal stuff, in the law library. He was taken to "the hole." Not surprisingly, I was grateful. With him leaving, I had the cell to my cell. He left all of his clothes in a cabinet. He thought, he was going to make his way back, to the cell.

I was sick of hearing constantly, how he wanted to bomb America. This was coming from the same guy, who called Dr. Martin Luther King Jr. a "faggot." It was during an annual event, held in the late civil rights leader's honor. Obviously, Abdul-Raheem wanted to see my reaction. I didn't give him the satisfaction. I didn't speak to him, the whole day over that.

Abdul-Raheem was a terrorist, if I ever saw one. The early successors of Islam never acted that way. So why should he? Hearing his remarks daily, made me constipated. I was sick to my stomach.

"I'm so glad he's gone! I'm so glad he's gone!" I said, crying like a baby, when it was official.

He was like a Canadian coin in America. There was no use. He was a loose goose, who continued to give Islam a bad name. I was happy to see him, kept in "the back."

My Christian friend, Hassan, had the audacity. He told the correctional officers, Abdul-Raheem left his clothes purposely, in the cell. So, they came and took his clothes out as well.

This was after, only one conversation with Hassan. What a way to bring in the new year 2004, huh?

So, when everything was said and done, Shakur corresponded, he wanted to move in with me. Merely, because I was Muslim as well. I reluctantly, dispensed an "Okay." My faith in the brotherhood was on the verge of extinction. How could I say "No?" Before I could recant my statement, he was assigned to the same cell, I was assigned to.

Shakur fabricated little conversation with me. It was counterintuitive. I didn't know what he expected from me. It made me very uncomfortable. It really disturbed me. Why was he so quiet? In return, I wasn't being social myself.

I didn't think it was fair. Why the hell, did he move in with me? I asked myself, "Was it me?" At any rate, I talked it over with Black Man.

"Give him time. He's just quiet," advised Black Man, in his usual cowboy stance.

It'll have to do. It wasn't his typical, fancy long-winded answer. However, it was a great domestic way of looking at it.

I was fast becoming, an outcast, with the other Muslims. I was hanging around Christians. They weren't harsh, or acted hard. I held my feelings about it to Black Man. I needed insight. I needed answers. He was once Muslim himself. I expressed how, it was such a double-standard.

# RESIDUE

Particularly, because the Brothers talked to whoever, they wanted to. No one questioned them, or said anything about it.

"Why don't I fit in?" I asked Black Man.

"They're disappointed in you, because you've been Muslim a long time. They don't think you're serious," he said.

All in which, made their actions towards me feasible. I felt double-crossed. I had a broken heart. I had a loss of hope. I felt downtrodden. Without a feminine touch, to help me cope, with this cold, cruel world, it was difficult. I could only dream of a better tomorrow. I missed being around good, humble Muslims, like it was at the mosque. It was so superficial, what I had to endure.

"Just do you. Don't let nobody control you. Talk to, who you want to talk to. Don't worry about them," he said.

I was appointed the Muslim community's muezzin again. It was under another Bilal's leadership. Yet, I was treated as though, I was young and dumb. My heart dropped. I felt so "unfulfilled," whenever I was around the Brothers. I didn't "feel them" any longer. They certainly, didn't "act spiritual." I didn't view them as "custodians of the faith." I began to see them, as "just dudes," in the same, fine institution, as I was.

Somehow, I resented the ghetto attitude. Especially, the amount of criminals it produced from its environment. I had a hunch, it was going to be along ride. I merely, went to Taleem class, and Jumuah prayer on Fridays, because I felt, it was my duty as the prayer caller. I was a fish out of water. Prison was the hook. I simply, wanted to go to the nearest dark room, and cry.

I'd often get, an earful of free advice, from Black Man. He'd get on me about having self-respect. Regardless, if I wasn't necessarily, trying to impress anyone. I'd flame up the iron, over the iron board, and started to iron my clothes, more often than not. I'd clean myself up, as though I was meeting a deadline.

I'd have my usual chat, with my counselor, during my annual review. I put a transfer request in for James River Correctional Center. It was considerably, closer to home.

On April 22, 2004 my plan came to fruition. I was happy to flee from the mountain terrain. I had little under, a decade more, to go. So, I wanted visitation, to be as less cost effective as possible, for my family.

I was flooded with a sense of home. I couldn't believe, I was only 30 minutes away from it all. I was assigned to Building One. It was a smoking pod, which contaminated my lungs. I needed elbow grease, for my heavy bags. Before I could unpack, the imam noticed my prayer rug. Under the fluorescent lights, he introduced himself.

"As-Salaamu alaikum, I'm Shaheed. I'm the imam here."

That made all the difference. Looking around, the place looked as old as Queen Elizabeth. Immediately, other Brothers fell in line, to shake my hand. They deliberately, made me feel comfortable. They welcomed me with food, or whatever I may need.

"I think, I'm going to like it here," I thought.

Quickly, I merged with the Muslims there. I decided to rid myself of any hard feelings. Despite what I previously, endured with the Augusta Correctional Center believers. They demonstrated a willingness for brotherhood, without the hardline, I was looking for. Without a compass, they assured me, I was facing Makkah. I wondered if things would change.

Particularly, before I arrived at James River, I had a conversations with my Christian buddies. They were eagerly, shaking my hand.

"I admire your peacefulness," said Eddy to me. "You're a credit, to your religion."

Others shook my hand as well. I felt fortunate. I was the only Muslim, the Christians at Augusta were comfortable with, to be around. I admired their sincerity. I liked their compassion, which was lacking in my own Muslim community.

I entertained the thought of whether the Muslims I was near was going to be just as intolerant, frail in faith, like the ones at Augusta. I was willing to give it a try. At best, I wanted to give the Brothers at James River the benefit of the doubt. I couldn't bear the rhetoric, the cursing or the "wailing" or lying epidemic any longer. I wanted to be free, to be me. Anything else would have been detrimental.

I was wishing to erase the cigarette smoke, along with the other fringe benefits. I requested the non-smoking dormitory.

# RESIDUE

I met Jihad. Right away, we dialogued. He established the fact, it was "us against them." He genuinely, had my back, as the only Muslim in Dorm 5. He had no love for "kafirs" or nonbelievers. What did I get myself into? He told me, what I should be eating, for my dietary needs, almost immediately. He watched me pray. He quickly, told me how certain aspects of my prayer was wrong. It got on my nerves, with him, judging me, and watching me, for errors. He was the exact opposite of what, I didn't want.

"Hey! You look real familiar!" said Shaheed.

He was from Dorm 6, next door. I would get that, "You look familiar," all the time, from people. Especially, if a guy happened to transfer from Powhatan Correctional Center. Minhajj from Augusta said the same thing. I actually, remembered him when I was a correctional officer.

"Was you at Powhatan?" Shaheed said to me.

As usual, I went into denial. Somehow this was different.

"Man, I ain't trying to offend you, but you look, just like this C/O at Powhatan! Just like him! Ya'll could be twins," he also said.

"Oh no," I thought. "He recognized me."

My future seemed dim. I decided to avoid an evil eye. I looked below. I didn't give him eye contact. Instead of using a "shank" or homemade knife on me, Shareef got more excited.

"He was a young dude," he went on. "Dude was a good dude! He ain't bother nobody! He won't on that stupid stuff."

That dude was me. Shareef gave me great compliments. He didn't know it. Somehow, he picked up on how I was disconnected from the ghetto. He was a no-nonsense Brother, who spoke his mind.

"You're naïve too," he said.

What was that supposed to mean? From the way, I was looking, Shareef saw, it must've struck a chord.

"No, I don't mean it like that. You didn't have to grow up, like we did. I wish I was naïve."

Laughing, Jihad agreed. I kept in harmony. Especially, with Jihad's idea of how Muslims should conduct themselves. Particularly, he suggested we walk, and be together during chow. He was a little demanding, as I tried to explain.

Jihad and I was so different from each other. We virtually, had nothing in common, except the same religion. So, I didn't necessarily, see the need to "hang with him." In general, I didn't mind. Yet, on principle, he was trying to force it, which I resented. There was nothing there, except Islam, our common denominator.

Synchronizing my time, I'd walk almost daily. I wanted something to do. James River was great at allowing inmates outside all day, except count-time, of course.

My bunkee Ray knew little, about the meaning of housekeeping, and Dove soap. He lived like a ghoul. He had a "shaving profile" from medical. Due to sensitivity to skin, razor blades, or razor bumps. He had somewhat of a beard. Most of us had to shave. On a humdrum, we were science fiction fans. Despite the concrete jungle of ours.

Being in a dormitory was like chewing on chicken gizzards. It had an acquired taste. It took getting used to. There was absolutely, no privacy. Otherwise, it was a cinch. I kept in mind, how open it was. I'd usually, lock my stuff up, whenever I was on the go. I'd frequent the religious library, to study. I'd go to Black History class. I'd remember to take my identification with me.

## CHAPTER 19, PART 20

# Redeemed

SEEING MY FAMILY, in the visiting room, was always a pleasure. I felt so redeemed, holding my nephew, Cory. I felt like a human being again. Especially, holding a baby, since Paris' death. That moment was everything to me! It was worth more than a mountain of gold. My sister didn't flinch at all. Particularly, with me holding her son in my arms.

"I know you wouldn't try to hurt a baby," said Drika. "And I'd let you babysit him too."

I nearly, cried. I was so touched by this. I thanked her, for believing in me. The child's father was a different story. With illicit behavior, he obviously, cheated on Drika. He was often, nowhere near my nephew. My sister was a knockout. I couldn't understand, why she allowed herself, to be in those hurtful relationships. She was too smart for that. My daughter Kandi was always on my mind. She had a first-cousin, Cory, she has yet to meet.

Back to the lab again. I insisted on not losing myself, or who I was, in that penitentiary environment. I used proper grammar, no matter how compelling the jail slang might be.

I wanted to divorce my wife, Mary, because of her unladylike behavior. I was grateful for the 3 years she hung in there, supporting me. However, after we were married, she soon left me. I'd often ponder over her whereabouts, and who was loving her. Ironically, I still had feelings for her. I felt, I wanted to be with her. Yet, I was sitting in prison, for homicide.

Jihad, formerly known as E. Green, was loud as any bullhorn.

"Yo!" he would say on impulse. "Stinking kufar!"

He was reeking with bitterness, for anyone who wasn't Muslim. I couldn't disagree more. It wasn't our way, to spew contempt, anger and hatred towards people, who were not Muslim. I was hip on the Ebonics or jailhouse slang, but I detested bigotry. More importantly, I hated the fact, others had to hear it, and think that was okay. It was grossly, inappropriate.

Going against the grain was one thing. However, I thought it was totally, hypothetical for Jihad to be calling nonbelievers "Kafir," behind their back, and smile in their face, over sports. I thought it was insane. I laid in the background, watching his two-faces.

There was another thing, which was guaranteed to cause controversy. Sometimes, my bunkee and I decided, to make ourselves meals together. I contributed the food. Ray did the cooking. Of course, Jihad had a problem with that. He was constantly, on my case, for eating with him.

Jihad would run to Shaheed, to tell him about it. I resented being treated like a child. Just because, I didn't live a life of gunfire, like they did. We actually, had a meeting over me, sharing and eating food with a non-Muslim.

"I don't see what the big deal is," I said. "It's just food."

I couldn't understand. I couldn't identify with them.

"It's intimate," said Jihad, with all the legitimacy, he could muster. "I only eat with the Muslims."

"These people don't care about you!" heckled Shaheed. "They're just using you."

I felt like, I was being indoctrinated, inside of a street gang, no less.

"I'm not going to baby you," said Shaheed, who had little tolerance for insubordination, of what he thought a Muslim should be.

This was coming from the same dude, unbeknownst to him, who spoke highly, of me. "The good C/O dude from Powhatan." I lacked so-called street credibility. I had common sense. I didn't want Shaheed to baby me. Nobody asked him to. I just wanted respect. Sure, I wasn't a hood rat, or sold drugs in the hood. Yet, it didn't make me, any less of a man. I certainly, didn't have a halo over my head. However, I wasn't a complete geek either.

I simply, learned to keep my distance from Shaheed. I took the less of the two evils. I hung with Jihad, some more. It was inexplicable, how he had a problem with me, walking to chow, with someone else. I complied, because I didn't want to hear it.

I was a liberal. Meanwhile, Jihad seemingly, wanted to hang anyone, who didn't agree with his religious, geopolitical views. I was tired of his inflammatory remarks. Especially, when it came to gay people. For the life of me, I didn't understand it. Homosexuality was the furthest thing from my mind. Jihad was always on guard about it.

"He talks to Boys," Jihad would wholeheartedly, warn about someone. "He's a faggot."

It was like a bite in the ass. I was sick of hearing it. Sometimes, it could be rather comical. The likelihood, of a gay guy talking to him, was next to none.

I on the other hand, was the kind of guy, to bury the hatchet. I wasn't inquiring about someone's past. I didn't care.

"They're here! They're queer! Get used to it!" I wanted to say.

I kept myself in line at James River. I went to congregational, Jumuah prayer, every Friday. It was the only time I'd wear my white kufi cap, respectfully.

I suffered from insomnia. I couldn't get comfortable. I couldn't lick the feeling, of being surrounded by thieves. Especially, after someone stole my mono adapter, which I plugged into my tv. It gave it stereo sound. Not only that, the summer heat was unbearable. Someone possibly, having a heat stroke wasn't out of the question.

Sure, I was closer to home. However, there was nothing like struggling, to pay car insurance, on a mediocre salary. I wanted to take a date out to Red Lobster. I felt so alone. Particularly, with no one to rely on. I wanted a friend. I wanted someone, who could interpret my feelings. I wanted a buddy to know what I was going through.

Soon after, despite the lopsided drama, I met Barry. We got along great. Instantly, we hit it off in friendship. He admitted to me, he used to get high, smoking crack. I was an introvert. He was a great listener. He was an older man, 50-years-old. Sitting behind his spectacles, he gave me such good advice.

I'd confide in Barry about the Muslims there. It made his eyebrows go up. I'd complain about the hypocrisy. I'd explain how some, who took their oath or covenant with Allah, didn't seem to care. I didn't necessarily, feel involved. I was sick of Jihad, correcting me all the time. Especially, in my lust of women. Meanwhile, he hogged the King Magazine himself.

"They think you're stupid," said Barry. "They want to control you. They're using you."

I nicknamed Jihad, "Osama Bin Laden," because of his extremism. I nicknamed Shaheed, "Sadam Hussein" because of his sternness. Barry nicknames Shaheed, "Big head" which caused us both to laugh.

I thought of Barry as a disgruntled Christian. He was always showing me passages in the Bible. He'd show me people's misconception of certain versus.

"What do y'all be talking about?" asked Shaheed.

Obviously, Jihad reported me. Not that it was any of his business.

"Stuff that's wrong in the Bible," I'd say, remaining patient.

My faith in Islam was irreversible. It would have been insane to convert to anything else. I admitted to Barry, I went to college. He wanted me to further my studies, and get a Master's degree. He was a great motivational speaker. He wanted to help people. He wanted it to be his life's mission.

I refused to disclose to Barry, I was a "cop" for Powhatan Correctional Center. I didn't think he was ready for that. I could actually, see my old job, from my window. What irony!

Despite it all, I liked Barry so much, I wanted to introduce him to my mother. I'd possibly, let them date, I thought to myself. He treated me like I was a grown ass man. I respected him for that. He showed his ivory teeth to everyone. Getting mail, every so often, from the women in our lives, we complained about our so-called wives.

Barry taught me to think outside the box. He taught me, not to take things at face-value. "Phooey on religion," was basically, his outtake on it. We'd sip our java coffee.

I let him believe, I was locked up for abusing Mary. It was an easier pill to swallow. Of course, being the male in the relationship, the police was quick to lock me up. It didn't matter, if I was being attacked first. It certainly, wasn't what I was currently, in prison for. It was a little, white lie. However, it was the horse I rode on, and I was sticking to it.

I was scared of Barry's reaction, if I dished out the truth. Especially, of me accidentally, hurting my baby. He was my best friend at the time. Yet, I couldn't take the chance of him saying something, to somebody else. Not trusting anyone was a mandate, I placed on myself. I never lost focus. I was in prison, man.

It wasn't until Tyson, moved into our dormitory, people started to take notice. He was a very intimidating, big, muscular guy, who liked to work out. More importantly, we quickly, became friends. Worth mentioning, we was a Muslim. He rarely, performed his prayers. Like a phantom, he walked alone. Of course, he was marked by the Brothers, with going against the grain. However, with that mean mug of his, they didn't dare approach him.

I didn't judge Tyson. To put things in perspective, he didn't judge me. Giving him the subliminal message, or proverbial middle finger, Jihad refused to talk to him.

"He's using you," said Jihad, noting the oatmeal cakes, I gave him. "And he doesn't pray."

Picking up from where I left off, why did he care? Jihad treated me no better, than a doormat. It was though, I was up to my old tricks. He treated me like, I was an adolescent. To put it gently, soft as a pillow. Regardless of the mean looks, I ignored the Brothers mediocre concerns. I hung out with Tyson, anyway.

Being a friend, I had to listen to Tyson, tell his tales, about the ladies he knew. It was only befitting, I share some of the things, I like doing too. When the mood was right, I asked him, how did he get the nickname, Tyson.

"From the fights, I used to get into. I used to knock 'em out," he said, proudly.

Tyson was constantly, trying to get me to write my daughter. From one father, to another. He volunteered to write Mary a letter, on my behalf. For the sake of my daughter.

If memory serves me correctly, Tyson and Barry got along great. We often talked about God, the Ever Present. Food for thought, our meaningful conversations me a plateful to think about.

Besides the food, and "freak books" or nudity magazines, we were usually, in our merry talks. Tyson admitted to me, he watches The Potter's House. It was a mega church, with TD Jakes presiding. It was on Sunday mornings. I was open-minded. I thought, I'd check it out too. The pastor had a way of working the crowd. I witnessed their pleas of hope.

Methodically, TD Jakes was an optimist. I really, enjoyed it. With his telecast, it plunged me into the inspiration, I desperately, needed.

"Eat the meat, and not the bones," Brother Kasib would offer to me, and he was Muslim.

Meaning, if I didn't agree with a certain thing, throw it away. TD Jakes was a middle-aged man. He was a little overweight. However, he was organized and poised. A Christian? Yes. I didn't view him as a run-of-the-mill guy.

When it came to other people's religion, I wasn't here to judge. I respected their sincerity and enthusiasm. Especially, one's compassion, should they believe. I braced myself for Muslim backlash. Tyson didn't care. They didn't like him anyway.

It wasn't often, I found someone, I had something in common with. In spite of my sensibilities, I tried. I simply, didn't fit in with the Muslims there. They didn't like Tyson, because of his dishonesty, and lack of performing prayers. Not to mention, calling himself Muslim, when he clearly, wasn't doing that much. In a perfect world, I'd be in a polo lounge, sipping on warm tea. Yet, it wasn't the case.

"That's why, your wife left you! You fat bitch!" Barry once said to me.

What? I was shocked. I couldn't believe, he was talking to me like that. Barry was under the impression, I was talking about him, behind his back. I wasn't. This man ministered to me. It was outrageous! If anything, I always took up for our friendship. Unfortunately, he flat-out disrespected me like that. I didn't get it. Was he high? On dope or something?

Without overreacting himself, Tyson told me what happened. My bunkee, Ray told Barry, I was in prison, for raping my step-daughter. Of course, it wasn't true. Yet, Barry must've believed it. Blindly, without consulting me first.

I didn't discuss what, I was locked up for. So, Ray apparently, made it up. Particularly, with him noticing my wife, Mary, or step-daughter, Toya, didn't visit me anymore. I was betrayed by this guy. The same guy, who everyone talked about, behind his back, because of his stinky odor or lack of hygiene.

I admit, I was hurt. Especially, over something, I did not do. Our friendship was over. I never spoke to Barry after that. What I thought was priceless, was dropped like a hot potato.

"You want me to tell him to leave you alone?" Shaheed said, before our little incident. "I'll do it."

Shaheed thought, he was preaching his modern-day Christianity to me. Obviously, he wanted him to stop. Whenever he came around us, Barry would quietly, leave. Apparently, he was going outside, to get some oxygen.

Shaheed had this air about him. Especially, when it came to people he didn't like. Barry didn't want any problems. So, I wouldn't be surprised, if Shaheed went behind my back, and told him to leave me alone. I'd bet a honey bun on it. It was a page in my life, I didn't get. It felt so inconclusive, our friendship would end like that.

I had to get beyond the various mood swings, from other people. I'd pamper myself with food, music, and tv. It was ironic, seeing certain C/O's from my old job at Powhatan. I believed Allah set a veil over their eyes. They seemingly, didn't remember me. I certainly, didn't forget them.

I worked alongside Sergeant Jones and Lieutenant Larry. I actually, worked with C/O Palmore and C/O Buckles. I too, worked in the same environment as they. I too, had to do diabolical tasks, with inmates, as they did. I too, had the pleasure of once representing The Department of Corrections. However, they didn't know that.

"You look familiar," they would say to me. "Were you at Powhatan?"

As an inmate, I was quiet as a mouse, around some of my former colleagues. I hardly, gave them eyeballs.

Thinking of Paris, I blamed myself, for thinking something was wrong with her. Pretty much, if I didn't think something was wrong, maybe I'd still be working with my former coworkers. That is, if they didn't volunteer to transfer to James River. Particularly, I was ashamed of being a inmate in front of them. Yet, they didn't know. I was in the prime of my life. I was a correctional officer. I had my own place. I was merely, 29-years-old when I was locked up.

"But look at me now," I must've said to myself a hundred times.

My mother thought, maybe my former coworkers did remember me. Perhaps they were protecting me, by acknowledging the fact.

I learned to get over it. I didn't let my pride get the best of me. It stabbed like hell. What's a patriot to do? Self-pity produced nothing. The only thing self-pity was good for nasal tissues. So, I put my peachy-clean life behind me. I was hoping the years would go by progressively, fast.

I was surrounded by Neanderthals. I had to endure people, who had little tolerance for other people. Somehow, they saw themselves as outside of themselves.

I lived like a king. I wanted for nothing. I visited canteen every week. Many didn't.

Tyson prompted me into talking about things, which were un-Islamic. We gawked at magazines with beautiful women, in negligee. We laughed the whole night through. However, he had no idea. I was tired of the Muslims, namely him, pinning me down, begging for food.

They were using the hell out of me, because I'm Muslim too. Yet, we had nothing in common, outside of our religious beliefs. It was the touchstone, of how I was being taken advantage of. Their priorities weren't straight. It was so neurotic. Sometimes, Jihad and I would chip in, to make a meal together. He'd give, half of it away, to a Brother.

Tyson would ask to perform his prayers, with me. I was happy to oblige.

"Yeah," I said, protruding forth. "Of course."

I thought it was nifty. Afterwards, he'd make these delicious meals. As usual, the Muslims said, he was using me, but I was too blind to see it. I was merely, psyched for good company.

"Ali, you got something sweet?" the Brothers would often say.

All I could do was shake my noggin, in disgust. Whenever I'd hear, "Ali" I knew exactly, what they wanted. They wanted food. As pertinacious as they were, the Brothers wouldn't take a hint.

"I don't have it," was finally, my answer.

I had it up to here, with that stuff. My puppy dog eyes were of no use. I couldn't get Tyson, not to fight a rude fellow named Kirk. The two of them went at it, in the bathroom.

Needless to say, they went to "the hole" or segregation. Without Tyson around, I went into a slump. I had nobody to talk about women with.

I started to run with Jihad, a bit more. I was smitten with more of his intolerant slurs of "kufar." It seemed to be quadrupled this time around. I wanted a Star Wars light saber. So, I could cut the crap down. I wanted nothing to do with, those snide remarks about non-Muslims. It made me queasy. Especially, when I would look up and witness him talking, laughing and playing Scrabble, with the so-called "kufar" or nonbelievers. It was all a sham.

Once, after Jihad and I finished our prayer together, I noticed a new arrival. He was with a box, which read "A. Hassan."

"He has a Muslim name," I said to Jihad, with excitement.

"We'll see," said Jihad, cynical as usual.

Sure enough, Hassan introduced himself to us. He had a foreign accent. I assumed he loved soccer. He was from Somalia, East Africa. Jihad quizzed him on whether he practiced the Quran and Sunnah. He could've been Uncle Sam, for all I cared. I was glad, he wasn't criminal-minded. He wasn't a wanna-be thug, on the down and out.

"A real Muslim," my heart screamed.

It was great seeing Hassan in solitude, studying. He didn't use curse words. He had a radiant smile. He wasn't a total sap. He didn't walk around with an attitude. He was wrongly, accused of burglary conspiracy. He was unfortunately, working on a two-year bid.

When it rained, it poured. He could tell, how many things were falling my way. Hassan was the only one, who understood me. He'd quote the Quran to me. He had a way of dusting me off, or making the pain go away.

"Ali, you have to understand, the Brothers grew up different, from you and I," said my good, African friend. "Be patient."

Hassan was a computer programmer by trade. He lived in Falls Church, south of Washington DC. He was a proud Somalian. He came to the west, for college. He went to Florida State. He wanted to support his family. At random, he knew statistical data, on key sports figures.

He was a few years older than me. Hassan treated me like I was younger brother. He became my new best friend. Particularly, after Tyson was shipped, to another location. However, Hassan reported everything I did, to Jihad. Especially, because he was now the imam.

To make matters worse, Jihad would blab my business during Jumuah service, without actually, mentioning my name. I knew it. More importantly, Jihad knew, who he was anonymously, referring to. It was awful. I confronted Hassan, for ratting me out. Particularly, for everything he didn't like I was doing.

"Will you stop doing that?" I asked Hassan. "I hate it."

Supposedly, in his mind, he was trying to help me by exposing me. Everything I did, was up for grabs. The shows I watched, the science fiction books I read, was all used against me. It was worse than spell-check, on a word processor. I felt bound. I wasn't allowed to be myself.

"You're like my little brother," Hassan said. "I apologize."

He showed me his picture scrapbook of his family. His spirituality was higher, than any Muslim at James River, as far as I was concerned. Hassan was the only one I could relate to. Yet, making him scratch his skull, I wouldn't tell him what I was actually, in prison for. I didn't tell him, where I used to work at. I would try to give him hints, without telling him.

Eventually, I began to trust him. Much to his credit and character, I didn't trust anyone in prison, but him. Hassan was fluent in Arabic, of course. Fellow Muslims would often go to him for advice. Sometimes they would get him to recite an "ayah" or verse from the Quran.

"You're not a criminal, Ali," said Hassan. "I can tell, you don't belong here."

The second he was assigned to "bottom bunk status," he asked me, to move where he was. I was sprinkled with uncertainty. I didn't want our friendship to be ruined, somehow. I didn't want to indiscriminately, get on his nerves. I thought it could happen. Particularly, by spending too much time with him.

I declined to take his offer for awhile. Yet, seeing how much Hassan wanted me to move to his area, I gave it some thought. Eventually, it squeezed a Request Form out of me.

Everything turned out fine, when I was assigned to his bed area. I was being myself. We talked. We laughed. I was feeling comfortable. I joked, to no end. Hassan was curious about my writing. I explained, it was my life story. I was currently, working on. He wanted to read it.

I would rather fall down a stairwell, than share with an inmate. Especially, with what the prosecutors accused me of. However, Hassan was different. I let him read, bits and pieces. Yet, I shielded the parts, which referred to my case, or former job.

"You can write," he said. "It's good."

Hassan gave me lots of free, sometimes unwanted advice.

"I'm just a regular guy," I'd say in protest, to his kind words.

Hassan was four years older than me. We argued, like biological brothers. It was all in good fun, but I stood my ground to him. I felt relax with him. I told him all about my family. He'd tell me about his family as well. He loved the fact, my mother was a very, quiet woman. He wanted to meet her.

Meanwhile, my sister, Drika, was still friends with a guy, named Sir. I thought, he played mind games with her. Much like a kid at Station's Break, an arcade near VCU.

At any rate, my mother and I would reminisce about the family, during my visitation. It was very unsettling. Especially, to hear about Drika being sarcastically, to her, all the time. I could tell, it was taking a toll on her. In repercussion, I wanted to write letters cursing my sister for her behavior. Yet, my mama wouldn't let me. She wanted to keep the peace between us. I was sick of her repugnant attitude. Particularly, taking things out on mama.

As a resolution to the food, Jihad, Hassan and I would often put together "shindigs." We prayed our daily prayers together, whenever we could.

Yet, Hassan and I had a relationship, beyond a superficial appearance of Muslim-togetherness. We were like brothers. Once, when I finished writing my story for the day, he wanted to read it. Everything was now across the board.

"You have to promise me," I said. "You can't say nothing to nobody."

"I'll take it to my grave," said Hassan.

I wasn't expecting any restitution. I was simply, ready for the truth to be known. I studied him, reading about my case, carefully. Hassan looked up, as though the verdict was in.

"It was an accident," he said. "You didn't mean to do it."

Sweet as shortcake to my ears.

"You believe me?" I said.

"Of course I do, Ali. You're not a criminal," reassured Hassan.

It was like chocolate over cherries. I damned near cried. I nearly, cried in retrospect. I thanked him for believing me.

"It was an accident. It was an accident," I shrugged.

"I know," he said, looking me in the eyes.

It was great, having a friend, with no strings attached. I couldn't ask for a better companion.

"You're the first person in here, I told my case to, in 5 years," I informed him.

Without being sidetracked, Hassan couldn't believe, the bogus things, the prosecution used against me, for evidence. Riding in the car further, Hassan read about my case, more and more.

"Ali, the jury didn't know all of this," he said.

He was realizing, how I got thrown in jail for Capital Murder. If only, I had a chance to truly, explain my side of what happened.

"A misunderstanding," said Hassan, reading my mind.

It appeared he wanted to cry as well. He had two young daughters himself.

"Now, I wish I didn't know. You're innocent. All this time, you have to do."

It was water under the bridge. Yet, it was a nightmare. I didn't want to touch it, with a 10-foot pole. I had to deal with unspeakable pain, alone, for five years. For years, I looked for a sign. I merely, hoped everything was going to be okay. Finally, I confided in someone, other than family.

Hassan was that person.

"I trust you, and I don't trust nobody in here," I admitted to him.

"I appreciate that, Ali," he'd say. "That means a lot."

The talks we had, always steered me into the right direction. When I felt the time was right, I tried to give Hassan hints, of what I used to do for a career.

"one of the Brothers here, seen me on my job," I'd tease. "But they don't remember."

I said one evening, after dinner. It just so happened, we came across Shaheed.

"Ali, I was just telling the Brothers, when you first got here. You looked just like this C/O, that worked at Powhatan, when I was there," said Shaheed. "You remember that?"

"Yes, I remember," I said, playing it off.

How could I possibly, forget? Hassan started to smile. He single-handedly, figured it out. When everyone was out of earshot, he took me to the side.

"You were a C/O?" he said, putting the puzzle together.

It rocked his world. I didn't fit the typical profile.

"Yeah, but you can't say nothing," I said, swearing him to secrecy.

"I'm proud of you," Hassan said, in less than 60 seconds.

Suddenly, I knew, I told Hassan everything.

"What took you so long to tell me?" he said.

I was relieved. There was nothing else to hide, or drag behind. My African friend release date was in the summer. So, I didn't have long to enjoy his friendship. It was like playing Russian Roulette. Hassan could've really, had my reputation in a sling, if he opened his mouth. However, he didn't. It was surreal, how he had, all of that information, on me.

*CHAPTER 20, PART 21*

# Epilogue

IT WAS YEAR 2005. Surfing among the countless faces of inmates was Adib. He was a new arrival at James River. I met him years prior. We frequented the same mosque. The same Muslims on the street, where I had fond memories of. He knew them as well.

Adib cussed and fussed like the rest of them. He too was wearisome. Especially, when it came to food.

"I remember Ali, from the street," he'd say.

For future reference, I'd speak to Adib about some of his behavior, as his "older brother." In truth, we had virtually, nothing in common. We were from two different worlds. Yet, we acted like we knew each other well, because of our mosque, Masjidullah. Sweetening the deal, he wanted to know about my case. I refused to tell him.

He was like a kid, with a turbocharger. He was too explosive. He was too unpredictable, for his own good. I grabbed the wheel, sort of speak, when things got of hand. I cared about Adib. He had great potential. I knew he could do better. He'd often let his short temper get the best of him. Despite his mood swings, Adib would pull up a chair, and ask advice from Hassan. Everyone did.

Hassan symbolized rationality. He was like a steady turtle, willing to stick his neck out. He was a whistleblower, on behalf of the Muslim community there. Adding more on his plate, he tried to get Jihad and I closer.

I wasn't perfect. I wasn't consistent or conservative. I wasn't the type of guy, who'd go along with anything, without proof. I wasn't the sort, to follow the script, word for word. I'd look out the window at a female's bottom, at the spin of a dime.

# EPILOGUE

"Uhm, hm," Hassan would say, to get me to stop staring out of the window.

It was a pain in the ass. I respected the guy. He certainly, wasn't tall. Yet, he carried himself as an unassuming giant. Hassan got on me about my favorite show, Charmed. It was about witchcraft. It was entertaining. I didn't see that the big deal was. He also tapped on my nerves, about me watching The Jerry Springer show. I knew he meant well, and was going by faith.

Adib and I didn't have half, or nearly, the connection Hassan and I had. I wasn't ghetto or a wannabe gangster. I didn't necessarily, consider myself "better than," but I couldn't relate. I worked for a living. I paid my taxes. I wasn't in and out of overpopulated jails. I wasn't stationed on a street corner, selling drugs, like some people I knew.

I'd usually, get on the prison telephone, or during a visit, and complain to my mother. I'd tell her, how unethical it was. I was uneasy, how wretched the people were.

"Marco, you're in a prison," she said. "What do you expect?"

For the life of me, I couldn't understand them. I wanted to go on the nearest airport terminal, and fly away from those "immoral people."

"You have to know, it's a test, Ali," reminded Hassan.

Meanwhile, I continued reading National Geographic magazine. I loved the stories, the beautiful pictures. I appreciated the scientific discoveries. I was fascinated with the their journalists and photographers zigzagging, all across the world. Not only did the magazine cover history, but what was going on now. For example, some reporters followed tornado twisters in Kansas. Others were knee-deep in an Amazon rainforest. I took it upon myself to learn the world, I was very much, still apart of.

Thoughtfully, I'd pour myself a cup of coffee, which often made me run to the urinal. Coffee, which I newly acquired, usually, went through me. Yet, it was a must-have in the mornings. Especially, when I didn't have a soda at night.

Hassan's vacation in jail was soon over. He didn't have to get a bus ticket. His lovely, family was at the front gate waiting for him. They were all Muslim as well.

BEHOLD

"I'll never forget you, Ali. Remember all I told you," said Hassan, before he walked out the door.

He promised to keep in touch. He wanted to get my daughter, to pay me a visit. My best friend was gone. I actually, cried in my Drafting class. It was a computerized, architecturally designed trade on blueprints. I was going to miss him. Hassan did so much during his stay at James River. He helped unite the Brothers. He also got Shaheed and I to settle our differences.

"I'm going to hook you up, Ali," said Adib.

Sometimes he was nice as vanilla ice cream. Other times, he was like a tired, old shoe, who needed to sit down somewhere. I felt lonely as hell. So, talking to a lady friend couldn't have come at a better time.

My life was in a vacuum. I welcomed the thought of having a woman in it.

My only concern was actually, telling her the truth about why, I was in prison in the first place. I wasn't sure, if I told her about my baby, she'd grab a tissue and sympathize? Would she wish I'd burn in hell? Whatever the case may be, I certainly, didn't want Adib to know. His mouth was fast as a tollbooth. Women were my only vice. They were my weakest strength at temptation. I told him to do it.

Her name was April. She had three small boys. She was living on welfare.

"What are you locked up for?" April wrote me, of course.

Pulling my coattails, she naturally, wanted to know. I didn't want to lose her. Especially, by not being straightforward. So, I told her. Surprisingly, April took the news well.

"Only God can judge," she replied.

Besides that, she was Adib's son's aunt, or baby mama's sister. I didn't want to lie. Yet, Adib was so vindictive. I wanted to touch a woman, and have her visit me.

Knowing fully, Adib was bound to know my case through April, I admitted to him as well. With his volcanic behavior, he could easily, betray me, backbite or expose me. It was like wading in the water, and come what may. I told him against my better judgment.

# EPILOGUE

I ran it by him. He actually, became mad, hearing how unfairly, the trial was. Having

Adib believing in me was all the treasure I needed. I finally, washed my hands of it. I tried to be colorful to April. I tried to be talkative and attentive, but she was stiff as waffles. She said, she didn't like to write. Next thing I knew, her phone was suddenly, blocked from "inmate collect calls." So, that was that.

However, Adib now knew, what I was in prison for. With Hassan gone, he was about the closest thing I had, to being a friend. We were so opposite, to each other. I tried to give him, the benefit of the doubt.

The other, older Ali decided to move over. Particularly, to where I was, to be my bunkee. He would ask astounding questions about Islam. I'd try my best to answer them. His Arabic, or religious usage of it anyway, was next to none. Sometimes, he was beside himself. He was moody. He'd pout, because his spending in canteen was rather limited. Also, he wanted to learn a trade, which wasn't readily, available.

"Ali, you're smart. Why don't you take some of those college courses?" he said to me.

He was noticing the notice, about J. Sergeant Reynolds Community College. It was posted on a bulletin board.

"I'm alright," I would say.

I usually, didn't disclose, I was once a college student. Not to mention, with a bachelor degree. Perhaps, I was arming myself with modesty. I didn't want to brag. Many people in prison were high school dropouts. Let alone, went to college.

"I want to see one of us in there, like them White boys," he said.

Suddenly, I was compelled to tell Ali. I wanted to make him proud. Especially, with him taking into account, I was a Black man, who successfully, graduated from VCU.

Nothing was artificial or superficial, by the way Ali would act. He fussed about this. He complained about that. It drove me batty. I needed an aspirin, with all of his victim stories. He could be a pain. Sometimes, he would make me uncomfortable. In depth, it was the way he would simply, sit there, in our bed area, and say nothing at all. I felt, he would surely, go astray. Especially, once he was out of a controlled environment, such as prison, and be on the street. It made my blood curl, how he acted. I could've strangled him, but what good would it do?

The way things were, fixed or situated, I didn't feel comfortable. I'd continue my daily walk, under the August sun. I was forced to be near the other inmates. I hated being bombarded with stares. Essentially, from the Muslims, because I wasn't "working out," particularly with weights.

Finally, Jihad was transferred, and taking his radical-version of Islam with him. It was simply, agonizing, with him aviation's over my shoulders all the time. Kasib was voted in, as the new imam. It made things turn out for the better.

On the other hand, I had to deal with Adib. He decidedly, sold cheap, bootleg prayer oil, to any unsuspecting person. I knew the difference between the genuine, thick, smell-good oil, and what he was peddling. It was an atrocity. Usually, he had a rude batch of ugly remarks for me.

"He thinks he's better than us, because he went to college," Adib would say. "He's from the suburbs."

Among other things, that was the very reason, I didn't like to disclose any of my accomplishments.

"What, you jealous?" I'd say, bouncing back.

When things got really bad, I'd tell Adib where he could go. Especially, for trying to embarrass me. He drove me to the point of nearly, cursing him out.

"Go rob somebody. Go sell something," I'd tell him. "When you get out of here, you're going to go 'Daleen.' I know it, and you know it."

It was practically, the worst thing you could say, to a fellow Muslim in prison. Particularly, telling him, he's going to "go astray" anyhow.

It wasn't long before I made an alliance, with a guy named, Roberto. He was someone, outside the Sunni Muslim community. Of course, the Brothers would constantly, tell me how bad he was. He had a reputation, or rumor following him, he was a "faggot." It was their word, not mind. They certainly, didn't like him being a coordinator, and member of the Nation of Islam. I wasn't there to judge him, for whatever he may have, or may not have done.

# EPILOGUE

"Not again," I thought.

I was getting tired of their judgmental attitude . Especially, with them telling me who, I was allowed to hang with. They were free to be with their non-Muslim friends. No one questioned their ability, to make right decisions.

All together, it gave me palmy hands. Brothers were sweating me so much.

"Give me a break," I'd think.

"What do y'all talk about?" they wanted to know. "He's a 'kufar'."

"He makes me laugh," I'd say, hoping for amnesty.

The more, I tried to explain our friendship, the more sanctimonious they behaved. With me, trying to bridge the gap was a hopeless cause. Ali was anchored in his chair. He too, was full of sin, much like anyone else. He too, hated for Roberto to come around.

"If looks could kill," Roberto said, playfully.

He knew they didn't care for him. I for one, was tired of the crap. Especially, with the audacity of who could talk with.

I wanted to be home, with a nice young lady, with an anklet on. Anything, but tip-toe around the mess, I had to endure. Don't get me wrong. Islam was my beacon of light. I tried to be an example. It was extremely, hard to be around the jail, strict and often difficult, tight-lip version of it.

Roberto sought any opportunity, to get on people's nerves. Yet, he liked me. So, he'd pull me into talking about the "Original Man." Anthropology agreed it was the Black man. As a religious person, I certainly, didn't believe we somehow morphed from monkeys. I knew unlike him, the Black man was not God. My bunkee, Ali was becoming more, and more agitated, with my new friend.

"I don't trust those people," I'd say, referring to the inflammatory teachings of the Nation of Islam.

However, Ali didn't know that. He mentioned to the other Muslims, Roberto and I hanging out so much.

Roberto wanted to pray with us. Soon, that fell to pieces. Somehow, he purposely, got into my head, making me laugh. Particularly, when I was calling the "iqamah" or announcing prayer was about to commence.

Needless to say, it was the excuse the Brothers needed for me to leave Roberto alone. I became stubborn. I was even more so determined, to decide with who, I wanted to be with. Quickly, that idea crashed and burned.

"What are you looking at?" said Ali to Roberto, suddenly pushing the envelope.

"I can look anywhere I want," Roberto said, under the circumstance.

"You like me?" Ali said in a convulsion, drawing closer to him still. "You must like me or something. I owe you something?"

Before I knew it, the two of them started fighting, like hungry cattle near the bathroom.

"Hey, hey!" I said, wanting to stop it.

I needed clarity. It was short and sweet. Ali and Roberto stopped fighting, before the correctional officers witnessed who were actually, fighting. With the guard merely, seeing a cut at the corner of Roberto's eye, they put them both into "the hole" or Special Housing Unit, anyway.

"This wouldn't have happened, if you won't messing with Roberto!" Adib said, dragging my name into it.

"I didn't tell Ali, to over there, and start fighting him!" I said, wanting clemency.

"I told you to leave Roberto alone," the others echoed.

As though holding a candlelight vigil, we all knew, Roberto wasn't going to take the fall, by himself. It was a matter of time, before Ali would be confined too. Information about him would surely, come out of the closet. Names would be dropped on somebody else, but who?

Ali was actually, proud of what he done. We waited a couple of days. So far, nothing happened. Firstly, after Jumuah prayer, one afternoon, I saw Adib being taken away, in handcuffs.

Suddenly, at his own expense, Ali was then taken to jail as well. Initially, I thought they must've been horse playing, in the Treatment Building. Which of course, was a no-no.

"You're next, Ali," said Wali, a fellow Muslim in our dorm, to me.

"Why? I ain't do nothing," I replied.

# EPILOGUE

A few minutes later, a few guards came in the area, as though they were searching someone out.

"Mr. Martin, will you come with us, please?" said one of them.

"Why? What did I do?" I objected.

"We'll talk about it outside," said the correctional officer.

"Are you going to tell me what this is about?" I said, trying to clear the cobwebs, in a fog of confusion.

"I'm not going to tell you again."

Outside in handcuffs, the story unfolded.

"We have witnesses in the building that said, you had something to do with the fight, or knows what happened," said the investigating officer.

My case flashed before my eyes. I became mad as hell. Soon, I was thrown in an isolated cell. I was then, behind bars.

"This is bullshit!...This is bullshit," I said.

Feeling crabby, I had more to say.

"I didn't do anything! I'm being confined unjustly!"

"They said, you had something to do with it," said my jailer.

"They're lying!" I yelled.

I was careful, not to overstep my bounds. Yet, I was hurt. I thought, I'd get an infraction, for no apparent reason. I was in a fly-infested, roach-infested room. Already, I was missing the small comforts, I've gotten accustomed to. Namely, my Coca-Cola drinks.

Hearing me curse for the first time, in a cell next to mine, Ali spoke up.

"If I say what happened, will you let them two go?" Ali said to the guard, in his usual raspy voice.

"Tell us what happened, and we'll let them go. Yeah," the guard said.

At that moment, I vowed to go to a predominantly, Arab or immigrant masjid, when I got out of prison. I was sick of all the drama from the "penitentiary" Muslims. Particularly, from the hood.

"It was me. I got to fighting with Roberto," admitted Ali. "Let Marzuk and Martin go. They had nothing to do with it."

Eventually, I calmed down.

"You hear that, Ali?" he said to me. "They should let y'all go."

Obviously, his guilt got the best of him. Ali was adding cream to it.

"Yeah," I said sadly, not believing it, until I see it.

The investigator made an empty promise too. Soon after, the dinner cart, with its bland food was slowly, rolled in. I knew deep down, I was in, for the weekend. I was an innocent bystander, caught in the crossfire.

I learned to cope and be casual about it. I began to take it all in stride. Being in isolation too, I had something in common with the other inmates there. I talked. I laughed with them in that place.

I had to deal with a crusty sink and toilet. It was all I had to show for it. Everyone put in their two cents. What was going to happen, with Ali and Roberto, was anyone's guess. Borrowed books and library magazines became a companion too.

Without a chair, I sat on the bed, most of the time. I was in a compromising position. Once, I saw a copperhead serpent, in the middle of the hallway. With chap lips, any and everything was up for discussion.

Daily, I watched counselors being chaperoned, past my cell. I read National Geographic. I needed something uplifting, not confusing, or insane.

"Bastards!" I wanted to yell, whenever I saw my dorm, going to chow hall, for something chewy to eat.

Consequently, I learned to go numb from hearing the people outside, being so cheerful. Though nobody was around, I still practiced my prayers. I was still consulting with God in faith. Members from the Muslim community sent us food. They let us know, they were thinking about us.

Later on, Ali and D-Nice, were laughing. Especially, because of my cursing, when I was initially, thrown in isolation. Seemingly, it was so out of my character, for me to use language like that.

"This is bullshit!" they teased, in good fun.

I deflated my ego. I refused to let solitary confinement, effect me. I told myself, it was all, only a flash in the pan. "This too shall pass."

I wasn't criminal-minded. I wasn't a delinquent. So, I was electrified, when I was eventually, released from my cell. I wasn't charged with anything. However, five days were flicked away from me, for nothing.

I was nearly, misty-eyed when I returned to the same dorm, and same bed. My name and handshakes pulsated from the people. I was floored how quickly, the guys there were willing to give me food. Meanwhile, my own food was depreciating in value, in a Personal Property cardboard box, somewhere.

It felt being treated like an emperor who finally, came home.

"No, not Ali," people flopped, when they heard I too, went to "the hole."

Their random acts of kindness, changed me for the better. Words couldn't describe it. I had an epiphany. Suddenly, it reoccurred to me, not everyone is the same, or acts the same.

"Everyone is not out, to hurt me. Everyone is not out, to get me," I told myself.

My close-minded definition of some people seemed foolish, at the moment. I was ashamed of my overgeneralization, of most of the inmates there. It was simply, destructive. I was engulfed in reassessment of my thinking. I continued to humble myself. Not scared, not acting hard. HearI afforded the people, the benefit of the doubt, from then on.

"They simply, need someone to teach them," I would say. "Be the example."

"You're the next imam," some of the Muslims would say to me.

What in the world? I wasn't exactly, sure about that. Sure, I knew the practicalities for prayer, but I didn't know, if I'd be comfortable enough. Particularly, with my diametrical size, and being around, often pissed-off people. Especially, with those who say they were Muslim.

Soon, I found myself with a new bunkee. To make matters worse, he happened to be, in The Nation of Islam. I felt at ease, when he looked at erotica or adult magazines, like any other dude. He went by the name, Shabazz. He had a smorgasbord of food. So, I didn't have to worry about him, asking me all the time. He also, made himself dinner, every night.

As predicted, Roberto and I's friendship pulled apart. We were great friends, but he was disappointed, I didn't stop people from talking badly, about him. He began to get sarcastic with me. I'd snap back. I didn't judge him, when he evaded my question. Particularly, when I inquired him about his once-sexual orientation. Our days of frolicking together went down the drain.

I finally, discovered why Ali picked a fight with Roberto.

"I was protecting you," Ali said, in his exact words. "I guess, I was overprotective. You were like, my little brother, being with this guy, that was no good."

Roberto was still annoyingly, a practical joker. He was also, an argumentative troublemaker. To say the least, he went back to his roots. He slid to the criminal elements.

Another headache in the dorm was Kirk. He had an ingenious way of getting on my nerves. He'd purposefully, bump shoulders with me, picking a fight. I wouldn't bite.

Kirk had his ass beat, twice, since his arrival at James River. I witnessed Tyson "carrying" him, as though he was a furry, little animal. No contest there. He exposed his fighting techniques. He exposed the coward, for what he really, was.

I was absorbed in wanting to eventually, go home. I certainly, didn't want to prolong my stay, with an additional institutional charge. I ignored Kirk, as best I could. I stayed out of his way. My mind was focused, outside of the penitentiary front gate. So, I forgot about him. Naturally, I wanted to slap the taste out of his mouth.

Besides Kirk, I had no other opponents. I stayed away from the garbage, which came out of most folks mouths. I dove, head-first into my own world, which was writing, tv time, and chitchatting with buddies. Regardless, of my lack of extra-curriculum activities.

Of course, what haunted me, more than anything was my case. I could still hear, the doctors on the stand, describing what happened to Paris. Sometimes, I'd go in a bathroom stall, cover my face, and cry. My daughter carried my genes. It never fallen on me, one day I'd be in jail. Let alone, for trying to help my daughter somehow. My mother was main supporter. She sent money and visited me every two weeks, like clockwork.

I couldn't help but wonder, where people like Jerry was doing, on the street. I wasn't expecting any dough from him. A letter every blue moon would've been nice. I was far from giggling all the time, when we were children.

Prison was such a drag. Being a free man seemed fathoms ago. I was

# EPILOGUE

glad to see my nice family. Yet, I was sad, I couldn't go with them. It was the little things I missed. I wanted to be free, to dress in whatever I desired. I miss being around people who weren't necessarily, explicit, criminal masterminds.

Instead, I was in a place, which often smelled like feces. The floors were anything but glossy. Most people there, were for drug-related charges.

"I'm a criminal," I'd hear.

"I'm an addict," some would admit.

It was a bumpy road, to say the least. Adib treated me as though, everything I said was nonsensical. He ridiculed me often. Especially, for my love of fictional novels. So, it wasn't hard to say goodbye, when he was finally, transferred to another facility.

What was more astonishing was how, I filled my day. I was going about it, easily. I wasn't paying bills. I didn't have a financial care in the world.

My remaining paternal grandparents were getting sick, and older. Meanwhile, America was at war with Iraq. The economy was suffering, with outrageously, high gasoline prices.

I wasn't fit. I didn't want grey hair. All I wanted to do was go home. I was merely, 34-years-old. I was given 15 years, with hopes of doing only 13 years, with good behavior. Naturally, I blamed Mary somewhat. Initially, she told the prosecutors, I didn't "show any remorse."

"Good grief," I thought to myself.

I met another Muslim brother, named Hassan. He was totally, against America's "imperialism" on the world. I wasn't the most knowledgeable person. However, I knew blowing up buildings, from Ground Zero wasn't Islam. He was proud of his Indian heritage, and bad posture. He wanted nothing more than to go on a suicide-mission. Perhaps, die in hail of bullets.

"Where do you get this stuff?" I'd try to correct him.

Over time, we became close. Some of his ideas were pretty lame. There was one thing I noticed, in all my penitentiary travels. Allah always sent me one, good friend at a time. It gave me gusto. So, this was no different, I thought.

"If I told you something, you'll probably, never look at me the same way again," Hassan said.

He was being indecisive, whether to tell me or not. I practically, begged him, like a kid on Santa's lap.

"You can tell me. I wouldn't tell anybody," I said. "Who am I going to tell? I don't trust these people."

After enough persuasion and "Ha! Ha," Hassan felt he corrupted his life. Particularly, by sleeping with a lot of men on the street. He once had a latitude of male sex-partners. Also, he locked himself in with transsexuals. He felt, he let his country, India down. With all, the ink on the wall, he disclosed, he also laid with a man in prison.

Again, I didn't judge Hassan. If the Brothers only knew! They would want to hang him. I inducted his secret inside my brain. I promised, not to release it.

Yet, it explained, why he had his mind set, on suicide-bombings. He took his past, sexual orientation, badly. He hated himself for it. He obviously, felt guilty. Somehow, he concocted the idea, blowing himself up would, "make it up." He romanticized it. He was infatuated with it. To him, a leg up would have been, to take some Americans along with him.

Ironically, Hassan uttered the word "faggot," often. Supposedly, a lot of it was a safe-haven, or play-off, to throw suspicion away from him. Meanwhile, he was actually, talking about himself. He was living a lie.

I would frequent so many questions at him. I mean, wasn't he scared of catching something lethal? Such as HIV. Also, I had another question for him. So, I just went ahead and said it.

"Do you consider yourself gay?" I said.

"A homosexual? Yes," he said.

"Well, at least you admit it."

He treated it like a malfunction. Hassan said, he still had "urges." He admitted, he'd probably, have them the rest of his life. He had lived a double life. It was some heavy duty stuff to deal with. A lot of weight was on my shoulders.

Do I still be his friend? Do I tell the Muslim community, there's a gay guy in our midst? Is he attracted to me?

# EPILOGUE

"You're taking it well," he said, after trusting me.

"I got gay people in my family," I said, dissecting the truth. "I'm used to it."

A great burden seemed to be lifted off from him. I helpless, to repeat it. The instant I would, I knew the Brothers were sure, to shellac him, up against the wall. Some hero, I would've been. Using my intellect and imagination, I finally, decided NOT to say anything.

I didn't want to hear the language. I didn't want to hear the judgement from high society. Nor, did I want to see the raised eyebrows. I didn't want to interfere. I just wanted to live. More importantly, I wanted to make my stay in the place, history one day.

If I would've disclosed anything about Hassan, it would've started an interstellar war. So, I kept it in my pocket, well-hidden. However, I did look at Hassan, differently. It was a vacuum, I wished I never had known.

I admired my long-haired brother, Mel. He was a homosexual. He wasn't afraid to live his truth. He was being himself. I seen my brother go through ups and downs. At least, he didn't give a hoot, what anybody else had to say.

Going back an isle of time, I felt good to have Mel as my brother. There were times, when we were younger, I may have been hostile towards him. It was because, my own life was jacked up, with the fat shaming, insecurities and self-loathing.

I didn't have much to speak of. All I had was the dawn of a new day. I too, wanted a significant other to say "hey" to.

Mel thought, I didn't like his new, White friends, after he joined the Gay Alliance at school. It certainly, wasn't because they were White. I too, wanted real friends, like he had. Not the superficial, judgmental, so-called friendships, I endured.

I too, wanted a red car, like his brand, new GeoTracker. It was a chick-magnet, but the girls didn't know that. He wasn't interested. I too, wanted a friend, knowing she had my back.

I too, saw my life as a journey. It was one, big maze. It was filled with helium, and everyone seemed to talk funny. I felt, no one was willing to take my picture. I dreaded going to the mall, with the guys, from my neighborhood. In my mind, the girls treated me, cold as ice.

Much like the jurors, at my jury trial. I was thrown in a place, mangled in idle talk. The steel bars told me, it was a keeper. A mop in my hand, meant it was home for now. The inmates illustrated, how much they were willing to kill, if necessary. A marquee, in bright lights, which read CRIMINAL. It was completely, immoral. It was something I wanted no parts of. So, what was I doing there? It was the kiss of death. I was around people, I normally, wouldn't have met. All I could do was muster up courage, and master my mind.

God, after all, was something to behold.


THE END

www.ingramcontent.com/pod-product-compliance
Lightning Source LLC
Chambersburg PA
CBHW050835230426
43667CB00012B/2012